Deep Run Roots

Stories and Recipes from My Corner of the South

Vivian Howard

PHOTOGRAPHS BY REX MILLER

Deep Run Roots

Stories and Recipes from My Corner of the South

Vivian Howard

PHOTOGRAPHS BY REX MILLER

DESIGN BY DON MORRIS DESIGN

Ⓛ Ⓑ

LITTLE, BROWN AND COMPANY

New York Boston London

Little, Brown and Company
Hachette Book Group
1290 Avenue of the Americas, New York, NY 10104
littlebrown.com

First Edition: October 2016

Little, Brown and Company is a division of Hachette Book Group, Inc. The Little, Brown name and logo are trademarks of Hachette Book Group, Inc.

The publisher is not responsible for websites (or their content) that are not owned by the publisher.

The Hachette Speakers Bureau provides a wide range of authors for speaking events. To find out more, go to hachettespeakersbureau.com or call (866) 376-6591.

ISBN 978-0-316-38110-9
LCCN 2016931447

10 9 8 7 6

Q-MA

Printed in the United States of America

To Theo and Flo:

I had to leave Deep Run
before I learned how special
this part of the world is.
I hope you will understand
that long before I did.

To Ben:

Thanks for making
this place your home, too.

CONTENTS

RECIPE GUIDE

AS I MENTION LATER in this book, the way I ordered the chapters and recipes is personal, driven more by story than anything else. But it's a cookbook, after all, and I want you to cook from it, and that's why I've included this more practical guide. If you're looking for a new salad or casserole or all the chicken recipes in the book, this should help.

CONTENTS

CONTENTS

EASTERN NORTH CAROLINA TRADITIONS

I grew up with these dishes, and they'll always taste like home to me.

INTRODUCTION

"Don't You Dare Skip This Introduction!"

THIS BOOK IS THE STORY OF MY LIFE so far, told through the ingredients that fill the plates and pantries of my home: Deep Run, North Carolina. A tiny farming community about halfway between Raleigh and the Atlantic Ocean, Deep Run is a nondescript dot on Eastern North Carolina's flat coastal plain. No stoplights, no strip malls—Deep Run is not a town; it's a fire district.

I used to dream about living somewhere more exciting, and for a while I did. But after I'd worked in restaurant kitchens and dining rooms in New York City, my roots called me back.

Eastern North Carolina is my Tuscany, my Szechuan, my Provence. This is a Southern cookbook, but not one that treats the South like one big region where everybody eats the same fried chicken, ribs, shrimp and grits, collard greens, and gumbo. Instead, I interpret Southern cooking the way we understand French, Italian, and Chinese food: as a complex cuisine with abundant variations shaped by terrain, climate, and people.

NORTH CAROLINA

This is a storybook as much as it is a cookbook, where the ingredients are characters who shape my life. Crafting a narrative wasn't my initial plan. Rather, I set out to write an informative essay about each ingredient and found that I could not, for the life of me, teach anything before I explained why turnips, figs, and corn rose above all the lettuces and berries of the world to claim a place in these pages. Those stories are how the book unfolds; not seasonal or alphabetical, but personal.

After purging myself of each story, I was able to share some information. Instead of basic tips you can find anywhere, I offer advice gleaned from my relationships with farmers and seasoned home cooks and my experience in a professional kitchen. I call this "wisdom," in the hope it teaches things you can't pick up from Google.

There are recipes too. A lot of them—one for every skill and interest level in each chapter. The first preparation documents how the people of North Carolina's coastal plain treat the ingredient. These dishes set the tables of our past, and today they connect us to a culture of resourceful cooks who prepared year-round to feed their families. Many of these recipes were considered too mundane to merit writing down. Now they risk being forgotten.

From those traditions, the recipes grow from simple things you might make on a weeknight to more elaborate dishes I serve in our restaurant. In some cases I extract the core idea from a traditional dish and dress it in modern sensibilities, such as acid, texture, and color—things my forefathers didn't always contemplate—and that's it. In others I showcase the ingredient in a way my forefathers would never have dreamed of. These recipes are familiar, rooted in the region's larder, but novel in a way that calls out to the rest of the world. They take an ingredient out and do an acid-induced, multitextured dance with it. These dishes best represent my personal style as a cook.

There's something for everyone here. I hope you find the dishes that best suit your kitchen.

VIVIAN'S RULES

EVERY CHEF COOKS by a set of rules specific to his or her kitchen. Here are the rules I never break and the tools I always have. They'll help make my recipes work for you.

Ingredients

ASIDE FROM FLAKY finishing salts that add texture to a completed dish, the only salt I use is **Diamond Crystal kosher salt.** I don't mess with iodized, pickling, or sea salt unless I'm trapped in someone else's kitchen. Diamond Crystal's particle isn't so big it flakes off meat before it hits the pan, and it's not so minuscule and heavy that it packs a saltier punch per teaspoon.

I have two **olive oils:** one for cooking and one for finishing. I use regular extra-virgin from an average supermarket in heated applications. For dressings or drizzling on top of dishes before I serve them, I use an extra-virgin whose taste I enjoy.

I have nightmares about my time spent **peeling garlic** in the basement of the cutting-edge restaurant WD-50 while the magic of service went on upstairs. My distaste for the process overrides a love for sticky, just-peeled cloves, so I buy pre-peeled whole cloves. These guys are not as agreeable raw, so in my recipes garlic almost always meets heat. When it stays raw, I bite my lip and peel some.

I'm into **fresh herbs.** If a recipe calls for herbs, they're fresh unless I specify dried. For cooked preparations, if you don't have the fresh herbs I suggest, use half the amount dried. But no matter what kind of apocalypse is upon you, never substitute dried herbs for fresh as a garnish or in a salad. Instead, freely swap fresh cilantro, mint, tarragon, basil, dill, chervil (my favorite herb), and parsley for one another. Do the same with "hard" herbs: rosemary, thyme, sage, lavender, oregano, and marjoram.

Whenever I call for **dairy,** I use the kind with fat: **whole milk, buttermilk, Greek yogurt,** and **sour cream** that's rich the way the cow intended it. **Unsalted butter** is the only butter I consider. If I want salty butter on my bread, I still start with unsalted. A kitchen without salted butter has fewer too-salty surprises. And as for those other items that masquerade as butter, I'm working to rid the world of them.

Your eyes may glaze over at this, but start with **whole spices** and grind them as you need them. I have two cheap coffee grinders, one for coffee and one for spices.

In the words of a friend, I'm "acid-dicted." I use a lot of **vinegar** and **fresh citrus**—never from concentrate.

I don't have the word *organic* tattooed on my body. I usually buy

VIVIAN'S RULES

organic meats and produce, but not always. Most farmers I work with are not certified organic, but many of them farm organically. I know they're growing food they'd feed their families, and that's good enough for me. Talking to the person who grew what I'm about to cook inspires me and gives me a tangible connection to my community.

Beyond that, I like **ingredients at their peak.** A peach should taste and smell like a peach. I want a chicken to look like a chicken, not a turkey. I like when roots are attached to their greens, and know that bright, plump berries taste better than ones that are shriveled and dull. I like fat pigs, salty oysters, and crisp sweet apples—the good stuff.

Tools

I HAVE SIMPLE TASTE in gadgets. I use three knives: a **10-inch chef's knife,** a **serrated paring knife,** and an **8-inch boning knife.** I like **big rubber cutting boards** for most of my work and **smaller plastic boards** that fit in the dishwasher for breaking down meats and fish, because the dishwasher kills bacteria that my little scrubber doesn't.

I have an emotional attachment to my **Microplane,** and even though I've cut the crap out of my hands a hundred times, I believe the risk of a **Japanese**

mandoline is worth the reward. I turn things with **tongs** but wince when people treat tongs like spoons. **Y-shaped peelers** are the best peelers. Companies should stop making the other ones.

I got a gift from heaven when I used my first **stainless-steel fish spatula.** It's the last spatula, except for a **small offset spatula,** I'll ever need. My favorite kitchen tool is a **serving spoon.** A close second is a **fine-mesh sieve** (not really, but they *are* good for refining sauces and soups).

My mom's "can't do without" kitchen gadget is a **collard chopper.** It looks like a biscuit cutter with a handle and a serrated bottom edge. And I've always got **butcher's twine, kitchen shears,** and **cheesecloth** shoved in a drawer nearby.

With some finagling, you could cook everything in this giant book using a **5-quart Dutch oven,** a **12-inch cast-iron skillet,** and a **half-sheet tray** with a lip around the edge. But if you want to enjoy the experience, you'll need **small, medium, and large mixing bowls,** a **10-inch saucepan or skillet,** a **3-quart brazier or 9 x 13-inch baking dish,** and a **3-quart saucepan.** And while just about everything but the ice cream can be done with elbow grease if that's the grease you've got, a **standing mixer, food processor, blender,** and **ice cream machine** are nice to have.

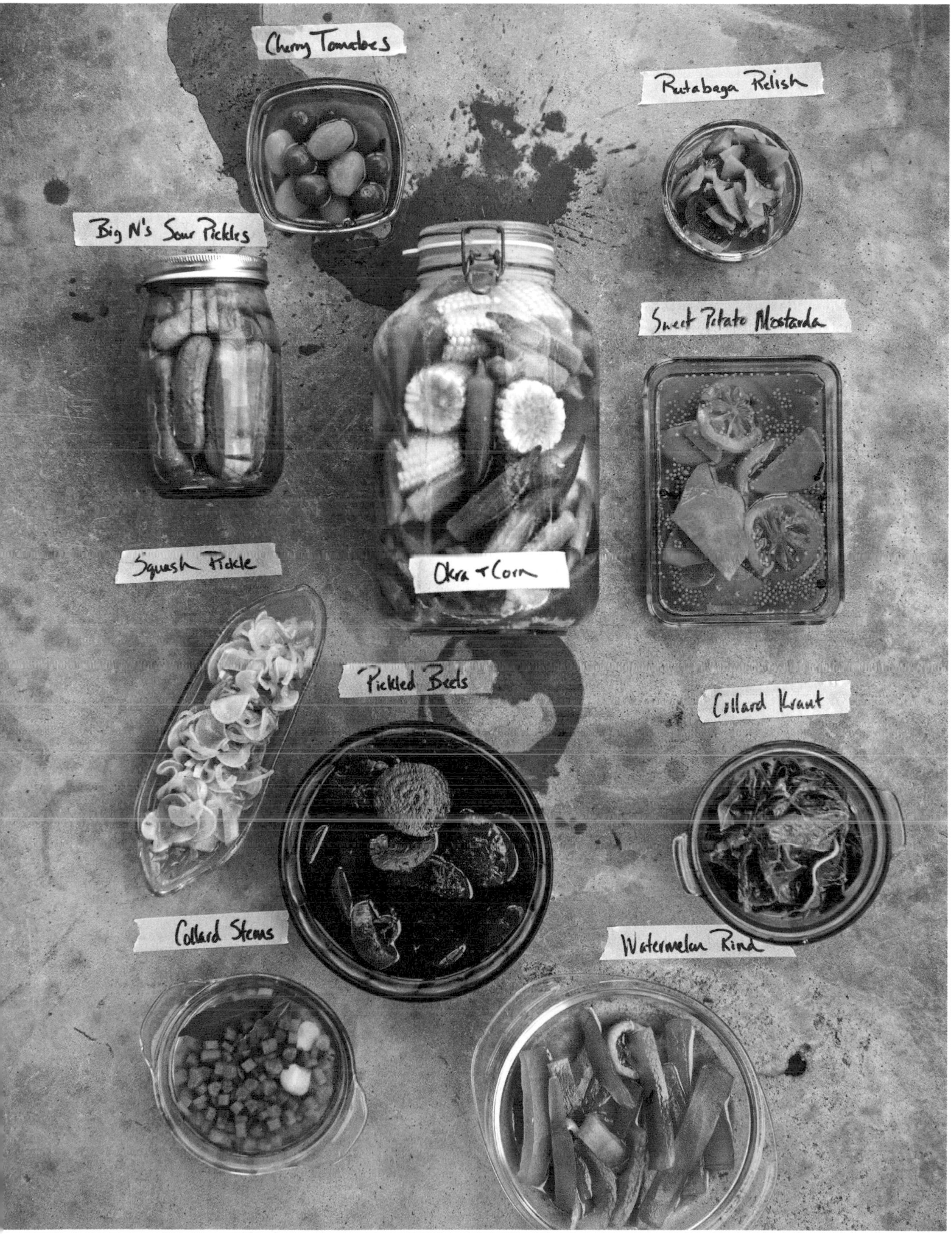

Cherry Tomatoes

Rutabaga Relish

Big N's Sour Pickles

Sweet Potato Mostarda

Squash Pickle

Okra + Corn

Pickled Beets

Collard Kraut

Collard Stems

Watermelon Rind

AN ODE TO SEASONING MEAT

TOO MANY PEOPLE THINK MEAT, often fried meat, sits at the center of the Southern plate. Maybe it does today, but historically we ate large pieces of meat once or twice a week. The rest of the time, cooks used "seasoning meat" as a condiment—a means to round out a vegetable-and-grain-focused meal. Seasoning meat is usually pork, but never a fancy cut. Instead, it is every nook, cranny, nugget, and bone salted, smoked, or ground into sausage to lend flavor to pots of anything you can boil.

We don't cook our beans and greens this way simply because we like it. The custom comes out of the need to preserve meat. Families came together after the first cold snap, slaughtered a few hogs, and turned those hogs into food for the frigid months to come.

This tradition is responsible for beloved pork products like country ham, smoked side meat, jowl bacon, ham hocks, and sausage. Pig tails, feet, cubes of fat, neck bones, and noses got salted down, packed into crocks, and hung from rafters till a cook imitated Jesus with His loaves and fishes and called on a hunk of cartilage and bone to turn a bunch of nothing into supper. Often simmered in water and nothing else, seasoning meat produces a porky broth bubbling with white fat, smoke, and funk that transcends the days of hog killings to become an essential cooking medium.

Southern cooks have strong opinions. Since this is my book, I'm calling mine "wisdom." Here it is.

Seasoning-Meat Wisdom

Air-dried sausage: The seasoning meat of choice in Eastern North Carolina. Its funk, tang, and umami accentuate the bitter notes of turnips in an incomparable way. See page 364 for more.

Smoked pig tails and feet: These offer body as well as fat and flavor. Look for feet and tails that have been split in half. They'll give up their sticky-fingered, lip-smacking, body-building qualities faster and gnawing on the carnage will be less offensive. I like these for soups

and greens, not for beans and peas.

Smoked ham hocks: A cross-section of what you could call the pig's calf, ham hocks are the quintessential collard-green seasoning machine. Hocks offer flavor, body, and good-size chunks of meat to their companions. It takes a lot of cooking to coax meat from hocks, but the result is luscious pink pearls bobbing in your pot.

Country ham: To me, country ham's place is in a biscuit or next to grits, not in a pot of greens. In a pinch, I'll use it as

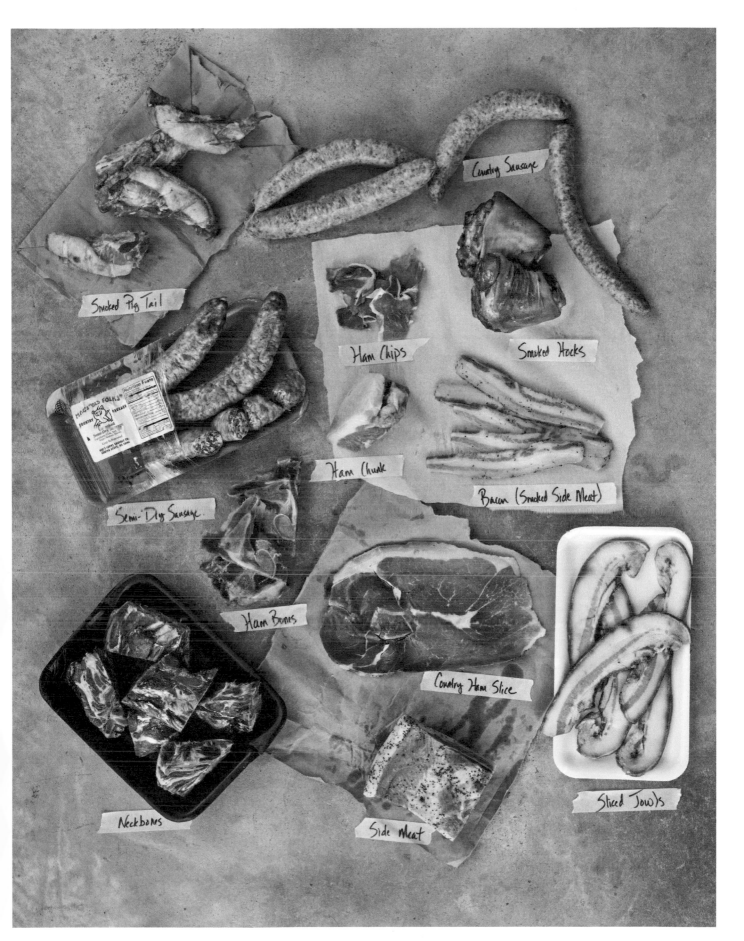

Country Sausage

Smoked Pig Tail

Ham Chips

Smoked Hocks

Ham Chunk

Bacon (Smoked Side Meat)

Semi-Dry Sausage

Ham Bones

Country Ham Slice

Sliced Jowls

Neckbones

Side Meat

AN ODE TO SEASONING MEAT

seasoning meat, along with its skin and bone. Country ham is short on fat and broth-body-building qualities, so look for chunks with the large pieces of fat and skin that we call "chips."

Smoked neck bones: These have a devoted following. Cross-sections of the neck studded with fatty nuggets of meat get simmered and gnawed on like a chicken leg. They do double duty as seasoning and centerpiece.

Belly bacon, side meat, streak of lean, and jowl bacon: Bacon is generally cured, smoked pork belly, but a fattier bacon with a stronger flavor is made from a pig's jowl. That's jowl bacon.

Pork belly that's cured but not smoked is side meat or streak of lean. The term refers to the strip of meat between

the two pillows of fat on every pork belly. I like when it's rubbed with black pepper on top of the salt cure and sold in slabs. It's my go-to for soups and beans because I find too much smoke distracting.

There are two ways to use bacon and side meat for seasoning. You can render it in your pan and set the crispy meat aside before you add water to make the broth, or put the meat straight in with the water like a ham hock. Usually I render some and leave a few whole chunks or slices for the water.

Fatback: Just what it sounds like, this is fat taken from the back of a pig. It is hard, flavorful, and great for rendering into lard. To make it seasoning meat, the skin is left on and the fat is cured in salt. Like pork belly, it can be rendered crisp or dropped straight into the pot.

Roots

I DIDN'T LEARN TO MAKE biscuits and elaborate Sunday lunches at my mother's knee. Nope; growing up, I was busy plotting my grand exit from the middle of nowhere, Deep Run.

I had big dreams, the kind I believed you could never realize in a community that was home to more pigs than people. I didn't aspire to be a chef. I wasn't thinking about becoming a big-city lawyer or an opera singer either. I just wanted night to sound like car horns and people instead of frogs and crickets. I wanted traffic, not tractors, and to walk somewhere other than to the car. And was an Applebee's too much to ask for?

My family made their living in tobacco, and when that industry faded we farmed hogs instead. My mom's parents, Buck and Lorraine Hill, and my paternal grandparents, Iris and Currin Howard, grew, harvested, and preserved much of their own food. Until I was four or five, my parents did too. It now sounds like a locavore's dream, but I thought our barbecue, creamed corn, and butterbeans were boring. I felt I deserved greater sophistication: regular dinners at Chili's, perhaps?

I got my wish at age fourteen, when I left home for an all-girls boarding school. I was finally off the farm, out of the country, with miles between me and Bethel Baptist Church. At school, my affluent new friends highlighted my countrified background. I suddenly realized that my parents said things like "It don't matter," "The collards are over yonder," "I might could carry you to town," and "I reckon that'll do." Our modest home and rural way of life became a source of shame for me.

Over the summers spanning high school and college, I spent as little time in Deep Run as possible. I found my way to camp in Connecticut and to the Senate as a page. I was a writing student at Choate Rosemary Hall, a waitress at Sticky Fingers Ribhouse in Charleston, and a student in Buenos Aires. I traipsed across Europe, took classes at NC State to "get ahead," and finally secured a summer internship at CBS News in New York.

Big City, Little Pocketbook

That year was 1999, and I was an English major interested in journalism. It's hard to imagine a more strategic starting point for an aspiring anchorwoman than an internship down the hall from Charles Osgood and Paula Zahn, but instead of devoting my energies to headlines and schmoozing, I was laser-focused on my lunch hour. New York fanned my smoldering obsession with food, tempting me with flat, crispy pizza slices, cold sesame noodles, brightly lit diners, my first sushi, and delis that served pastrami, smoked fish, and bagels. I was long over Applebee's.

After college, hell-bent on settling in New York, I moved there without a job. Soon I found a position in advertising, a Manhattan apartment, and that special pep in my step that marked me as a fabulous young professional. I walked to work at Grey Worldwide in the morning and ate falafel, curries, orecchiette, and dumplings at night. I partied, shopped, and maxed out three credit cards in what seemed like minutes.

But when the newness wore off, and my office job grew so unbearable I started hiding on a vacant floor after lunch to take a nap, I quit. Following stints as a cocktail waitress, a dog walker, and a delivery girl, I was lost and desperate for direction. Then fate intervened. I had just left a promising interview at a biker hangout called Hogs and Heifers when I stumbled across a Now Hiring sign in front of a restaurant on a perfect little corner in the West Village. The restaurant's name was Voyage and the concept was Southern food via the African diaspora. I got a job as a server. The chef, Scott Barton, became my mentor, and many of the waitstaff became lifelong friends. One in the group, Ben Knight, a painter who dressed in leather and chains, became my husband.

This was that time in my life—we all have one—when everything shimmered in the light of possibility. Scott was as much a storyteller as he was a chef, and I gobbled

HOWARD FAMILY TREE

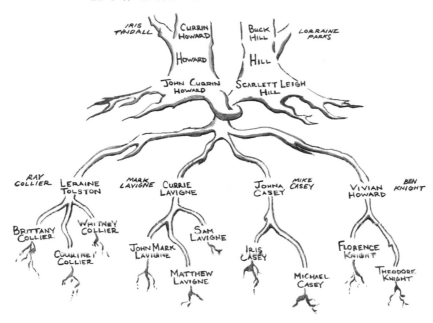

up his every word. Inspired by the way the two skills played together, I started working in the kitchen in hopes of turning that experience into a career in food writing. What I turned it into was a job as a line cook. First as an intern at WD-50 and later as a big shot earning $10 an hour at Spice Market, I struggled to make ends meet and fumbled awkwardly to excel among my more meticulous peers.

After more than a year and a half lost in the grind, I needed to do more. I'd been an entrepreneur since age eight, when I sold a roll of raffle tickets to eager third graders in exchange for the promise of one amazing (and imaginary) grand prize, but this time I decided to sell something real.

Ben and I "opened" Viv's Kitchen in the fall of 2004. We made big, delicious batches of soup, chilled them down in our ice-filled bathtub in Harlem, and delivered pints and quarts to subscribers on days off from our jobs. They garnered us a pretty good following and, out of the blue, a customer offered to invest in a legitimate storefront for our startup. I was ecstatic. My family was not.

This Part Gets a Little Fuzzy

A few months later, I took Ben to Deep Run. I thought that Ben, a Jewish artist born to a yogi vegetarian in Chicago, might seem like an alien to my hog-farming, Southern Baptist parents. But the Howards loved Ben, and Ben loved the Howards.

Over supper, we talked about our plans to open a Manhattan storefront. My then-brother-in-law Ray proposed that we move back home instead, to open a restaurant in partnership with him and my sister Leraine. Ben and I would start it, make it successful, and move on. I scoffed at the idea, knowing it had been planted by my parents in hopes we'd settle in and stay forever. Meanwhile, Ben processed the proposal. He had grown up in a small, broken home, so my in-your-face family appealed to him. And having lived in cities his whole life, he found Eastern Carolina's pace and landscape exotic.

When we returned to New York, there was snow on the ground. Not that pretty white snow you see in movies but the dirty, stinky kind that puts you in a foul mood. We blew forty bucks on a cab to our apartment and trudged up four flights of stairs only to find that the heat was out. That night, we began to toss around the idea of leaving the city.

I did my best to warn Ben that there was more to "back home" than what he'd seen. *Fine dining* meant steaks, baked potatoes, and salad bars, not tasting menus with wine pairings. Our competition would be all-you-can-eat buffets and barbecue. No one would understand his abstract, wildly colorful paintings. And Eastern North Carolina had shrunk into one of the poorest regions in the country. Our kind of restaurant could never be lucrative there.

But we decided to do it anyway.

Leaving New York felt like failure. I was the flip side of the catchphrase "if you can make it here, you can make it anywhere." I hated that weight, and as I packed up my New York City life, I struck a deal with myself to make the most of every new opportunity, to dedicate myself to my craft, and to never let my location determine the quality of my work.

Seeing Deep Run for the First Time

Ben and I opened Chef and the Farmer in June 2006 to a lukewarm reception. What was supposed to be a soup-and-sandwich shop in the town of Kinston, about fifteen minutes from Deep Run, had morphed into an ambitious, high-end dining experience. People came in droves…to speculate on how long it would take us to fail. Diners grumbled that our tea was too expensive and moaned about our unfamiliar and complicated food. We started thinking about where to go next.

At the same time, Ben and I grew closer to my family. My parents offered thoughtful advice and filled two seats at Chef and the Farmer nearly every night for the first few years, paying full price for more food than they could eat. Having always considered me a spoiled brat with a wild streak, my older sisters began to see me as an adult struggling to succeed. I gained their empathy, followed by their respect. Then Johna, Currie, Leraine, and I became friends.

Those first years were hard. There was a heaping dose of truth in the criticism. I had never led a restaurant kitchen, nor had I given one thought to developing a cuisine of my own. I was cooking washed-out versions of food I had seen in New York, forcing someone else's style on folks who didn't like it.

One thing we did have going for us was a commitment to buying everything we could from local farmers. I had hoped to convince them to grow artichokes, lemongrass, and purple potatoes. Instead, season after season, they presented me with collards, rutabagas, and sweet potatoes. I was forced to develop savory recipes around fruits, treat meat like a condiment, and imagine new ways to use rice and cornmeal. Our food no longer imitated a fancy New York accent, but it still didn't have a distinct personality. I hadn't looked deep into the food ways of Eastern North Carolina, so I set out to learn what I had been missing. That turned my life around.

We started eating at the buffets and barbecue haunts I had once avoided, thinking that nothing good could sit on a steam table or be slung into a Styrofoam bowl. Now I saw that these places represented years of recipe development shaped by our common place and ingredients. I could approach this food honestly. I could speak its language—in fact, it was my native tongue.

I interrogated my dad about the table of his youth. I learned about annual hog killings and their all-but-lost roster of products like liver pudding, Tom Thumb, pickled pork, and souse. I rendered my own lard, made cracklins, and baked biscuits that were thin and crispy instead of tall and fluffy. I found out why rice and not grits was a staple on our table. I spent the morning in a shed making collard kraut. I layered my first fish stew. And I finally got to the bottom of what a butterbean was.

With my eyes open to the realities of country living and sustenance farming, I realized my parents, grandparents, and neighbors owned a wealth of practical knowledge that in no way proved embarrassing. Instead, they were cool and smart. They had not, in fact, "just fallen off the turnip truck."

At Chef and the Farmer, I began to combine the techniques I learned from my mom, remembered from my grandmother, and deciphered from steam tables and barbecue sheds with what I knew about balance, color, texture, and presentation. I had finally found my center, and was sinking some roots of my own. I was exalting these ingredients season after season. I preserved, stewed, and manipulated the foods of my childhood into something that reflected my new personal style.

The rewards have been plentiful. Through opening the restaurant and getting to know the place I grew up as an adult, I've become best friends with my family. To honor them and their roots is a tremendous gift. Not many sons and daughters get to do that in such a tangible way, and I know that. And I'm grateful.

HOW TO CAN IN A HOT-WATER BATH

BEFORE OUR GRAPES came through Walmart from Chile and our lettuce grew out of water in a greenhouse, people spent much of their time preparing to grow, growing, and harvesting their food. Then they put a lot of time and energy into preserving it. Except for the very brief time around the harvest or slaughter of something, most of what people ate was preserved in some way. Often it was salted down and cured. Sometimes it was fermented. At a certain point, a lot of things were frozen. And in many cases, ingredients were transformed by sugar, acid, and heat and preserved in a jar.

Canning made me a hoarder. Now I'm freakish about squirreling away pickles, fruit preserves, relishes, and tomatoes for the winter. And I know for certain a jar of something I preserved with my own hands and then sealed between glass and a lid is the best, most thoughtful gift I can give.

Glass preserving jars

2-piece lids

Hot-water canner or a deep and wide saucepan with a lid and rack

A second deep and wide saucepan for sterilizing the jars

Ladle or a measuring cup with a handle

Jar lifter

A heavy-duty, slip-resistant hot pad

Jar funnel

Kitchen towels

Sterilize the jars: Fill your jars halfway with water and stand them up in a large deep pot. Fill the pot halfway with water and bring it up to just under a simmer. Keep the jars hot until you fill them, at least ten minutes. Hot food needs to go into hot jars to prevent breakage. Alternatively, you could run the jars through your dishwasher and fill them while they are still hot from the cycle.

While the jars sit in the hot water, wash their lids and bands in hot soapy water or run them through the dishwasher. Once sterilized they can be at room temperature.

Fill and process the jars: Fill your canning pot halfway with water and bring it up to a simmer. Keep it covered and simmering until you're ready to process your jars.

Remove the jars from the water using the jar lifter and the hot pad. Using the funnel, fill them with whatever it is you're canning, leaving about half an inch of space between the product and the lid. I like to use a measuring cup with a handle, but a ladle also works well. Make sure that whatever you put in the jars is hot. For instance, if you made a relish the day before, reheat it before canning.

Wipe the rim of the jar with a clean damp towel and secure the lid. If you have a traditional canning pot, pull the rack up and secure it on the sides of the pan. Place your

filled jars on the rack, leaving about an inch of space between each jar. Once the rack is full, lower it into the pot. The water should cover the jars by at least one inch and up to two inches. If you don't have enough water, take some of the hot water from your sterilizing pot and adjust the level. Cover the pot and bring it up to a boil. Once it's boiling, process for the time suggested in your recipe.

Cool and store: Once the jars are done, turn off the heat and lift up the rack. Secure it on the sides of the pot and let the jars rest for five minutes. Then remove the jars and place them upright on a kitchen towel, leaving at least an inch of space between them. Let

them cool, undisturbed, for twelve hours.

After twelve hours, check the lids for a seal. If you are using an American-style canning jar, like a Mason or Ball, press on the lid. If it moves up and down, you do not have a good seal. If it appears slightly inverted and doesn't move with the pressure of your finger, it's sealed. If you are using a European-style jar, such as a Weck, look at the red tongue of the rubber seal. On a properly sealed jar, it will point down. To test, take off the clamps and try to push the lid off with your finger. If you can't do this, you have a safe seal.

If you do not get a good seal, you can refrigerate the product or reprocess.

GROUND CORN

White Fine Cornmeal

Dried Corn

ABBITT'S
WHITE CORN MEAL

Yellow Medium Cornmeal

ATKINSON'S
CORN MEAL

Yellow Fine Cornmeal

LAKE SIDE
YELLOW GRITS

Yellow Grits

Rosebank Gold Grits

White Grits

CATTAIL
CORN MEAL

INDIAN HEAD
STONE GROUND
YELLOW
CORN MEAL

RGG-10

Rosebank Gold
Grits

I LIVE TODAY ON THE SAME WINDING RURAL ROAD I grew up on. It's named for a water-powered gristmill a half mile from my house. Every tiny community in Eastern Carolina used to have a mill like this, where people gathered to grind corn into grits, meal, and flour. A hundred years ago, these mills were bustling community hubs that often operated on barter and usually hid a moonshine still somewhere on the property.

But by my childhood in the 1980s, the farmers and housewives of Deep Run had been turned on to the joys of one-stop shopping at the Piggly Wiggly. The mill still made grits, but it was no longer a center of commerce. My family's kitchen, like many others, had begun to straddle the growing space between tradition and convenience, with one of Mom's feet planted in an old cast-iron skillet of cornbread and the other in a box of Bisquick.

The daughter of farmers who had to grow most of their own food, Mom saw the Piggly Wiggly as a promised land of peas she didn't have to shell, chickens whose necks she didn't have to wring, and tomatoes she didn't have to can. Never mind that the mill's corn was probably grown around the corner from our house, a detail some people would get teary-eyed over today. She looked instead to the promise of a whole fluorescent-lit aisle of white- and yellow-corn stuffs.

Mom appreciated the convenience of buying her cornmeal in the same place she bought her dish soap, but like her own mother, she preferred her cornbread simple, unadulterated, and made from scratch. She made us cornbread every day and chicken and rice once a week, and she added variety to our diet with vegetables stewed with cured pork, sweet potatoes roasted in their jackets, and, when she wanted to show off, deviled eggs or banana pudding. We called lunch "dinner" and dinner "supper." And instead of grits for breakfast, we ate rice because that's what my Granddaddy Howard had eaten. I assumed that's what everybody did.

RECIPES

Mom's Cornpone

Grandma Hill's Hoecakes

Lillie's Fried Cornbread

Foolproof Grits

Charred Spring Vegetables
with Creamy Scallion Dressing
and Hushpuppy Croutons

Grits and Greens with Hot Sauce
and Pork Rinds

Pimento Cheese Grits with
Salsa and Chips

Cheesy Grit Fritters

Spoonbread with Sausage Ragout

Then one day when I was six years old, my sister Johna described a bowl of grits she had had at a friend's house; it was loaded with butter, Velveeta singles, and crumbled sausage. Right away I wanted that new invention more than anything I'd ever wanted in all my six years, but Mom refused my petitions. Grits took too long to make and burned too quickly, she said, and I could just as easily put Velveeta and sausage in a bowl of rice.

But I was tired of rice and wanted the dream dish Johna had had over at Suzanne's. The next time I went to the store with Mom, I did it with purpose. At the grits end of the cornmeal aisle, the word *instant* caught my eye. I had a feeling Mom might like that. We had just gotten our first microwave and she had enrolled in a class on how to cook a whole meal in it, so I had both timing and technology on my side. I grabbed the Quaker instants and handed them up for consideration. Mom looked the box over and dropped it in the cart with a thud of approval.

Saturday morning, Johna dumped her packet of instants into a bowl and slid it into our shiny microwave. When she pulled them out, she laid a slice of Velveeta on top and crumbled in a link of sausage. I peered into the bowl and met cheesy steam. At first bite, these grits were everything I'd hoped they'd be.

For years, instant grits with Velveeta and crumbled sausage were my gold-standard Saturday-morning experience, a bowl of comfort only a kid could feel good about eating. I knew even then that there had to be something unwholesome about grits that swallowed up water in a mere minute, but my cheese-filled gut told me that there would be more highbrow food in my future once I made it out of Deep Run.

The irony is not lost on me that I moved to New York to escape my upbringing on a farm in Eastern North Carolina and then went to work in a hip downtown restaurant that celebrated Southern food. But at the time, I didn't see a connection between *my* food and the food we served at Voyage. What we put on the table back home seemed way too basic to be held up as beautiful or important.

Scott Barton was celebrating a different South—one that was far more storied and sophisticated than my own. I privately topped my grits with fake cheese and

Jimmy Dean sausage, while he treated grits as though they were precious, cooking them slowly into a plump, creamy porridge and serving them under truffled scallops and redeye gravy. Once again, I was ashamed of where I came from.

During the year I worked for Scott, I fell in love with the stories behind his food, and I fell in love with cooking. Like a woman who never went to college looks at a sister with a PhD, I admired the South he talked about, and I had issues with it. The South we celebrated at Voyage was about Anson Mills grits ground from heirloom corn, not pulled from a Quaker pouch. It was a place where the biscuits were tall and fluffy and made from scratch. Mom's biscuits came from a can. It was a land where people ate gumbo and duck and raw oysters. We didn't eat any of that at home. Scott's South, with its low country and bayou and Appalachian Mountains, was not Deep Run. Deep Run was different.

I've learned a lot since then. Yes, Deep Run is different than other parts of the South, but it's not worse. Our region's food traditions are unique, shaped more by rural sensibilities, resourcefulness, and preservation than by ports or mountains. Our grits had not always been instant. After all, I grew up on a road named after a gristmill! Instead, my *generation's* grits were instant. We grew up with parents so in love with not having to grow, pick, and pickle everything that they often chose not to grow, pick, preserve, or cook anything.

In a way, my life began that year at Voyage, and it has been marked by moments of discovery, delight, and dumbfounded awe at the gold mine of history, wisdom, and tradition living quietly around me. Maybe that's what it means to grow up. If so, I'm glad I got to do it here.

GROUND CORN WISDOM

No Corn, No America

GROUND CORN DISTINGUISHES the food of the Americas from that of the rest of the world. Sweet corn—bursting with sugar, begging for a pat of butter—is not what we're talking about here. We'll talk about that later *(pages 216–34)*. When we talk about ground corn, we're talking corn that matures in late summer and dries out in the field, or field ripens, before it is harvested and finally ground into cornmeal, grits, polenta, or masa.

Corn, or maize, is indigenous to the Americas. Native people relied on it as a major source of nutrition till it and the continent were discovered by Europeans. Then those Europeans relied on corn in the same way. Americans survived on corn's bulk and nutrition year round. It's like the role of rice in Asia. In many ways we are here because it was here first. Now corn is responsible for more food products worldwide than any other grain.

Cornmeal versus Grits

AS I MENTIONED ABOVE, ground corn shows up in a lot of places these days. In Eastern Carolina though, ground corn is cornmeal or grits and that's it. Both products are dried corn ground to different consistencies. **Cornmeal** is ground very fine: sometimes like flour, other times like sand. Cornmeal's tiny particle size allows it to absorb liquid quickly, making it the foundation for cornbread, dumplings, breaders, or batters. Cornmeal's particle size varies across brands, so you may have to adjust recipes slightly to reach the desired consistency.

Grits are coarser, with an often irregular granular texture. Their larger particle size requires coaxing with gentle heat to fully absorb liquid. The larger the particles, the longer they take to cook.

Don't bread a piece of fish or attempt to make cornbread with something labeled grits. Instead transfer those grits to a food processor or blender and let it rip till they resemble coarse sand. Voilà! Cornmeal!

Instant grits are precooked, then dried. They come in individual packs and are rehydrated by pouring boiling water over top. They have lots of sodium and a processed taste. Instant grits will not work in these recipes.

Quick grits, the most common being Quaker, are finely milled. They cook in five to twenty minutes because their particle size is small. They will work in these recipes but don't have the nuanced flavor and rustic texture of coarse artisan grits.

Coarse grits come in different sizes and take twenty minutes to an hour to cook. They're my favorite because every brand has its own approach. Sometimes the variety of corn is the point. Other times it's the way they're ground. Some are creamy with larger corn particles mixed in, and some are hearty, almost chewy when cooked. Reputable artisan mills include Anson Mills, Geechie Boy Mill, Barkley's Mill, Palmetto Farms, Hagood Mill, and Bob's Red Mill.

Yellow versus White

MOST OLD-SCHOOL COOKS in the Southeast prefer white cornmeal and grits. It's all I grew up eating. Dried white corn tastes elegant, with mineral notes and floral qualities. Sometimes when I eat plain-as-possible cornbread made with white cornmeal, I could swear there's dairy or cheese in there.

Yellow corn is more popular just about everywhere else in the United States. A chef friend of mine once told me he preferred yellow grits because they looked like they already had butter in them, which explains a lot. To me, dried yellow corn is overtly corny. In Eastern Carolina, it's what we feed livestock.

That being said, in these recipes you can swap yellow for white or vice versa.

Dried Corn's Future

MY MOM ALWAYS HAD A BAG of opened cornmeal tucked inside the door of our fridge. The women in my family deemed it perishable and worthy of the icebox space. Today, after decades of us looking at ground meals and flours as if they were dead dusts, many premium mills recommend storing their products in the refrigerator or freezer. This is a good sign. It means those meals are fresh and preservative-free. It also means people are favoring nutritional value and taste over preservatives and shelf life.

What Cornbread Means

CORNBREAD STARTED OUT as poor-people food, a way to stretch a meal, and it evolved into soul food, a way to celebrate it. There is perhaps nothing more deeply ingrained in the Southern table than the tradition of moistened cornmeal baked or fried to a pleasing texture and taste. And although the South is known for barbecue, fried chicken, and sweet tea, every confident Southern cook has a way of making cornbread that speaks to how he or she likes to eat and organize time in the kitchen.

In my house growing up, we sometimes ate yeast rolls from the freezer or, on special occasions, biscuits from a can, but we had homemade cornbread every day. That tells you how little effort it takes to throw together a no-frills batch of cornbread.

The cornbread we make in Eastern Carolina is starkly simple. Our recipes don't always include eggs, lots of sugar, baking powder, or flour, but we still make countless versions of the basic formula. Hushpuppies with margarine, corn sticks, flat crispy rounds or squares cut from a thick chewy slab: nobody here serves somebody else's recipe. Your cornbread is a window into your soul.

Mom's Cornpone

Grandma Hill's
Hoecakes

Lillie's Fried
Cornbread

Mom's Cornpone

Makes a 10-inch skillet

MOM NEVER CALLED THIS CORNPONE, but I now know cornbread baked in a round skillet without dairy or eggs is most accurately referred to as *pone*. Dense, with an extremely crisp exterior and chewy moist crumb, this is not the fluffy corn cake most people call cornbread. Mom made this nearly every day when I was a kid, and if it were not for the big dollop of bacon fat I watched her spoon into the screaming-hot pan, I would have dismissed it. It's one of the few things Mom still cooks regularly. She swears it soothes an angry belly.

Eat this cornbread straight out of the oven if you can. I love it with molasses. See the photograph on page 27.

2½ cups cornmeal	2 teaspoons granulated sugar	¼ cup bacon fat or butter
1¼ teaspoons salt	1⅔ cups water	

Place a 10-inch cast-iron skillet in your oven and preheat the oven to 475°F. Sift together the cornmeal, salt, and sugar. Stir in the water. You should have a thick, spoonable dough.

Carefully but quickly place the bacon fat in the screaming-hot cast-iron skillet and let it melt. You can do this in the oven or on the stovetop, just don't let it go longer than it takes to barely melt. You don't want to burn and waste something as precious as salvaged smoked pork grease.

Spoon the cornmeal mixture into the bottom of your pan and spread it out to the edges. The hot fat will bubble up around the sides and start to fry at the edges. Using a spoon, move some of that fat to the center top portion of the cornbread. Ideally, before you put the skillet back in the oven, fat will have touched every square inch of the pone.

Bake the cornbread on the center rack of your oven for 15 minutes. Bring it out and, using a spatula, flip it over. Slide the pan back in the oven and cook an additional 10 minutes.

The cornpone should be brown, beautiful, and fragrant all over with especially thick, crisp edges. Serve hot and fast, if you can.

Grandma Hill's Hoecakes

Makes 12 to 16 sand-dollar-size cornbreads

GRANDMA HILL PROBABLY NEVER HEARD the term *hoecake,* but that's what she made for every Sunday lunch at her house. They were flavored with onion, delicate and addictive, and we called them little cornbreads. Grandma hid these till we sat down to eat and never took them outside her own kitchen.

Their preparation was such a mystery that none of her children knew the recipe. I became determined to figure out how to make these for myself ten years ago, and, by piecing together memories and research, I've come pretty close.

The one memory we all share is of Grandma bringing the little cornbreads out of the oven on a baking sheet. We never saw her fry them, but I know they had to be fried because I've tried the alternative, with sad results. Grandma must have fried her hoecakes before church and heated them up just before lunch. She was smart…and a little sneaky. See the photograph on page 27.

1 cup cornmeal	½ cup buttermilk	¾ cup water, divided
½ teaspoon salt	¼ yellow onion, diced	¼ cup vegetable oil, divided
½ teaspoon granulated sugar		

If you plan to serve these within 20 minutes of cooking, preheat your oven to 200°F. In a medium bowl, sift together the cornmeal, salt, and sugar. Put the buttermilk and the onion in a blender and puree till it's a homogenous liquid. Pour that plus ½ cup of the water into the cornmeal mixture and whisk to combine.

You're looking for something akin to slightly loose pancake batter—a batter that, when you drop it into the skillet, spreads on its own, bubbles up around the edges, and spatters a little. If you need to add more water to accomplish this, add the remaining water in increments.

Heat 1 tablespoon of the oil in a 10-inch cast-iron skillet over medium heat. Spoon 2 tablespoons of batter onto the edge of the pan to form 1 corn cake. If the batter sizzles a little, the pan's ready. Continue to drop the batter around the perimeter of the pan, finishing off with one in the middle. Make sure you get as many of them in there as you can without letting them touch. Lower your heat slightly and cook on one side for about 3 minutes. When they're brown on the cast-iron side and little bubbles are shooting up through the center of the batter, flip and cook an additional 3 minutes. Transfer the browned hoecakes to a baking sheet and hold them in the oven till you're ready to eat. Add another tablespoon of oil and continue with the next batch.

If you, like my grandma, want to make these ahead and serve them a few hours later, warm them in a 375°F oven for 12 to 15 minutes. Do not use a microwave. The results will disappoint.

Lillie's Fried Cornbread

Makes 10 1-ounce pieces

MS. LILLIE HARDY, my friend and home-cook mentor, shocked me when she broke out this technique during a lesson on stewed rutabagas. She called it cornbread, but everything I knew led me to believe she was frying hushpuppies.

Hushpuppies are another of our region's cornmeal creations. Deep-fried, slightly sweet, onion-flavored dough, hushpuppies are the bread you'd often eat next to barbecue or fried fish. Ms. Lillie makes them at home, but hushpuppies are something I always associate with restaurants. Although a few spots still make slabs of cornbread or corn sticks, most barbecue joints and seafood haunts fry hushpuppies. Ms. Lillie's are bare-bones simple, but you could add buttermilk, grated onion, or onion powder to jazz them up. Some people even add flour or eggs—although no purist would do that. See the photograph on page 27.

2½ cups vegetable oil for frying	1 tablespoon baking powder	½ cup plus 2 tablespoons water
1 cup cornmeal	1 teaspoon granulated sugar	
1 teaspoon salt		

Heat the oil over medium heat in a 10-inch cast-iron skillet. In a medium bowl, sift together the cornmeal, salt, baking powder, and sugar. Stir in the water. The cornbread batter will be thick, pasty, and spoonable. You should be able to scoop a little football-shaped piece with your spoon and have it hold its shape when you drop it into the oil. If it's too loose or seems dry, adjust with more cornmeal or water.

I would typically recommend a thermometer for checking the temperature of the oil, but Lillie would never do that. So test the oil by dropping a small piece of the batter into it. If it immediately starts sizzling, you're good to go. You're looking for oil that is roughly 350°F.

Spoon the cornmeal footballs around the perimeter of the pan and into the center. Do not crowd the oil, making sure each fritter has a little space on either side of it to fry. If your cornbread is not completely submerged, turn it over after about 3 minutes to fry on the other side. It will take close to 6 minutes to cook the cornbread properly. When it's done, it will have a thick brown crust and a chewy interior. Drain on paper towels. Serve as soon as possible.

Foolproof Grits

Makes 3 cups

THERE'S NOTHING SIMPLER than a bowl of grits. Still, very few people I know, except for chefs, cook grits from scratch at home. Instant grits became so popular in the 1980s and '90s that generations of Southerners have no idea what good grits taste like or how to prepare them.

I'd like to empower a new generation to make grits at home. I employ a double-boiler situation because I can't bear standing over something for more than thirty seconds, and the gentler heat safeguards against a burned breakfast. I think it also produces a creamier grit. But you could absolutely do this in a two- or three-quart saucepan over low heat with a watchful eye.

I cook grits in milk, but that's just personal preference. You could use stock of any kind, water, or heavy cream. What's important is starting with a quality product. If more than two ingredients are listed on the package, choose different grits.

1 cup grits	10 turns of the pepper mill or ¼ teaspoon black pepper	1 tablespoon butter
3 ¼ cups milk		
1 ½ teaspoons salt		

Note: *I don't have a legitimate double boiler, so for this recipe, I rig one up. I fill the bottom of a 4-quart saucepan with 2 inches of water, then I position a 2- to 3-quart glass or metal bowl on top of that. There you have it, a double boiler.*

In the top section of your double boiler, stir together the grits and the milk. Take a fine-mesh tea strainer and skim away the hulls that float to the top. Getting rid of these will prevent you from having hard, uncooked bits in what should be a creamy finished product. Heat the double boiler over medium high. Whisking every few minutes, run the whisk or spoon around the edges to make sure the grits aren't sticking. After about 10 minutes, the milk will start to take hold of the starch, and the mixture will thicken slightly. Depending on the grind of your grits, between 25 and 40 minutes in, they will have completely swollen and become one with the milk.

Stir in the salt, pepper, and butter. Serve warm. If they thicken up like cement before you're able to get them on the table, whisk in warm water or milk to loosen them up. They should be thick, not runny, but should spread when you portion them out.

Charred Spring Vegetables with Creamy Scallion Dressing and Hushpuppy Croutons

Serves 4

IT OCCURRED TO ME a few years ago that little hushpuppies would make clever croutons. And they do, flavored with onion and lightened by club soda. Here, the thumbnail-size fritters dot a salad made with the first things I get in a tizzy over every spring.

Charring scallions, asparagus, radishes, and just about every other fresh vegetable in a blazing-hot skillet will develop their sweetness and add a note of bitterness to round out their finish. If it's not spring where you are, char something else and pair it with the same elements. Eggplant, okra, squash, corn, Romaine lettuce, even sweet potatoes love to be charred. Take my advice and char your veggies with abandon.

Note: *If you want to skip the salad, the hushpuppies themselves are a worthwhile easy venture; serve them with the dressing as a dip.*

1 bunch asparagus, tough ends trimmed	***Creamy Scallion Dressing***	***Hushpuppy Croutons***
1 bunch scallions, greens and whites separated	Makes 1 cup	Makes about 30 tiny puppies
5 radishes of your choice, halved lengthwise	⅓ cup mayonnaise	1 quart vegetable oil for frying
	⅓ cup Greek yogurt	¾ cup cornmeal
2 tablespoons extra-virgin olive oil	¼ cup buttermilk	3 teaspoons baking powder
1 tablespoon lemon juice	3 tablespoons minced scallions, green part only	1 teaspoon salt
1 teaspoon salt	⅓ cup Parmigiano-Reggiano, grated on a Microplane	1 teaspoon granulated sugar
1 cup Creamy Scallion Dressing	15 turns of the pepper mill or scant ½ teaspoon black pepper	3 tablespoons grated yellow onion
30 Hushpuppy Croutons	Zest of 1 lemon	2 tablespoons buttermilk
	2 teaspoons lemon juice	½ cup plus 2 tablespoons club soda
	Scant ½ teaspoon salt	

Make the dressing: Whisk all the dressing ingredients together in a medium bowl and let them marry for at least 30 minutes before serving. The dressing will keep up to a week in a sealed container in the refrigerator.

Char the vegetables: Heat a 10- or 12-inch cast-iron skillet over high heat. Toss the asparagus, scallions, and radishes with the oil and position about a third of them in a single layer in the skillet. Char the asparagus and radishes hard on one

side, and take them out of the pan. Char the scallions so that they're browned on two sides. Continue with the remaining batches. Toss all the vegetables with the lemon juice and salt and let them cool in a single layer, ideally on a rack, before serving. Not crowding your vegetables while they cool will prevent them from further steaming one another.

Make the hushpuppies: Preheat your oven to 200°F. In a 4-quart Dutch oven, heat your oil to 350°F. Sift together the cornmeal, baking powder, salt, and sugar in a medium bowl. In a smaller bowl, whisk the onion into the buttermilk and add the club soda. Stir the wet into the dry, and get ready to fry your puppies. The batter should be spoonable, not drippy but not pasty either. This batter is slightly more loose than the batter for Lillie's Fried Cornbread because I like a more irregular shape and crisper exterior

here. It's important you cook these within half an hour of mixing them, otherwise the club soda will lose all its fizz, and the hushpuppies will be more dense than they should be—good, but dense.

In 3 batches, drop ½ teaspoon rounds or annoyingly minuscule scoops of batter into the hot oil. Carefully stir them around after about 15 seconds and cook a full minute and a half to 2 minutes. Once they're a deep golden brown on the outside, use a slotted spoon to lift them out of the oil and drain them on paper towels. Follow up with the next batch. Hold the hushpuppies in a warm oven till you're ready to serve.

Serve: Serve the vegetables with the dressing drizzled over the top. Finish with as many croutons as you like.

Pimp My Grits

FOR CLOSE to two years we had a section of our menu called Pimp My Grits. The idea was to use grits as a blank canvas to express all the elements of taste and texture. In one six-inch cast-iron skillet, the humble grit was paired with something bitter, sour, sweet, salty, umami, and crunchy. The section was a fun way to think about a complete dish and a clever way to encourage guests to try new combinations. We dropped the section from the menu eventually because I became self-conscious about the *pimp* part of it, but we still keep one grit with gravitas, if you will, on the menu at all times. The recipes on pages 36–38 are two of our most popular renditions.

Both are a great way to begin a party because they're easy-to-share conversation starters. Plus, you can assemble them ahead of time and bake them off just before your guests arrive.

Grits and Greens
with Hot Sauce and
Pork Rinds

Pimento Cheese Grits
with Salsa

Grits and Greens with Hot Sauce and Pork Rinds

Serves 6

GRITS AND GREENS, a combination introduced by American Indians, are a classic for a reason. They are typically made with collards, but I chose turnips because I'm a turnip disciple. Use any leafy green that you believe in. This Brown-Butter Hot-Sauce Vinaigrette couples my obsession with brown butter and all its nutty nose love with my people's penchant for dousing stewed greens with chili-laced vinegar. Don't skip it, please. The acidity, the heat, and the additional fat are all big players here.

These are obvious as a hearty side, but I like to serve them as a shared appetizer. Wherever it shows up in your meal's progression, don't miss the chance to treat the pork rinds like chips and the grits like dip! See the photograph on page 35.

Grits and Greens

- 1 pound turnip greens
- 4 garlic cloves, minced
- 2 tablespoons extra-virgin olive oil
- 2 teaspoons salt, divided
- ¼ teaspoon chili flakes

- 1 batch Foolproof Grits *(page 31)*
- 1 cup chicken stock
- 15 turns of the pepper mill or scant ½ teaspoon black pepper
- 1 tablespoon butter, divided
- 1 cup grated Parmigiano-Reggiano

  Pork rinds

Brown-Butter Hot-Sauce Vinaigrette

- 4 tablespoons butter
- 2 tablespoons lemon juice
- 1 tablespoon hot sauce
- ¼ teaspoon salt

Cook the greens and assemble the grits: Preheat the oven to 400°F. Cut the tough end off the turnip greens and slice the remaining stem and leaves into ½-inch pieces. In a 10-inch cast-iron skillet, the skillet you will bake the grits in, cook the garlic in the oil over medium heat till it just starts to sizzle. Quickly, because brown garlic is bitter burned garlic, add the greens, 1 teaspoon salt, and the chili flakes. Using tongs, toss the greens around as they wilt.

Once the greens are just wilted, dump them in a large bowl with the grits, chicken stock, black pepper, 2 teaspoons butter and Parm. Rub the inside of the cast-iron skillet with the remaining 1 teaspoon butter and spoon the grits and greens into it. Slide the skillet onto the middle rack of the oven and bake uncovered for 40 minutes.

Make the vinaigrette and serve: In an 8-inch sauté pan or skillet, melt the butter. Do not use a cast-iron black-bottomed skillet here, because you will not be able to see the butter browning. Once the butter melts, it will foam and fizz and eventually start to brown a little on the bottom. When you see this beginning to happen, make sure you swirl the pan around so that all the milk solids brown evenly. Do not walk away. Once the butter is nutty in color as well as aroma, carefully stir in the lemon juice, hot sauce, and salt. Let it bubble up for about 15 seconds, then spoon the hot vinaigrette over the baked grits. Serve right away with the pork rinds.

Pimento Cheese Grits with Salsa and Chips

Serves 4 to 6

THESE ARE BY FAR THE MOST POPULAR pimped grits we ever served. Think of this like a layered dip with both hot and room-temperature components, or forgo the chips and serve it as a starter or side.

Here I recommend a tomato-based salsa, but depending on the season, you could use snow peas, charred asparagus, or radishes in the place of the tomato. The point is to have something bright, vegetal, and acidic with every bite of rich cheesy grits. If you choose to go the dip route, use your favorite tortilla chips or make Grandma Hill's Hoecakes *(page 29)*. See the photograph on page 34.

2 teaspoons butter

1 batch Foolproof Grits *(page 31)*, at room temperature or chilled

1½ cups Pimento Cheese *(page 370)*

2 cups Tomato Salsa

Tomato Salsa
Makes 2 cups

½ medium red onion, peeled, halved, and sliced paper-thin

½ jalapeño, seeded and sliced paper-thin

2 tablespoons lemon juice

2 medium tomatoes, small-diced

3 tablespoons chopped cilantro

¼ teaspoon salt

Make the salsa: In a medium bowl, marinate the onion and jalapeño in the lemon juice for 30 minutes. Stir in the diced tomatoes, cilantro, and salt. Let that marinate a minimum of 15 minutes and up to 2 hours before serving.

Assemble and bake the grits: Preheat your oven to 400°F and grease the inside of a 10-inch cast-iron skillet liberally with the butter. Spoon the grits into the pan and spread them into a flat circle that spans the entire skillet.

If your pimento cheese is soft and you feel up to the task of spreading it on top of the grits in an even layer, please do so. But I go about it this way: Cut 2 pieces of parchment or waxed paper into 12-inch squares. Place 1½ cups thoroughly chilled pimento cheese onto the center of one of the squares. Lay the other square on top of that and quickly press the cheese out into a 10-inch circle. Peel the top layer of paper off and lay the side with the exposed cheese down on the grits. Carefully peel the paper off, revealing a disk of cheese on top of the grits.

Just before you're ready to serve, bake on the middle rack of your oven for 20 to 25 minutes, then set the oven on broil and cook 2 additional minutes. The grits should be bubbling vigorously around the edges and splotchy brown on top. Serve warm with salsa on top and chips if you like.

Cheesy Grit Fritters

Makes 30 fritters

ARANCINI, stuffed and fried rice balls from Italy, are hard to say no to. So are their Southern U.S. brothers. Loaded with Monterey Jack, dredged in cornmeal, and fried, these little grit balls are fun as finger food with Refried Field Peas (*page 168*) or Stewed Tomatoes (*page 270*) or Basil Pesto (*page 346*).

Note: *When I serve these fritters with Refried Field Peas, I choose Monterey Jack, but you could use any good melting cheese. One of my favorite combinations is stuffing the grits with something creamy and funky like Brie and pairing the fritters with Apple Chips (page 490) for dipping. I've also added ingredients like chopped scallions, country ham, and roasted mushrooms to the grit mix. The trick is to keep the mixture stiff. Too much moisture can cause the fritters to fall apart while they're frying.*

1½ **cups cooked grits or ½ batch Foolproof Grits (page 31)**	1 **cup Monterey Jack cheese, grated** 1 **cup cornmeal**	4 **cups vegetable oil for frying**

In a medium bowl, stir together the cooled grits with the cheese. The mixture should be stiff and should hold its shape when portioned. Using a 1-ounce scoop or a spoon, roll the grit mixture into fritters, each about half the size of a golf ball. Then roll the fritters in cornmeal. Refrigerate or freeze the fritters in a single layer until you're ready to fry them up. They will keep in the fridge for up to 3 days and in the freezer for a month.

Heat the oil in a 4-quart Dutch oven till a thermometer reads 350°F. Fry the fritters in 3 batches, gently dropping them in the oil using a metal slotted spoon or a Chinese-style spider. Cook the fritters till they are golden brown on the outside. This will take about 2 minutes if they are not frozen and up to 4 minutes if they are. Drain the fritters on paper towels. Serve warm.

Spoonbread with Sausage Ragout

Serves 4

MY CHILDHOOD SATURDAY-MORNING RITUAL of instant grits, breakfast sausage, and Velveeta left a lasting impression, so much so that when we opened the restaurant and everybody urged us to serve shrimp and grits, I did the only thing that seemed appropriate: I put shrimp over sausage ragout and cheese grits. We kept that on the menu for close to seven years.

Now I prefer the same ragout perched on an airy pudding we call spoonbread. Spoonbread is not bread at all. This version is more like a cornmeal soufflé. It's magnificent right out of the oven, puffed up and proud, and it's still pretty wonderful once the eggy pudding falls.

Note: *Depending on the sausage you use and whether or not your chicken stock is store-bought, you may need to adjust the salt level in this recipe. The recipe provided assumes you'll make the fresh sausage on page 363 and use homemade stock.*

Spoonbread

- 5 tablespoons room-temperature butter, divided
- 2 cups milk
- 2 teaspoons salt
- 2 teaspoons granulated sugar
- ¼ teaspoon cayenne
- ¾ cup cornmeal
- 3 eggs, separated, at room temperature
- ½ cup heavy cream

Sausage Ragout

- 1 teaspoon vegetable oil
- 1 pound Fresh Sausage *(page 363)* or your favorite breakfast sausage
- 8 ounces button mushrooms, quartered
- 1½ teaspoons salt, divided
- 1 medium yellow onion, small-diced
- 1 large green or red bell pepper, diced
- 3 cloves garlic, minced
- ¼ teaspoon chili flakes
- 1 medium tomato, small-diced
- 1½ cups chicken stock
- 1 tablespoon butter

Make the spoonbread: Preheat your oven to 375°F and grease a 2-quart baking dish with 1 tablespoon butter. Heat the milk, salt, sugar, and cayenne in a 2-quart saucepan until bubbles form around the edges. Whisk in the cornmeal and cook for about 2 minutes or until the starch grabs hold of the milk and thickens up tremendously. Remove it from the heat and stir in 4 tablespoons butter, 1 piece at a time.

In a large bowl, whisk together the egg yolks and heavy cream until the yolks are fully incorporated and the cream is a pale pretty yellow. Then, in the bowl of your mixer fitted with the whisk attachment, beat the egg whites till they reach soft peaks.

Once the cornmeal mixture has cooled for at least 5 minutes, whisk a third of it into the egg yolks and cream. Follow up with the remaining thickened cornmeal, making sure you achieve a homogenous, pourable batter. Using a spatula, fold a

third of the whipped egg whites gently into the batter. Continue with the remaining egg whites. Pour the spoonbread batter into the greased baking pan and slide it onto the middle rack of the oven. Bake for 30 to 35 minutes. Make the ragout while the spoonbread bakes.

The spoonbread will puff up and turn a golden brown on top but be slightly moist in the center. This is the way it's intended to be, but if you prefer it cooked all the way through, increase the baking time by 5 minutes.

Make the ragout: In a 12-inch skillet or sauté pan, heat the oil over medium-high heat. Add the sausage, crumbling it into pieces as you drop it in. You should be able to add all the sausage in a single batch, but be careful not to overcrowd your pan; sausage that's sitting on top of itself in a hot pan is not sausage that's browning—it's

sausage that's steaming. Once the sausage is in the pan, don't shake it around like you're Gordon Ramsay. Let it sit there for a good 3 minutes to take on color. When the first side is a caramelized crisp brown, shake the pan, turn the sausage over with a spoon or spatula, and brown the other side. Once the sausage is brown on 2 sides, lift it out of the pan and set it aside. Pour off the fat, reserving 2 tablespoons.

Pour 1 tablespoon sausage fat back into the skillet and add the mushrooms. Follow the same principle I laid out for the sausage: Do not shake and stir it like I know you want to. Let it sit and sizzle instead. The mushrooms will brown on one side over the course of about 3 minutes. Once they are caramelized, give the pan a shake. Add ½ teaspoon salt and cook an additional minute. Take the mushrooms out of the pan. Add them to the reserved sausage and lower the heat.

Add the remaining 1 tablespoon sausage fat as well as the onions, bell pepper, and 1 teaspoon salt. Let that sweat for about 5 minutes without browning. Stir in the garlic and chili flakes and cook for 1 minute. Add the tomatoes, chicken stock, sausage-and-mushroom mixture, and the remaining ½ teaspoon salt. Bring all that up to a brisk simmer and cook uncovered till the liquid is reduced by about two-thirds. Stir in the butter. The ragout should be shiny and juicy, not brothy. If you let too much liquid cook out and the ragout appears dry, add ¼ cup of water with the butter to glisten things up.

Serve the warm spoonbread alongside or underneath the sausage ragout.

EGGS

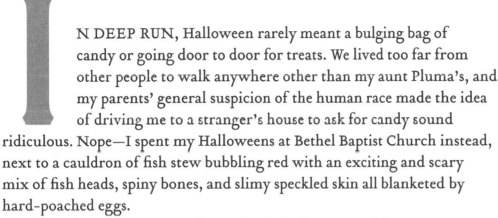

IN DEEP RUN, Halloween rarely meant a bulging bag of
candy or going door to door for treats. We lived too far from
other people to walk anywhere other than my aunt Pluma's, and
my parents' general suspicion of the human race made the idea
of driving me to a stranger's house to ask for candy sound
ridiculous. Nope—I spent my Halloweens at Bethel Baptist Church instead,
next to a cauldron of fish stew bubbling red with an exciting and scary
mix of fish heads, spiny bones, and slimy speckled skin all blanketed by
hard-poached eggs.

For a lot of country people, particularly for women like my mom,
whose day-to-day life revolved around home and the farm, church meant
community. For just about every activity other than school and shopping,
we went to Bethel Baptist. The fellowship hall, a simple building adjacent
to the sanctuary, was where all the eating happened.

Fain Reeves, a quiet man with carpet-thick black hair, oversaw the stew and
much of the cooking that went on at church. On Halloween, he built a big fire out
back and suspended an unimaginably large cast-iron pot above its flames. As the
families of Bethel arrived, the men and women separated. The men stayed outside
with the cauldron, slicing potatoes, peeling onions, and smoking cigarettes, while
the women went inside to make tea, set up the desserts, and glance sideways at one
another's work. The children fluttered around, admiring their friends' homemade
costumes. Two years in a row I dressed up as a bumblebee; I wore a black trash bag
dotted with yellow circles and stuffed with paper, with two holes cut out of the
bottom so my legs could go through—a cross between a fire hazard and a choking
hazard, with construction-paper wings.

To make the stew, Fain first rendered several pounds of bacon in the giant black
cauldron. The unmistakable smell of sizzling smoked pork drew everyone within nose-shot

EGG WISDOM

Shelf Life and Storage

IF YOU BUY EGGS directly from a farmer, ask if they have been refrigerated. If they have not, you too can leave them at room temperature for up to five weeks from harvest. If they've spent any time in the refrigerator at all, they do have to stay there.

Always store your eggs pointy side down. This reduces the amount of oxygen the eggs are exposed to and will keep them fresher longer.

Super-fresh eggs are harder to peel when boiled, so keep that in mind when you're making something like deviled eggs. There's nothing wrong with a two- to three-week-old egg that's easy to peel.

Color

WE MAKE FAR TOO big a fuss about the color of an egg's shell. There is absolutely no difference in the taste or quality of the egg based on the color of its shell. Many small farmers, though, favor brown eggs because customers at markets and restaurants turn their noses up at white ones.

Pastured, Cage-Free, and Free-Range Eggs

PASTURED EGGS come from birds that have unlimited access to grass or pasture, and they are the best you can find. *Cage-free* and *free-range eggs* are not the same. These terms refer to the amount of space a chicken has to live. Because a pastured hen's diet includes not only grain but also grasses and insects, pastured eggs have a vibrant orange yolk and fuller flavor. When you use pastured eggs, you can really taste the difference in foods that rely primarily on yolks, like pasta doughs or custards. They also have a superior nutritional makeup with more beta-carotene and protein and less cholesterol than other eggs.

Guinea Eggs

ONCE UPON A TIME, every home place around here had guineas. Sometimes called watchdogs, guineas traveled in small flocks, hid their nests, roamed the yard foraging for insects, and made a lot of noise at the sight of intruders. They were social birds who were a working part of small family farms.

Guinea eggs were revered by my grandmother's generation for their performance in cakes. They are about a third smaller than chicken eggs, but because of the guinea hens' diet, based almost entirely on bugs and seeds, their eggs have rich, full-flavored yolks. This allows the baker to add less volume in eggs while still achieving ethereal results. If you are using a full-size guinea egg, follow a one-to-one ratio in the recipes below.

near. We all knew when Fain lifted the bacon out to drain, he doled out a few pieces.

The Eastern Carolina fish stew is a traditional food event that, like pig pickings, oyster roasts, and clambakes, follows a set of rules. If you break a rule, you might make something tasty, but you're making a different dish.

First, for a proper fish stew, it has to be chilly outside. This is not a hot-weather affair. Second, you need the right type of fish, something meaty and full-flavored, like rockfish, sheepshead, or drum. Flounder, catfish, and grouper make soup, not stew. Third, potatoes, onions, and fish must be layered with salt and chili flakes. And no matter what, not even if Jesus Himself walks on water over to you and asks nicely, you will never stir a fish stew. That would make it a muddle, an inferior dish from farther east. Bethel's bubbling cauldron was always red from tomato paste. That's not a defining quality—just a superior preference. But the thing I've always found most distinctly satisfying, and the addition that sets Eastern Carolina fish stew apart, is the egg.

RECIPES

Fish Stew

*Breakfast of a Busy Mom
Who's Trying to Be Healthy*

Deviled Eggs

*Stewed Tomato Shirred Eggs
with Ham Chips*

*Avocado and Tomato with
Broken-Egg Dressing*

Warm Banana Pudding

Unlike bouillabaisse and cioppino, other regional stews that celebrate bounty, our stew developed out of the need to stretch a weekend's catch and feed more people than five pounds of fish should. Potatoes and onions, always plentiful and cheap, filled the pot. Bacon, that little bit of salted smoked pork my people call on often for flavor, made the broth complex, and eggs, an ingredient every farm family had in excess, made it substantial. When that first farmer-fisherman dropped whole eggs into his stew to stretch it further, I'm sure he had no idea he was adding the thing that would make it memorable and unique.

Some churches did a lot of singing and clapping and rejoicing, but Bethel Baptists from Deep Run were more melancholy. While other congregations might have bobbed for apples or had marble races, we watched stone-faced as Fain assembled the stew and filled the cauldron just barely to the top with water. When the crowd broke up and the kids began to play, men shuffled around and talked farming and tobacco prices. Women untied loaves of Sunbeam Queen white bread and put ice in Styrofoam cups. And once the cauldron came to a gentle boil, Fain called a child over to count how many heads we were feeding. This number determined how many eggs got cracked into the stew. I always wanted more than one egg—everybody did. On the one occasion I got to count, even though I was at church and had been warned about an eternity in hell, I lied and told Fain we had about forty-five people to feed.

He looked down at me knowingly and smiled.

Barely tall enough to see all the way into the bubbling pot, I counted as Fain cracked fifty eggs over the top of the stew. Minutes now, and it would be ready. I was first in line. The stew was so thick with fish, potatoes, and onions that the eggs didn't sink. They floated together and formed a raft over the top.

"I'd like three eggs, three potatoes, juice, and bacon; that's all. No fish, no onions. Okay?" I asked, peering up, bumblebee antennae bobbing around.

"You got it, Vivyen," Fain answered, pronouncing my name like everyone at church did, with two syllables instead of three.

He handed me the stew, and I smiled with gratitude. Mom would have made me eat the fish and the onions. I turned on my heel, grabbed three slices of Sunbeam Queen, and settled down in a corner to slurp and sop a country girl's Halloween treat.

Fish Stew

Serves 12

THIS RECIPE mirrors the Deep Run classic, but some people add flourishes like fish heads, garlic, sausage, shrimp, and additional spices. In the words of my friend Warren, "I've seen it done every which-a-way." In that spirit, don't get caught up with specific knife cuts, portion sizes, or equipment. If you want to add something extra, add it.

What makes this stew unique is the layering of the ingredients, the water level, the type of fish, the cooking time, the way you add the eggs, and the soft white sandwich bread for sopping up the broth.

- 1 pound sliced smoked bacon
- 1 6-ounce can tomato paste
- 3 pounds white or red potatoes, peeled and sliced into ½-inch rounds
- 2 pounds yellow onions, peeled, halved, and cut into ¼-inch slices
- 6 garlic cloves, sliced (optional)
- 3 pounds fish steaks, about 3 ounces each, with bones intact (red drum, rockfish, or sheepshead are good options)
- 1 fish head, rinsed well (optional)
- 2½ tablespoons salt
- 1½ teaspoons chili flakes
- 1 dozen eggs
- 1 loaf white bread

Cut the bacon slices into 1-inch squares. Brown it in the bottom of an 8- to 10-quart Dutch oven or cast-iron pot. Once it's crisp, remove it and reserve. Whisk the tomato paste into the bacon fat, making sure you scrape up all the scattlings left from browning the bacon (another nugget of wisdom from Warren).

With the heat off, begin layering the ingredients. Keep in mind you want to end up with three layers. Start with a layer of potatoes, followed by a layer of onions and of garlic, if using, followed by a layer of fish. Top the fish with a third of the salt and a third of the chili flakes. Repeat with two more layers. Fill the pot with enough water to just *barely* reach the top of the fish. If there's a little fish peeking out over the top, that's okay—better than if it's swimming in water. Cover the pot with a tight-fitting lid and bring it up to a boil slowly over medium heat. Once it starts to boil, reduce the heat and let it cook at a high simmer for about 15 minutes. Check the potatoes for doneness. They should be barely tender, not falling apart.

Taste the broth and add more salt if needed. Then, with the stew at a good simmer, add the eggs one by one in a single layer over the top of the stew. I like to crack the eggs into a small cup before I drop them in. What you're trying to do is cook whole eggs in the broth.

Once the eggs are cooked through, use a large ladle to portion the stew. A proper serving is at least one piece of fish, two potatoes, some onions, and an egg swimming in broth. Shower each bowl with some bacon and set it up with a slice or two of white bread.

Breakfast of a Busy Mom
Who's Trying to Be Healthy

Serves 1

PEOPLE HAVE WRITTEN WHOLE BOOKS about eggs and how to cook them, so my method for hard-boiling might get spit on. Nevertheless, here's how I cook my breakfast about three times a week. Paired with a mouthful of broccoli sprouts dressed in lemon juice, it feels healthy. Boiling some eggs is also the first step in two of the recipes in this chapter.

2 eggs

Flaky sea salt
     (I use Maldon)

Black pepper

Hot sauce, if you're
     feeling bored

1 teaspoon lemon
     juice

Broccoli sprouts,
     as many as you
     can manage

Put the eggs in a 2-quart saucepan. Cover them with cool water by 1 inch. Bring the eggs up to a boil and cook for 1 minute. Remove the pot from the heat, cover, and let it sit for 10 minutes. Drain the eggs and run cold water over them till they are cool enough for you to handle.

I find boiled eggs more satisfying warm, so go ahead and peel them. Slice the eggs into quarters and sprinkle both the plate underneath and the top of the eggs with way more salt and pepper than seems reasonable. Add the hot sauce if you're using it. Eat them up. Chase with the lemon-juice-dressed sprouts, and go to work.

Deviled Eggs

Makes 12

MAKING DEVILED EGGS IS TEDIOUS. When we do them at the restaurant, moans, groans, and sighs accompany the hunched-over work of peeling, carefully scooping, and finally stuffing the little cups. Still, deviled eggs have been and continue to be among the most admired of all the South's hors d'oeuvres.

Like a layer cake, a deviled egg is a gift, an offering of affection that reflects the tastes of its maker. Some shine psychedelic yellow with French's mustard, and many are chunky and sweet from pickle relish; my favorites are sprinkled red with paprika. Others (the sad ones, in my opinion) are pale from a blinding but understandable obsession with mayonnaise. My mom's version, which I happen to favor, is tangy with more vinegar than usual. As for mayo, she uses Miracle Whip. I like Duke's.

Use this recipe as a blank canvas. Add flair, like pickles of any kind, blue cheese, herbs, bacon, or all of that at once if that's what you want. I don't, but I'm a purist.

8 large eggs	½ teaspoon salt	¼ teaspoon hot sauce
3 tablespoons softened butter	½ teaspoon granulated sugar	1 teaspoon paprika
2 tablespoons mayonnaise	5 turns of the pepper mill or scant ⅛ teaspoon black pepper	
2 tablespoons white wine vinegar		

Cook the eggs as instructed on page 50 and cool them under running water. Peel the eggs carefully. Have someone who gives a darn do this. Otherwise your gifts will look like someone hacked away at them with his or her fingernails.

Slice the peeled eggs in half down the middle. You can do this one of two ways—lengthwise (most common) or through the equator. Either way, depending on the serving vessel, you may need to slice a tiny piece of white off the bottom to create a flat place for the eggs to rest.

Carefully scoop the yolks into a bowl. I like to use a small spoon to help this along. Once you've scooped your yolks out, select the 12 prettiest whites. You won't need the other 4 halves, so discard them or eat them for some flavorless protein.

Stir the remaining ingredients (except for the paprika) together with the yolks and pass it all through a fine-mesh sieve. I think this mildly tedious step makes the filling slightly more fluffy than just blending everything in the food processor or mashing it with a fork, but those methods work too. In the end you should have a homogenous, smooth yellow filling.

Transfer it to a piping bag fitted with a star tip; a Ziploc bag with the corner cut off will also work. Of course, you could forgo the tip and the bag altogether and use a spoon. Just before you're ready to serve the eggs, pipe the filling into the whites. There should be just enough to overfill each egg.

Sprinkle with paprika and serve at room temperature.

Stewed Tomato Shirred Eggs with Ham Chips

Serves 4

I'LL COME RIGHT OUT and admit that I eat eggs with ketchup. This is not a recipe for that, thankfully, but rich eggs bubbled together slowly with the tart sweetness of stewed tomatoes is like my guilty pleasure went out and got a good job.

Shirred is the Scottish way to say "baked in a pan with a flat bottom." The tricky part of this dream breakfast is the ham chips. They have become staples at the restaurant, and given a very thin slice of ham or prosciutto, they're easy to make. Check your fanciest grocery store for sliced prosciutto or ask your butcher to slice country ham to a sixteenth of an inch thick.

This dish does need a sharp, salty counterpoint, so if you can't make the ham chips happen, substitute shaved Parmigiano-Reggiano.

8 slices country ham or prosciutto, ¹⁄₁₆ of an inch thick	4 to 5 eggs	Whole basil, parsley, or chervil leaves
3 cups Stewed Tomatoes *(page 270)*	½ teaspoon salt	
	10 turns of the pepper mill or scant ¼ teaspoon black pepper	

Make the Ham Chips: Preheat your oven to 350°F. Line a baking sheet with a Silpat-style pan liner or parchment paper. Lay each piece of ham in a single layer on the parchment. Top the ham with another piece of parchment. Set a second baking sheet on top of the parchment to weight it down. Bake in the middle rack of your oven for 12 to 15 minutes, or until the ham is crisp and two shades browner. If you're using Silpats, increase the baking time by 5 minutes. Bring the ham out of the oven and let it cool to room temperature. It will crisp up more as it cools. Peel the parchment away from the ham. Store the ham in a sealed container for up to 2 days before using.

Assemble and bake the eggs: Warm the stewed tomatoes to a simmer and spoon them into a 1½- to 2-quart baking dish. Carefully crack the eggs and position them on the tomatoes with plenty of room between them to cook separately. Bake uncovered on the center rack of the oven for 12 minutes. The whites will be a little jiggly and the yolks will be barely set. If you like more runny yolks, cook the eggs for 10 minutes.

Sprinkle with salt, pepper, herbs, and ham just before serving. Wilted bitter greens, crusty bread, or grits complete the arc of perfection.

Avocado and Tomato with Broken-Egg Dressing

Serves 4

IN 2011 I GAVE BIRTH TO TWINS. Theo and Flo came into the world four weeks early, and their arrival turned every routine Ben and I ever had on its head. One afternoon, right after we brought them home from the hospital, Ben made me a snack. I was depressed and hooked up to a milker, so nothing anyone did for or around me was appreciated. But I do remember this.

The egg, lemon juice, and olive oil in this rudimentary salad came together to make a satisfying puddle of stuff to drag the tomatoes and avocados through. The snack is the first thing other than the tormented-lucky-new-mom feeling I remember from that time. It's like the first food memory of my new life.

¼ small red onion, cut into very thin julienne	2 tablespoons olive oil for finishing	1 large avocado, peeled, pit removed, and sliced
2 eggs, cooked and peeled as on page 50	1 teaspoon Dijon mustard	5 turns of the pepper mill or ⅛ teaspoon black pepper
2½ tablespoons lemon juice	1½ teaspoons salt, divided	
	2 medium tomatoes, cut into small wedges	4 large basil leaves, chiffonade

Place your onion julienne in a little ice water while you get everything else ready. It will take off some of the sharp oniony edge.

Cut each egg into 8 pieces. Place the eggs in a small bowl and stir them together with the lemon juice, oil, Dijon, and ½ teaspoon of the salt. This will be your dressing.

Divide the tomatoes among 4 plates or flat-bottomed bowls. Do the same with the avocado, making sure those ingredients are in a single layer. Spoon the egg dressing over the top. Use all of it even if it seems

like a lot. Season the top of the salad with the remaining salt and the pepper. If you have it, substitute a flaky finishing salt here. Finish with the drained red onion and basil.

I like to tell people how to eat things, and if you are also so inclined, make sure you tell your guests to drag the tomatoes and avocado through the dressing, lifting up any they can. Bread may also help. If you don't want to go to the trouble to arrange the ingredients as suggested, toss everything together in a bowl and go to town.

Warm Banana Pudding

Makes a 3-quart pudding

BANANA PUDDING WAS WARM and sacred at my house, by far Mom's favorite dessert. She treated every covered-dish obligation as a chance to bake a banana pudding. We had a three-quart Pyrex we called the banana-pudding dish. It was deep with rounded sides, so Mom could stuff three good layers of Nilla Wafers between sliced bananas and pudding she had cooked on the stove. She topped it all with mounds of voluptuous meringue.

When the toasted spectacle came out of the oven, hot and fragrant, no matter where the pudding was going or when, Mom scooped a tiny portion into a coffee cup and ate it in a corner of the kitchen with her back to the family. The pudding at that point was jiggly, so she was able to slide all the elements back into place. No one ever knew the difference, I guess.

This is an ode to my mom's pudding, but different. Eat it warm if you can.

Banana Puree

- 5 or 6 ripe bananas
- 2 tablespoons vegetable oil
- ¼ cup 99 Bananas liqueur (optional)

Pudding and Meringue

- 1⅓ cups granulated sugar, divided
- ⅓ cup plus 1 tablespoon cornstarch
- 3 cups milk
- 3 cups heavy cream
- 1 tablespoon vanilla extract

- 8 large eggs, separated
- 4 tablespoons butter
- ¼ teaspoon cream of tartar
- 4 to 5 very ripe bananas, peeled and sliced into ¼-inch rounds

Sesame Wafers

Makes 36 wafers

- 2 cups all-purpose flour
- ½ teaspoon baking powder
- ¼ teaspoon salt

- ⅔ cup sesame or benne seeds, toasted
- 1 cup (2 sticks) butter at room temperature
- 1 cup granulated sugar
- 1 tablespoon light brown sugar
- 1 tablespoon sesame oil
- 1 egg
- 1½ teaspoons vanilla extract

Warm Banana Pudding

Continued from the previous page

Roast the bananas: Preheat your oven to 350°F. Place 5 or 6 peel-on bananas on a cookie sheet about 1 inch apart and rub them with 2 tablespoons vegetable oil. Slide the cookie sheet into the oven and roast for 15 to 20 minutes. The bananas will be extremely dark and soft to the touch. Let them cool enough to handle and transfer the banana flesh and any banana ooze to a food processor. Discard the skins. Add the 99 Bananas, if using, and blend till smooth. Set aside.

Make the wafers: Preheat your oven to 375°F. In a medium bowl, whisk together the flour, baking powder, salt, and sesame seeds. Set aside.

In a mixer fitted with the whisk attachment, cream the butter and sugars till lightened in color and fluffy, about 2 minutes. Add the sesame oil, egg, and vanilla. Scraping down the sides as needed, beat on medium until everything is combined. Reduce the mixer to low and add the dry ingredients and beat until it just forms a dough. The dough will keep in the fridge for 3 days or in the freezer for 3 months.

Using a 1-ounce scoop or a tablespoon, portion out the cookies and roll them into balls. Position the balls 1 inch from one another on two greased cookie sheets. Flatten each cookie to roughly ¼ of an inch thickness. Slide the cookie sheets into the two middle racks of your oven and bake for 10 to 15 minutes or until the

cookies are caramel brown around the edges. Let them cool thoroughly before assembling the pudding.

Make the pudding: In a 4- to 6-quart saucepan, combine 1 cup of sugar along with the cornstarch, milk, heavy cream, and vanilla extract. Stirring constantly, bring it up to a simmer over medium heat until things thicken slightly. Make sure to slide your spatula around the lower edges of the pan periodically. These edges are the hottest part and they'll burn before you know it. Once the mixture has thickened slightly, remove the pan from the heat.

In a medium bowl whisk the yolks until they lighten a little in color. Slowly, a little at a time, whisk in roughly ⅓ of the hot cream mixture. Pour the tempered yolks back into the saucepan and return that pan to medium heat. Stirring constantly, bring it up to a simmer and cook gently for two minutes. Look for it to thicken up even more.

Remove the pudding from the heat and whisk in the butter. If you notice lots of lumps and bumps, strain the pudding through a fine-mesh sieve. If not, go ahead and stir in the roasted banana puree.

Make the meringue: Bring your egg whites to room temperature and add them to a mixer fitted with the whisk attachment. Whisk until they are frothy, and add the cream of tartar. Continue whisking until soft peaks form. Slowly add the remaining ⅓ cup sugar and whisk on, till you have nice stiff peaks.

Assemble and bake the pudding: While both the cookies and the pudding can be made several days in advance, the meringue should be whipped up just before baking. I personally like to assemble this using warm pudding so that things have the chance to heat all the way through as the meringue bakes. But that's not mandatory—just a suggestion per my mother, Scarlett.

Begin by spooning a thin layer of pudding on the bottom of your dish. Top that with a single layer of cookies followed by the sliced bananas. Top those with a little less than half of the remaining pudding followed by another round of cookies and bananas. Spread the last of the pudding on top of that layer and finish with the final round of cookies and bananas. Spoon the meringue on top of it all and feel good accentuating all its height and volume with your spatula. Bake the big pudding on the bottom rack of your oven for about 30 minutes or until the meringue is chestnut brown all over. Serve warm.

TURNIPS

THERE ARE BASICALLY TWO TYPES OF PEOPLE in the South: turnip eaters and collard eaters. I grew up in a turnip-eating house because my mom prefers the bitter, nose-burning notes of turnips to the sweeter ones of collards. For collard eaters, it's simple: You eat the greens because that's all there is. For turnip lovers, what simmers in the pot is more complicated. A lot of people only think of fat white root vegetables when they consider turnips, but here, we celebrate an entire family of bitter greens we call turnips, and only a few of them sprout from a swollen edible taproot. When our turnips carry that big earthy root, we cook it too. When they don't, we stew a "mess of salad." Yes, for some reason folks in Eastern Carolina call all varieties of turnip and mustard greens "salad." Not salad like Caesar or Cobb or Wedge, because lots of turnip greens are fuzzy and not anybody's favorite thing to eat raw, but salad like a tangle of tender, mildly spicy stewing greens.

I didn't share my mom's appreciation for turnips as a kid. Their distinct smell stewing from the back burner of the stove crinkled my nose, and when we sat down to eat supper, I winced as my parents slurped and sopped up their pot liquor like it had healing powers.

Our house was built in the late 1960s, and its family kitchen was square, dark, and small. A mustard-and-avocado-green flower-patterned linoleum floor supported wood cabinets stained dark red. Brown Formica countertops ran from the refrigerator around a corner to an aluminum sink sitting under a little window that seemed to let out more light than it brought in. The countertop picked up to the left of the sink and ran around another corner to meet the workhorse of our house, a four-burner, electric-coil Frigidaire stove.

TURNIP WISDOM

Purple Tops versus Hakureis

I WORK PRIMARILY with two varieties of root-bearing turnips: Purple Top and Hakurei. Purple Top is prized for storage and the most common variety grown in the United States. Out of the ground, they are crisp, sweet, and thin-skinned, but as the roots sit in storage, their skin toughens and their flesh grows bitter. They are fine to eat but need to be peeled and cooked rather than eaten raw. Mature Purple Top roots should not exceed three inches in diameter. If you run across a bigger one, it's going to be "piffy." That's what my mom calls it when the root seems woody and suffers streaky holes at its core.

Hakureis, sometimes called Japanese or Tokyo turnips, are now popping up at farmers' markets and restaurants. They are more elegant than other roots favored for storage. Mature Hakureis are smaller than mature Purple Tops and rarely require peeling. Raw they remind me more of a cross between jicama and an apple than a turnip, and when roasted, they burst with juice.

Turnip Season

WE THINK OF TURNIPS as fall crops because Purple Top roots are often harvested in fall and stored for winter use, but they produce equally well in spring. Turnips do not fare well in temperatures above eighty degrees, and their roots can't withstand frost.

How to Make a Turnip Look Like a Turnip

IF YOU PLAN to serve a whole or halved turnip root, leave about half an inch of the green attached. This will make the end product look the way you always thought a turnip should.

How to Wash Furry Greens

BECAUSE TO ME there's nothing worse than a gritty green and several varieties of turnip greens are covered in little grit-trapping hairs, I wash the bejesus out of them. This is not a rinse-and-run scenario. You've got to commit to the process.

Do what my mom does: Place the greens in the bottom of your sink or in a

---

After breakfast about once a week, my mom geared up to cook a pot of greens. I say "geared up" because although Scarlett Howard loves a mess of salad more than anything other than banana pudding, she thought cooking greens was a whole lot of work.

Drinking coffee from a petite teacup, Mom filled a giant metal pot a third of the way up with water. Then she plucked out one long, shriveled link of funky-smelling sausage from a parcel wrapped in butcher paper. She glanced from the pot to the link, made a judgment call, and cut a sizable piece to drop in.

Mom's policy on greens was to cook a lot of them. Otherwise it wasn't worth the time. Her unit of measurement was a sinkful, about five pounds. She stopped

large bowl. Fill it with water and agitate the turnips to loosen the sand. Drain it and do it again. After the third time, pick the greens up out of the water. Drain. Take a gander at the sand at the bottom and smile. None of that dirt will be crunching between your teeth.

Turnips and Sausage

AIR-DRIED COUNTRY-STYLE sausage brings out the best in turnips. Something about the bitter edge and faint horseradish-like spice of turnip greens cuddles the earthy notes of sage, thyme, and age in a warm-blanket kind of way. I liken it to broccoli rabe's affinity for Italian sausage. A cousin of the turnip, broccoli rabe gets slapped together with fennel and chili-spiced pork all the time. Our tradition pulls the same cords

If you don't live in the Southeast and don't choose to make the air-dried sausage on page 364, it may be hard for you to find this specific style. Don't worry; you can substitute any slightly spicy link sausage in these recipes.

RECIPES

Turnip Roots and Greens

Turnip Root and Green Gratin

Marinated Turnips with Orange and Pumpkin Seeds

Turnip Run-Ups in Parmesan Pot Liquor with Ricotta Cornmeal Dumplings and Tomato Jam

Slow-Roasted Beef Short Ribs with Herb-Scented Turnip Puree and Turnip Gremolata

up the sink, stuffed it to the brim with greens, and filled it with water. Using both hands, she swished the leaves around to loosen the dirt, drained the sink, and did it three more times. By then, the little kitchen was full of boiling-sausage smell, and she dropped turnip salad by the handful into the pot. She did this in steps, allowing the last batch to wilt enough for her to fit more in the pot. If there were roots, she dropped them in too. When all the turnips were tucked under a lid, she slid the pot to a back coil and let it cook on low. About thirty minutes in, Mom dumped out her cold coffee, rinsed that little teacup, and dipped it down into the greens for some pot liquor. Holding it with both hands, she sipped that broth like it was a delicious tonic. Based on its flavor, Mom knew if the greens needed more time or seasoning.

Even after Mom stopped tending a garden, she grew turnips. The year I turned thirty, she filled our family pool with dirt and planted it with salad. At the time, only Mom and Dad, neither of whom know how to swim, cared for the idea. But now that I, too, cook more than I swim, the diving board in the garden makes a little more sense.

Turnip Roots and Greens

Makes 5 cups

THIS IS THE CLASSIC WAY people here cook fresh, just-pulled turnips with their roots still attached. Mom used sausage to season the dish but took it out before chopping it up. Ms. Lillie taught me to chop the sausage in with everything else, and to that I say: Hell yeah!

8 ounces semidry country-style link sausage	2 quarts water 2 pounds turnip roots with their greens attached	1 teaspoon salt

Combine the sausage and the water in a 4-quart saucepan. Cover and bring it up to a boil. Cook for 15 minutes.

Meanwhile, wash the roots and greens thoroughly. If you're using Purple Top or another variety of large turnip, separate the roots from the greens and cut the roots into quarters. If you're using Hakureis, you can leave them whole.

Make sure you still have about 2 quarts of water in the saucepan and add the roots and greens at the same time. They will not be completely submerged right away, but check back in a minute or two and stir things around. The greens will have cooked down, and both the roots and greens should be submerged in the cooking liquid. If they are not, add just enough water to barely cover them.

Simmer covered for about 30 minutes. You're looking for the roots to be quite tender and the greens to be soft. Once they're done, drain off all but ½ cup of pot liquor, but by all means drink it. Pot liquor is the life-fixing chicken soup of the South.

Add the salt. If you have a collard chopper, roughly work through the roots, greens, and sausage. The end product ain't gonna be pretty, but it is delicious. If you don't have a collard chopper, get one, and use a large fork in the meantime. Serve warm.

Turnip Root and Green Gratin

Serves 6 to 8

EVEN PEOPLE WHO CAN'T STAND turnips of any kind will like this because when you bake roots, greens, cream, cheese, and bread together, the bubbling, crunchy thing that emerges from the oven is magic. Serve it with roasted meats or instead of dressing at Thanksgiving, and for ease of entertaining, assemble the gratin the night before and bake it off when you're ready.

2 tablespoons butter, divided	2 cups heavy cream	1 cup Fontina, grated on a box grater
3 medium onions, halved and sliced with the grain	5 garlic cloves, sliced thin	10 turns of the pepper mill or scant ¼ teaspoon black pepper
1½ teaspoons salt, divided	½ teaspoon dried thyme	
2 cups turnip roots (about 2 to 3 medium turnips), peeled and cut into ¼ inch dice	8 ounces greens (4 cups), wilted to 1 cup	3 cups stale crusty bread cut into ½-inch cubes
	1 egg	
	1 cup Parmigiano-Reggiano, grated on a Microplane	

Preheat your oven to 375°F and rub the inside of a 2- to 3-quart baking dish with 2 teaspoons butter.

Melt 1 tablespoon butter in an 8- to 10-inch sauté pan or skillet and add the onions plus ½ teaspoon salt. Cook over medium heat, stirring frequently, until the onions are caramelized and chestnut brown, about 30 minutes. If the onions stick and the bottom of the pan looks dangerous, add ⅓ cup water. Scrape up all the dark bits and cook out the water. You should end up with about ⅔ cup caramelized onions.

Bring a 6-quart pot of heavily salted water up to a rolling boil and set up an ice bath nearby. Add the turnip roots and cook them for 2 to 3 minutes. Transfer them to the ice bath to stop the cooking. Once they're cool, drain and dry the turnips.

Meanwhile, in a 2-quart saucepan, gently heat the cream with the garlic and the thyme to just under a simmer. The goal is to let the cream steep, not boil, for about 30 minutes. Once it's done, set it aside and let it cool slightly.

If you want to wash as few dishes as possible, like I do, melt the remaining butter in the same sauté pan you used for your onions. Add the turnip greens and ½ teaspoon salt. Let them wilt down for about two minutes. Transfer the greens to a colander and press as much liquid out as you can. Transfer the greens to your cutting board and run your knife through them.

In a large bowl, whisk together the egg, cooled cream, cheeses, remaining salt, black pepper, and onions. Stir in the roots, greens, and bread. Transfer the gloppy mess to your baking dish and let it rest for about 10 minutes (or overnight) before baking uncovered for 45 minutes. Serve warm.

Marinated Turnips with Orange and Pumpkin Seeds

Serves 4

TURNIPS AND ORANGES BRING OUT THE BEST in each other in this salad that lightens the sometimes heavy combination of roots and greens. Make this bright version of the combo with baby turnips of any kind, but Hakureis are my favorite. Mature turnips or turnips that have been sitting in a root cellar or grocery store for any length of time will disappoint. Baby beets work too.

This salad needs to marinate before you serve it, so it's great to make when you're entertaining or going to a potluck. I like the way I feel when I eat something like this for lunch, but I also favor it for spring menus focused around the grill.

1½ pounds turnips with their roots attached

½ teaspoon salt

½ cup orange supremes, roughly 2 medium oranges

½ cup salt-roasted pumpkin seeds

Orange-Ginger Dressing
Makes 1 cup

¼ cup thinly sliced scallions, white part only

Zest of 1 orange, removed with a Microplane

Juice of 2 oranges, about ½ cup

1 tablespoon ginger, grated on the Microplane

1 teaspoon fresh garlic, grated on the Microplane

2 dashes hot sauce

2 tablespoons soy sauce

2 tablespoons honey

¼ cup rice vinegar

¼ cup olive oil for finishing

¼ teaspoon salt

Make the dressing: Whisk together the scallions, zest, orange juice, ginger, garlic, and hot sauce. Let this hang out for 5 minutes while the flavors bloom. Whisk in the remaining ingredients and set aside while you prepare the turnips.

Prepare the turnips: Bring a 4- to 6-quart pot of heavily salted water up to a rolling boil and set up an ice bath nearby. Wash the turnips thoroughly and separate the roots from the greens.

Using a mandoline, slice the turnip roots in ⅛-inch rounds. Transfer them to a 2-quart bowl. If the greens are young, small, and tender, blanch them for a generous 60 seconds and shock in your ice bath. If they are more mature, increase the blanching time up to 3 minutes. You want your greens to still have texture, but you don't want your jaw to get a workout.

Once the greens have cooled down, drain them well and chop roughly with your knife.

Transfer the greens to the bowl with the roots. Toss them with ½ teaspoon salt and pour the dressing over top. Stir it all up and refrigerate for a minimum of an hour. Just before serving, top with the orange supremes and pumpkin seeds.

Turnip Run-Ups in Parmesan Pot Liquor with Ricotta Cornmeal Dumplings and Tomato Jam

Serves 4 to 6

RUN-UPS ARE THE GOLD STANDARD of turnip greens. Basically the second coming of the Seven Top turnip, run-ups shoot out of the ground in late March from what appears to be a cold-killed turnip plant. They have a floret and look a whole heck of a lot like broccoli rabe. They are sweeter than their first coming and produce the absolute best pot liquor possible.

The classic way to cook run-ups is boiled with sausage, then they're eaten in a bowl with cornbread to sop up their pot liquor. This dish fiddles with the concept of what's in that bowl. My recipe tester Anna says it "looks like matzo ball soup had a Christmas party."

This might sound like a chef-y take on a basic dish, but don't be intimidated—it's not hard to make. If you don't have run-ups, use regular turnip greens and don't look back. The tomato jam is great to have on hand and will brighten up any number of winter soups or rich meat dishes, so don't skip it.

Tomato Jam
Makes 1 cup

Note: *This is a bare-bones recipe designed for convenience. Feel free to add herbs, onions, or spices to make a more complex condiment.*

- 1 14.5-ounce can strained tomatoes or 1⅔ cups tomato puree
- ¼ cup granulated sugar
- ½ teaspoon salt
- 2 sprigs thyme
- ⅛ teaspoon chili flakes

Parmesan Pot Liquor
Makes 6 cups

- 2 tablespoons extra virgin olive oil
- 4 medium yellow onions, peeled and sliced thin with the grain
- 1 teaspoon salt
- 7 garlic cloves, smashed
- ½ teaspoon chili flakes
- 8 ounces Parmesan rinds
- Zest of 1 lemon, removed with a vegetable peeler in strips
- 3 quarts water
- 8 ounces turnip greens, about 3 cups
- 1 tablespoon butter

Ricotta Dumplings
Makes 12 dumplings

- 1 cup of the highest-quality ricotta you can find or homemade, drained over a fine-mesh sieve for 1 hour
- 1 medium egg
- ½ cup Parmigiano-Reggiano, grated on a Microplane
- 1 teaspoon salt
- ½ cup fine cornmeal
- ⅛ teaspoon nutmeg

Turnip Run-Ups in Parmesan Pot Liquor with Ricotta Cornmeal Dumplings and Tomato Jam

Continued from the previous page

Make the tomato jam: Combine everything in a 2-quart saucepan and bring it up to a simmer over medium-low heat. Cook uncovered for 40 minutes, stirring every 10 minutes or so to make sure it doesn't burn on the bottom. When it's done, it will have a deep sweet tomato flavor and a jammy consistency. Transfer to a sealed container and store in the fridge for up to 2 weeks. Serve at room temperature.

Make the pot liquor: Heat the olive oil over medium heat in a 4-quart Dutch oven or a saucepan with a lid. Add the onions and 1 teaspoon salt. Cook the onions, stirring now and then, until they caramelize. This should take about 40 minutes. You're looking for dark golden-brown onions. If they begin to stick and the bottom of the pan looks dangerous, add ½ cup water and, using a wooden spoon, scrape up the browned bits. Let the water cook out and continue to caramelize until you reach the desired color.

Once you do, add the garlic, chili flakes, Parmesan rinds, zest, and water. Bring it up to a boil. Reduce to a simmer and cook covered for about 45 minutes. Stir the broth occasionally to make sure the rinds are not sticking to the bottom of the pan. You should end up with an aromatic, slightly reduced, chestnut-colored broth. Strain the broth and discard the solids. Return the broth to its original pan and add the turnip greens. If the greens are more than 2 inches long, run your knife through them. Cook the greens uncovered at a simmer about 15 minutes or until they are quite tender.

Make the dumplings: Using a spoon, in a medium bowl, mix the drained ricotta, egg, Parmigiano-Reggiano, salt, cornmeal, and nutmeg until homogenous. The ricotta mixture should be quite thick, almost pasty. Refrigerate until you're ready to use. You can make it up to this point a day in advance.

Cook the dumplings and serve: Bring the broth and greens up to a simmer and season it with 1 teaspoon salt. Using your hand or a 2-ounce scoop, pull off rounds of the dumpling mixture and drop them into the broth and greens, leaving about ½ inch of space between each dumpling. Once you've dropped all the dumplings in they should be nearly submerged. If they are not, add a little water to help cover. Put the top on the pot and cook for about 5 minutes. Don't freak out when the broth becomes cloudy. That's supposed to happen.

To serve, whisk the butter into the broth and then spoon 5 dumplings into each bowl. Nestle turnip greens next to the dumplings, and ladle broth over the top. Finish with a heaping tablespoon tomato jam.

Slow-Roasted Beef Short Ribs with Herb-Scented Turnip Puree and Turnip Gremolata

Serves 4

BRAISED SHORT RIBS are like a soft wool scarf on a cold night: silky and comforting. On a warm night, they seem like a wool scarf worn the wrong time of year. This dish takes a cut of meat I love and dresses it for any weather.

This sounds like a lot of turnips, but hear me out: Think of the puree as low-carb mashed potatoes. Serve it here, or try it with roast chicken or as a base for a pile of roasted root vegetables. Envision the gremolata, typically a simple condiment made with lemon zest, parsley, and garlic, as that punchy bright thing that's going to keep you going back for another bite. Both preparations are useful additions to your repertoire.

4 bone-in beef short ribs, roughly 10 ounces each	1 tablespoon butter	Zest and juice of 1 lemon
4 teaspoons salt	1 garlic clove, smashed	¼ teaspoon hot sauce
20 turns of the pepper mill or 1 teaspoon black pepper	2 sprigs thyme	1 large garlic clove, grated on a Microplane
2 pounds turnip roots	1 sprig rosemary	3 tablespoons chopped flat-leaf parsley
1 tablespoon extra-virgin olive oil	1 bay leaf	2 tablespoons chopped mint
⅓ cup milk	1 teaspoon granulated sugar	1 tablespoon honey
⅓ cup heavy cream	⅛ teaspoon chili flakes	
	Zest and juice of 1 small orange	

Roast the ribs and the turnips: Preheat your oven to 300°F. Season the short ribs on both sides with 3 teaspoons salt and 1 teaspoon of black pepper. Place two of them in a 3-quart or 9 x 13-inch baking dish and the other two in another similar dish. Cover with foil and slide them onto the top and bottom racks of your oven. Roast for 1 hour.

Meanwhile, wash and cut the turnip roots into ⅔-inch-wide wedges.

Toss the turnips with the olive oil and 1 teaspoon salt. After the ribs' first hour

in the oven, bring them out, divide the turnips in half, and spread them evenly over each dish. Make sure the turnips are spread out and have plenty of room to breathe. Turnips that are piled on top of one another are steaming turnips, not roasting turnips. Roast uncovered for 40 minutes. Bring the dishes out and toss the turnips around to coat them in the fat from the short ribs. Return them to the oven, rotating the top and bottom dishes, and continue roasting for 50 more minutes.

When everything is tucked into the oven, heat the milk, cream, butter, smashed garlic, thyme, rosemary, bay leaf,

one half in the blender and the other half in a bowl. Turn off the oven, cover the ribs with foil, and slide them back into the oven to keep warm. They should be nicely browned and tender but with enough texture that they require a knife and fork to eat.

Assemble the gremolata: Toss the turnips that are in the bowl with the citrus zests and juice, hot sauce, grated garlic, parsley, mint, and honey. Set aside. It's fine to let the gremolata cool slightly, but don't let it get so cold that the beef fat solidifies.

Make the puree and serve: Pluck the rosemary, thyme, garlic, and bay leaf out of the steeped cream mixture and add the liquid to the turnips in the blender. Cover the blender carefully, making sure the lid is secure, and blend the turnips up till they are totally smooth.

Serve the ribs over the turnip puree and under the gremolata.

sugar, and chili flakes in a saucepan over low heat. Let it steep just under a simmer for 30 minutes.

After 2½ hours total oven time, take the pans out of the oven. The turnips should be caramelized and shiny with beef fat, like the most appealing turnips you've ever seen. Divide them in half. Put

WATERMELON

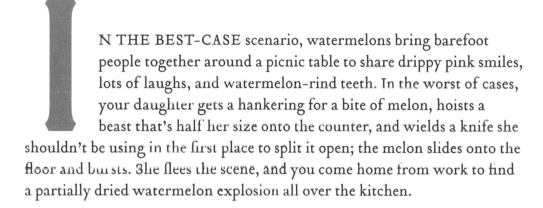

IN THE BEST-CASE scenario, watermelons bring barefoot people together around a picnic table to share drippy pink smiles, lots of laughs, and watermelon-rind teeth. In the worst of cases, your daughter gets a hankering for a bite of melon, hoists a beast that's half her size onto the counter, and wields a knife she shouldn't be using in the first place to split it open; the melon slides onto the floor and bursts. She flees the scene, and you come home from work to find a partially dried watermelon explosion all over the kitchen.

I find it pretty inconsiderate that the fruit that benefits the most from being cold won't fit into the average refrigerator. This was a big problem in my house growing up because my sisters and I believed in the power of a cold watermelon. In the Howard house we cooled watermelons down by storing them on top of the floor air-conditioning vents. It didn't matter how hot the house got so long as the watermelons were cold.

I feel shorted, too, that the diva who sings summer the loudest doesn't ripen till that season's on the wane. When I was a kid, I wanted every day in the sun to be bookended by watermelon: cold watermelon for breakfast and cold watermelon for supper. But in the 1980s in Deep Run, we had to wait for our own local watermelons to ripen, and that never happened before the middle of July.

I really get bent out of shape, though, when I consider watermelon seeds. I'm thinking God made a mistake here. Watermelon's scent, juice, and texture are so intoxicating, so all-consuming, that you want to savor and slurp every bite, every lick of juice. But because of the fruit's anatomy, you have to stop over and over to spit out seeds. There are more seedless watermelons available at this point than bikinis in July, but have you ever tasted a seeded watermelon side by side with one of its seedless cousins? Try it and see how it makes you feel.

For a kid, it takes a certain amount of skill and dedication to eat watermelon while avoiding the seeds. I, for one, struggled with the idea and the execution of it.

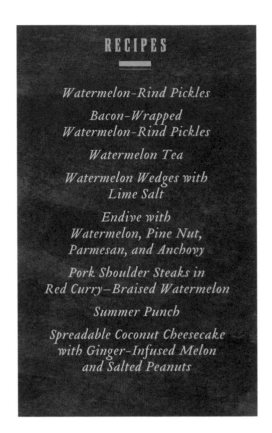

In the beginning, I just ignored them, swallowing happily till Granddaddy Howard told me too many watermelon seeds would rot my gut. This little pearl of (untrue) wisdom scared the seeds out of me and sent this five-year-old on a search for a new way of eating the best thing about summer.

It didn't take long to figure out there was one part of the watermelon that was oddly free of seeds and even sweeter than the rest. My mom called it the heart, and just the mention of it made her smile.

One day my sister Johna had friends over for a pool party. They were in high school and I was in kindergarten, but I insisted on lurking around the shallow end, lapping up any intel I could use for blackmail later.

Late that afternoon, Johna's boyfriend, Greg, showed up in his pickup truck with the Guns N' Roses song "Sweet Child o' Mine" blaring and one tan, muscular arm hanging out the window. He looked like a Ken doll in cutoff jeans, and once he'd voluntarily taken me fishing. I was smitten. Greg lifted a huge watermelon out of the back of the truck and brought it over to a table next to the pool. He split it in half and cut one half into wedges. Johna and her friends all helped themselves to a wedge, and I, eager to show off and thinking I was privy to some knowledge the teenagers were not, scooped my right hand down deep into the other half of the melon, extracted its heart, and shoved it into my mouth like a Neanderthal.

The teenagers, even Greg, looked at me like I had ripped out a human heart and eaten it. And Johna, who didn't want me out there anyway, stood up, pointed me to the house, and chided: "You don't just eat the heart of the watermelon, Vivian! And you *certainly* don't use your grubby little hand to ruin it for everybody else!"

I was mortified in front of Greg, my future husband. I knew I had screwed up. Had I just reached in and grabbed a seed-riddled wedge like everybody else, I would have been swimming instead of sulking. But no…I was seduced by a watermelon, and betrayed.

WATERMELON WISDOM

How to Find the Perfect Melon

WATERMELONS, cucumbers, pumpkins, and summer squash are members of the same family, but a watermelon, unlike its cousins, doesn't necessarily lose flavor as it gets bigger. Instead, the eating quality of a watermelon depends on when it's harvested and that particular year's growing conditions. A summer packed with rain means waterlogged, faintly sweet melons.

When we look at a cucumber on a vine, we know within a day or two when that cucumber is at its prime based on its size. Watermelons are less forthright. If the melon is still in the field, check the stem end that connects it to the vine. If it's a ripe melon, a curled portion of the stem, called the pig tail, will have turned brown. If the watermelon is in the market, check its bottom. If it's flat and yellow, chances are the inside is sweet and crisp. If the bottom is a bright white, the melon was probably harvested early and won't be ideal. If the whole melon looks bleached out by the sun, it most likely sat in the field too long and will be mushy and just plain bad.

Older folks around here say another way to tell if a melon is at its prime is to rub the melon perpendicular to its stripes. If you feel ridges, you're holding a tasty melon.

Seeds or No Seeds

I THINK we'll soon think of seedless watermelons the way we now think of seedless grapes—we will eat them every day for convenience, but watermelons with seeds will be prized for their unique flavor profiles and exceptional crisp texture.

No matter what, the seeded watermelon isn't going anywhere. It takes seeded watermelons to pollinate seedless ones, and while watermelons with seeds and names like Moon and Stars and Bogue Sound are hard to find in supermarkets these days, they're usually readily available at farmers' markets and roadside stands.

Silly Games
We Actually Played

I KNOW THE URGE is to buy seedless melons, but if you're entertaining and plan on eating your melon outside, consider an old-school seeded one. As a kid, I used to have seed-spitting contests with my siblings all the time. It's clean fun that encourages you to do something that's not normally acceptable. We also used to carve fake teeth out of the watermelon rind. This is kind of silly, but it's not a bad way to spend an afternoon in the sun.

Watermelon-Rind Pickles

Makes 4 to 5 pints

EVEN WHEN SUMMER GETS AWAY FROM US at the restaurant and we're not able to pickle and preserve everything in our path, we somehow find a way to make these pickles. It's a traditional recipe that highlights the home cook's need to waste nothing, and it feels good to make something translucent and crispy out of stuff that's potentially trash. That's one reason we go to the trouble. The other is that they're a pork chop's soul mate.

If you know before you cut into a watermelon that you're going to use its rind to make pickles, go ahead and peel the outside while it's still whole. It's easier to use a vegetable peeler on something big and round than on something small and sloped.

Sometimes I leave the slightest bit of watermelon flesh attached to the rind. It looks so darn pretty when pickled and doesn't seem to make much of a difference in the texture of the finished product. Use the spices I've listed here as suggestions, adding or subtracting anything you want to. What's important is cooking time, acid level, and sugar content. The rest is up to you.

½ cup salt

2 quarts plus 2 cups water

Rind from 1 medium to large watermelon, peeled and cut into roughly 1×3-inch strips

2 cups white wine vinegar

1 cup lemon juice

4 cups granulated sugar

1 tablespoon coriander seeds

10 cloves

5 star anise

3-inch piece ginger, peeled and sliced into ⅛-inch rings

1 cinnamon stick

Zest of 1 orange, removed with a vegetable peeler

1 lemon, thinly sliced

Dissolve the salt in 2 quarts of the water, and submerge the watermelon rind in the salt water overnight. Weigh the rind down with a plate to make sure it's completely submerged in the brine.

The next day combine the remaining 2 cups of water, vinegar, lemon juice, sugar, and spices in a 6-quart Dutch oven. Cover and bring it up to a boil over medium-high heat and simmer hard for 10 minutes.

Drain and rinse the watermelon rind. Add it along with the orange zest and lemon slices. Bring this up to a boil and simmer, covered, until half the rinds are translucent. At that point the others will follow suit as they cool in the brine or are further processed in a hot-water bath. This is the trickiest part because you don't want the brine to boil down to a thick syrup,

but you do want the pickles to be cooked through. If the liquid starts to reduce significantly and darken in color before at least half your rinds are translucent, add up to a half a cup of water and continue cooking.

If you plan to can your pickles, proceed with the directions on page 16 and process for 10 minutes. If you don't wish to can the pickles, let them cool to room temperature. You can store them in the fridge, submerged in their brine and sealed in a container, for up to 3 months.

Bacon-Wrapped Watermelon-Rind Pickles

Makes 24 skewers

ASSUMING YOU HAVE THE PICKLES on hand, this could be the easiest and most gratifying finger food you ever make. They don't have to be served hot, but they ain't that good cold, so try and find a warm spot for these to hang out while they last... which will be all of about a minute.

24	short pieces of your thickest watermelon-rind pickles	12	slices smoked bacon (thick-cut slices will not work)

Preheat your oven to 375°F. Cut each slice of bacon in half and wrap the slices around the watermelon pickles. Wrap around the pickles leaving a little extra on either end so that when the bacon shrinks, you're not left with naked pickles. Don't take that as a cue to wrap the pickles two and three times, though; the bacon won't render properly.

Lay the wrapped pickles in a single layer on a baking sheet with at least a half an inch of space in between them. Just before you're ready to serve them, bake for about 15 minutes on the middle rack of your oven until the bacon is shrunken, fragrant, and caramelized.

Sometimes I like to take a little of the pickling liquid and stir it together with the bacon fat that's rendered out onto the pan and drizzle the tops. But that's just when I have time to spare. It's not necessary.

Serve warm with skewers, so folks can pick them up.

Watermelon Tea

Makes 6 cups

HERE'S ANOTHER CONFESSION: I don't drink sweet tea. Admitting that in a book about Southern food is akin to announcing I've just sold my children on eBay, but I prefer the dry tannins of cold black tea to simple syrup over ice. Every now and then, if I'm feeling skinny, I'll order my tea half and half. That's half sweet, half unsweet, for those of you who don't know.

This watermelon tea reminds me of that but with another, very pleasing dimension not offered by plain sugar. It's a perfect way to use up a watermelon that has mealy flesh but decent flavor.

Let the tea chill in your refrigerator overnight. A small amount of sediment will settle in the bottom, leaving the tea pristine, clear, and cold.

Note: *If you're a sweet-tea drinker, this is not going to trick your trigger, so add sugar or honey to suit your tastes. The watermelon flavor will still come through.*

---

1 quart diced watermelon flesh (seeds are fine)

2 family-size Lipton-style tea bags

1 quart water

1 tablespoon lemon juice, optional

In a blender, process the watermelon until completely pulverized. Strain it through a fine-mesh sieve or a larger colander fitted with cheesecloth. Discard the pulp and reserve 2 cups of the juice.

Place the tea bags in the pitcher you plan to serve it from. Boil the water and pour it over. Let the bags steep for 4 to 5 minutes. Remove and discard the bags (although my mom uses them a second time). Stir in the reserved watermelon juice and lemon juice, if using. Chill the tea until you're ready to serve. Serve over ice.

Watermelon Wedges with Lime Salt

Makes enough salt for 24 wedges

I WAS SEVEN or eight years old the first time I ever saw someone put salt on a slice of watermelon. The experience confused me so deeply that I went home and asked my mom about it. She answered by saying that "some people just don't know how to leave a good thing alone." I grew up to be one of those people.

| 2 tablespoons Maldon sea salt or other coarse sea salt | Zest of 3 limes, removed with a Microplane | Half of 1 large watermelon |

In a small bowl, combine the salt and lime zest. Using your fingers, pinch it roughly to combine and slightly crush. The idea is to "bruise" the zest but also preserve the nice flaky texture of the salt.

Slice the watermelon half into 1-inch, rind-on wedges. Chill the wedges thoroughly because warm watermelon is a letdown. Just before serving, remove them from the fridge and sprinkle one side with the salt. Serve immediately.

Endive with Watermelon, Pine Nut, Parmesan, and Anchovy

Makes 24 spears or 1½ cups watermelon filling

TWENTY YEARS AGO, no one in the States thought of throwing watermelon into anything other than a fruit salad. But in the past two decades, Americans have come to accept it underneath salty cheeses, amplified by spicy chilies, or grilled alongside shrimp. I'm going a step further to recommend you throw some anchovy into the mix.

This snack is healthy, addictive, and startlingly refreshing. Spoon it into the endive spears for a more formal presentation, or serve the spears piled high next to a bowl of the relish to evoke chips and dip.

1 cup watermelon, diced into ¼-inch cubes, seeds removed

¼ cup pine nuts, toasted

3 tablespoons Parmigiano-Reggiano, cut into ¼-inch cubes

2 tablespoons lemon juice

1 tablespoon dill, picked and roughly chopped

2 teaspoons boquerones or regular anchovy fillets, finely minced

1 teaspoon salt, divided

4 heads Belgian endive

Zest and juice of 2 oranges, whisked together

In a small bowl combine the first 6 ingredients plus ½ teaspoon salt. Stir to thoroughly combine and store in the fridge till you're ready to serve. It will hold up to 3 hours before the watermelon begins to soften.

Cut the root off the endive and discard the outer leaves. Separate the spears, reserving the medium to large ones for this dish. Chop up the remaining spears and save them for your mixed green salads. Toss the endive with the orange zest, juice, and the remaining ½ teaspoon salt. It's going to seem like a lot of orange product,

but I want it juicy. Reserve the leftover juice that leaches off the spears.

If you choose to stuff the endive, spoon 1 to 2 tablespoons of the watermelon mix on the wispy tipped end of each spear and drizzle the remaining OJ over the top of the whole presentation. If you choose to serve it like chips and dip, make sure the leaves are wet with OJ before you dip. That little bit of juicy elegance makes it great. And make sure all the components are really cold.

Pork Shoulder Steaks in
Red Curry–Braised Watermelon

Serves 4

LIKE CUCUMBER, watermelon loses much of its spirit when subjected to heat, so I almost never recommend it any way other than cold and raw. I've made an exception here because more people need to know about the wizardry that happens when watermelon and pork cook slowly together. Everybody who eats this will think the watermelon is tomato. Everybody.

Serve it alongside Perfect Rice with Herb Butter (*page 292*) or Stewed Fresh Butterbeans (*page 153*).

1 tablespoon vegetable oil	⅔ cup red wine vinegar	5 cups watermelon, cut into 1½-inch cubes, seeds removed
4 8-ounce pork shoulder or blade steaks	⅓ cup honey	
3 teaspoons salt	3 tablespoons red curry paste	
1 teaspoon black pepper	2 teaspoons fish sauce	

Preheat your oven to 350°F. Heat the oil in a 12-inch brazier, cast-iron skillet, or Dutch oven over medium-high heat until almost smoking. Season the pork with salt and pepper on both sides and put it in a single snug layer in the bottom of the pan to brown. Maintaining medium-high heat, brown the steaks on all four sides, and I mean that. The more caramelization your steaks take on, the more flavor the end braise will have.

While the pork is browning, whisk together the vinegar, honey, red curry paste, and fish sauce. Once the pork looks like something I'd be happy with, turn off the heat and drain away the excess fat. Scatter the watermelon over the top and pour the vinegar mixture over that. Either

with foil or a lid that fits snugly, cover and slide the pork onto the middle rack of your oven. Bake for 1½ hours. Remove the lid and bake an additional 30 minutes.

After 2 hours in the oven, the pork will be tender and the watermelon will look like shriveled tomatoes. There will be a good amount of juicy aromatic liquid pooled around it all. It should be more brothy than saucy.

To serve, spoon the watermelon chunks and some of the red curry broth on top of the pork steaks and know that if you don't serve this on top of something with the ability to soak up the red juice, you've totally missed the point.

Summer Punch

Makes 8 cups

THIS IS THE WAY I want to end every meal. Hell, it's the way I want to end everything I do. It's so refreshing, I slurp it up like a dog drinking water…when I'm alone. Otherwise I use a spoon.

1 quart watermelon rosemary sorbet

1 bottle sparkling rosé, chilled

2 cups seedless watermelon, cut into small dice

Watermelon Rosemary Sorbet

1½ cups granulated sugar

1 cup water

3 sprigs rosemary

3 pounds seedless watermelon cut into cubes (about 10 cups)

½ cup lime juice

¼ cup plus 2 tablespoons tequila

Make the sorbet: In a small saucepan bring the sugar, water, and rosemary up to a boil. Remove it from the heat and let it cool to room temperature, then strain.

Combine the rosemary syrup, watermelon, lime juice, and tequila in the blender and process till it's smooth. Strain it through a fine-mesh sieve and refrigerate overnight.

The day you want to serve the punch, freeze the sorbet according to the directions on your ice cream machine and transfer it to your freezer for about 2 hours.

Serve: Spoon a nice scoop of the sorbet into the bottom of a chilled glass and top with a tablespoon or so of the watermelon dice. Pour the bubbly over and stick a spoon in it. Slurp or spoon up immediately.

Spreadable Coconut Cheesecake with Ginger-Infused Melon and Salted Peanuts

Serves 4

I'M A POSTMODERNIST when it comes to cooking. I was an intern at WD-50, a restaurant that was for a long time Manhattan's most notable temple to modernist cuisine. Chef Wylie Dufresne foamed, sous-vided, and compressed everything that would fit into a bag or a siphon. He deconstructed American comfort foods such as corned beef sandwiches and eggs Benedict to the point that the average diner had to be told that the delicious work of art in front of him was in fact an homage to something he'd eaten a hundred times.

Today I admire the modernist approach, but my heart doesn't beat for it. This is my very simple ode to my not-so-humble beginnings.

The cheesecake and the melon will take you all of thirty minutes to put together. If you'd like to just make those and serve them with some store-bought graham crackers or gingersnaps, it's fine by me. Otherwise, know that you can make all of these components up to three days in advance and assemble them just before you're ready to serve. If you think of it that way, it's actually quite convenient.

1½ cups White Chocolate Coconut Cheesecake, at room temperature

1½ cups ginger-infused melon, chilled

1 cup salted peanuts, roughly chopped

Graham crackers

Ginger-Infused Melon

Makes a scant 1½ cups

Note: *Any syrup left over is a great addition to cocktails. Try substituting it for simple syrup in any of your favorite summer drinks.*

1 cup water

¼ cup fresh ginger, roughly chopped

⅓ cup granulated sugar

¼ cup lime juice

⅛ teaspoon salt

1½ cups watermelon cut into ½-inch dice, seeds removed

White Chocolate Coconut Cheesecake

Makes 1½ cups

1 small ripe banana

½ pound (1 cup) cream cheese, at room temperature

¼ cup cream of coconut (Coco López)

¼ cup white chocolate, roughly chopped

⅛ teaspoon salt

Graham Crackers

Makes about 15 roughly broken crackers

½ cup plus 2 teaspoons all-purpose flour

2 tablespoons whole wheat flour

¼ cup dark brown sugar, lightly packed

¼ teaspoon baking soda

¼ teaspoon salt

1½ tablespoons butter, cut into cubes and very cold

1½ tablespoons honey

1½ tablespoons milk

1 teaspoon vanilla extract

Infuse the melon: In a 2-quart saucepan, bring the water, ginger, and sugar up to a simmer over medium heat. Simmer, covered, for 15 minutes. Remove from the heat and let steep an additional 10 minutes. Strain out the ginger. Stir in the lime juice and salt, followed by the watermelon. Transfer the watermelon and the marinade to a container. Cover and let it marry and mingle refrigerated overnight before serving.

Make the cheesecake: In a mixer fitted with the paddle attachment, drop the banana in and paddle on medium till the banana is broken. Add the remaining ingredients and keep going until everything is incorporated and smooth except for the little chunks of white chocolate. Transfer

the cheesecake to the fridge and store in a sealed container until about 30 minutes before you're ready to serve. It will keep for up to a week.

Make the graham crackers: Pulse the flours, sugar, soda, and salt together in the bowl of a food processor. Add the butter and continue to pulse until it looks like very coarse cornmeal.

In a separate bowl, whisk together the honey, milk, and vanilla. Pour this into the flour mix and pulse a few more times, just until the dough starts to come together. It will be quite soft and sticky. Wrap the dough in a heavily floured piece of plastic and refrigerate for about an hour.

Preheat your oven to 350°F and line a cookie sheet with parchment paper. Dust your work surface with flour. Roll the dough into a rectangle an eighth of an inch thick. It's gonna be sticky, so don't be afraid to add flour as necessary.

Carefully transfer the rectangle to your cookie sheet and slide it onto the middle rack of your oven. Bake for 7 to 10 minutes. It will be a bit browner than it was when it went into the oven, and the edges will crinkle slightly. Let the large cracker cool completely before breaking it into irregular pieces.

Assemble and serve: I like to serve this family-style. Make a large puddle of spreadable cheesecake on the bottom of a plate. Spoon the melon and a little of the syrup over the top. Sprinkle it all with the peanuts and surround the whole thing with broken graham crackers.

OYSTERS

WORSHIP OYSTERS. Almost nothing else calls my name year-round the way they do. On days it's so hot and humid the air conditioner sweats, I crave an icy tray of briny raws next to a glass of champagne. As soon as I feel that first cold snap and Deep Run starts to get dark early, I want a bonfire, a jean jacket, and an oyster roast. When January threatens an ice storm and we're trapped at home with the promise of no school or work the next day, I open a bottle of red, make an oyster pan roast, and spoon it over crusty bread.

Oysters shape my adult fantasies, but I didn't like them as a kid. My distaste went beyond the way they looked, smelled, and felt in my mouth. I hated oyster-eating culture. It was crass and fast, and most important, it came between me and a Shirley Temple.

During my childhood, our family economics changed. Mom and Dad went from rarely spending money on anything other than the farm to going out to eat on weekends. My sisters are a generation older than me, so by the time my parents started to cap off a workweek with a meal in town, I was the only one left to tag along.

Most Friday nights, we got dressed up to eat at Baron and the Beef, a smoke-filled steak house with a low ceiling and nary a window. Aside from the county's best steak and baked potatoes, Mom loved the salad bar. Baron and the Beef offered smoked oysters from a can and fresh spinach—delicacies of the era. Dad loved the crock of meatballs bobbing in grape jelly–mustard sauce that came free with the salad bar. I liked Frances.

Frances was our waitress. She wore a flower in her hair, and her compliments made me feel like the prettiest little girl to ever eat beef. She brought me free Shirley Temples and extra spiced apple rings. Frances worked awfully hard for that dollar my dad reluctantly left on the table after dinner, and I would have happily eaten with her every week. But that was not to be.

After the first cold snap of the year, my parents started craving oysters instead of steak. Mom would start with "I can't wait to get some good oysters," and Dad would follow up with "It sure has been a long time." And then I knew it would be spring before I'd see Frances and sip my next Shirley Temple. Friday nights now meant a two-hour round trip to the T&W Oyster Bar in Swansboro.

Steamed oysters are what we do here in Eastern North Carolina. The coast is full of oyster beds, but until recently, the idea of eating a jiggly cold oyster straight out of our brackish water was not our thing. We prefer oysters steamed till their shells barely pop open. I'm guessing it started as a way to get at them easily and evolved into an appreciation of a warm oyster with a salty edge. People do eat fried oysters as an appetizer, and they might take a bowl of oyster stew instead of a salad, but the point of the oyster has long been the steamed peck.

The term *peck* is useless nowadays. Grandma Hill said she loved me "a bushel and a peck and a hug around the neck," and I knew that was a lot. But an actual peck refers to a dry volume measurement of a quarter of a bushel, which is the number of pieces that fit into two gallons. That's usually between twenty-five and thirty-five oysters.

At T&W, I appreciated the basket of hot hushpuppies and packs of margarine that slid my way the moment we sat down. What bothered me was the culture of the place: its frenetic pace, the overtly masculine way the shuckers looked, and the uncultured way my parents acted. T&W was and still is a sprawling fried-seafood restaurant with more than a hundred seats, but for steamed oysters, you sat at the oyster bar. Friday nights at the T&W meant waiting in a long line for three of the bar's twenty or so stools.

John Howard hated, hates, and always will hate waiting. He fidgeted in line as he scarfed down pack after pack of saltines, discreetly dropping their plastic wrappers on the floor behind him. Finally, probably because she was tired of looking at my dad clean out his ear with a car key, the hostess called our name and escorted us to the crowded, rowdy bar. The working side of the counter was fitted with a trough where the shucking happened. Burly men who looked like Popeye moved with purpose, slinging hot buckets, shells, and grunts at one another. Waitresses (none of whom had flowers in their hair) carried pitchers of beer, ducked under swinging steamer doors and darted around arms ending in oyster knives.

We took our seats and without so much as a glance at the menu, Dad waved over a waitress.

"We'll have a peck of oysters, medium, a small fried-seafood platter, and two salads."

"Anything to drink?"

"Water."

"What about for the girl?"

"Water."

Annoyed that we were a group of water drinkers, our waitress turned on her heel to go put our order in. Her goal from that point forward was to get us out of there as fast as possible. I didn't know then that restaurants don't love it when you drink only water. The best margins are in beverages, and a family of water swillers, like mine, held seats hostage from beer drinkers. My dad didn't care. We could drink tea and soda at home.

Barely half a glass of water in, our food landed in front of us: my fried shrimp, deviled crab, and french fries, the salads, and Mom and Dad's oyster "setups."

An oyster setup came on a melamine plate with three compartments. Cocktail sauce, "drawn" butter that I'm pretty sure was margarine, lemon slices, and two packs of saltines filled the largest compartment. Creamy white slaw sat in the next section. The third spot sat empty for oysters.

Like people coming off a juice cleanse, my parents went to town, scarfing down salad, shoveling in slaw—heads down, mouths open. Then our personal Popeye lumbered over, steaming bucket in tow, and dumped the hot, gnarly, cement-shelled oysters into his trough. Oysters shot rapid-fire from his knife to my parents' plates. My parents slurped them up as quickly as they landed, dipping each oyster into butter, laying it on a saltine, and topping it with cocktail sauce. It was a dizzying, exhausting show, like a tennis pro feeding ball after ball into my parents' open mouths. I couldn't

OYSTER WISDOM

What You Won't Find Here

THE SUBJECT OF OYSTERS is vast, and I'll only touch on a portion of it. I'm not going to wax on about the flavor profiles and cup shapes of East versus West Coast oysters. I'm not going to pontificate on the virtues of wild versus farm-raised. I'm not about to trace the history of the oyster from peasant food to privileged food. I'm not qualified to talk about how they might possibly have the ability to save our oceans. What I will do is recommend a few ways to get an oyster into your mouth. That, I understand.

The Myth of R

JUST TO BE CLEAR, eating oysters in a month without an *R* will not hurt you. The rule grew out of the fact that wild oysters spawn from May through August, making them watery, kind of flavorless, and flaccid in those months—but not dangerous. Farm-raised oysters do not spawn and are perfectly acceptable for that summertime oyster craving.

Shucking, Storing, and Cleaning

SHUCKING AN OYSTER, either raw or steamed, is a learned skill honed by practice. If you're honestly interested in becoming adept, buy about fifty oysters, watch a YouTube video on the process, and go to it. Don't try to open an oyster with a screwdriver or a steak knife. Get the right tool for the job and protect your hand with a towel. Here are a couple of things you may not find on YouTube.

1. When stored, oysters like to be cold and crowded. Pile them up in a dark spot of your refrigerator. Do not store them on ice, which will melt and eventually drown them.

2. Farm-raised oysters are cleaner than wild, but both will need the highest-pressure rinse you can manage as well as a brief scrub from a kitchen brush. The idea is to eliminate grit from your eating experience and prevent pushing mud into the shell as you shuck.

Eating Them Raw

RAW-OYSTER CULTURE reminds me a little of wine culture. If you don't know much about it, the experience can be intimidating and disappointing. Here's a primer on how to approach oysters on the half shell.

1. Always ask your server what his or her favorites are. Not only have the servers tasted all the oysters, but they know what diners respond most positively to.

2. Order at least two different oysters and ask for varieties that are distinct from one another. I'll often request an East Coast and a West Coast oyster, or a Northeast and a Southeast oyster. It's also fun to taste wild and cultivated side by side. And if you're in a region that's known specifically for its oysters, it can be enlightening to taste oysters grown in the same body of water but in different parts of it.

3. Try to order two of each oyster for every person. I geek out over the flavor, texture, salinity, and finish of raw oysters, so I'm often hesitant to gild them with mignonette or cocktail sauce. If you order two of each, you can eat one naked and enjoy it the way nature intended. Then you can eat one with stuff and experience it the way the chef suggests.

4. This last one is nitpicky, but it will make you look like you know what you're doing. After you slurp down an oyster, return the empty shell to the tray but turn it over so the open side faces down. That just lets everybody know where you are with your oysters.

Entertaining with Oysters

IF YOU'RE SERVING OYSTERS for a party and have to shuck a bunch ahead of time, here are a few things to keep in mind.

1. If you need a certain number of oysters to make a recipe work, start out with 10 percent more than what's called for. Inevitably, there are casualties from the shucking process, whether caused by the hand of the shucker or due to the quality of the oyster itself.

2. Shuck oysters over a bowl to make sure you catch all the liquor. Then refrigerate the oysters in that juice in a container or on the half shell. The oyster liquor will keep the oysters fresh-tasting, plump, and briny.

3. If you choose to store the oysters in their shells, you'll need something underneath each shell to stabilize it. I like to use rock salt. It holds them steady and is less likely to end up in your mouth than regular salt.

4. After you shuck oysters, you have a window of about three hours before their eating quality starts to suffer.

Bucket Oysters

OYSTERS ARE AVAILABLE for purchase in two forms: in their shells or in a bucket. In-shell oysters are self-explanatory. They are living bivalves, and once they are shucked, they have an extremely limited shelf life.

Bucket oysters, available in fish markets and grocery stores, have been shucked and treated with a saline solution to extend their shelf life. They are not a bad thing, but they are not suitable for any sort of raw application. I favor buckets for frying because they're convenient and I don't need the oyster liquor.

My Oyster Pet Peeves

1. Sand or shell or mud in an otherwise pristine briny raw

2. Attempting to shoot one back only to find it hasn't been cut loose from its shell

3. Raw oysters that aren't cold

4. Shucked half shells that look like they were torn up with a hacksaw

focus on my fried shrimp. The oysters looked like giant, jiggly boogers. Gosh, I needed a Shirley Temple.

Before I finished my last french fry, my parents polished off the slaw, wiped their mouths, and took in a deep, post-workout breath. We'd been seated less than twenty minutes and were already done. But my dad paid the bill, left a dollar for service, and grabbed a toothpick on the way out, satisfied.

It took me years to see a trip to T&W for the unique, badass dining experience it is. Eventually Ben and I coupled our reverence for this cultural phenomenon with our love for oysters and naively opened an homage to the T&Ws of the region.

The Boiler Room, our second restaurant, is a modern take on the shell-slinging steamed-oyster bar. Our waiters are polite young people who shuck oysters painfully slowly and drop them in a warm bowl so you don't have to scarf them down before they cool off. Our oyster setup comes with homemade saltines, citrus-infused butter, and cocktail sauce made with our house ketchup. We offer the steamed-oyster service all over the restaurant, not just at the oyster bar, and we serve burgers so there's something for everybody. But it just ain't the T&W.

RECIPES

*ENC-Style
Steamed Oyster Party*

Pork-Rind Roosters

*Oysters on the Half Shell with
Mignonette-Marinated Orange*

Apple and Scallion Oyster Ceviche

*Roasted Oysters
with Brown-Butter
Hot Sauce and Bacon*

Oyster Pie

*Fried Popcorn Oysters with
Kitchen-Sink Mayo*

*Oyster and Clam Pan Roast
with Bacon-Fat Toast*

ENC-Style Steamed Oyster Party

ALTHOUGH THE HOWARDS ATE OYSTERS only at the oyster bar, lots of people here host oyster roasts or steams at home. It's a popular thing to do in the late fall, when handling hot oyster shells helps balance a chilly evening. I personally think it's one of those brilliant outdoor parties that by its nature gives everyone something to do.

For something like this, buy oysters by the bushel from a trusted source. Unless you're me and have a walk-in refrigerator, buy them late in the afternoon on the evening you plan to serve them and do your best to keep them cold till they steam.

Note: *There are 4 pecks and roughly 100 oysters in a bushel. A bushel of oysters will feed anywhere from 5 to 7 people, depending on whether or not you're serving other food.*

In-shell washed oysters

6- to 10-gallon pot fitted with a basket and lid

Cocktail sauce

Sliced lemons

Melted butter, kept warm in a fondue pot or chafing dish

Hot sauce

Saltines

Newspaper

Several pairs of rubber gloves (you want more than one person doing the shucking)

Multiple oyster knives

A stack of dish towels

A sturdy trash can

Paper towels

Worktables

Beer (optional)

To cook the oysters, you need a large steamer situation. We use a turkey fryer or seafood boil set up at my house. This type of pot is for cooking outside and comes fitted with a basket, a handle, and a lid. In a pinch, you could put a brick in the bottom of a large pot and rest a colander on top of that. I've even used a hot-water-bath canner. Once you select your cooking vessel, pour water in the bottom of the pot but don't let the water reach the bottom of the basket. Cover the pot and bring the water up to a boil.

Lay your oysters in no more than a double layer in the bottom of the basket and lower it into the bottom of the pot.

Cover and steam for about 4 minutes for just warmed oysters whose shells are barely beginning to open. Hard-core oyster lovers prefer them at this stage. We call it rare, but there's no right or wrong here. When rare, they're still plump with liquor but warm and comforting. If you have some guests who are unsure about oysters, steam them for about 8 minutes. They're less jiggly and more like chicken that way.

Drain the steamed oysters and dump them onto newspaper. The faint sea smell and poof of steam will draw people over. Shuck, garnish, and eat. Serve with beer or water.

Pork-Rind Roosters

Makes 24 roosters

AN OYSTER-BAR TRADITION I didn't know about till I started going to them on my own is that of the rooster. Let me set the stage. You and a buddy settle in at the bar for the evening. You plan to drink pitchers of beer and eat pecks upon pecks of oysters. After the second pitcher, your buddy says, "I'll eat a rooster if you eat one." You say okay, and the two of you clink Budweiser bottles to celebrate. A server brings you a saltine topped with a steamed oyster, about a tablespoon of horseradish, and several sliced jalapeños. You shoot one back, grimace, and chase it with some beer. Your buddy does the same. Before you know it, you've each eaten a dozen and you've got a T-shirt to prove it.

This is not that. This tastes good. Instead of something you'd eat only after partying a bit, this version of the rooster is an adept way to start a party. If you don't have fried puffy pork rinds, use saltines. But for me the pork rinds are half the point.

¼ cup minced pickled jalapeños	2 tablespoons mayonnaise	24 fried pork rinds, each about the size of a saltine cracker
¼ cup prepared horseradish	1 large jalapeño sliced into 24 rounds	24 shucked oysters (small or medium ones work best)
¼ cup cocktail sauce	Juice of 1 lemon	

In a small bowl stir together the pickled jalapeños, horseradish, and mayonnaise. Refrigerate for a minimum of 30 minutes before using and up to 3 days.

An hour before you plan on serving the roosters, marinate the jalapeño slices in the lemon juice. Just before serving, stir 1 tablespoon of that lemon juice into the pickled jalapeño mixture.

To serve, spoon a heaping teaspoon of the pickled jalapeño tartar on top of a pork rind. Place an oyster on top of that and crown that oyster with a teaspoon of cocktail sauce. Top it off with a jalapeño slice. Serve these immediately, because pork rinds (or saltines, if you're using them) get soggy very fast.

Oysters on the Half Shell with Mignonette-Marinated Orange

Makes 12 to 14 oysters

MIGNONETTE IS A TRADITIONAL SAUCE for raw oysters made from shallots, black pepper, and vinegar. I'm going against the grain here, but classic mignonette, even from the most revered kitchen, is a little too bracing for me. These marinated oranges tamp the acidity down a bit and offer a clean, fruity finish.

- 1 Valencia orange
- 2 teaspoons rice vinegar
- 2 teaspoons lemon juice
- ½ teaspoon grated shallot
- 4 turns of the pepper mill or scant ⅛ teaspoon black pepper
- 1 sprig tarragon
- 12 to 14 oysters

Supreme your orange over a bowl large enough to catch all the juice that leaches off in the process. Rather than removing whole orange sections, cut each section in half lengthwise. This will give you a thin strip of orange instead of a large chunk.

Squeeze the tarragon in the palm of your hand to bruise it a bit and gently stir it, the vinegar, lemon juice, shallot, and black pepper into the oranges. Let this marinate in the refrigerator for at least 30 minutes and up to overnight. Discard the tarragon before serving.

To serve, shuck your oysters (*page 106*) and, depending on their size, spoon one orange supreme and about a half teaspoon of juice over each oyster. If you have really small oysters, you may want to cut the oranges in half again, but one whole slice should be good for medium to large bivalves. Serve cold and soon.

Apple and Scallion Oyster Ceviche

Makes 20 oysters

WE STARTED MAKING THIS CEVICHE in the dead of winter when both oysters and citrus are at their absolute best. In a season when a lot of our food is rich, warm, and brown, this ceviche wakes up your senses. It's best with small to medium oysters that are easy to eat in one bite. Big ones just don't translate well unless you cut them in half.

I love this ceviche as a passed snack or a first course because anything that marinates for a bit before I have to serve it gives me time to put other things in motion.

- 2 scallions
- 2 tablespoons plus 2 teaspoons extra-virgin olive oil
- 1 small garlic clove, grated on a Microplane
- 2 tablespoons finely chopped cilantro stems
- Zest of 1 lime

- 1 tablespoon lime juice
- Zest of 1 lemon
- 1 tablespoon lemon juice
- ¼ teaspoon hot sauce, such as Texas Pete or Tabasco
- ¼ teaspoon salt
- ¼ teaspoon granulated sugar

- ¼ cup small-diced, crisp, sweet eating apple plus 1 tablespoon of that same apple grated on a Microplane
- 20 small shucked oysters, half of each shell washed, soaked, and reserved

---

Start by making the ceviche cure. Minus the apple, this can be done up to a day in advance and will benefit from the relaxation time. Heat a grill, grill pan, or 10-inch cast-iron skillet to almost smoking. Cut the green top off the scallions and split the white end in half lengthwise. Toss the green tops as well as the white bottoms with 2 teaspoons olive oil and go about charring the heck out of them. I'm not talking about mild caramelization; I'm talking about a char that's close to making an ash. The green parts will likely get done before the whites, and that's fine. Just remove them from the pan and set aside while the white ends continue to char on all sides.

In a small bowl, whisk the remaining olive oil, garlic, cilantro, zests and juices, hot sauce, salt, and sugar. Mince the scallions and add them to the bowl. Refrigerate until it's time to put the ceviche together.

Just before you're ready to marinate the ceviche, add the apple and stir in the oysters and their liquor. The liquor is important, so I often drain it off and measure it to make sure all the components will be balanced. You're looking for about a third of a cup of oyster liquor.

Let the ceviche "cook" for a minimum of 10 minutes and up to 1 hour. To serve, spoon the chilled oysters along with about 1 tablespoon of the cure into each shell. In lieu of shells, you can serve the ceviche in individual spoons or a bowl.

Roasted Oysters with
Brown-Butter Hot Sauce and Bacon

Makes 16 oysters

I LIKE OYSTERS ROCKEFELLER as much as anybody, but I'm willing to bet you could take the oyster out and nobody would know. This is my ode to an oyster roasted in the shell where the oyster matters. These work on the grill or in the oven. Either way, what you'll taste is oyster, spice, nutty butter, and smoky bacon.

I serve these with a fork and encourage people to shoot back the liquor left behind.

4 tablespoons butter	⅛ teaspoon salt	3 slices bacon, cooked till crisp and roughly crumbled
Zest of 1 lemon	16 shucked oysters, half of each shell reserved and washed	
1 tablespoon lemon juice		1 tablespoon chopped parsley
1½ teaspoons hot sauce, such as Tabasco or Texas Pete		

Make the butter: In a 6-inch sauté pan, melt the butter over medium heat. Watch closely and swirl the butter around in the pan. Once it takes on a nutty aroma and the bottom of the pan is speckled with brown dots, pour the butter into a small clear glass bowl.

Transfer the butter to the refrigerator and let it chill for about 10 minutes. Take it out and stir, making sure you scoop up the browned bits that have sunk to the bottom. The idea is to evenly distribute the browned solids throughout the butter, so continue to stir as it cools. The butter itself will become pale brown, similar to the color of bacon fat. Once it's room temperature, stir in the zest, lemon juice, hot sauce, and salt. Cover and refrigerate till you're ready to use. It will keep for up to a month.

Roast the oysters: Preheat your oven to 500°F or your grill to medium high. Put one oyster in each shell and top with a teaspoon-size slice of the butter. If you're grilling the oysters, they should fit nicely between the grates. If you're roasting them, put a layer of rock salt over the bottom of your baking sheet and nestle the shells on the salt. For both methods, it's important the oysters sit up straight and don't tip over. The last thing you want to do is lose the buttery juice.

Roast for 4 to 6 minutes or until the butter is bubbly and the edges of the oysters have just started to curl. Top with crispy bacon and chopped parsley. Serve immediately.

Oyster Pie

Serves 6

WHEN I STARTED THINKING about the oyster portion of the Boiler Room menu, I questioned locals about their family recipes. Oyster pie and scalloped oysters kept coming up. Best I can tell, the two dishes are basically the same thing: luxurious sides reserved for holidays. This is my revamped version. It's silky, comforting, and too good to be put in the holiday corner. If you don't have Cocktail Tomatoes (*page 280*), use the same amount of diced tomatoes marinated in a little rice vinegar plus three dashes of hot sauce.

- 2 sleeves saltine crackers
- ⅔ cup grated Parmigiano-Reggiano
- 2 teaspoons smoked paprika
- 6 tablespoons butter, divided
- 2 cups diced leeks, white and light green parts only
- 1½ teaspoons salt, divided
- 2 cloves garlic, minced
- 2 tablespoons all-purpose flour
- 2 cups Cocktail Tomatoes (*page 280*)
- 1 teaspoon Worcestershire sauce
- 1 cup milk
- 3 cups oysters, plus their liquor (bucket oysters are fine here)
- ⅓ cup heavy cream
- 2 teaspoons chopped tarragon
- 1 tablespoon chopped parsley

Note: *You can make the oyster filling and butter the saltines up to a day before you plan to bake the pie, but don't assemble the whole thing till you're ready to cook unless you want a soggy topping.*

Preheat your oven to 350°F. In a medium bowl crush the saltines into small pieces. You're not looking for crumbs or saltine sand. Instead, you want broken recognizable pieces. Pour the Parm, paprika, and 4 tablespoons melted butter over the crackers and stir to incorporate. Set aside.

In a 10- to 12-inch sauté pan or skillet, melt 2 tablespoons of butter and heat till foaming. Add the leeks and ½ teaspoon salt. Sweat the leeks over medium-low heat for about 10 minutes. Add the garlic and the flour and cook an additional minute. The mixture will be quite dry and will form a film over the bottom of the pan. Don't you dare walk away from this because it's a burned mess waiting to happen.

Stir in the tomatoes, Worcestershire, and milk. Bring it up to a boil and watch things thicken up to a paste-like consistency. Add the oysters, their liquor, the heavy cream, tarragon, parsley, and remaining 1 teaspoon salt. Take the pan off the heat and mix to bring everything together. The filling should be loose with raw oysters and creamy from the incorporated roux.

Transfer the filling to a 2-quart baking dish or consider baking it right in the skillet you built it in. Top with the saltines and bake in the center of your oven for 30 minutes. Serve warm.

Fried Popcorn Oysters with Kitchen-Sink Mayo

Serves 4

MY MOM IS A CONNOISSEUR OF SWEET TEA and fried oysters. If the latter is on the menu, she orders it and passes judgment. After decades of hearing Mom's critiques, I distilled her grievances down to one core symptom: different-size oysters. Much like my mom, I prefer fried oysters that are all about the same size because they cook evenly. At the Boiler Room we satisfy my mom by cutting large oysters in half and keeping small oysters whole in order to guarantee consistency. What you end up with is something akin to popcorn shrimp, but instead of giving way to a rubbery shrimp, the delicate crust reveals a creamy oyster.

Kitchen-Sink Mayo is twice what the name implies. You throw in everything but the kitchen sink, and it's good on everything but the kitchen sink.

Kitchen-Sink Mayo
Makes 1½ cups

- 1 egg yolk
- 3 teaspoons lemon juice
- 1 tablespoon rice vinegar
- 3 anchovy fillets
- 2 teaspoons hot sauce
- 2 teaspoons Worcestershire sauce
- 1 tablespoon Garlic Confit (*page 156*)
- 2 cloves fresh garlic

- 1 tablespoon prepared horseradish
- 2 teaspoons soy sauce
- ½ teaspoon salt
- 1 tablespoon honey
- 1 cup vegetable oil

Fried Oysters

- ½ cup panko crumbs
- ½ cup cornmeal
- 2 teaspoons salt, divided
- 1 teaspoon garlic powder

- 1 teaspoon paprika
- 1 teaspoon onion powder
- ½ teaspoon cayenne
- 2 quarts vegetable oil
- 2 cups shucked oysters, drained of their liquor but damp
- ¼ cup picked soft herbs such as parsley, chervil, chives, basil, tarragon

Make the mayonnaise: I'm aware it's annoying to use both the blender and the food processor in one recipe, but in this case it's necessary. Sorry.

Combine everything but the oil in a blender and blend till smooth. Transfer this mixture to your food processor. Turn it on and begin slowly streaming in the oil. This should emulsify and produce a sauce that's

not as thick as Duke's or Kraft but thicker than bottled salad dressing. The mayo will keep, sealed in the fridge, for up to 3 days.

For the oysters: In a food processor, pulverize the panko crumbs until they resemble stone-ground cornmeal. Since you're already working with the food processor, add all the other dry ingredients and pulse until well combined. Set this

aside. It will keep indefinitely in a sealed container.

Preheat your oven to 200°F. In a Dutch oven, heat the oil to 350°F. Lightly dredge each oyster in the panko mix, shake off any excess, and drop them carefully in the oil using a slotted spoon. Do not crowd the oil. Each oyster should have a little room to sizzle privately. Every batch of oysters will take about 60 seconds, and you will probably need to drop them in three batches.

Remove the oysters from the oil, drain on paper towels, and season them lightly with the remaining salt. Hold them in the warm oven while you fry off the remaining batches.

Scatter the fried oysters with the herbs and serve with the mayonnaise.

Oyster and Clam Pan Roast
with Bacon-Fat Toast

Serves 4

I MAKE THIS IF IT'S COLD and raw outside and I want to serve something sexy (forgive me for using that word, but nothing else really works). Both brothy and rich, my pan roast weaves the New Orleans tradition of decadent creamed oysters over toast with that coastal winter staple, steamed clams. I throw in turnip greens because they make it feel like a meal.

I use bacon fat for the toast. It adds more sexy (used it again!), but olive oil and butter work too.

- 1 loaf rustic crusty bread
- ⅓ cup bacon fat, divided
- 1 teaspoon salt, divided
- 2 cups sliced leeks (roughly 2 leeks), white and light green parts only
- 2 cloves garlic, sliced
- 3 cups turnip greens, roughly chopped
- 4 sprigs thyme
- ¼ teaspoon chili flakes
- 1 cup dry vermouth
- 24 littleneck clams, scrubbed
- 25 oysters and their liquor (bucket oysters are an okay substitute)
- 1 teaspoon lemon juice
- 2 dashes hot sauce
- 2 tablespoons butter
- 2 tablespoons heavy cream
- 2 tablespoons chopped parsley

Preheat your oven to 375°F. Slice the loaf of bread into 1- or 2-inch slices. Brush them with all but 1 tablespoon of the bacon fat and sprinkle with ½ teaspoon salt. Lay the bread out on a baking sheet and put it in the oven just before you start to make your pan roast. The two will take about the same amount of time.

In a 12-inch brazier, Dutch oven, or skillet fitted with a lid, melt 1 tablespoon bacon fat over medium-low heat. Add the leeks and ¼ teaspoon salt. Sweat for 10 minutes. Add the garlic, turnip greens, thyme, and chili flakes. Toss around and wilt for 2 minutes. Add the vermouth and the clams. Raise the heat to medium.

Cover and steam. Check the clams after about 5 minutes. They will probably need more time and may take up to 10 minutes to open, but you want to be vigilant about catching them just as they do. Once about ¾ of the clams have just popped open, lower the heat slightly and stir in the oysters, lemon juice, hot sauce, butter, heavy cream, remaining salt, and chopped parsley. Continue to heat just until the oysters barely begin to curl around the edges. If you have clams that never open, throw them out. Serve immediately over or next to ultra-crunchy bacon-fat toast.

PECANS

MY PARENTS WOULD NEVER describe their upbringing as poor, but the stories they tell about their childhoods suggests something different to me.

When John and Scarlett read this, they're gonna say, "Vivian, we were never poor." And I'm gonna say, "Did you grow most of your own food? From the day you could dress yourself, did you contribute to the household income? Did you get up before dawn and go out on the road to pick up the pecans that had fallen overnight before a car or truck could crush them so your mom could sell those pecans in town and accumulate what she called your Christmas money? Today, we'd call that poor."

My parents call it frugal. They'd call themselves, their parents, and their grandparents all frugal farmers—people who lived a ways from town, worked the land, and wasted nothing. In their kitchens, they exalted spoiled milk and relished things like liver pudding and chitterlings, scraps I can't imagine eating twice. They worked all summer fattening pigs, growing vegetables, and preserving fruit. So when something like a pecan, a fatty foraged delicacy, fell from tall trees in late fall, it was truly special.

I'd go so far as to call pecans the truffles of our kitchens. Pecans fell from trees for about a month each year, and every pecan that wasn't picked up lay in danger of getting squashed, toted away by a squirrel, or infested by a worm. That's why my mom and her siblings were up at the crack of dawn rescuing pecans from the dirt road before the school bus or farm trucks rushed through and crushed them. That's why, till the day Grandma Hill died, nobody pulled a car into her driveway between October and early December. She was a frugal, practical woman who valued pecans. And her driveway sat under a vast pecan tree whose roots had pushed through and split the concrete the way the Incredible Hulk's arms split his shirt.

By the time I was born, John and Scarlett were almost forty and not nearly as frugal as their parents would have liked. They ate at restaurants on the weekends, dabbled in processed food, and, for the most part, bought meat instead of slaughtering it. But come holiday time in our house, we still worshipped the pecan. The deep sweet nut, the only nut the Howard girls knew, was meant for gifts, pies, and a crystal snack bowl but once a year. Only my teacher, not my teacher's assistant, got a jar of Mom's Salt-and-Butter-Roasted Pecans (*page 134*). Her assistant got peanuts. And Mom's pecan pie was a luxury too because she put two times more pecans in the filling than the Karo Syrup bottle called for. It was the holidays, and we could be extravagant.

The Christmas of my eighth-grade year, Grandma Hill started giving all her grandchildren bags of shelled pecans instead of real presents. Her gifts had never been all that great, but by this time I was tired of the frugal-farm thing and the freezer bag of nuts for Christmas set me off.

Didn't my redneck family understand there was more to the world than turnip greens, pecans, and *Hee Haw*? Weren't they curious about these highly populated places called cities? Places where you could order Chinese food and have a Chinese person bring it to your door? I wanted to live in a place like that. I wanted to unpack and unfold the little white cartons full of noodles and rice and egg rolls, pull out my chopsticks, sit cross-legged right in front of the TV, and eat like a chopstick expert while I watched *Beverly Hills 90210*! That's what I thought a cosmopolitan life meant at the time, and I knew my family was not cosmopolitan.

The following fall I went to boarding school—not because I was forced to, but because I was dying to. I had to get out of Deep Run. The farm thing was shameful and backward, and I was thankful to escape before my tastes and talents were fully formed.

Salem Academy, an all-girls school in Winston-Salem, a four-hour drive from Deep Run, met me with everything I'd longed for and more. I could take a cab (a cab!) to Applebee's, TGI Fridays, Bennigan's, and the largest mall in North Carolina. I could order Chinese food and watch *90210* with a bunch of squealing girls in the TV lounge on our hall. And I quickly learned that although a lot of these girls were from the South, none of them had grown up praising the pecan or showing pigs at the livestock

show and sale like me. They were *Southern*. I was *country,* and I was ashamed.

I tailored my story to be just a little different than it was. I didn't even have to tell lies to shape my image. I was already at boarding school, the second of the Howard girls to attend this institution. My sister Currie had been Salem's valedictorian nine years prior, so my status as an affluent landowner's kid was assumed. I just never let on my parents were actually farmers who had sacrificed things for themselves because they believed my education was their most important investment. Then, my sophomore year, I brought home an exchange student from Switzerland. With

PECAN WISDOM

Our Native Nut

PECANS ARE OUR COUNTRY'S only native nut. From North Carolina to Texas to New Mexico and Arizona, fifteen states produce pecans. Georgia grows the most.

Pecans come from large trees, need a warm climate, and require a lot of water for production. Desirable, Stewart, and Cape Fear are popular varieties in North Carolina. These trees produce their first nuts after about seven years and can continue producing for up to a hundred years.

Every pecan as it exists on a tree is two kernels separated by a woody, inedible membrane. The nutmeats, as nut people call them, are surrounded by an oval shell, and that shell is surrounded by a hull. Once the hull can be shaken off the shell, the pecans are ready to be harvested. Pecan harvest begins in late October and goes through November.

How to Keep Them Fresh

PECANS HAVE MORE FAT than nearly any other nut. That makes them tasty but incredibly perishable. If you get your pecans from the grocery store, they've been dehydrated enough to keep them fresh in the sealed bag. But once you open the bag, put them in the refrigerator or freezer in a sealed container. In the fridge they'll stay fresh for about two months, but they tend to absorb odors there, so I prefer the freezer, where they can stay for up to a year (some say two years).

Broken Nuts

PECANS ARE NOT CHEAP. Nuts in general are pricey, in part because of how difficult it is to extract an intact nut from its shell. Because a lot of perfect pecans are broken in the process, you can often find pieces at a better price than intact halves.

The good news is that all the recipes in this chapter work with pecan pieces and some of them, like Viv's Addiction (*page 133*) and Spiced Pecan and Pumpkin Seed Crumble (*page 135*), work better with pieces than halves. Really the only time I would seek out whole pecan halves is if I were preparing a gift for someone I wanted to impress.

everything I had allowed her to believe about my aristocratic parents, she was shocked when she saw our modest home and likened it to an apartment. I guess I would have been surprised too!

I'd like to say I wised up and embraced my upbringing earlier than I did, but the truth is, I continued to tweak my story and even my accent for a long time. I didn't tell lies. I just didn't let on my parents said things like "I reckon," "over yonder," and "*pee*-can." I told stories about my friends from boarding school instead of my friends from the trailer park. During my early days in New York, terrified I'd be dismissed

Grocery Store Nuts Are Sad and Shriveled

I RECENTLY GOT A PACKAGE of fresh macadamia nuts from a couple in Hawaii. They had been harvested from the couple's tree and were like no macadamia nut I had ever seen. Plump, shiny, fatty, and sweet, they reminded me of pecans—or at least of the pecans we get around here in late fall. Then it occurred to me the pecans that the couple had access to in Hawaii were probably a lot like the macadamia nuts I plucked out of a snack mix here in North Carolina. The conclusion: fresh nuts are different nuts, and the nuts from the grocery store are sad, dry examples of their kind. We are fast to think about the seasonality of tomatoes, peaches, and apples, but we are conditioned to believe nuts are nuts, consistent from a can or a bag.

If you have the opportunity to buy fresh nuts of any kind from a roadside stand or farmers' market in season, do it, and open your mind to what a nut at its prime can be. Then treat the uneaten nuts like the perishable produce they are and store them in the fridge or freezer.

RECIPES

Viv's Addiction

Salt-and-Butter-Roasted Pecans

Spiced Pecan and Pumpkin Seed Crumble

Pecan–Chewy Pie

Party Magnet

Breakfast in the Car

Pecan, Pepper Jelly, and Stinky Cheese Panini

Butter-Baked Turkey with Pecan Cranberry Relish and Warm Sorghum Vinaigrette

as a redneck, I altered my speech to the point that people mistook me for British, "peh *cahn*" and all.

Today I wear my pride in my place and my people like a badge. I believe my parents, with all their country ways, are some of the smartest people I've met anywhere. When I think back to my fake persona and British accent, I wince and have to remind myself I was just a kid trying to make my way. Thankfully I just covered up the values, work ethic, and principles my parents gave me; I didn't lose them. I'm a hard worker. I'm honest, kind, resourceful, and compassionate. But I am not frugal. I'm gonna blame it on my generation, or maybe on my parents' desire for me to have more than they had, but I didn't get the frugal gene. I wish I had. I even *pretend* I did, saving vegetable scraps for stock or boiling a chicken carcass a second time to make broth. But when no one's looking, I crush pecans in the driveway.

Spiced Pecan and
Pumpkin Seed Crumble

Salt-and-Butter
Roasted Pecans

Viv's Addiction

Viv's Addiction

Makes 4 cups

I CALL THESE Viv's Addiction because they are. Once I decided nuts were good for me and might actually curb my appetite, I started having a handful of these every time I wanted a snack at work. Now they're one of my five food groups.

I learned how to do pecans this way from Ben and Karen Barker's *Not Afraid of Flavor* cookbook. Prior to that I had gone through four different steps to make nuts that were almost this good. Over the years, I adapted the Barkers' recipe to fit the needs of our kitchen. At any given time, we have some kind of egg-white-coated spiced nut on the menu, and most of the time, there's a sealed container of these nuts at my house. Except now Amelia, our nanny, is addicted too. Why not...they're healthy and they curb your appetite.

2	egg whites	1	tablespoon ground chipotle	1	tablespoon ground cumin
2	teaspoons salt	1	tablespoon ground coriander	2	teaspoons paprika
½	cup granulated sugar			4	cups pecan halves or pieces

Preheat your oven to 350°F. In your mixer fitted with the whisk attachment, beat the whites till they are very foamy. Continue whisking and slowly add the salt and sugar. Bring the egg whites to stiff peaks. Then whisk in the chipotle, coriander, cumin, and paprika.

Using a spatula, fold in the pecans, taking care to coat them evenly in the egg-white mixture. Transfer the egg-white-coated nuts to a baking sheet lined with either parchment paper or a Silpat. Spread the nuts out into a single layer so they cook evenly.

Bake the pecans on the center rack of your oven for 10 minutes. Remove the tray from the oven and, using a metal spatula, turn them over and break up any nut clumps you see. Do this a couple more times over the course of 20 more minutes. The pecans will be dark brown and should sound dry and flat rather than muddled and moist when you tap them with your spatula. This should take about 30 minutes in total, but the freshness of your pecans will really determine their cook time. Just-shelled pecans will require more time in the oven than those from the grocery store.

Remove the pecans from the oven and let them cool on the sheet tray. Break them up once they're cool. Store the pecans in an airtight container for up to 5 days.

Salt-and-Butter-Roasted Pecans

Makes 2 cups

INSTEAD OF HANDING OUT tins brimming with homemade Christmas candy, my mom gave these as gifts for the holidays. The deep smell of butter and pecans roasting in our little kitchen meant Santa was coming soon, and we'd have a fancy crystal bowl of salty plump pecans before our Christmas Eve dinner. In a family that never ate hors d'oeuvres or mingled, that bowl of nuts was a big deal. Today we're more likely to eat these on a salad than from a crystal bowl.

2 cups pecan halves or pieces	2 tablespoons melted butter	¾ teaspoon salt, divided

Preheat your oven to 350°F. Toss the pecans thoroughly with the melted butter and ½ teaspoon of the salt. Spread them out in a single layer on a baking sheet and slide that sheet onto the middle rack of your oven. Roast the pecans for 11 minutes if using pecan halves and 10 minutes if you're using pieces.

Bring the slightly darkened and toasty-smelling pecans out of the oven and hit them with the remaining salt. Let them cool 5 minutes before you eat them. These will keep for 2 weeks in an airtight container at room temperature.

Spiced Pecan and Pumpkin Seed Crumble

Makes 5 cups

LIKE A SAVORY GRANOLA meant for a snack, salad, or cheese plate, this crumble maximizes the pecan's appeal without totally relying on it. In other words, it's affordable to make and it's tasty. Sub in another nut like almonds or walnuts and achieve the same effect.

In addition to this crumble's obvious uses, think about folding it into muffin or zucchini-bread batter or tossing it with cooked faro, rice, or quinoa for a dish with lots of texture. Think outside the granola.

2 cups rolled oats	2 egg whites	2 teaspoons Worcestershire sauce
½ cup steel-cut oats	½ cup granulated sugar	
1¼ cups roughly chopped pecans	3 teaspoons cayenne	¼ cup grapeseed or sunflower oil
1 cup pumpkin seeds	3 teaspoons ground fennel	¾ teaspoon salt

Preheat the oven to 300°F. In a large bowl, stir together the oats, the pecans, and the pumpkin seeds. In your mixer fitted with the whisk attachment, whisk the egg whites till they're quite foamy. Then slowly add the sugar, cayenne, fennel, Worcestershire, oil, and salt. Continue whisking till you have stiff peaks. Pour the egg-white mix over the nut mix and stir it to combine. Spread the whole thing out in a thin layer on a baking sheet lined with parchment or a Silpat and bake on the center rack of your oven for 15 minutes. Using a metal spatula, turn it over on itself and bake an additional 15 minutes.

Take the crumble out of the oven and let it cool completely before breaking it into pieces. Store in an airtight container for up to 2 weeks.

Pecan-Chewy Pie

Makes two 8-inch pies

MOM MADE THREE SWEETS: Warm Banana Pudding when she wanted to treat herself (*page 59*), pecan pie when we celebrated as a family, and chewies when she was in a bind and needed a quick dessert. This combines her pecan pie and her chewies, which are basically chocolate-less brownies. She never made just one pie, so this recipe is for two. You could also treat this like a bar; follow the same recipe and instructions, but use a 9 x 13-inch baking dish instead of pie pans.

Crust and Streusel

- 1¼ cups all-purpose flour
- 1 cup granulated sugar
- 2 cups finely chopped pecans (they should resemble coarse grits)
- 4 tablespoons cold butter, divided
- 1 tablespoon water
- 1 egg, whisked

Pecan-Chewy Filling

- 1 cup white chocolate chips
- 8 tablespoons (1 stick) butter
- 4 egg yolks, at room temperature
- ½ cup dark brown sugar
- 1 cup heavy cream, at room temperature
- ⅔ cup all-purpose flour
- 1½ cups toasted pecans, roughly chopped
- 1 teaspoon salt

Make the crust and streusel: Preheat your oven to 350°F. In a medium bowl, stir together the flour, sugar, and pecans. Using a fork, pastry cutter, or cold hands, cut in 3 tablespoons butter until it all resembles pebbly sand. Stir in the water and egg until the mixture is damp.

Using 1 tablespoon of butter, grease the pie pans. Take half the streusel mixture and split it between the pans. Press along the bottom and up the sides to form a crust. Set aside the other half of the streusel. Blind-bake the crust on the middle rack of your oven for 15 minutes. It will just begin to take on a little color around the edges only. Let it cool before filling it.

Make the filling: While the crust bakes and cools make the filling. Using a double boiler, melt the white chocolate and the butter over low heat. It may separate and give you the impression something has gone wrong, but it will be fine. In a medium bowl, whisk together the yolks and the sugar until thoroughly combined. Pour the melted white chocolate mixture into the egg and sugar mixture and whisk it to combine. Whisk in the heavy cream.

In another small bowl, stir together the flour, pecans, and salt. Fold that into the egg mixture just until everything is incorporated.

Assemble and bake: Lower the oven to 325°F. Divide the filling between two crusts. Sprinkle the remaining streusel on top. Bake the pies in the center of the oven for about 40 minutes, or until they are golden brown and set in the middle.

Serve warm or at room temperature. I prefer it warm with a scoop of chocolate ice cream. The pie will keep, covered with plastic wrap, for up to 3 days.

Party Magnet

Makes 1 large cheese ball or 2 small ones

THE CHEESE BALL IS A CLICHÉ. I believe, however, that like the pig in a blanket and the baked potato, cheese balls are so clichéd they've actually become cool. Socially acceptable or not, when this thing is put out at a party of any kind, people hover over it like it's a crystal ball.

Once you get used to the idea of making a cheese ball, keep a few things in mind. Bring it out at least thirty minutes before you plan on serving. This forethought will make it spreadable and allow the complexity of its flavor to come through. Also, consider doubling the recipe. A fully formed cheese ball freezes and travels nicely. And, last, keep your cracker choice simple. This is not the place for roasted-garlic Asiago Triscuits. Sea salt or plain Jane is the way to go here, possibly everywhere.

Note: *This recipe calls for dates. Please do not use pre-chopped dates from a bag. They are covered in sugar and taste like sweet cardboard. Use whole, dried dates and remove the pits.*

- ¼ cup high-quality blue cheese (I like Maytag)
- ⅓ cup (5½ tablespoons) butter
- ¼ cup fresh goat cheese
- ¼ cup plus 2 tablespoons cream cheese
- ¼ cup chopped dates
- 2 tablespoons finely chopped scallions (both white and green parts work here)
- ½ teaspoon hot sauce
- ¼ teaspoon salt
- ⅓ cup Salt-and-Butter-Roasted Pecans (*page 134*), roughly chopped
- 2 tablespoons chopped flat-leaf parsley

Take the blue cheese, butter, goat cheese, and cream cheese out of the refrigerator to soften 30 minutes before making your cheese-ball mixture.

In the bowl of a mixer fitted with the paddle attachment, combine all the ingredients except for the pecans and parsley. Paddle it up till homogenous. It will be loose and sticky and you'll wonder how you're ever going to form that mess into a ball. The answer is, you transfer the bowl to the refrigerator for 15 minutes or so. During that time the cheese mix will firm up enough for you to pat it into a sphere. Once it's stiff enough to hold up, form the ball and roll that ball in the pecans, followed by parsley. Serve with Curried Peach Preserves (*page 458*), Whole-Fruit Fig and Lemon Preserves (*page 178*), or Apple Chips (*page 490*).

Breakfast in the Car

Makes 2 roll-ups

WE LIVE A FORTY-MINUTE DRIVE from Theo and Flo's school, and while I preach that every meal should be savored, sometimes it's savored in the backseat of the car. Our friend David Brody shared how he used to make PB&J sandwiches for his kids by flattening slices of bread with a rolling pin, spreading the PB&J on thin, and rolling it up like a pinwheel. I've adapted that lightbulb idea for a one-hand roll-up with banana and vanilla pecan butter and no sticky jelly. Both my kids eat it without complaining, and that's saying something.

Nut butters are my new thing. They're easy to make and it's worth washing an extra dish just to have this one around for apple snacks. The key step in making an excellent nut butter is to toast the nuts properly and let them cool down completely before you let the food processor rip. Too toasted, and that burned flavor really rears its head; too warm, and the pecan butter becomes separated nut sludge.

- 2 slices whole wheat sandwich bread of your choice
- ¼ cup vanilla pecan butter
- ½ ripe banana, sliced into ¼-inch rounds or strips

Vanilla Pecan Butter
Makes ½ cup

- 2 cups pecans
- ½ vanilla bean, split and scraped

- 1 teaspoon honey
- ¼ teaspoon salt

Make the pecan butter: In a 10- to 12-inch skillet or sauté pan, toast the pecans over medium heat for about 2 minutes or until they are just becoming fragrant. They may darken slightly in color but do not let them get noticeably darker in places. If you find a few spots where this happens, pluck those pecans out.

Let the pecans cool completely, then transfer them to the bowl of a food processor along with all the little dark seeds from the center of the vanilla bean. Process the pecans for 1 minute. Stop and scrape down the sides. Process another minute. Scrape down the sides again and add the honey and salt. Continue processing for a third minute or until the pecan butter is quite smooth and loose. The end product will be much looser than any peanut butter

you've ever seen and a bit less viscous than almond butter. It will pour off a spoon.

Depending on the power of your food processor or the sharpness of its blade, making the pecan butter may take longer than 3 minutes. Just keep an eye out for separation of nut and fat. If this starts to happen, let the pecan butter cool down before blending further. Store the pecan butter, sealed, at room temperature for up to 2 weeks. Stir well before using.

Make the roll-ups: Use a rolling pin, flatten each slice of bread to an eighth of an inch thick. Spread roughly 2 tablespoons pecan butter over each flat piece and lay the banana slices over the top. Roll the bread up in a pinwheel and take it wherever you need to eat.

Pecan, Pepper Jelly, and Stinky Cheese Panini

Serves 4

THIS ASSERTIVE SANDWICH IS A TRIBUTE to my first teacher at the Institute of Culinary Education in Manhattan. I attended a six-month program there, and, lucky for me, Alexandra Guarnaschelli taught my basics class. Chef Alex talked a lot about her time cooking in France and, in particular, of the astounding dairy there. She said she chugged heavy cream from glass bottles and ate lollipops of Époisses, one of the stinkiest cheeses on the planet. Those stinky lollipops still haunt me. Here's the result.

I recommend Époisses, which is creamy and pungent, but any stinky or slightly stinky cheese works fine. What makes the sandwich work, I think, is the pecans. They have a salty, savory quality as well as a round sweetness that brings the pungent cheese and tangy spread together in harmony. This sandwich next to a green salad makes a fun lunch, but my favorite way to serve it is cut into little triangles as a party snack.

8 slices rustic sourdough or ciabatta bread, ½ to ¾ inch thick	4 tablespoons Jalapeño Peach Glaze *(page 452)* or hot pepper jelly	8 ounces Époisses round (Taleggio, Roquefort, or a triple-crème Brie are also good options)
3 tablespoons butter, softened	⅔ cup Salt-and-Butter-Roasted Pecans *(page 134)*, roughly chopped	

Spread one side of each slice of bread with the butter. That's the side that will get toasted. Spread the opposite side of each slice with the glaze or jelly. Divide the slices into tops and bottoms. Set the tops aside. On the glaze-smeared side of the 4 bottoms, divide the pecans evenly. Slice the Époisses into ¼-inch slices and position them in a single layer on top of the pecans. Make sure you don't use extra cheese; it will overwhelm...even if you like cheese. Put the tops on, glaze-side down, and cover the sandwiches with plastic wrap till you're ready to toast.

Preheat your oven to 200°F. Toast the sandwiches in a 10- to 12-inch cast-iron skillet over low heat, making sure each side becomes a nice golden brown. Alternatively, you could use a sandwich grill or panini press if you happen to have one.

Hold the grilled cheeses in the oven up to 15 minutes till you're ready to serve. Serve warm, sliced in half.

Butter-Baked Turkey with Pecan Cranberry Relish and Warm Sorghum Vinaigrette

Serves 6

THIS COMBINATION OF turkey, cranberry, pecan, and sorghum will likely make you hide your gravy boat for a year or two. Add the Citrus Sweet Potato Butter (*page 316*) and cover almost all the Thanksgiving flavor bases on one platter.

The relish and sorghum vinaigrette are two components that make everything they're near taste like autumn. If sorghum is hard for you to find, substitute equal parts blackstrap molasses and honey for a similar sweet. Together the relish and vinaigrette pair wonderfully with any kind of poultry, roasted Brussels sprouts, Stewed Rutabagas (*page 470*), or Turnip Roots and Greens (*page 68*).

Butter-Baked Turkey

A fresh 8- to 10-pound turkey

2 tablespoons salt

20 turns of the pepper mill or scant ½ teaspoon black pepper

4 sprigs rosemary

4 sprigs thyme

1 orange, halved

2 pounds butter

1 lemon, halved

2 x 2-foot piece of cheesecloth folded to cover the breast portion of your bird

Pecan Cranberry Relish

Makes 2 cups

2 tablespoons butter

1 cup pecans, roughly chopped with a knife

⅓ cup dried cranberries

⅓ cup leeks sliced thin, white part only

¼ teaspoon salt

5 turns of the pepper mill or ⅛ teaspoon black pepper

Sorghum Vinaigrette

Makes 1 cup

2 tablespoons butter

¼ red onion, minced

¼ teaspoon salt

5 turns of the pepper mill or ⅛ teaspoon black pepper

¼ teaspoon nutmeg

½ cup cider vinegar

⅓ cup sorghum syrup

¼ cup honey

Cook the turkey: Preheat your oven to 325°F. Remove the giblets from your turkey and rinse the inside as well as the outside of the bird. Pat the turkey dry and season its skin and cavity thoroughly with salt and pepper.

Stuff the cavity with the rosemary, thyme, and halved orange. Place the turkey in a roasting pan and slide it into the oven.

Meanwhile, melt the butter along with the halved lemon in a small saucepan. After about 30 minutes of roasting, dip the cheesecloth into the butter and lay it over top of the turkey's breast. Repeat this every thirty minutes until the last 30 minutes of cooking time. For the final 30 minutes, leave the turkey uncovered to encourage even browning. The turkey is done when the juices run clear between the leg and the thigh, between 2½ and 3 hours.

Once it's done, take the turkey from the oven and allow to rest for 20 minutes. Carve the turkey and top with the relish and vinaigrette.

Make the relish: In a 10-inch sauté pan, melt the butter. Add the pecans and toast them for about 4 minutes, but watch closely and stir often to prevent them from burning. Add the cranberries, leeks, salt, and pepper. Continue sautéing and stirring for 2 minutes. Set aside and keep warm.

This will keep in a sealed container in the fridge for up to a week. Warm gently on a baking sheet or in a sauté pan before serving.

Make the vinaigrette: In a small saucepan, melt the butter. Add the red onion and the salt. Cook until onions are soft and translucent. Throw in the pepper, nutmeg, and vinegar. Bring it up to a boil and add the syrup and honey. Reduce by half. Serve immediately or store it in the fridge for up to a week and heat before serving.

BEANS & PEAS

Dried Limas

Speckled Butterbeans

Dixie Lee Peas

Butterbeans

Dried One Hill

Dried Field Peas

Fresh Red Ripper

WAY BEFORE I STEPPED FOOT in a professional kitchen, even before I microwaved my first bowl of instant grits, I worshipped butterbeans. Not quite a vegetable, not rice, and most definitely not the burpy peas my mom and dad favored, butterbeans lived in a category I couldn't identify. Decadent tiny green packages of creamy comfort wrapped in a sheath of tight but tender skin, butterbeans were one of the few things I craved that my mom approved of.

Mom always worried about my weight. Scarlett, a waif whose one brush with being plump was solved by voluntarily leaving sugar off her morning cornflakes, gave birth to four girls, three of whom inherited her husband's appetite and naturally heavy genes. (Currie was the lucky one.) And though my mother tried to keep an eye on everything her chubby daughters ate, her rheumatoid arthritis made it impossible. Diagnosed at seventeen when she opened the door of the school bus—a school bus she drove, by the way—and her shoulder popped out of its socket, Mom suffered through numerous surgeries and experimental treatments as a young parent. But despite her fatigue and frequent trips to the Mayo Clinic, believe me, she tried to keep us skinny. We never ever bought Lucky Charms, Fruity Pebbles, Snickers bars, Twix, Mountain Dew, Pringles, or ice cream. Our sugar cereal was Raisin Bran and our lusty junk foods were sausage biscuits and the peanut butter crackers we called nabs.

All this restriction made me one heck of a houseguest. When I slept over at Tara's, Jessica's, or Crystal's, I slurped down Kool-Aid and marveled at the two whole cups of sugar it took to make every pitcher. I zapped Moon Pies for a few seconds in the microwave and ate entire bags of Doritos and Cheetos in front of the TV. I ate hot dogs at Ma's Hot Dog House, and Nachos Bel Grande and fried cinnamon puffy things at Taco Bell.

Then I went home, acted famished like we'd played outside the whole weekend, and requested butterbeans for supper. Even though the general public thinks of

beans as modest food, a staple intended to round out a meager offering, we treated
butterbeans differently. No commonplace filler, they were a precious ingredient, with
our stash stowed away in the locker (freezer) to be rationed out till the following
summer. Butterbeans were sherbet green and pleasantly plump, like me. Moist with a
vegetal smell, they came to us late every summer on a pickup truck, stacks and stacks
of them, hiding inside shiny pods.

    We held butterbeans up high because we shelled most of our ration by hand, one
shiny pod at a time. For a few weeks every summer, I joined in as my mom, grandma,
and sisters sat both inside and out, pans flush with beans in their laps, shelling and
talking. After the first day, we'd barely made a dent in the endless pile of beans stacked
under the carport, and the nailbed of my thumb ached from prying open the flat green
pods over and over again. The youngest helper, and not much help at all, I shelled in
spurts but always stayed nearby as my family told stories and laughed. It was work
that felt like pleasure.

I put butterbeans on a pedestal through high school and college, an ingredient in a category of its own. When I got serious about losing weight, I cut them out of my diet. Anything that creamy, that plush, that tasty, couldn't possibly help me shed pounds. I understood beans and legumes to be health foods, carbohydrates that were high in fiber and low in fat. But those were the beans I saw at the grocery store, not my beloved butterbeans. Although they shared a name, they seemed like opposites. Healthy beans came pre-shelled in bags of dusty shades of brown, red, and black. They were dry, in need of a soak before cooking. They even looked healthy, not creamy and delicious.

When I started working at Voyage and became friends with Scott, the chef, I took the opportunity to boast about Eastern Carolina's unique bean. He'd waxed on about crawfish, country ham, and ramps—now it was my turn.

"Have you ever had butterbeans?" I asked.

"Sure. I like lima beans."

"Limas? No, I mean butterbeans. They're tiny and green and creamy."

"Yeah, Vivian. They're immature, fresh lima beans. If you left them on the plant, they'd get bigger, fade to white, and dry out. Then they'd be limas."

What? I was crestfallen. I liked limas just fine. My friend Crystal's mom made them with ham hocks and black pepper, and they fell apart and made a white stew I spooned up after I'd finished the bag of Doritos and pitcher of Kool-Aid. But limas were ordinary, even maligned—like Brussels sprouts and okra, the foods kids are forced to eat. Butterbeans were so much more than that to me. I was trying to reconcile who I was with where I came from, and butterbeans were the lone item in the category of things that had the potential to make Deep Run cool. They weren't just delicious to eat; I believed they were unique to my part of the world. And here Scott was telling me that what I loved were just immature versions of the most boring bean on earth. I guess you could call that a life lesson. Go figure.

RECIPES

FRESH BEANS & PEAS

Stewed Fresh Butterbeans

Shrimp Succotash Salad

Butterbean Hummus with Charred Okra and Marinated Peppers

Boiler Room Butterbean Burger

Baked Peas

DRIED BEANS & PEAS

Winter Caviar

Hamburger Steak with Red Pea and Onion Gravy

Sprouted Field Peas

Slow-Cooked Limas

Dried Field Peas Over Rice

Refried Field Peas with Cheesy Grit Fritters and Celery Cilantro Salad

BEAN & PEA WISDOM

Dried Beans and Peas

BEANS AND PEAS are legumes, seeds we eat that grow in a pod. Other legumes are peanuts, lentils, soybeans, alfalfa, tamarind, and clover. Most legumes we eat are dried, often by hanging on the plant till the sun and wind pull out their moisture.

To Soak or Not to Soak

THERE'S SOME DEBATE over whether it's best to soak dried legumes before you cook them. I soak sometimes and sometimes I don't. The difference is nuanced, not mind-blowing.

Fresh Beans and Peas

OCCASIONALLY, like with butterbeans and peas, we eat legumes fresh or harvest them fresh and freeze them. Fresh legumes are extremely perishable and hold their shape better than their dried brothers when cooked. They have a sweeter, greener taste and a softer, less grainy texture.

Butterbeans

I'LL SAY IT DEFINITIVELY: Butterbeans are indeed baby lima beans. They are harvested small and prized for their tender, young-tasting flesh. As Scott Barton told me, if we didn't harvest them as butterbeans, they would continue to grow and dry out in the field to become a lima.

An older person once told me that a true butterbean was no larger than the nail on your pinkie finger. Most butterbeans I see today are the size of my thumbnail or a little bigger, so I fear we are lowering our standards.

Field Peas

ONE OF THE LOWLIEST yet most crucial elements of our cuisine, the combination of field peas and rice proved sustaining for generations of rural families here. The category contains varieties like Crowder, Black-eye, Pink-eye, Red, Lady Cream, Greasall. Although Black-eye peas are the most common of all the field peas, they're my least favorite to eat. I prefer more petite, deeply flavored varieties like Red peas and the very rare Greasall.

Cooking Legumes

I PREACH THE GOSPEL of seasoning with salt through every stage of the cooking process—except when cooking legumes. Salt added too early makes the skin tough. The general rule is to season once the legumes are cooked through. Then let them sit in their cooking liquid for about twenty minutes to soak up the salt.

Some cooks painstakingly skim off every bit of scum from the top of the pot. They say it gives you gas. I have no idea if that's true, but just to be safe, I do the same.

Stewed Fresh Butterbeans

Makes 3½ cups

MOST PEOPLE FROM MY PLACE would put some sort of smoked pork product in this pot. Sometimes I would too. But on the rare occasion that you have fresh butterbeans or field peas, you might as well taste everything they've got to offer.

Note: *This technique works for field peas too.*

3 cups beans, fresh or frozen	2 bay leaves	1 tablespoon salt
6 cups cool water	5 turns of the pepper mill or ⅛ teaspoon black pepper	

If using fresh beans or peas, rinse them well under cool water. In a 3- to 4-quart saucepan, combine the beans, water, bay leaves, and pepper. Bring it up to a boil and skim off any scum that rises to the top during the first 10 minutes.

Cover the pot and reduce the heat slightly. Let it cook at a quick simmer for 15 to 20 minutes more, or until the beans are tender. Turn off the heat and stir in the salt. Let the beans sit in the seasoned cooking liquid for 20 minutes before serving.

Several of the recipes in this chapter call for the beans just like this, but if I were serving them on their own as a side, I'd stir in a pat of butter beforehand.

Shrimp Succotash Salad

Serves 4

THE FIRST COOKBOOKS I ever flipped through were church compilations of favorite family recipes. Titles like "Bake and Smile Churchwoman-Style" and "Casserole Blessings" have a way of drawing you in. Even today I can't resist the magnetic pull of an old church cookbook.

A recipe that repeatedly shows up in these books is a three-bean salad or marinated bean salad that takes a bunch of canned beans, sometimes corn, and marinates them overnight in oil, vinegar, and sugar. It was an obvious choice for covered-dish functions, because you made it the day before and it improved overnight—a homemaker's dream.

This chilled succotash combines that spirit with fresh field peas or butterbeans and pickled shrimp. Make it for lunch or as the opening to a summertime supper.

Succotash
Makes 5 cups

- ½ **pound large shrimp, 21/25 count, peeled and deveined**
- 1½ **cups Stewed Fresh Butterbeans** *(page 153)*, **drained and rinsed of their cooking liquid**
- 1 **cup fresh corn**
- ½ **cup celery, small-diced**
- ⅓ **cup picked parsley leaves**
- ½ **teaspoon salt**
- 1 **medium tomato, diced**

Dressing
Makes ½ cup

- 3 **tablespoons extra-virgin olive oil**
- 3 **tablespoons minced red onion**
- 1 **garlic clove, grated on a Microplane**
- 1 **teaspoon coriander seeds**
- 1 **teaspoon mustard seeds**
- ⅛ **teaspoon chili flakes**
- 3 **tablespoons red wine vinegar**
- **Zest of 1 lemon**
- 2 **tablespoons lemon juice**
- 1 **tablespoon honey**
- ½ **teaspoon salt**
- ¼ **teaspoon hot sauce**

Make the dressing: In a 6- to 8-inch sauté pan, heat the olive oil over medium heat. Add the onion and cook gently for 3 minutes. You do not want the onion to brown, only to soften. Stir in the garlic, coriander seeds, mustard seeds, and chili flakes. Toast for 45 seconds. Transfer the oil mixture to a small bowl.

Whisk in the remaining ingredients and let it hang out while you assemble the salad.

Make the succotash: Bring a large pot of heavily salted water up to a boil in a saucepan. Slice the shrimp in half lengthwise and drop them into the boiling water. Turn the heat off, stir the shrimp, and cook for 30 seconds. They should be opaque and barely cooked through.

Transfer the shrimp to a plate and slide that plate into the fridge to cool.

In a medium bowl, stir together the shrimp, butterbeans, corn, celery, parsley, and salt. Pour the dressing over the top and refrigerate. Let the salad marinate a minimum of 3 hours and up to overnight. Give it a stir as often as you're able. Just before serving, stir in the tomato. I like to eat this cold, but room temperature is totally acceptable.

Butterbean Hummus with Charred Okra and Marinated Peppers

Serves 5

THIS BUTTERBEAN HUMMUS is something we put on the menu in 2006 and kept there for five consecutive summers. We don't generally do that, but our waitstaff requested it and I craved it. I probably ate butterbean hummus seven days a week every summer for five straight years. I love bean dips and spreads because their creamy texture implies decadence, fat, calories, and sin, but they're actually not awful for you. If more foods delivered on that premise, I'd be a happier person.

This composition raises up the stars of late summer, things that come off the same time, like okra and peppers. But this hummus could just as easily be made from frozen beans and paired with Grandma Hill's Hoecakes (*page 29*), Turnip Gremolata (*page 78*), Collard Kraut (*page 425*), or simply with some store-bought pita bread.

Note: *Garlic Confit is a key ingredient in this hummus and a building block for several recipes in this book. By making it, you end up with two really useful products: soft, spreadable poached garlic and a flavorful oil. I like to make more than I need, just to have some around. I throw the oil and the garlic into vegetable purees, stews, dips of all kinds, and scrambled eggs.*

Garlic Confit
Makes ½ cup

- **20** cloves garlic, or 2 heads cloves separated and peeled
- ⅓ cup extra-virgin olive oil
- **2** sprigs thyme

Butterbean Hummus
Makes 3½ cups

- **3** cups Stewed Fresh Butterbeans (*page 153*)
- ½ cup Garlic Confit
- ¼ cup lemon juice
- **3** tablespoons olive oil for finishing
- **2** tablespoons water
- ⅓ cup tahini
- **1** tablespoon honey
- 1 to 1½ teaspoons salt
- ¼ teaspoon cayenne

Marinated Peppers
Makes 1½ cups

- **3** large bell peppers, roasted, peeled, and cut into 1-inch strips (substitute jarred if you like)
- **2** tablespoons aged balsamic vinegar
- **1** tablespoon olive oil for finishing
- **1** tablespoon finely chopped parsley
- **1** teaspoon salt

Charred Okra

- **1** pound small to medium okra (about 45 pieces)
- **3** tablespoons extra-virgin olive oil
- 1½ teaspoons salt
- ¼ teaspoon cayenne

Make the garlic confit: Preheat your oven to 350°F. Combine the garlic, oil, and thyme in an ovenproof ramekin. Cover with foil. Slide it onto the middle rack of your oven and bake for 45 minutes. The garlic will be a toasted blond color and quite soft. Store the confit in the fridge for up to 2 weeks. When a recipe calls for confit, use equal parts oil and garlic cloves unless the instructions state otherwise.

Make the hummus: In the bowl of your food processor, combine all the cooled ingredients and let her rip. We want the hummus to be smooth, so keep it going for about 3 minutes or until most of the skins have broken down. If you have some skins left in there and they bother you, pass the hummus through a fine-mesh sieve.

Marinate the peppers: Combine all the ingredients in a small bowl. Let them marinate at least 30 minutes before serving.

Char the okra: Toss the okra with the olive oil and preheat a grill, grill pan, or cast-iron skillet to medium-high heat. Char the okra on all sides, making sure about ⅔ of every okra is a nice dark brown and the remaining flesh is green.

Once you've cooked all the okra, toss them with the salt and cayenne and lay them out on a serving dish. If you refrigerate these, they'll lose any texture they gained from charring.

Serve: Serve a big mound of room-temperature hummus next to the okra. Treat the peppers like gravy over mashed potatoes and nestle them in a little indentation atop the bean puree. Use the okra to scoop it all up.

Boiler Room Butterbean Burger

Makes 4 burgers

BEFORE I STARTED DEVELOPING the menu for the Boiler Room, the only veggie burger I had ever eaten was a Boca Burger frozen patty at three o'clock in the morning at a Rastafarian's house. So my exposure to the genre was limited.

I knew right out of the gate, though, that I wanted my burger to be about butterbeans. The first iteration had about thirty ingredients and was so wet and limp, I had to pack it with three cups of bread crumbs to form a patty. My next try was pretty much what you see here.

I don't always eat this on a bun; the whole starch-on-starch thing is still a little weird for me. But I do love it on top of a salad, with a piece of fish sauced by Sun Gold Tomato Soup (*page 279*), or with Everyday Cucumbers (*page 246*). My dad, who says he doesn't eat bread (till he sees a biscuit or a slice of pizza), has the patty with all the burger toppings and bacon.

4 **Butterbean Patties**

4 **burger buns**

4 **slices smoked Gouda**

1 **red onion, peeled and sliced into ¼-inch rings**

½ **cup Big N's Sour Pickles** (*page 242*), **sliced into ¼-inch rounds**

¼ **cup mayonnaise**

1 **tomato, sliced into ½-inch rounds and seasoned with salt and pepper**

Butterbean Patties

3 **tablespoons extra-virgin olive oil, divided**

1 **medium yellow onion, split and sliced thinly with the grain**

½ **teaspoon salt**

½ **teaspoon ground cumin**

½ **teaspoon smoked paprika**

½ **teaspoon chipotle powder**

2 **cups Stewed Fresh Butterbeans** (*page 153*), **completely drained of any cooking liquid**

¼ **cup Garlic Confit** (*page 156*)

½ **cup overcooked brown rice**

¼ **cup panko bread crumbs**

Make the patties: In a 10- to 12-inch sauté pan, heat 1 tablespoon olive oil over medium heat. Add the onion and the salt and cook until the onions start to caramelize, about 10 to 15 minutes. With the pan still on the heat, stir in the cumin, paprika, and chipotle powder and toast for 30 seconds.

Transfer the spiced onion mixture to a large bowl and stir in the butterbeans, Garlic Confit, and brown rice. Using an immersion blender, carefully blend about ⅔ of the bean mixture. It needs to have a chunky texture, so don't get carried away with the electronics. Once it's blended, stir in the panko and let the mixture rest in the refrigerator for 30 minutes.

The bread crumbs and time will have thickened the mixture even more. At this point it should be pretty stiff and malleable. If it's too loose or sticky, stir in another tablespoon of panko and let it sit another 20 minutes.

Divide the bean mixture into 4 equal portions and press them into patties. At this point they can be stored in the refrigerator for up to 6 hours or in the freezer for up to a month. If left in the fridge longer they'll oxidize and change for the worse. At the Boiler Room we cook all of our butterbean burgers from frozen.

Cook and serve: Preheat your oven to 400°F. In a 10- to 12-inch skillet, heat the remaining 2 tablespoons olive oil.

Panfry the patties on both sides for about 4 minutes or until they are dark brown and crisp.

If the patties were not frozen, top them with the Gouda and slide them along with the buns into the oven for 4 minutes. A well-toasted bun provides a lot of texture to the eating experience, so don't skip this step. If the patties were frozen, transfer the burgers into the oven for 3 minutes before adding the cheese and toasting your buns.

Assemble the burgers with the onions, pickles, mayo, and tomato to your liking and serve.

Baked Peas

Serves 5

THIS MARRIES AMERICA'S TRADITION of sweet tomatoey baked beans with a depth of flavor and texture you don't expect. Instead of a side for hot dogs and hamburgers, these beans make more sense next to the Day-at-the-Beach Pork Picnic (*page 455*) or Spice-Rubbed Flank Steak with Cucumber and Charred Onion Relish (*page 252*). They're a great choice for summertime entertaining if you put the dish together the day before and bake it off just before the party starts.

½ cup extra-virgin olive oil, divided

2 medium yellow onions, halved and sliced ¼-inch thick with the grain

½ teaspoon salt

9 cloves of garlic, sliced thin

3 cups cherry or grape tomatoes

3 cups Stewed Fresh Butterbeans (*page 153*) with 1 cup reserved cooking liquid

2 roasted red bell peppers, peeled, seeded, and cut into ½-inch dice

¼ cup green olives, halved (optional)

2 tablespoons dark brown sugar

2 tablespoons sherry vinegar

1 tablespoon oregano, chopped

1 teaspoon rosemary, chopped

¼ teaspoon chili flakes

Preheat your oven to 350°F. In a 3-quart brazier or 12-inch cast-iron skillet, heat ¼ cup of the olive oil over medium heat. Add the onions and salt and cook for 5 minutes. Add the garlic and cook an additional minute.

Transfer the onion and garlic mixture to a bowl. Then add the tomatoes to the skillet. Give the pan a good shake and let the tomatoes cook till they start to blister and pop, about 2 minutes. Stir in the butterbeans, the reserved cooking liquid, remaining ¼ cup oil, onions, bell peppers, olives, if using, sugar, vinegar, herbs, and chili flakes.

Slide the pan onto the middle rack of the oven and bake for 1 hour and 45 minutes. The beans will begin to brown on the top and have a little moisture left in the pan. Take them out and let them rest 10 minutes before serving. Serve warm or at room temperature.

Winter Caviar

Makes 4 cups

"DIXIE CAVIAR" is a popular salsa made with lots of stuff from cans. Black-eyed peas, corn, and pimentos are dumped together with a bottle of store-bought Zesty Italian dressing to make something that ends up tasting pretty good, if mildly metallic. Problem is, I'm not a fan of the can.

Here I marinate cooked field peas, roasted sweet potatoes, and Cocktail Tomatoes (*page 280*) to mimic the look and purpose of Dixie caviar. This is generally thought of as a dip, but we serve it in the doldrums of winter as a punchy salad with fish or Hamburger Steak with Red Pea and Onion Gravy (*page 162*). See the photograph on page 163.

- 1 large sweet potato, peeled and cut into small dice
- 2 tablespoons extra-virgin olive oil
- 1½ teaspoons salt, divided
- 1 teaspoon light brown sugar

- 2 cups Dried Field Peas *(page 167)*, cooked, drained, and rinsed
- 1 cup small-diced Cocktail Tomatoes *(page 280)* plus ¼ cup of their liquid
- ½ cup thinly sliced scallion

- 2 tablespoons chopped parsley
- 1 tablespoon chopped oregano
- ¼ cup olive oil for finishing

Note: *If you don't have Cocktail Tomatoes and would still like to make this caviar, marinate 1 cup of quartered cherry tomatoes in 2 tablespoons rice vinegar, 1 teaspoon honey, 1 teaspoon lemon juice, and ½ teaspoon salt for 30 minutes.*

The idea is for all the ingredients in the caviar to be about the same size, so keep that in mind when you are doing your knife work. The sweet potatoes will shrink by ⅓ when they roast.

Preheat your oven to 350°F. Toss the sweet potatoes with the olive oil, ½ teaspoon salt, and sugar. Spread them out on a baking sheet in a single layer with as much space between the potatoes as possible. Slide the baking sheet onto the center rack of your oven and roast for 15 minutes. Then stir the potatoes around so they cook evenly on all sides and roast an additional 10 minutes if needed.

Take the potatoes out of the oven and let them cool. They should be slightly crisp and brown on a side or two and roasted through. In a medium bowl, gently stir together the remaining ingredients, including the remaining 1 teaspoon of salt. Let the caviar marinate, refrigerated, overnight or up to 3 days before serving. Serve at room temperature with chips, endive, celery, or as a side.

Hamburger Steak with Red Pea and Onion Gravy

Serves 4

MY PARENTS ALMOST NEVER COOKED an actual steak, which is most likely a good thing, since it probably would have tasted like warm beef jerky. What we did eat was hamburger steak, and I loved it.

Mom browned the beef in a cast-iron skillet and served it over rice, drowned in a pale thick blanket of gravy made with the pan drippings—a real treat in Mom's health-conscious household. Flash-forward twenty-five years, and we serve hamburger steak in lieu of real steak at Chef and the Farmer on occasion. Instead of onions, cloves of garlic confit stud the steak. They're little surprises you mine out as you eat. In place of a gravy made with flour, I cook red peas with caramelized onions and blend that till it looks just like my mom's gravy. The sum is comforting and nostalgic. Because we're always trying to balance rich stuff with bright stuff, we pair this with Winter Caviar (*page 161*).

Hamburger Steak
Serves 4

- 2 pounds ground beef
- 1 tablespoon salt
- 1 teaspoon black pepper
- 1 teaspoon picked thyme
- ¼ cup Garlic Confit cloves *(page 156)*
- 1 tablespoon vegetable oil

Red Pea and Onion Gravy
Makes 4 cups

- 2 medium onions, halved and sliced thinly with the grain
- 1½ teaspoons salt, divided
- 2 tablespoons bacon fat or butter

- 30 turns of the pepper mill or scant 1 teaspoon black pepper
- 2 cloves garlic, sliced
- ⅔ cup dried peas, soaked overnight (should yield about 2 cups)
- 5 cups beef stock or water
- 2 bay leaves
- 2 cups milk

Note: *At the restaurant, we grind chuck fresh through a large die for this preparation. High-quality beef that's just been ground makes a big difference here, and the larger die gives it a more toothsome steak-like quality. If you live in a town with a newfangled butcher shop, call ahead and tell them what you're doing. They'll gladly facilitate the process. If not, any lean ground beef will do.*

Make the gravy: In a 4-quart saucepan, cook the onions and ½ teaspoon of the salt in the bacon fat over medium-low heat till they caramelize, about 30 minutes. They should be a golden brown. Stir in the black pepper and garlic. Cook an additional 2 minutes.

Add the peas, beef stock, and bay leaves. Cover and bring it up to a boil. Cook for about 40 minutes or until the peas are extremely tender.

Transfer the peas, all their liquid, and the remaining 1 teaspoon salt to a blender. Add the milk and blend till it's super-smooth. Depending on how much liquid cooked out of the peas, you may have to add some additional water to achieve the proper consistency. It should look like gravy; adjust accordingly.

For the steak: Preheat your oven to 400°F. Season the beef with the salt, black pepper, and thyme. Sprinkle the garlic cloves over the top and fold them in. Divide the beef into 4 equal portions. We can't have anybody mistaking these for plain old hamburgers, so shape them into ovals or rectangles.

Heat the vegetable oil in a cast-iron skillet over medium-high heat. Add the steaks and cook on the first side about 4 minutes, or until they're nicely browned. Flip the steaks and slide the pan into the oven. Cook for 5 more minutes for a medium rare.

Serve the steaks smothered in the gravy.

Sprouted Field Peas

Makes 3 cups

I EAT SPROUTS BECAUSE THEY'RE GOOD FOR ME and because I enjoy the distinct sweet green flavor only plants in their earliest stage of life offer. I love them with my usual breakfast of hard-boiled eggs in the morning or on a sandwich to make me feel better about eating the sandwich. I used to buy all my sprouts, but recently I've been sprouting everything with a germ that I can find. Last winter, in need of something bright and fresh for a New Year's Eve salad, I decided to try and sprout field peas. The result was a nutty, colorful take on Hoppin' John *(page 296)*.

Not every bag of dried peas or beans is suitable. Because the act of sprouting carries with it the risk of bacterial growth, it's essential to buy organic peas or beans from a trusted source. I use organic Sea Island Red Peas here.

½ cup dried field peas	1-quart mason jar Cheesecloth	Rubber band

Rinse the peas, then cover them by 3 inches with cool water in the mason jar. Skim off any shriveled peas that float to the top; they will not sprout. Soak the peas at room temperature away from direct sunlight for 8 to 12 hours.

Drain off the soaking water. Rinse the peas and drain them again; if the peas are sitting in a puddle of water, they likely will not grow. Cover the top of the jar with cheesecloth and secure it with the rubber band. Put the jar in a room-temperature spot (70°F is ideal), away from direct sunlight but not in a closed cabinet. A countertop away from pets and children works great.

In 8 to 12 hours, rinse the peas. I run water right through the cheesecloth, swirling it around to make sure all the peas make contact with the water. Drain them well. Then turn the jar over onto a clean dish towel, cheesecloth down, to drain further for a minute or so. Turn it back over and set the peas back in their spot for another 8 to 12 hours.

Do the rinsing-and-draining thing again. This time you should start to see a few sprouts. After one more round of 8 to 12 hours, followed by another rinse and drain, your sprouts should be done. If not, wait another 8 to 12 hours. You're looking for sprouts that are roughly ¼ of an inch long. Your peas may sprout in as little as 24 hours (two rounds of rinsing and draining), or they may take up to 3 days to germinate. The age and variety of the pea are key factors.

Following the final rinse, drain the sprouts extremely well by dumping them out on paper towels and letting them sit there for a few minutes. Then transfer them back to the dry jar to sit at room temperature another 8 to 12 hours.

Transfer your field pea sprouts to a plastic bag or sealed container and refrigerate. They will keep for up to 1 week.

Slow-Cooked Limas

Makes 3 quarts

THE PARENTS OF MY CHILDHOOD FRIEND and neighbor Crystal Howard (no relation) made this during the dead of winter. They filled a cast-iron Dutch oven with cured pork and fat white limas and cooked them slowly on top of their wood heater all day. The beans didn't look like much when they were done, but their silky texture and satisfying porkiness haunts me. I suppose you could do these on the stove over really low heat, but the oven makes me think of their wood heater.

Believe it or not, I serve a version of this at the restaurant topped with Cocktail Tomatoes (*page 280*) and Basil Pesto (*page 346*).

1 **pound dried lima beans**

12 **ounces cured and smoked pork seasoning meat (*page 8*)**

1 **onion, peeled and halved**

1 **bay leaf**

1 **teaspoon black pepper**

1 **teaspoon dried thyme (optional)**

Preheat your oven to 300°F. In a 4- to 6-quart Dutch oven, combine the dried limas, the pork, onion, bay leaf, black pepper, thyme, and 10 cups of water. Bring the beans up to a simmer. Cover with a tight-fitting lid and transfer the pot to the oven.

Check the water level in the beans occasionally just to make sure the pot is not dry. After 3 hours, take the pot out of the oven and gaze down into swollen creamy white beans. Pluck out the bay leaf and the onion if you wish. I leave the pork in there in case people want to eat it with their beans.

Dried Field Peas Over Rice

Makes 3 cups

DRIED PEAS ARE A PILLAR of the Southern diet. Protein-rich, comforting, and shelf-stable, this is the kind of poor-people food we exalt in modern restaurant kitchens. I've made them vegetarian here, but go ahead and throw some cured pork or bones in there for additional flavor.

Lots of people cook peas in this fashion, then puree half of them, call it gravy, and serve it over rice. Many cultures have a tradition of combining a legume and a starch and considering it a complete meal: Mexican black beans with tortillas, Cajun red beans and rice, and Indian dal and rice. Red pea gravy over rice is the Eastern Carolina version.

1 cup dried field peas or black-eyed peas	2 garlic cloves, smashed	1 tablespoon salt
1 carrot, halved and split	2 bay leaves	1 tablespoon butter
½ yellow onion, peeled	15 turns of the pepper mill or scant ½ teaspoon black pepper	3 cups Perfect Rice (*page 292*)

In a 3-quart saucepan fitted with a lid, combine the dried peas, carrot, onion, garlic, bay leaves, and black pepper with 6 cups of water. Bring it up to a boil. Cover and reduce the heat to medium low. Cook for 2 hours, keeping an eye on the water level. If too much water evaporates, add a little in. Once the peas are tender, stir in the salt.

To serve, pluck out the spent vegetables and the bay leaves and stir in the butter. If you'd like to take it a step further and make it "gravy," transfer half the peas plus their liquid to the bowl of a food processor and blend until smooth. Stir the smooth mixture back into the peas. Serve warm over rice.

Refried Field Peas with Cheesy Grit Fritters and Celery Cilantro Salad

Serves 4

I'M A BIG BELIEVER in making vegetarian entrées that a meat eater would order. This one has proven to be our most popular of those dishes (outside of the cult-craved tomato pie). I had the idea for it when I was laid up on bed rest before I gave birth to my twins. I guess I was craving Mexican food.

This is a dish we usually pull out in late winter or early spring, when everybody in the kitchen is tired of cooking roots. Depending on when you make it, you can do a lot of different things with the salad. Try asparagus, snow peas, sugar snaps, or butternut squash in place of the celery. I use a mandoline for much of the knife work.

3 cups Refried Field Peas

1½ cups celery salad

12 Cheesy Grit Fritters *(page 39)*

Refried Field Peas
Makes 3 cups

¼ cup extra-virgin olive oil

1 medium yellow onion, small-diced

½ teaspoon salt

5 garlic cloves, grated on a Microplane

1 teaspoon ancho chili powder

¼ teaspoon turmeric

1 teaspoon ground coriander

1 teaspoon ground cumin

¼ cup minced cilantro stems

1 cup tomato puree

3 cups Dried Field Peas *(page 167)*

1 cup reserved liquid from cooking the peas, plus more, just in case

Celery Cilantro Salad
Makes 1½ cups

2 stalks celery, preferably from the heart

1 small red onion, peeled

2 radishes of your choice

2 tablespoons rice vinegar

½ cup picked light green and tender celery leaves

1 jalapeño, halved, seeded, and sliced very thin

Juice of 1 lime, about 1 tablespoon

½ teaspoon salt

1 tablespoon finely chopped cilantro stems

½ cup picked cilantro leaves

Make the peas: In a 10-inch sauté pan, heat the oil over medium heat. Add the onions and salt and cook for 10 minutes until the onions start to caramelize. Add the garlic, ancho, turmeric, coriander, and cumin. Let all that toast briefly, about 45 seconds. Stir in the cilantro stems, tomato, and field peas and their liquid. Cover and bring it up to a simmer. Cook for 15 minutes.

Take the top off and go about mashing the peas. You can use the back of a spoon, a potato masher, or an immersion blender. What's important is the end consistency, not how you got there. You're looking for ⅔ pureed peas and about ⅓ chunky peas. Luckily most of us know what refried beans look like at this point. If you need to add any liquid to get it going, use water or the reserved liquid from cooking the peas.

Make the salad: Slice the celery on a bias about ⅛ of an inch thick. If you can't get it that thin, don't fret. Just try. Using a mandoline or your knife, slice the onion and radishes into rounds about as thick as the celery. Marinate the onion in the rice vinegar while you put everything else together.

Just before serving, stir together everything but half the cilantro leaves. We want this to be like a crunchy salad, not a limp salsa, so don't do it in advance.

Serve: Spoon the peas onto the bottom of your plate. If you've cooked them ahead of time and let them sit at all, they will need to be livened up with some water or cooking liquid and heat, and maybe even a pat of butter if you like. Put the salad on top of the beans and the Grit Fritters on top of that. Finish with the remaining cilantro.

WHEN BEN AND I moved to North Carolina in 2005, we believed our stay would be temporary. Our little soup business in Harlem had given us a thirst for self-employment, but we were fatigued by New York. When my sister Leraine and her husband at the time, Ray, asked us to help open a soup-and-sandwich shop in Kinston, we felt it might be the launching pad we needed to save money, develop our own restaurant concept, and then settle down just about anywhere else.

Because we were only visiting—and because any place with central air and a driveway was an upgrade from our city life—we lived in what my family called the "river house." It was really a shack—actually, two shacks connected by a makeshift hallway that held a refrigerator. The house sat in the bend of a tributary of the Trent River, too close to the water to survive erosion long term. It had no foundation, no insulation, and was never meant to be a home. It was where my dad got a break from the buzz of family and the worry of work. He basically went there to take a nap.

When Ben and I moved in, my sisters placed bets on how long we would last. To their shock, we loved it. My sisters saw a rickety building held up by cinder blocks. Ben and I saw a free place to live with tranquil views of winding water. We went from paying fifteen hundred dollars a month for a small apartment to paying nothing for a house. Of course we loved it.

After a few months, when the rose tint wore off our glasses, we saw Kinston as the economically depressed place it was. The biggest town near Deep Run, fifteen miles away, Kinston was never where I wanted to end up. But at least when I left for high school twelve years earlier, it had some life. The tobacco trade was strong, and the DuPont textile mill was one of the largest factories in the state.

When we moved back, Kinston was a sad shell of its former self. Those economic engines had vanished, and they'd taken businesses and young families with them. It seemed that every person under the age of fifty who was able to leave had done so. As a kid, a trip to town from rural Deep Run meant getting dressed up. In 2005, it meant getting depressed. The downtown stretch that people once called the Magic Mile had become a streak of shuttered buildings, and that bleak view stretched beyond Lenoir County. If you made Eastern North Carolina its own state, it would have been the poorest state in the country.

The building Ray had selected for the sandwich shop was smack in the middle of Kinston's ruins. Even though 120 West Gordon Street had its own parking lot and was adjacent to the only business still open, I knew our sandwiches and soups didn't stand a chance. There wasn't anyone to buy them.

But I'm a dreamer to a fault. I began to long for somewhere other than Applebee's to have dinner (how ironic, since Applebee's was all I wanted in high school) and a place where I could find a decent glass of wine. Despite the hard economic facts, I became fixated on opening a bustling bistro that would serve food inspired by my experience in New York but grown by people who used to grow tobacco. It would have intentional ambience, the kind you create, not accumulate over time. It would set a new standard for service in an area where service was only something you had done to your car. We'd establish a name for ourselves, turn the town around, and split. Easy stuff for a twenty-six-year-old.

I steamrolled Ben, Leraine, and Ray into agreeing to open a high-end restaurant instead of a sandwich shop. Building out and opening Chef and the Farmer took a year and a half, so without a restaurant to run, Ben and I basically played house... river house. We cooked dinner every night, sat by the water, planted a garden that was six times too big to manage, and daydreamed about how our bistro would change the town. The plan was always: *Change the town, leave the town, do more than run a restaurant*—whatever *more* meant.

Late that summer, my parents had to move my grandma Hill from their house, where my mom had cared for her, to a rest home between Deep Run and Kinston. The week she moved in, I was busy. The restaurant, the garden, daydreams—they all got in between me and a depressing trip to Classic Country Care.

The following Sunday, Ben and I cooked for my parents at the river house. Supper with Mom and Dad had become a halfhearted ritual, a gesture offered when Ben and I had nothing else to do. That night, Mom seemed lower than I'd ever seen her. She was ashamed of putting her mom in a home. She questioned her choice. And I began to wonder if I had done enough myself to help Mom keep Grandma at home.

The next day, I drove Mom to see Grandma. We walked in and saw her—our protector of pecans, singer of songs that didn't rhyme, and baker of candied yams and flat cornbread—lying pale in a remote-controlled bed, her mouth open and eyes closed, as two nurses talked noisily over her.

The last time I'd seen Grandma, two months prior, she was alert and able to walk. Now, when Mom stroked her forehead, she stared through her without expression. Guilt and fear lined Mom's face.

This was not an assisted-living facility where folks took the elevator down to the dining hall for dinner and played card games before bed. This was where people went to stare at the ceiling and have their lips moistened.

All of it, even half of it, was too much for me.

I should have spent more time with her. I should have helped Mom feed her, dress her, take her to the doctor. I should have been there for both of them. Instead, I was off playing house.

I needed to get some air.

Wandering through a maze of hallways, I fought against my thoughts. I'd never lost anyone close to me. My other grandparents had passed away either before I was born or when I was too young to feel it. Boarding school, college, New York—all of them were vehicles to take me away from the discomfort and responsibility I just experienced. For my entire life, I'd done exactly what felt good at the time. I was the baby, and everybody took care of me.

Now, in a flash, I saw Grandma. I saw Mom. I saw me. I saw our future, and I saw all of our roles change. And I really needed to get some air.

FIG WISDOM

The Race to Use a Fig

I COMPARE THE PERISHABLE quality of fresh figs to that of picked flowers because figs are themselves inverted flowers. That explains why produce doesn't get more perishable than a ripe fig. Pick perfect figs, store them properly—unwashed, uncovered, in a single layer in the refrigerator—and you've got four days, tops, to make something happen.

Figs will not continue to ripen off the tree, so pick figs that are soft and fragrant, like a perfect peach. Ripe figs will let you know they're ripe by separating more easily from the stem end of the tree.

Sorting

WHEN I GET FIGS I immediately divide them into four categories for storage. Mushy figs, sticky with syrup, will affect the quality of the other ones in the batch, so it's important to sort them right away. Moldy, sour-smelling figs go in the trash. Soft, squished, bruised figs will be for jams and purees. Perfect specimens at the height of flavor go into salads and preserves or are eaten out of hand. And figs that are a little more firm and not completely ripe are reserved for roasting with sugar or caramelizing on the grill.

Mostly Brown Turkey

THE FIGS I TALK ABOUT are of the Brown Turkey variety. They are a rich copper color and have an elongated shape like a pear. Their flesh is soft and sweet like vegetal honey, and the texture is a cross between a strawberry and a peach. The best Brown Turkey substitutes are Mission and Celeste figs. The Celeste looks and tastes a whole lot like the Brown Turkey. Mission figs are dark purple and have a squat shape and muted sweetness. In these recipes, any fresh fig could be swapped out for a juicy peach with good results.

Figs, Bugs, and Insecticides

INSECTS LOVE TO MUNCH on figs, so it's a race to see who can get them first. As a result, some folks heavily spray their trees with insecticides. If you're buying figs from a farmers' market, ask whether they've been

The hallway spat me out into a parking lot, where I leaned against a brick wall and took a deep breath. Then I noticed buzzing nearby. June bugs, hundreds of them, whizzed around the base of a big tree. I walked closer, swatting through the shield of flying beetles, and saw a huge flush of pear-shaped figs so ripe that some of them dripped with syrup. I'd never seen anything like it.

Dodging bugs, I gathered a handful of figs and sat down under the tree's canopy. I've always turned to food for respite, so these figs, sticky with sugar, slowed my heart and offered escape. As I ate, I thought about my mom, Grandma Hill, and this intense, new feeling that I needed to stay in Deep Run. Like the tree I was leaning

sprayed. If they have, make sure they take a longer bath than your fruit typically does.

Dried Are Better Than None

Rehydrated dried figs will work in several of these recipes: Cornbread Coffee Cake *(page 182)*, Baked Figs *(page 186)*, Grandma Shirl's Survival Cookies *(page 184)*, and Chocolate Fig Gravy *(page 185)*. To rehydrate dried figs, place them in a saucepan, cover with water or apple cider, and simmer for several minutes.

Figs and Deep Run

UNTIL I WAS IN MY TWENTIES, I thought figs were food for people in California and Europe. The pope ate figs; I didn't. Then my dad explained to me that at one time, every home place here had three types of trees: apple trees for dried apples, peach trees for canned peaches, and a fig tree for whole fig preserves. They were a part of the wheel going round in pursuit of not only food but treats to eat all year long.

RECIPES

Whole-Fruit Fig and Lemon Preserves

Pancake Sunday

Fig and Honey Bourbon Slush

Cornbread Coffee Cake with Fresh Figs and Walnut Streusel

Grandma Shirl's Survival Cookies

Chocolate Fig Gravy

Baked Figs and Goat Cheese with Caramelized Onions and Pecans

Fried Chicken Livers with Balsamic-Marinated Figs

against, I was rooted here—not by a restaurant, but by my family. Despite what I had told myself, we had come back to Deep Run for more than a professional opportunity. It was the pull of home, the connection to my place, the impulse to be a contributing part of my family. That fig tree cast a powerful spell.

Grandma died about a year after the restaurant opened. And even though I passed the rest home several times a week, I didn't visit as much as I should have. It was too painful. But my mom sat with Grandma every day, brushing her hair, rubbing lotion on her hands, singing hymns, and loving her with deep and tender respect.

At some point that first year, Ben and I agreed that Deep Run wouldn't be our launchpad. It would be our home. We decided to stay here, build a new house where the river house sat, and do everything we could to make our family and business thrive. Then we planted a fig tree.

Whole-Fruit Fig and Lemon Preserves

Makes 3 pints

WITH WHOLE PIECES of fruit suspended in clear pristine syrup, preserves are the lacy-dress cousin to jean-cutoffs jam. The difference between the two is in both nature and nurture. For preserves, you're looking for perfect, plump examples of that fruit, but with jam, it's okay if the fruit is a little bruised up and past its prime. To produce preserves with intact fruit and see-through syrup, you have to cook them slow and low and be vigilant about skimming off any scum or foam that rises to the top.

Whole-fruit preserves hail from a time when fruit didn't fly in from Chile, an era when housewives were actually trying to preserve things like berries, cherries, and peaches in a fashion that would allow their hungry husbands to spoon real pieces of fruit (albeit swimming in syrup) over steaming biscuits in the dead of winter. The preserves were special then and they are special once again. We make preserves in the same manner described below with strawberries, peaches, pears, and apples, but whole, plump, fragile Brown Turkey figs glistening in lemon syrup are the crown jewel of our fruit preserve kingdom.

2	heaping quarts perfectly ripe figs (about 3 pounds)	
1	quart granulated sugar	
1	lemon, sliced thin, seeds removed	

Wash your figs thoroughly but gently. Broken figs will cloud the syrup and will not hold up during the cooking process. Lots of folks remove the stem; I do not. I like the way it looks in the finished product. That's your call.

In a large bowl, gently toss together the figs, the sugar, and the lemon slices. Cover the bowl and nestle it in the fridge for a minimum of 6 hours or up to overnight.

When you're ready to make the preserves, remove the bowl from the fridge and transfer its contents to a 4- to 6-quart Dutch oven. Bring the figs, sugar, and lemon up to a boil over medium heat and reduce it to a simmer. Cover and cook at a good simmer for up to an hour. Try not to bother them too much, as the more you stir, the more figs you'll potentially break.

Over the course of an hour, the preserves will take on the color of strong tea, and the figs themselves will shrivel but amazingly hold their shape. About 45 minutes in, check the preserves by dipping

a spoon into the syrup, removing it, and running your finger along the back of the spoon. If the syrup separates and holds its position briefly, your preserves are done. If the syrup is watery and runs together as soon as your finger is gone, cook the preserves a bit longer.

These preserves will keep, covered in the fridge, for up to two months. If you choose to can them, follow the basic canning instructions on page 16 and process them in your water bath for 10 minutes.

There are a lot of obvious things to do with these preserves. Spooning some over biscuits, cornbread, or tangy cheese immediately comes to mind. The housewives of Eastern Carolina would also recommend them with a scoop of ice cream. But feel free to surprise those ladies and simmer them down with a little of their syrup and some red wine, sherry, or balsamic vinegar and use the result as a condiment for grilled meats.

Pancake Sunday

Makes 6 large pancakes

BEN MAKES PANCAKES for Flo and Theo every Sunday morning. As of right now, Pancake Sundays are our little family's only food tradition. To immortalize it, I told Ben over a year ago I wanted to put his recipe in my book and pair it with fig preserves and pecans. From that Sunday on, Ben cooked, flipped, and tested his pancakes with perfection in mind. I finally had to threaten him with my missing my deadline to get him to settle on the details. Thank God this whole book wasn't a husband-and-wife collaboration. It would never have been published.

To be fair, Ben's endless testing turned out some spectacular pancakes with crispy edges. Ben says the trick is to use lots of butter in the pan and essentially fry the pancake.

On theirs, Theo and Flo prefer regular maple syrup and lots of it, but I think my Whole-Fruit Fig and Lemon Preserves (*page 178*) and the Spiced Pecan and Pumpkin Seed Crumble (*page 135*) give them the fancy touches they deserve.

½ cup all-purpose flour

½ cup buckwheat flour

1½ tablespoons granulated sugar

1 teaspoon baking powder

1 teaspoon salt

½ teaspoon baking soda

10 tablespoons butter, divided

1 egg, lightly beaten

1½ cups buttermilk

1 cup Whole-Fruit Fig and Lemon Preserves with their syrup (*page 178*)

1 cup Spiced Pecan and Pumpkin Seed Crumble (*page 135*)

In a medium bowl whisk together the flours, sugar, baking powder, salt, and baking soda. Melt 2 tablespoons of the butter and, in a separate bowl, whisk it into the egg and buttermilk. Add the wet to the dry and mix to barely combine. The batter will have a few lumps and bubbles.

Heat a 10-inch cast-iron skillet over medium-low heat. Melt 1 tablespoon of butter in the pan till it's foamy. Add ⅓ cup of the pancake batter to the pan. It should spread to 5 or 6 inches in diameter. Cook on the first side about 90 seconds or until the edges start to brown and little bubbles force their way up through the center of

the pancake. Flip and add a teaspoon or so of butter to give that side some love too. Cook for an additional minute. Follow up with the remaining batter, making sure you add a tablespoon of butter with each new pancake.

Ben cooks and serves these one at a time in the spirit of his uncle Bob, who did the same. All of us just wait our turn. He never holds them in a warm oven till they're all done, but you could certainly do that.

Serve with Whole-Fruit Fig and Lemon Preserves and the Spiced Pecan and Pumpkin Seed Crumble.

Fig and Honey Bourbon Slush

Makes 6 cups

I'M REALLY INTO boozy slushies. This is fun, interactive, and apropos for late summer when figs are in season. If you don't have an ice cream machine, you can make slush by putting the mixture in the freezer and stirring it every hour till it's right where you want it. Because of the alcohol, it's never going to freeze entirely— which makes the process both fool- and drunk-proof.

2 cups fresh figs, stemmed and halved

1 cup orange juice

½ cup honey

½ cup water

2 strips orange zest, removed with a vegetable peeler

1½ cups bourbon

2 tablespoons lemon juice

½ cup ginger beer

Combine the figs and the orange juice in a blender and process till you have a smooth puree. Set aside.

In a small saucepan, combine the honey, water, and orange zest. Simmer for 5 minutes. Remove the orange rind.

In a large pitcher, whisk the honey syrup with the remaining ingredients and allow the mix to chill thoroughly before freezing. This step will improve the texture of your slushy.

Depending on your ice cream maker, you will more than likely have to freeze this in 2 batches, so make sure to give each batch one last whisk before freezing because the fig puree may have sunk to the bottom. Freeze in your ice cream maker according to the manufacturer's instructions, and then transfer the slushy to your freezer for a minimum of 1 hour before serving. You'll end up with a partially frozen concoction that's fun to slurp.

Cornbread Coffee Cake with Fresh Figs and Walnut Streusel

Serves 8

THIS IS ONE OF THOSE BEAUTIFUL THINGS that could be either breakfast or dessert. I developed it with breakfast in mind, maybe something to be shared when family was in town over several pots of coffee. But when I first made it, my kids named it corn-candy cake and called for it after supper. I obliged and put some whipped cream on top.

Whenever you choose to eat it, feel good about baking it a day ahead. It keeps beautifully and is just as satisfying at room temperature as it is warm.

Walnut Streusel

- ⅔ cup sliced walnuts (or any nut you like, really)
- ⅔ cup light brown sugar, packed
- ½ cup rolled oats
- ¼ cup whole wheat flour
- 1 tablespoon cinnamon
- ½ teaspoon salt
- 8 tablespoons (1 stick) cold unsalted butter, cut into pieces

Cornbread Cake

- ½ cup plus 2 teaspoons room-temperature butter, divided
- 3 cups figs, divided
- ⅔ cup granulated sugar
- 2 large eggs
- 1½ cups cornmeal
- 1 cup whole wheat flour
- 2 teaspoons baking powder
- ½ teaspoon baking soda
- ½ teaspoon salt
- 1½ cups buttermilk
- ¼ cup apple cider
- 1 teaspoon vanilla paste or extract
- ½ cup sour cream

Make the streusel: In a medium bowl, toss together all the ingredients but the butter, taking care that everything is evenly distributed. Add the butter and pinch together with your fingers until it forms a wet crumb.

Make the cake: Preheat your oven to 375°F and grease a 12-inch cast-iron skillet with 2 teaspoons butter. Remove the stems from all the figs and cut 1 cup of them into eighths. Cut the remaining 2 cups in half lengthwise. Set aside.

In a mixer fitted with the paddle attachment, cream together ½ cup butter and the sugar until light and fluffy, about 4 minutes. Add the eggs one at a time, making sure the first egg is fully incorporated before adding the second. From this point forward, make sure you scrape down the sides of the bowl periodically with a spatula. Add the cornmeal, roughly a half a cup at a time, until it's just incorporated.

In a medium bowl, sift the flour, baking powder, baking soda, and salt. In another smaller bowl, whisk the buttermilk, cider, and vanilla. With the mixer on low, add the sifted flour and buttermilk alternately in three batches, ending with the flour. Using your spatula, fold in the sour cream and the cup of figs cut into eighths.

Assemble and bake: Spoon half the corn-cake mixture into the bottom of the skillet and spread it out with a spatula. Sprinkle the streusel evenly over the top and finish with the remaining corn-cake batter. Spread the halved figs over the top, pink-flesh-side up.

Bake uncovered, in the middle of your oven, for 40 to 45 minutes. Try to let it cool a little before people go to town on it. I like this even more the next day.

Grandma Shirl's Survival Cookies

Makes about 30 cookies

SOMEWHERE between a granola bar and a Fig Newton, these are a tweaked version of a cookie Ben grew up eating courtesy of his great-aunt by marriage Shirl Bernstein. They're full of stuff that gives you energy, like oats and nuts, and I'm guessing that's how Grandma Shirl (as she was known) came up with the name. Her recipe calls for dried dates. I've substituted fresh figs for a crispier cookie.

2	cups rolled oats
1	cup dark brown sugar, lightly packed
½	cup shredded coconut
½	cup chopped walnuts or pecans, plus about 30 nut halves
½	cup whole wheat flour
½	teaspoon salt
¼	teaspoon baking soda
1	cup fresh figs, finely chopped
8	tablespoons (1 stick) butter, melted
2	medium eggs
1	teaspoon vanilla extract

Preheat your oven to 350°F. In a large bowl, thoroughly combine the oats, sugar, coconut, chopped walnuts or pecans, flour, salt, and baking soda. In a separate bowl, whisk together the figs, butter, eggs, and vanilla. Pour that over the oatmeal mixture and stir to combine. Things will be kind of wet and loose, not like a typical cookie dough at all. Let the mix sit in the fridge for 30 minutes to firm up and come to terms with itself.

Grease a cookie sheet with whatever you like and scoop out tablespoon-size portions of dough. Roll the dough into balls and place the balls 2 inches apart on the sheet. Press down on each dough ball to flatten it out slightly and press a nut half into the center. Bake for 15 to 20 minutes or until the cookies have spread out and are brown and crispy around the edges. They will be quite fragile when they come out of the oven, so allow them to cool for about 10 minutes on the sheet.

Chocolate Fig Gravy

Makes 2 cups

I GREW UP HEARING ABOUT chocolate gravy but never eating it. I suspect a resourceful housewife with a bare pantry first threw it together in a pinch to make something sweet out of almost nothing at all. Like gravy of any kind, this is an easy and economical way to stretch flavor, and it's oddly satisfying.

Folding in fresh fig puree and warm spices makes it kind of taste like Mexican hot chocolate and gives the gravy's otherwise bland texture character. Traditionally, chocolate gravy graces biscuits at breakfast, and that works for sure. But I also adore it over Mom's Cornpone (*page 28*), ice cream, or pound cake. See the photograph on page 184.

- 1½ cups fresh figs, stemmed and halved
- ⅓ cup heavy cream
- ½ cup granulated sugar
- 2 tablespoons high-quality cocoa powder

- 1½ tablespoons all-purpose flour
- ½ teaspoon ground cinnamon
- ½ teaspoon nutmeg
- ¼ teaspoon salt

- Zest of 1 orange, grated on a Microplane
- 1 cup milk plus more for thinning out later
- 2½ tablespoons butter, cubed

Combine the figs and the heavy cream in a food processor and let rip till you have a textured puree.

In a 10-inch cast iron skillet, stir together the sugar, cocoa, flour, spices, salt, and zest. Whisk in the milk and the fig puree.

Over medium heat, stir the gravy until it thickens, making sure you pay close attention to the edges, as they burn most easily.

Take the gravy off the heat and whisk in the butter until it melts. Pour it over whatever you like or eat it straight from a spoon. If the gravy thickens up as it cools, feel free to whisk in a little milk to loosen it up.

Baked Figs and Goat Cheese with Caramelized Onions and Pecans

Serves 6 to 8

WHEN WE OPENED Chef and the Farmer in 2006, the pickings were slim in terms of farmers and artisans doing things on a small, quality-driven scale. So when a farmer from a place called In the Red showed up with his unusually creamy goat cheese, I vowed to help In the Red get in the black.

Then I had to figure out what to do with thirty pounds of fresh goat cheese every week. Out of that dilemma, this crowd-pleasing share plate was born. People often stuff figs with cheese and wrap them in salty pork, but this is equally satisfying and a lot easier to execute. I've omitted the pork part, but in lieu of pecans, you could indulge with bacon…or use both.

2	cups figs, sliced into ⅛-inch rounds
2½	tablespoons dark brown sugar
	Zest of 1 orange
	Scant ¼ cup orange juice (roughly the juice from 1 orange)

1	tablespoon butter
2	medium onions, halved and sliced with the grain ⅛ inch thick
2	teaspoons finely chopped rosemary
1	teaspoon salt

6	ounces fresh goat cheese
1	cup Salt-and-Butter-Roasted Pecans *(page 134)*, roughly chopped

Preheat your oven to 375°F. In a medium bowl, carefully stir together the figs, brown sugar, orange zest, and orange juice. Set aside.

In a 10-inch heavy-bottomed sauté pan, melt the butter over medium heat. Add the onions, rosemary, and salt. Cook the onions for 10 minutes. They should begin to brown. Lower the heat and allow the onions to caramelize over a period of 15 to 20 more minutes. You'll need to stir regularly and keep your eye on things to prevent a burning-onion scenario. The end product should have reduced to about ½ cup and be a deep caramel color.

Stir the figs into the onions to thoroughly combine. Transfer that mixture to a 2-quart baking dish and top with the crumbled goat cheese. Press down a little with your hands or the back of a spoon to make sure the two meet and mingle.

Bake uncovered for 30 minutes on the middle rack of your oven. Once the dish is done, the edges should be bubbling but the goat cheese will not necessarily have melted into the mixture and lost its shape.

Take the baked, fantastic stuff out of the oven, shower it with the pecans, and let it sit for 5 minutes before smearing on the best crostini you can toast.

Fried Chicken Livers
with Balsamic-Marinated Figs

Serves 4

I AM NOT A LIVER LOVER. I was fooled one too many times as a kid by the oddly intoxicating aroma of liver and onions frying on the stove. They smelled so good—somehow better than bacon and sweeter than cake. I tried them again and again only to push the sad livers and limp onions aside in favor of just about anything else on my plate.

For me to enjoy the distinct flavor and texture of chicken livers, all the stars have to align. The livers have to be crispy, not overcooked, and paired with the perfect sweet acidic condiment. That's where these marinated figs come in; they are the perfect counterpoint to everything off-putting about chicken liver. The figs are also nice with pork of any kind, ricotta cheese, or in an arugula salad with bacon.

Fried Livers

- ½ teaspoon fennel seed
- ½ teaspoon cumin seed
- ½ teaspoon coriander seed
- ¼ teaspoon ground cinnamon
- 1 teaspoon ground black pepper, divided
- 2 teaspoons salt, divided
- 1 cup buttermilk
- 1 pound chicken livers, trimmed and halved
- 1 cup all-purpose flour
- 2 cups vegetable oil for frying

Balsamic Figs

- 3 cups ripe figs, stemmed and quartered
- 1 tablespoon light brown sugar
- 3 teaspoons fresh ginger, grated on a Microplane
- 1½ teaspoons salt
- 1 teaspoon chopped rosemary
- 1 teaspoon picked thyme
- Zest of 1 orange
- 1 tablespoon honey
- ⅓ cup aged balsamic vinegar
- ¼ cup lemon juice

Note: *I'm about to tell you to toast and then grind whole spices, but please don't let that step deter you from trying this recipe.*
If you have ground fennel, cumin, and coriander on hand, it's okay to use them.

Marinate the figs: In a medium bowl, gently toss together the figs, brown sugar, ginger, salt, rosemary, thyme, and orange zest. Let this hang out at room temperature for about an hour. Some liquid will leach out and the flavors will begin to develop. After an hour, stir in the honey, balsamic vinegar, and lemon juice. Let this mingle another 30 minutes at room temperature before serving.

Prepare the livers: In an 8-inch skillet, toast the fennel, cumin, and coriander seeds over medium heat. Once you start to smell them, they're done. Let them cool, transfer them to a spice grinder, and grind till smooth.

Whisk those spices plus the cinnamon, ½ teaspoon black pepper, 1 teaspoon salt, and the buttermilk in a medium bowl. Add the livers, and let them marinate in the refrigerator a minimum of 30 minutes and up to overnight

Stir the flour together with the remaining salt and pepper and divide this mixture into two medium bowls. In batches, lift the livers out of the buttermilk, drain off any excess moisture, and toss them in half the flour until they are evenly coated. One by one, dip them back in the buttermilk, then toss them in the remaining flour. This is messy, I know, but the double dip is going to provide a good platform for the warm spices in the buttermilk to come through as well as give you a better crunch-to-liver ratio. Separate the livers in a single layer on a baking sheet and refrigerate up to 1 hour before you fry.

Fry and serve: Preheat your oven to 200°F and set a plate lined with paper towels next to your stove to drain the livers once they come out of the oil.

Pour the oil into a 10-inch cast-iron skillet or Dutch oven to a depth of 1 inch. Using a thermometer for best results, heat oil to 350°F. Using tongs, gently lay a third of the livers in the hot oil and fry them on one side until nice and brown, about 3 minutes. Make sure you don't crowd the pan, and keep an eye on the oil's temperature; it should not rise above 375°F or fall below 325°F. Carefully turn the livers and fry the other side an additional 2 to 3 minutes.

Transfer the beautiful brown livers to the paper towel to drain. Sprinkle them with a little salt and keep the livers warm in the oven while you fry the second batch.

I like to serve the livers and figs with pickled red onions and arugula drizzled with the fig marinade. This way, it kind of feels like a salad.

BLUEBERRIES

THE BLUEBERRY helped me find my voice.

When Ben and I opened the restaurant, Kinstonians made a lot out of my pedigree. A small group of people were thrilled to have a local girl who'd been trained in New York come home and open a restaurant, but most people were a little suspicious of Ben and me.

"That Howard girl thinks she's gonna come in here and cook all this fancy stuff for country folks and charge an arm and a leg fer it. She ain't gonna have no salad bar, no baked potato? Heard she thinks she's gon' teach us what's good. I give 'em three months. No…I give 'em a year. Her daddy'll foot the bill till then."

Sounds harsh now, but that was the word around town at the time. People either desperately wanted us to succeed or were certain (and weirdly hopeful) we'd fail.

That we came from New York enchanted some people and pissed others off. Both groups believed I'd brought back with me a different notion of how to cook, a refined palate, and a penchant for the sophisticated. What I brought back, unfortunately, were just other people's recipes. Sure, I knew how to work in a professional kitchen, and I'd grown to understand the importance of knife skills and realized that if you weren't constantly learning, you were losing. But I had no sense of the type of food I wanted to cook. And I certainly had no idea how to use food to connect with people.

The first year Chef and the Farmer was open, we did fine. I made seasonal, tweaked versions of other people's food, and they were fine. Did James Beard rise from the dead to give me an honorary medal? No. But we were making food from scratch and fostering relationships with local farmers, and I wasn't embarrassed by any of it. A small group of Kinstonians did everything they could to fill our seats. Some of them ate with us twice a week, terrified the new restaurant owned by actual young people

might fold on their watch. And we also had our haters—the same people from before, and maybe a few more because we had stayed open a whole year.

Then, in the summer of 2007, my dad, who never does anything on a small scale, called to say he had a blueberry connection who was willing to sell me berries for one dollar a pound.

A note about my dad: John Currin Howard, like a lot of men, loves a good project. But when most men would settle for fixing up an old car or building a fence around the property, my dad chose to move two dilapidated homes from polar ends of the county to our family farm, connect them with a hallway, and make it his nap shack— the river house Ben and I lived in when we moved back home.

So when John Currin told me he had a source for blueberries, I knew two things: He'd made a connection with someone he didn't want to let down, and I was going to

be buying a *lot* of blueberries. That Saturday at 4:30 p.m., the absolute worst time of the week to receive a massive produce delivery, he showed up with five hundred pounds of them.

On Saturdays, our crew runs around in a frenzy to get things ready for the restaurant's busiest night while simultaneously trying to wind down for their weekend (we're closed Sunday and Monday). But even if I had had a crew of five people dedicated only to those berries, there wasn't enough working refrigeration in all of downtown Kinston to store them. So the berries sat out in boxes stacked on top of one another for much longer than they should have, an unfortunate method of storage that has been known to shorten shelf life.

Sunday morning, when Ben and I would usually have been lying in bed talking about what we were going to cook on our day off, we instead lamented the quarter ton of blueberries sitting outside the walk-in at the restaurant. We went from discussing our frustration at my dad's manner of helping to trying to come up with something I could do with blueberries past their prime.

This was before someone could go to the Internet and learn how to pickle a pine tree, so I put my nose in a cookbook. I didn't even have to leave the bed, actually, because I went to sleep every night reading books about food and had a stack of twenty next to me. I found a story, not quite a recipe, about blueberry vinegar, and I'd just learned to make fruit vinegar, so I took that as a sign. Then the challenge became figuring out what to do with thirty gallons of blueberry vinegar. Neither my New York training nor my cookbook obsession pointed me anywhere useful, so I looked inward.

Eastern North Carolina is known to outsiders for whole-hog barbecue sauced with seasoned vinegar. Hogs are split in half and slowly smoked over a wood fire till their skin crackles and their meat falls apart. Then the meat is dressed with cider vinegar and spices and either left on the hog for people to pick or all chopped together. Pig pickings are memorable, cuisine-defining events, but they're not everyday food. What I actually ate at least once a week as a kid was chicken done with the same sauce.

A man named Tom Heath, a fixture from my childhood whose connection to my family I can't really explain, brought us three barbecued chickens every Saturday morning. Like the aroma of fresh-brewed coffee, the smell of vinegar and smoke pulled me out of my twin bed to our kitchen, the promise of chicken still warm from

RECIEPS

the coals much greater than the comfort of sleep. I ate two legs for breakfast and a cold breast for lunch. I suspect that my dad and Tom had some kind of business deal—my dad did something for Tom, and Tom paid him in food—but I never thought about it till that aromatic metal bowl stopped appearing on Saturdays.

Tom's chicken, cooked in smoke and bathed in a mildly sweet vinegar sauce—that was where I'd start. Blueberry barbecue chicken...the idea was born.

At the restaurant on Tuesday of that week, we replaced pan-roasted chicken in a sherry and thyme jus with blueberry barbecue chicken alongside squash casserole and peach slaw. The whole dish was a departure for us. On a menu that featured things like smoked goat-cheese ravioli in tomato petals, this dish made a statement, and was an instant hit.

Our fans loved the way it looked: crispy, crackly, caramelized purple. They responded to the way it smelled: sweet, smoky, intoxicating. But most of all, people loved that it made them remember something they had eaten many times before but that somehow complemented rather than competed with those memories. Even a few of our haters (the ones who were on the fence) came around.

The blueberry chicken was familiar, but different. It worked because I had an emotional connection to Tom Heath's original—its sweet vinegar smell, unevenly charred skin, and smoky meat were part of me. But as a chef versed in texture, balance, and eye appeal, I was able to raise it up and make it exciting for people.

No one was more surprised than me at its success. I remember going to my teensy office after service that night to absorb the idea that I wasn't necessarily a fake. I had been looking so hard outside myself and outside my place for inspiration that I assumed every idea out there was better than an idea from here. But, lo and behold, I had found my voice in that quarter ton blueberries, and I was bursting at the seams to sing with it.

BLUEBERRY WISDOM

Picking

WHEN I WAS A KID, my aunt Pluma had what seemed like a blueberry forest in her backyard. I remember running from my yard and through my grandfather's to her house with a bucket hanging around my neck. I ate and picked till my bucket was full. Then I ran home and handed my berries over to my mom to make a cobbler. Turns out that what came naturally to me as a kid, having the bucket hang around my neck, is an efficient way to pick blueberries.

Like figs, blueberries will not continue to ripen once picked, so select only those berries that are plump and sweet and come off the bush easily.

Frozen Boobies

WE FILL A LOCKER (chest freezer) under my parents' carport every year with blueberries and pecans. There's nothing to freezing a pecan, but to best freeze blueberries, spread them onto a baking sheet and freeze in a single layer. Once the berries are completely frozen, transfer them to zip-lock bags. This is actually the best method for freezing any ripe fruit.

Theo and Flo actually prefer blueberries frozen. When they were just learning to talk, I cut the berries in half and pretended they were bits of ice cream. They called them "boobies."

Frozen berries are suitable for any recipe where blueberries meet heat.

Little Round Suckers

Blueberries are round rascals that roll around your plate when chased by a fork. I know it's a pain to do this, but you can fix that problem by slicing blueberries in half, giving them a flat edge, for salsas or salads.

The Blueberry Conundrum

GENERALLY SPEAKING, we use blueberries in savory dishes less often than we use other fruits. I used to think it was because blueberries don't have the pointed acidity of raspberries or strawberries or the boozy, red-wine notes of blackberries. They don't have the intoxicating floral perfume of peaches or the snappy texture of apples. But now that I've swapped blueberries in for a variety of fruits in a ton of recipes to great effect, I believe it's because blueberries are indigenous to North America. The immigrants who settled here, making the United States the mishmash of cultures it is, had no experience with dusty, demure blueberries. Perhaps even more American than apple pie is blueberry anything. Cook with them.

Blueberry BBQ Chicken

Makes a 3-pound chicken with sauce left over

UNLIKE TRADITIONAL EASTERN CAROLINA–style barbecue sauce, Blue Q is useful on items beyond meat. Similar to a shrub—a fruit syrup punctuated by vinegar—it makes a bracing drink when mixed with club soda or booze or both. It's also the first step in a fruity vinaigrette. And as much as it loves smoke, this sauce sees my oven more than my grill.

Whether you're doing chicken or pork, keep in mind this is not a marinade. Brush it on toward the end of cooking and let it soak for a bit before serving. The final soak is key.

1	3-pound chicken
3	teaspoons salt
1½	teaspoons black pepper

Blue Q Sauce

3	cups blueberries
2	cups apple cider vinegar
2	cups granulated sugar

1	3-inch cinnamon stick
1	bay leaf
1	teaspoon salt
¼	teaspoon chili flakes

Make the sauce: Begin by combining the blueberries and a little of the vinegar in a food processor. Pulse the berries just to break them up. You're not trying to achieve smooth berries at this point. You just want to get some blue juice flowing.

In a 4-quart saucepan, combine all the ingredients. Bring them up to a simmer over medium heat and cook for 1 hour, covered. Give it a stir from time to time because it's possible to burn this. I know from experience.

Carefully transfer the sauce to a blender. Pull the little knob off the top of the lid and cover it with a dish towel to prevent an explosion. Blend the sauce to get it as smooth as you can. Strain it through a fine-mesh strainer and transfer it back to your saucepan. Bring it back to a boil, and reduce the sauce by a third. The Blue Q should coat the back of a spoon. Its

viscosity should be more like maple syrup than honey. Refrigerate overnight to let things mellow out. This sauce will keep for months, covered in the refrigerator.

Cook the chicken: Light your grill and heat it to roughly 350°F. If using charcoal, throw some water-soaked cherry-, pecan-, or apple-wood chips in with the charcoal for the smoke effect.

Ask your butcher to butterfly or spatchcock your chicken by cutting the backbone and sternum out and flattening. About 30 minutes before you plan to cook it, bring the chicken to room temperature and season it thoroughly with 3 teaspoons salt and 1½ teaspoons black pepper.

Place the chicken skin-side up on the grill and close the lid. Cook covered for 20 minutes. Begin basting with the blueberry sauce every 5 minutes for an additional 20 minutes. Keep the grill lid closed between

bastings. After 40 minutes, turn the chicken over to caramelize the skin and baste the other side for 10 more minutes. Using a thermometer, check the temperature of a meaty part of the leg. If it's at 165°F, remove it from the grill. If not, cook until it reaches the proper temperature, skin-side up.

Off the grill, douse the chicken in blueberry sauce and let it rest for 10 minutes. Once it's well rested, cut the chicken into 6 or 8 pieces and toss once more in sauce. Serve warm or at room temperature.

Blueberry Chutney

Makes 6 cups

THIS CHUTNEY ASSERTS THE blueberry's power to play a savory role. Inspired by a curry-flavored peach chutney, the blueberries here maintain their character next to all the aromatics. The obvious partners are pork, chicken, and even lamb—but a dollop of this over Stewed Rutabagas (*page 470*) or whipped into the salad dressing that follows this recipe are the real revelations.

1   medium red onion, peeled and sliced thin with the grain

¼   cup ginger, peeled and minced

½   teaspoon salt

1   tablespoon vegetable oil

1   teaspoon ground coriander

1   teaspoon curry powder

1   teaspoon ground cumin

½   teaspoon cayenne

½   teaspoon ground black pepper

6   cups blueberries

1½ cups granulated sugar

Zest and juice of ½ orange, zest removed with a Microplane

Zest and juice of 2 limes, zest removed with a Microplane

¼   cup rice vinegar

½   teaspoon salt

In a 4-quart Dutch oven or wide-mouthed saucepan, sweat the onion, ginger, and salt in the oil for about 5 minutes. Add the coriander, curry, cumin, cayenne, and black pepper and toast for roughly 30 seconds or until the spices are fragrant. Add the remaining ingredients. Bring it to a simmer and cook until it's chunky like jam, about 20 minutes.

If possible, serve this chutney at least a day after you make it. The flavors get to know one another and mellow overnight. This will keep, covered, in the fridge for up to 3 months. To preserve it for longer, follow the directions for canning (*page 16*) and process in a hot-water bath for 10 minutes.

Creamy, Tangy, and Sweet Blueberry Dressing

Makes 1½ cups

THE INITIAL INSPIRATION for this was the cream-cheesy, sweet fruit dip my mom made in the 1980s. Apples, pineapples, grapes—all the fruit tray's usual suspects are elevated by this complex, sweet, and savory purple stuff. It's also a nice surprise under sturdy lettuces dressed with lemon juice, fresh blueberries, and Spiced Pecan and Pumpkin Seed Crumble (*page 135*) or Viv's Addiction (*page 133*).

Blueberry Chutney

Creamy, Tangy, and Sweet
Blueberry Dressing

½ cup Blueberry Chutney (*opposite*)
½ cup fresh goat cheese
⅓ cup lemon juice
¼ cup orange juice
½ teaspoon salt

Combine all the ingredients in a blender and blend till totally smooth. Serve this underneath a green salad dressed with lemon juice, a little salt, and a nice olive oil. Top the salad with some fun nuts and fresh blueberries.

Blueberry-Rosemary Breakfast Pudding

Makes a 9 x 13-inch pudding

DEAR BLUEBERRY MUFFINS and Pancakes: I'm sorry. This bread pudding brings everything you do to the breakfast table *and* it can be assembled the night before.

14 ounces sourdough bread cut into 1-inch cubes (6 cups)	2 cups milk
	½ cup heavy cream
2½ cups blueberries	4 medium eggs
2 teaspoons chopped rosemary	½ plus ⅓ cup granulated sugar
Zest of 1 lemon, removed with a Microplane	1 teaspoon vanilla extract
	½ teaspoon salt
	1 teaspoon ground nutmeg

In a large bowl, toss together and thoroughly combine the bread, blueberries, rosemary, and lemon zest. Transfer the bread mixture to a greased, 9 x 13-inch baking dish and set aside.

In the same bowl you used to mix the bread, whisk together the milk, heavy cream, eggs, ½ cup sugar, vanilla, and salt. Pour this over the bread. Stir it up, cover, and refrigerate a minimum of 1 hour or up to overnight.

When you're ready to bake, preheat the oven to 350°F. Remove the bread pudding from the fridge and give it a stir. In a small bowl, combine the remaining sugar and nutmeg. Sprinkle it generously over the top of the pudding. It may seem like a lot of sugar, but this will make the top crunchy, sweet, and aromatic.

Bake for 1 hour uncovered. Your kitchen will smell like French toast and the pudding itself will be brown and crisp on top and firm throughout. Serve warm and be glad you're not flipping pancakes to order.

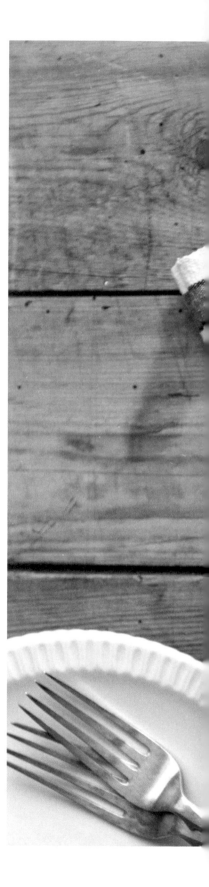

Blueberry Cobbler with a Cornmeal Sugar-Cookie Crust

Makes a 9 x 13-inch cobbler

BLUEBERRY COBBLER WAS THE GO-TO EASY DESSERT of my childhood. A box of Bisquick, some less-than-perfect fruit, a little sugar, and a scoop of ice cream to cool it down...the cobbler worked hard for its reputation as the lazy country cousin to the pie.

The large number of mediocre cobblers in the world adds validity to this label, and those cobblers' problems are easy to identify: The filling is too runny or there's too much of it. The topping is too cakey and there's too much or too little of it.

At the restaurant we've worked to perfect our cobbler science for years. What we've come up with is a crust that's crispy and chewy and smells like vanilla, and a filling that's syrupy and bright. It translates equally well to any combination of fruits.

You're going to look at this recipe and assume the three sticks of butter the crust calls for is a mistake. It's not. Roll with it. This is dessert, not salad.

Note: *We've used the obvious, like blackberries, cherries, strawberries, plums, apricots, figs, muscadines, and peaches here. But we've also made festive holiday versions with dried figs, fresh apples, and cranberries. Feel free to combine fruits and add spices to suit the occasion. Cloves, allspice, and cinnamon work well with fruits like fig and apple.*

Blueberry Filling

- 2 pounds of very ripe blueberries (imperfect fruit is okay here)
- ¾ cup granulated sugar
- Zest of 2 lemons, removed with Microplane
- 4 tablespoons lemon juice
- 1 teaspoon salt

Cornmeal Sugar-Cookie Crust

- 1 cup all-purpose flour
- 1 cup cornmeal
- ½ teaspoon baking powder
- ½ teaspoon salt
- 1½ cups (3 sticks) butter, softened
- 1 cup granulated sugar
- 1 tablespoon light brown sugar
- 1 large egg
- 2 teaspoons vanilla extract

Blueberry Cobbler with a Cornmeal Sugar-Cookie Crust

Continued from the previous page

Make the filling: Put all the ingredients in a large bowl and press down with the back of a spoon to burst about half the berries. Stir it all together and cover. Let the berries and sugar hang out in the refrigerator for about 2 hours or overnight, stirring when it's convenient.

After about 2 hours, lots of juice will have leached out of your fruit. Strain the juice and add it to a small saucepan. Reduce the juice by half, or until it's nice and syrupy. Add the syrupy stuff back to your fruit and stir to combine. It should coat and cling to the fruit like that scary cherry-pie filling from the can.

Make the crust: Combine the flour, cornmeal, baking powder, and salt in a small bowl. Cream together the butter and sugars in a mixer fitted with the paddle attachment until light and fluffy. Add the egg and vanilla and paddle to incorporate. Slowly add the dry mixture till it's just incorporated.

Remove the dough from the bowl, cover it well with plastic wrap, and let it rest. The cookie dough can be made several days in advance. You could even make a larger batch, freeze it, and whip it out when you have some dying fruit or unexpected guests on your hands.

Assemble the cobbler: Butter your 9 x 13-inch baking dish and spoon the fruity velvet into it. Alternatively, if you have a lot of cute dishes you'd like to use, make sure they can stand the oven and go for it. What's important is the filling-to-topping ratio. For every 1½ inches of filling, you want ½ inch of cookie crust. If your dishes go deeper, just increase both using the same ratio.

If your topping is chilled, allow it to come to room temperature. Generally for something like this, you would be instructed to flour your work surface and roll out the dough, but for this recipe, that doesn't really work. So just take your hands, grab a nice ball of the soft, kind of sticky dough, and flatten it between your palms until it's approximately ½ inch thick. Lay that flattened, irregular disk on top of the fruit and move on to your next handful. The goal is to pretty much cover the filling without overlap but with very little exposed fruit in between.

Place the baking dish on top of a larger cookie sheet because, chances are, it's going to bubble over, and that's a good thing (unless I'm washing the dishes). Bake it at 350°F for about an hour. The top should be on the dark side of golden brown with crispy-looking edges. Serve warm with a scoop of vanilla ice cream.

Blueberries and Cucumbers with Pistachios and Yogurt

Serves 4

BLUEBERRIES AND CUCUMBERS respect each other. Both come off in early summer here, so their surprising harmonious marriage lends credibility to the locavore mantra "What grows together, goes together."

Up close, this is a refreshing salad with lots of texture, but zoom out and you'll see something that resembles a substantial Southern tzatziki. Serve it cold.

½ cup plain Greek yogurt

¼ cup buttermilk

Zest and juice of 1 lemon

2 tablespoons orange juice

4 tablespoons extra-virgin olive oil, divided

1½ teaspoons salt, divided

1 scant tablespoon honey

¼ teaspoon hot sauce

2 medium cucumbers or 1 English cucumber

1 cup blueberries

1 tablespoon picked dill

1 tablespoon minced chives

2 teaspoons torn mint

2 tablespoons rice wine vinegar

¼ cup toasted pistachios, roughly chopped

In a small bowl, whisk together the yogurt, buttermilk, citrus, 2 tablespoons of olive oil, ½ teaspoon salt, honey, and hot sauce. Store it, covered in the fridge, till you're ready to serve.

If you are using traditional slicing cucumbers, peel or mostly peel them. If you are using an English cucumber, feel free to leave the skin on. Either way, split it and use a small spoon to remove the seeds. Then slice the cukes into ⅓-inch half-moons. You should end up with roughly 2 cups of cucumber slices.

In a medium bowl, just before serving, toss together the cucumber, blueberries, the dill, chives, mint, remaining 1 teaspoon salt, vinegar, and remaining 2 tablespoons olive oil. Puddle half the yogurt sauce on the bottom of your plate. Mound the salad on top of that. Drizzle with the remaining sauce and finish with the pistachios.

Crab Hoecakes with Blueberry Corn Salsa

Makes 6 tostadas with a little salsa left over

FISH TACOS ARE CURRENTLY my favorite thing to cook and eat at home. So, several years ago, when it occurred to me that my grandma Hill's hoecakes were oddly similar to a crispy tortilla, I was thrilled to make the fish-taco concept Southern. Unlike a taco, this is knife-and-fork fare. Take the idea and switch out the protein or change the ingredients in the salsa. Just make sure you've got the flat cornbread, something creamy, and something fresh and crunchy.

Lemony Crab

- ⅓ cup mayonnaise
- 2 tablespoons minced chives
- 2 tablespoons extra-virgin olive oil
- Zest of 1 lemon
- 2 tablespoons lemon juice
- 2 teaspoons Dijon mustard
- 2 teaspoons ground coriander seeds
- 1 garlic clove, grated with a Microplane
- ½ teaspoon hot sauce
- ½ teaspoon salt
- 1 pound fresh or pasteurized lump crabmeat, picked through for shells

Salsa

Makes 4 cups

- ½ medium red onion, minced
- 3 tablespoons lemon juice
- 2 cups blueberries
- 2 cups fresh corn and corn milk, from roughly 4 ears
- 1 medium tomato, diced
- ¼ cup chopped cilantro
- 1 tablespoon chopped mint
- 2 tablespoons extra-virgin olive oil
- 1 teaspoon salt

Grandma Hill's Hoecakes *(page 29)*, made into six 4-inch circles

Make the salsa: In a medium bowl, combine the red onion and the lemon juice. Let this hang out while you prepare the remaining ingredients. Once everything's chopped and ready, throw all of it into the bowl with the onions and stir to combine. The salsa should marry a minimum of an hour before you serve it. Leftovers are tasty on chips and will keep covered in the fridge for three days.

Dress the crab: In a medium bowl, whisk the mayonnaise, chives, olive oil, lemon zest and juice, Dijon, coriander, garlic, hot sauce, and salt. Stir in the crab, and refrigerate till you're ready to serve.

To serve: Top each corn cake with a heaping third of a cup marinated crab. Top the crab with an equal portion salsa. Serve soon with knife and fork because you don't want the hoecake to get too soggy.

Blueberry, Buttermilk, and Lime Parfait

Makes six 8-ounce parfaits

DAZZLING TO LOOK AT, creamy layers of buttermilk, lime, and blueberry make these parfaits a fun study in eating similar textures punctuated by bright complementary flavors. It's the kind of dessert I want to eat slowly with a long spoon and a moment of silence.

You'll need clear eight-ounce glasses or jars to do this right.

Blueberry Layer

- 4½ cups blueberries
- 1 cup granulated sugar
- Zest of 2 limes
- ⅛ teaspoon salt
- ½ envelope powdered gelatin
- ¼ cup cold water

Buttermilk Panna Cotta

- ½ envelope powdered gelatin
- ¼ cup cold water
- ¾ cup heavy cream
- 1⅔ cups full-fat buttermilk
- ⅓ cup granulated sugar
- 1 teaspoon vanilla extract
- 1 teaspoon lemon juice

Lime Curd

- 8 egg yolks
- 2 teaspoons lime zest, removed with a Microplane
- ½ cup plus 2 tablespoons lime juice
- 1 cup granulated sugar
- ⅛ teaspoon salt
- 8 tablespoons (1 stick) room-temperature butter, cut into pieces

Buttermilk Whipped Cream

- 1 cup heavy cream
- ¼ cup buttermilk
- ¼ cup powdered sugar
- ½ teaspoon vanilla extract

Note: *Make the whipped cream the day you serve the parfaits.*

Make the blueberry layer: Combine the first 4 ingredients in a medium saucepan. Bring it up to a boil, reduce it to a simmer, and cook for about 10 minutes.

Bloom the gelatin by stirring it into ¼ cup cold water. Let it sit for about 5 minutes.

Pour the blueberry mixture into a blender and process until it's completely smooth. Strain it through a fine-mesh sieve and whisk in the bloomed gelatin.

Pour ⅓ cup blueberry mix into the bottom of each of your glasses, then transfer the glasses to your refrigerator to set up. It should take about 1½ hours in a cold refrigerator to firm up enough to withstand the next layer. If you're pushed for time, stick them in the freezer for 30 minutes.

Make the buttermilk panna cotta: In a medium bowl, bloom the gelatin into ¼ cup cold water. In a small saucepan, whisk together the cream, buttermilk, sugar, and vanilla. Heat it just until the sugar dissolves. Add this mixture to the bloomed gelatin and stir in the lemon juice. Things will curdle up a bit at this point, so strain the mix through a fine-mesh sieve.

Once the blueberry layer is relatively firm, pour about 1 inch of the buttermilk mix on top. Chill the jars till the panna cotta is set.

Make the lime curd: In a medium metal or glass bowl, whisk together the first 5 ingredients. Fill a 4-quart saucepan with roughly 2 inches of water and bring that to a boil. Set the bowl holding the yolk mixture over the water in order to create a double boiler. Whisk the yolk mix constantly until it reaches 180 degrees or until it thickens. This should take about 12 minutes. Remove the bowl from the heat and whisk in the butter, one piece at a time, until it's fully incorporated.

Once the buttermilk panna cotta has set, spoon ¼ cup of the curd over the top and store, covered, till you're ready to serve.

Make the whipped cream: In a mixer fitted with the whisk attachment, combine all the ingredients. Whisk on high until you reach stiff peaks.

Spoon enough of the whipped cream on top of the lime-curd layer to fill the glass, then wipe it off flush. Finish the parfaits with a few blueberries and Spiced Pecan and Pumpkin Seed Crumble (*page 135*) if you like. Serve cold and encourage folks to dig down deep in order to get all the flavor sensations at once.

SWEET CORN

ALMOST NOTHING in the summer garden requires as much urgent attention as the sweet corn harvest. If you plant a bunch of corn at the same time, it's going to mature and need to be picked and processed at the same time, roughly twenty-one days after the plant produces a tassel. You don't go out to the field, pluck an ear or two for dinner, and wait a few days for the next ear on the stalk to ripen. We're not talking about strawberries and tomatoes here. Corn comes off all at once, and timing is crucial.

The way people here once dealt with this is different than the way we approach sweet corn today. We sate our sweet corn hunger with a few ears plucked from the farmers' market during summer because we know we should, but the ritual used to be that families came together for one or two days before the tobacco work started each summer to put up, otherwise known as hoard, hundreds of ears of sweet corn. Before modern refrigeration, folks fermented corn like I do with collards on page 425 or pressure-canned it. But when I was a kid, my family froze corn by the truckload.

I remember riding my bike up the driveway to meet a pickup truck backed up to the carport, its bed brimming with what looked to me like a thousand green husks. Work started just after sunrise as the boys and the occasional man shucked and silked ears of corn outside on the doorstep between swigs of Pepsi or pulls on their cigarettes. Inside, the women did the work of getting the corn off the cob and into freezer bags.

There's more than one way to do this part, and each family had its preferred system. Some cut the corn off the cob, cooked it in a big pot, then added salt and butter

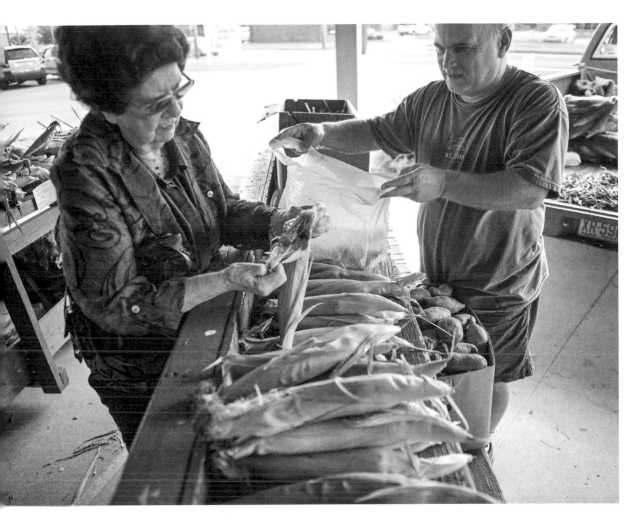

to taste. Others cut the corn off the cob and froze it raw. If someone was a gadget kind of person, he or she probably had a special brush for removing the silks or a special scraper for mining the corn milk, but my family was minimalist. We removed pesky silks with our hands, then blanched the cobs in boiling water on the stove. My sisters and grandmother cut the corn off the cob at the kitchen table with small knives. And I scooped the blanched, cob-free corn into freezer bags with a measuring cup, squeezed the air out, and walked pans across the carport to the lockers. We had one locker to freeze corn and butterbeans and one for pecans. Like the name suggests, we kept them locked.

The stove ran full blast all day, and by the end of it, corn milk, silk, and blanching water covered every surface of our little kitchen. It was hot work, but no one ever questioned whether it was worth it. We ate and savored that corn, stewed simply with a little butter, at every holiday beginning with Thanksgiving and almost every Sunday till the next sweet corn harvest rolled around.

After that, my family stopped putting up corn. We no longer had a garden, and frozen corn, albeit a far cry from our put-ups, was readily available in the grocery store. But I always missed those little freezer bags of broken-up sweet kernels mixed together with a slurry of fragrant, creamy corn milk.

SWEET CORN WISDOM

What Is Sweet Corn?

YOU HEARD ME SAY IT in the first chapter, but to clarify, sweet corn and field corn are not the same. Field corn stays on the plant to dry and is ground and used as a grain. Sweet corn is a genetic mutation of field corn discovered by American Indians. It has more sugar, which makes it very perishable, so we harvest it when it's immature and eat it like a vegetable.

Varieties, Maturity, and Obsession

WITHIN THE SWEET-CORN GENRE, there are a lot of subcategories that elicit prejudice, worship, reverence, and ridicule.

White corn has a lot of crazed fans in Eastern Carolina. Varieties like Silver Queen, Treasure, How Sweet It Is, Captivate, and Country Gentleman taste like their names suggest—delicate, mineral-driven, and one-note sweet. **Yellow corn**, such as Bodacious, Golden Buns, and Incredible, is what I'd call "corny." Deep yellow kernels imply the taste of butter. It's sweet, but more complex and robust than its genteel white sister. Then there's the **bicolor** phenomenon. Obsession, Peaches and Cream, Serendipity, and Mystique give eaters the best of both worlds, with both yellow and white kernels on every ear. The combination of the little pop of the super-sweet white kernel against the tenuous burst of the yellow one absolutely thrills me.

Then there's the question of maturity. Once the corn plant produces a tassel, twenty-one days sit between you and a ripe ear of corn. Problem is, there's a window of about a week at the end of that twenty-one days where the size and eating quality of the ears morph; the small, immature kernels with little character become swollen, tight, and sometimes tough. I'm not a fan of immature corn, but farmers harvest it this way early on in the season because consumers are so ravenous they'll pay money for anything in a green husk. Some cooks revere the immature corn's fragile kernels for their creaming quality. At the other end of the spectrum are ears I call "horsey." They are just on the edge of being overripe and going bad, but some people love them this way.

Select the Best, Keep It Fresh

ONCE CORN HAS BEEN PICKED, it is extremely important to cool it down and keep it that way till you prepare it. To avoid starchy, dry

A few years ago, three generations of Howard women and children came together again to put up four hundred ears of corn. I wanted to relive some of the food rituals I had read about or remembered, and even though putting up corn is a bit of a production, it's less involved than slaughtering a hog or canning tomatoes.

This time, instead of a hot kitchen, we did it outside under a shed with a nice breeze. We used a turkey fryer to boil the water, and no one worried about the mess

kernels, don't waste time transferring ears to your refrigerator. If you're buying corn from a farmers' market, go early in the morning. The longer corn sits out at summertime temperatures, the more it suffers.

The first corn of the summer is the best and least likely to have been sprayed with pesticides. As summer moves along, insects and worms become harder to control. If you buy organic corn, which is not sprayed with pesticides, late in the summer, it will likely be riddled with worms.

Look for bright green, moist-looking husks. If the husks have started to dry or turn brown, you're dealing with corn that's been out of the field for a while.

Corn Milk

CORN MILK IS THE CREAMY liquid scraped from the cob after you've cut the kernels off. I'm obsessed with this by-product and tailor how I cut kernels off the cob for maximum corn-milk extraction.

Instead of cutting kernels as close to the core of the cob as you can, leave a little of the kernel attached. Then go back around and scrape all that milk into the corn. This is where the term *creamed corn* comes from.

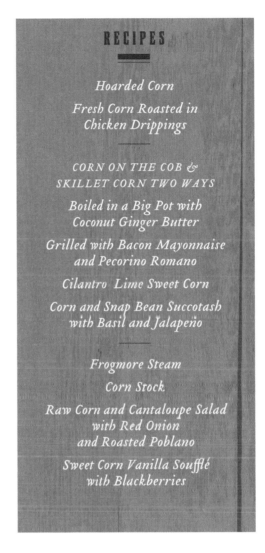

RECIPES

Hoarded Corn

Fresh Corn Roasted in Chicken Drippings

CORN ON THE COB & SKILLET CORN TWO WAYS

Boiled in a Big Pot with Coconut Ginger Butter

Grilled with Bacon Mayonnaise and Pecorino Romano

Cilantro Lime Sweet Corn

Corn and Snap Bean Succotash with Basil and Jalapeño

Frogmore Steam

Corn Stock

Raw Corn and Cantaloupe Salad with Red Onion and Roasted Poblano

Sweet Corn Vanilla Soufflé with Blackberries

we were making. It was so much fun telling stories, laughing, eating, and teaching, the afternoon didn't feel like work at all.

It occurred to me as the day moved along that putting up corn was just one of many food rituals that required the hands and attention of the whole family. It was one of the ways families once worked together toward a common goal. It made me more than a little sad that we don't do it, or things like it, anymore, and it raised the question of what kind of family-building exercises we've replaced these experiences with.

Hoarded Corn

200 ears will yield about 20 quarts

THIS IS A PROCESS, so make sure you hoard enough corn for it to matter. I recommend no fewer than 200 ears. Sounds like a lot, but with several sets of hands and lots of life to discuss, the work goes fast.

An afternoon

Trash bags

Pint or quart freezer bags

Fresh in-husk ears of corn

A large box of kosher salt

The biggest pot you have

A set of long tongs

A big ice bath

A measuring cup with a handle

1 or 2 large casserole dishes

A sharp or perforated paring knife

A Sharpie marker

Begin by shucking each ear of corn and removing the silk. People have all kinds of gadgets for this. I've even heard of people putting corn in the microwave to speed the process along, but I find all that stuff a distraction. I use two hands. That's it.

Meanwhile, fill your pot halfway up with water and add salt until it tastes like the sea. Bring this up to a rapid boil. Next to the boiling water, set up your ice bath and sprinkle some salt in there as well.

Drop 10 or so ears of corn into the boiling water. Once it comes back to the boil, let it go for another

3 minutes. Transfer the corn to the ice bath to shock it, stop the cooking process, and cool it down.

Using the casserole dish as the base, cut the corn off the cob, making sure you scrape every little bit of milk off with it. Discard the cobs, or reserve some for Corn Stock (*page 232*). Using a large spoon or 1-cup measure, spoon the corn into freezer bags and squeeze as much air out of the bags as possible.

Label each bag with the date and variety. Stack the bags on top of one another in the freezer. They'll keep for up to a year.

Fresh Corn Roasted in Chicken Drippings

Serves 4

WHEN I STARTED WRITING THIS BOOK, my sisters had a lot to say about which family heirlooms to include. One dish from my grandma Iris kept coming up: corn roasted under a chicken. Problem was, I had never eaten it, and no one could give me a straight answer about how Iris made it. But Currie, the queen of memory and details, described corn that was savory, caramelized, chewy in some places, creamy in others, and spicy with black pepper. This description—and the way Currie looked when she talked about it, twirling her hands in a wizardly motion reserved for things that are greater than the sum of their parts—made me determined to figure it out.

This dish is deceptively simple, and, like my mom's chicken and rice, it goes against what I consider to be "correct" cooking technique, but it pleases anyway. The pan, the temperature, and the size of the chicken legs matter very much here.

- 4 chicken-leg quarters, about 10 ounces each (this means drumettes and thighs attached)
- 3 teaspoons salt, divided
- 30 turns of the pepper mill or scant 1 teaspoon black pepper, divided
- 2 tablespoons vegetable oil
- 4 cups fresh corn
- 1 teaspoon granulated sugar
- 4 thyme sprigs

Preheat your oven to 400°F and season both sides of the chicken with 2 teaspoons salt and 10 turns of the pepper mill. In a 12-inch skillet, heat the vegetable oil over medium heat until it shimmers. Add the chicken, skin-side down, to the pan and let it begin to brown slowly. You do not want the oil smoking, volatile, and wild; the process should sound like a gentle rendering of fat and caramelizing of skin.

As the legs brown, toss the corn with the remaining salt, black pepper, and sugar. Spread it out on a 13 x 18-inch baking sheet with no more than a 1-inch lip. The corn should reach to the edges and be in a ½-inch layer. Put the 4 sprigs of thyme on top of the corn to mark the spot where you plan to lay the chicken.

Once the skin side of the legs is golden brown, lay the chicken skin-side up on top of each sprig of thyme. There should be an inch or two between the legs. Slide the sheet pan onto the middle rack of your oven and roast for 45 minutes. I know that sounds like a long time, but chicken legs can take it, and the corn requires it.

When you take the chicken out of the oven, the corn should be cooked inconsistently over the pan. The edges will be dry and caramelized and the corn under the chicken will be juicy and fragrant.

Remove the leg quarters. Set them aside and discard the thyme. Using a spoon or spatula, stir all the corn together and serve under the chicken.

Corn on the Cob & Skillet Corn Two Ways

WHETHER they gnaw it off the cob or stew it in a skillet, my people enhance sweet corn only really with butter. And I get it. It's hard to improve on that nearly perfect marriage, but sweet corn has an affinity for so many ingredients, it seems unfair to make her monogamous. Herbs, peppers, cheese, bacon, garlic, ginger, and citrus all deserve a moment with the most American food there is. Here are four recipes that make the argument.

Cilantro-Lime Sweet Corn

Boiled in a Big Pot
with Coconut
Ginger Butter

Corn and Snap Bean
Succotash with
Basil and Jalapeño

Grilled with Bacon Mayonnaise
and Pecorino Romano

Boiled in a Big Pot with Coconut Ginger Butter

Serves 5

I SWAP IN COCONUT butter all the time on toast and in the skillet. Turns out it's a stunning companion for sweet corn too. Make sure you use unrefined. It's got a subtle but beautiful aroma and taste that the refining process diminishes.

- 5 shucked ears of corn
- 1 teaspoon salt
- 2 tablespoons chopped scallions
- 1 tablespoon chopped mint

Coconut Ginger Butter
Makes ½ cup

- 3 tablespoons unrefined coconut oil, at room temperature
- 3 tablespoons butter, at room temperature

- 1 tablespoon plus 2 teaspoons fresh ginger, grated on a Microplane
- Zest of 1 orange
- 1 teaspoon lemon juice
- ¼ teaspoon salt
- 2 dashes hot sauce

Make the butter: In a small bowl, combine all the ingredients and mix well with the back of a spoon. You could use a mixer or food processor for this part, but if everything is truly room temperature, you shouldn't need to.

Set the butter aside at room temperature till you're ready to use it. Typically I preach that you should make compound butters in advance, chill them,

and bring them out to use on a whim, but fresh ginger loses something shortly after it's been grated or minced.

Cook and serve the corn: Bring a large pot of heavily salted water up to a boil. Meanwhile, using a sharp knife, cut a notch in the center of each cob. Grab both ends and break the cob in half. For boiling, I just think half cobs are easier to deal with.

Drop the cobs into the boiling water just before people are ready to eat. Boil them for 3 to 5 minutes, depending on how tender your corn is, and drain them well. It's important to get as much water off the corn as you can. Add the hot corn, salt, and half the Coconut Ginger Butter to a bowl and toss it around madly so that the butter melts all over the cobs. Stack corn on a platter; top with more butter if you like. Finish with scallions and mint.

Grilled with Bacon Mayonnaise and Pecorino Romano

Serves 5

GRILLED CORN tossed in mayonnaise, covered in cheese, and squirted with lime is a classic Mexican preparation. This is my nod to the tradition. If you can't find Pecorino Romano, any hard cheese, like Parmigiano-Reggiano, will work.

To make this or any of the other recipes in this book that call for bacon fat, just get yourself a heatproof vessel and start saving all the slightly cooled grease that renders off your bacon. I use a mason jar. Keep it in the refrigerator, and you've salvaged a beautiful and useful thing. Even my mom, a fat hater, saves all her bacon grease. It's careless not to.

- 5 shucked ears of corn
- 1 tablespoon extra-virgin olive oil
- 2 teaspoons salt
- 3 tablespoons Pecorino Romano, grated on the Microplane
- 1 teaspoon paprika

Bacon Mayonnaise
Makes ⅔ cup mayonnaise

- ¼ cup mayonnaise
- ¼ cup reserved, room-temperature bacon fat

- Zest of 1 lemon, removed with a Microplane
- 1 tablespoon lemon juice
- ½ teaspoon granulated sugar

Make the mayonnaise: In a small bowl, combine all the ingredients and stir vigorously to incorporate. As you might imagine, this is good on a lot of stuff.

Cook and serve the corn: Preheat your grill to medium high. You need the grates to be quite hot in order to achieve the char you're looking for, but you don't want jumping blue flames.

Toss the corn with the olive oil and salt and position the ears perpendicular on the grates. Grill 2 to 3 minutes on each side or until you see spotty caramelized kernels. It should take about 10 minutes to get it right all the way around.

Combine the corn and about ⅓ cup of the mayo in a large bowl. Toss it around and get it good and coated. Lay the corn in a single layer on a serving tray. Top with the cheese and paprika.

Cilantro-Lime Sweet Corn

Makes 4 cups

MAKE SURE YOU STIR this bright green butter in just before serving. The flavor and color will be more vibrant than if you let it sit and grow tired.

4	tablespoons butter, softened
1½	teaspoons salt, divided
	Zest of 2 limes, removed with a Microplane
3	tablespoons lime juice
½	cup cilantro, stems and leaves chopped very fine
¼	teaspoon cayenne
4	cups corn (cut from about 8 ears)
1½	cups water or corn stock

In a food processor pulse the butter, ½ teaspoon salt, lime zest and juice, cilantro, and cayenne till the mixture comes together. Set aside. You could make this up to a week in advance and store it sealed in the refrigerator.

Combine the corn, water, and remaining 1 teaspoon salt in a 10-inch skillet or a medium saucepan. Bring it up to a simmer and let it cook, uncovered, stirring occasionally, for about 15 minutes. You want all but about 2 tablespoons of liquid to evaporate out of the pan. I know that's nearly impossible to measure, so don't try. Look for moist corn that's not swimming in liquid.

Just before serving, stir all the compound butter into the hot corn. The remaining liquid should come together with the butter to make things a little creamy. If this is not happening and your pan is too dry, add a couple tablespoons of water. Serve soon.

Corn and Snap Bean Succotash
with Basil and Jalapeño

Makes 5 cups

AT ITS MOST BASIC, succotash is a dish of corn and beans stewed together.

This one lands a long way from its humble roots. I chop the beans into pieces roughly the same size as the corn; that way, all the little elements of this dynamic succotash fit in the cradle of a spoon. Make sure you add the basil just before serving so it has a shot at hitting the plate while it's still green.

- 1 cup leeks, sliced into ⅓-inch rounds
- 2 tablespoons minced ginger
- 1 tablespoon vegetable oil
- 3 garlic cloves, sliced thin

- 3 cups corn, cut from 6–7 ears
- 2 cups snap beans (we call them string beans), cut into ⅓-inch pieces
- 1 tablespoon minced jalapeño, seeds removed, if you like

- 1 teaspoon salt
- 2 cups water or corn stock
- ⅓ cup whole basil leaves
- 1 tablespoon lemon juice
- 3 tablespoons butter

In a 10- or 12-inch skillet or sauté pan, sweat the leeks and ginger in the vegetable oil for 2 minutes. Add the garlic, corn, beans, jalapeño, salt, and water. Bring it up to a simmer and cook until all but ¼ cup of the water has evaporated. I know that is impossible to measure, so just eyeball it. Stir in the basil leaves, lemon juice, and the butter. Serve warm.

Frogmore Steam

Serves 4

FROGMORE STEW IS ONE OF SEVERAL NAMES people assign to seafood boils that include potatoes, sausage, corn, and shrimp.

It's a summertime tradition everybody in my family enjoys: all of us eating communally, using our hands, and grabbing the ingredients we crave the most. But I'm never knocked over by how awesome any of it tastes. Food boiling away in a massive pot of water, no matter how heavily seasoned, can always taste better. This Frogmore Steam retains the elements we loved about the original stew—eating with our hands, prioritizing which calories we consume, and the surf-and-turf summer feel of it all—but it sits in a broth made from the fat and flavor of the ingredients themselves. I bet if you try it, you too will be changing your ways.

Note: *We toss our peel-and-eat shrimp in this rub at the Boiler Room. I describe it as a cross between a BBQ rub and Old Bay. It's a welcome change for any type of boil and makes a versatile seasoning for fish. If you don't get around to making it for this recipe, you can substitute Old Bay.*

BBQ Shrimp Rub
Makes just over 1 cup

- 3 tablespoons smoked paprika
- 1½ tablespoons ancho chili powder
- 2½ tablespoons kosher salt
- 2 tablespoons ground celery seed
- 2½ tablespoons ground coriander
- 1½ tablespoons ground cumin
- 1 tablespoon chipotle powder
- 2 tablespoons brown sugar

Frogmore Steam

- 2 cups corn stock (water is a fine substitute)
- ¼ cup BBQ Shrimp Rub plus more for dusting
- 1 pound smoked sausage of your choice, sliced into 2-inch rounds
- 1 pound new potatoes, halved (about 3 cups)
- 4 ears of corn, halved
- 1 pound deveined, peel-on large shrimp, 21/25 count
- 3 tablespoons butter
- 2 tablespoons lemon juice
- 1 teaspoon salt

Make the rub: Stir everything together, taking care to break up stubborn clumps of brown sugar. Store in a sealed container at room temperature for up to 2 months.

Make the Frogmore Steam: Preheat your oven to 400°F. Combine the corn stock and 1 tablespoon of the shrimp rub in the bottom of a 6- to 9-quart Dutch oven. Bring it up to a boil. Add the sausage, the potatoes, and the corn. Cover the Dutch oven and slide it into the oven. Let it bake

for approximately 40 minutes. You're looking for the potatoes to be just tender, and that really depends on how big and old they are. Once the potatoes are ready, take the Frogmore out of the oven and add the shrimp. Cover again and slide it into the oven for an additional 5 minutes.

Take the vessel out of the oven and remove the lid. Add almost all the remaining rub and the butter, lemon juice, and salt. Toss it all together, making sure everything gets coated. Some of the seasoning will drip down into the broth. That's a good thing. Dump the whole awesome-smelling mess out onto a serving platter with a rim. Sprinkle it with a little more rub. Put it in the middle of the table with a big spoon for serving, and arm all your diners with bowls and napkins. Make sure everyone gets some broth and knows to dip all the components down into it for extra flavor.

Corn Stock

Makes 3 quarts

CORN STOCK IS A STAPLE in our summertime kitchen. Like corn itself, this liquid is incredibly versatile and a resourceful way to deepen the flavor of vegetable dishes.

Try swapping corn stock in for absolutely any savory dish that calls for water, or substitute it for chicken stock anytime to enjoy lighter, more focused flavors.

When I'm shucking corn and cutting it off the cob, I set my stockpot right next to me. Building the stock as you go kills two birds with one stone and produces a better stock. The fresher the husks and cobs are, the more flavor they'll have.

	Inner husks from 10 ears of corn	1	medium onion, diced	2	sprigs thyme
20	corncobs, corn removed	5	garlic cloves, smashed	2	bay leaves

When you shuck your ears of corn, remove the outside layer of husk and throw it away. Reserve the inner husks, minus the silk, from roughly 10 ears and place them in the bottom of an 8-quart stockpot. Lay 20 corn-less cobs, the onion, garlic, thyme, and bay leaves on top of the husks and add water to cover by one inch. You can use cobs that have already been blanched as you would for putting up corn. What's important is that corn was cut from the cob recently.

Bring the stock up to a boil and cover. Reduce to a simmer and cook for 1 hour. Strain and reserve the liquid. Return the stock to your pot and reduce by half. If you'd like to freeze it and space is an issue, reduce the stock further and freeze for up to 4 months.

Raw Corn and Cantaloupe Salad with Red Onion and Roasted Poblano

Serves 4

I TEST THE QUALITY OF SWEET CORN by peeling back the husk and silk and biting into the raw kernels. At some point over the last nine summers of doing this at the restaurant, I decided I liked raw corn just as much as, if not more than, cooked corn.

When sweet corn is at its peak and your farmer tells you this is as good as it's gonna get, run home and make this salad.

1 medium poblano pepper	¼ teaspoon granulated sugar	2 tablespoons olive oil for finishing
½ small red onion, halved and sliced super-thin with the grain	2 cups raw corn, cut from about 5 ears	1 teaspoon salt
	1 cup cantaloupe, diced just slightly larger than a corn kernel	2 tablespoons mint, roughly torn
¼ cup red wine vinegar		1 tablespoon tarragon, picked and roughly torn
¼ cup water	3 tablespoons lemon juice	
¼ teaspoon salt		

Roast the poblano over an open flame, on the grill, or under the broiler in your oven. Peel and discard most of the char. Remove the pepper's seeds and stem and slice the remaining flesh into a 1-inch julienne or matchsticks.

In a small bowl, combine the poblano, onion, vinegar, water, salt, and sugar and let it hang out or "pickle" for at least an hour before assembling the salad.

To assemble the salad, drain the onions and poblano and discard the liquid. In a medium bowl, combine them with the corn, cantaloupe, lemon juice, olive oil, and salt. Just before serving, stir in the herbs.

Sweet Corn Vanilla Soufflé with Blackberries

Serves 6

YOU'LL OFTEN SEE CORN PUDDINGS or soufflés on a savory table, but unless they're topped with cheese or cut with garlic, corn's overt sweetness sometimes seems out of place here. I've added vanilla bean and blackberries to prevent any confusion around where this delicate dessert belongs.

Floured nonstick baking spray, such as Baker's Joy

2 cups sweet corn, divided

1 cup heavy cream, divided

½ cup granulated sugar

⅛ teaspoon salt

1 vanilla bean

½ cup all-purpose flour

2 teaspoons baking powder

8 tablespoons (1 stick) butter, at room temperature

2 eggs, separated

Zest of ½ lemon, removed with a Microplane

½ teaspoon nutmeg

1 cup sliced blackberries

Preheat your oven to 350°F and spray a 6x6-inch baking dish, a 10-inch cast-iron skillet, or 6 individual ramekins with copious amounts of nonstick cooking spray. In a 2-quart saucepan, combine 1 cup corn, ½ cup cream, the sugar, and the salt. Using a knife, split the vanilla bean down the center lengthwise and scrape out all the little seeds. Add those along with the pod to the pot. Bring all this up to a simmer and cook for 5 minutes. Remove it from the heat and let it steep 10 minutes more. Pluck out the vanilla pod and discard. Transfer all the contents to the blender and process till totally smooth. Set aside.

Stir together the flour and baking powder and set aside. In the same saucepan, heat the remaining cream over medium heat till bubbles form around the edges. Whisk in the flour mixture and continue cooking till it thickens up. It will be very pasty. Remove it from the heat and stir in the butter, 2 tablespoons at a time.

Once the flour mixture is close to room temperature, add the pureed corn, egg yolks, lemon zest, and reserved corn. Stir it all up well to make a nice homogenous mixture.

In a mixer fitted with the whisk attachment, beat the egg whites till they reach stiff peaks. Fold them gently into the corn. Fill your baking dish or ramekins ⅔ of the way up with soufflé. Sprinkle with nutmeg and bake, uncovered, in the center of your oven. The large dish will take about 35 minutes. The small ramekins will require roughly 25. The soufflé should rise up just above the edge of the vessel. Take out of the oven. Top with blackberries and serve right away if you can. If you can't, that's okay too. The soufflé won't be as poofy, but it will be just as tasty.

CUCUMBERS

EVERY YOUNG CHEF IN AMERICA waits for the moment when the phone rings or an e-mail arrives from a magazine asking for a spread of his or her recipes. Having started out in the hype-driven world of Manhattan restaurants, I understood such a request as a rite of passage, a mark that you had finally made it. So after Ben and I moved to the boondocks, opened Chef and the Farmer, and finally started turning out food I felt deserved recognition, I too began waiting for that request.

As you might have guessed, no one called. No one e-mailed. *Food & Wine* didn't care whether I had revolutionized chicken and pastry with the use of acid and herbs. *Bon Appétit* wasn't looking to me for a primer on a million ways to use fruit in savory form. I was waiting for the proverbial pot to boil, and the burner wasn't even on. Tallying up the number of times my peers had been featured in glossy magazines against my big fat goose egg made me resentful, angry, and unfocused. I knew I should worry more about my own work and less about others' press, but I struggled to do it.

When the phone finally rang, well into our sixth year of business, I got freaking *excited*. Hunter Lewis, then the new food editor of *Southern Living* (and now the editor of *Cooking Light*), sent Ben an e-mail asking to speak to me about contributing some recipes for their June food issue. He would call me the next day to talk.

That night's service at the restaurant was a messy blur as ideas I planned to share with him rushed through my little brain...old techniques made new again, with red velvet beet cake, air-dried country-style sausages, braised pork shoulder, and sweet potato lasagna. This was going to be my moment to show the world—or at least the readers of *Southern Living*—how skilled and creative I was.

After work, I rushed home, got in bed, and Googled Hunter's name. I was certain a picture of a gray-haired man wearing an ascot and swirling a glass of sherry would pop up—and I was shocked to see that Hunter Lewis was in fact a young guy who had recently left *Saveur* to help update the image of *Southern Living*. That made me nervous. For some reason, I felt more comfortable in the hands of a gentle old guy with an ascot.

The next day Hunter did call and laid out the meat of the business. They were doing a big package on summer bounty with a lot of other chefs and wanted a few recipes from me. Keep in mind, these publications do their planning way in advance, so we're talking summer bounty in February.

Clearly this wasn't going to be my opportunity to tell folks about my love for laying hens or mullet roe, but I thought I could certainly weigh in on something that spoke to who I was, like charred okra or stewed tomatoes. But no. They wanted me to do…*cucumbers*. And they needed nine ideas by Monday—just three days away.

I nearly lost it. Cucumbers? Really? You don't even cook them. I didn't have anything to say about a dang cucumber. It felt like a cosmic joke.

At that point I really just needed to get off the phone, so I told Hunter I was honored and as excited as anything to write about the cucumber, but someone was calling my name in the kitchen and I had to go.

I got off the phone, raced to the Piggly Wiggly, and bought an armful of cucumbers. I had heard that French people sautéed them. I thought I might also try grilling them. Either way, I was going to cook the bejesus out of some cucumbers.

Turns out that didn't work. Each time I applied heat to the cukes, they instantly lost the qualities I like most about them—their cooling properties gone; their crisp snap flabby; their unmistakable bouquet muted; their shy friendly flavor watery.

I walked away from the stove that day pissed as hell at Hunter for giving me such a limited assignment. But I had found a new appreciation for the cucumber and a new understanding of what it meant to respect the ingredient.

That night in bed I thought about what the cucumbers lost when I cooked them, and I decided to change my approach for the package. I would develop recipes to exalt the crisp, shy, cooling, and aromatic qualities of the raw cucumber. I would let the ingredient really do its thing, rather than try desperately to show how well I could do mine. Right then and there, I changed my approach to cooking, and maybe even to life. The cucumber moment was a big one for me. Thanks, Hunter.

CUCUMBER WISDOM

Shrink Wrap Gets a Bad Rap

EVEN THOUGH I GREW UP eating what we called slicing cukes and substituting pickling cukes when there were no slicing ones to be found, I do appreciate the ease and function of shrink-wrapped English cucumbers, also known as hothouse or seedless cukes. While their flavor tends to be a little more watery than a Kirby straight from the vine, I love that the skin is pleasant to eat. Not to state the obvious, but the green of an English cuke's skin adds a lot to the appearance of certain recipes.

Another variety to keep your eyes open for is the lemon cucumber. They are shaped like lemons and have yellow, sometimes bristly skin. Maybe it's me eating with my eyes, but I think they offer a lemony aftertaste.

If you use English cucumbers for any of these recipes, forgo peeling if you wish.

They Don't Like It Hot

CUCUMBERS don't like it too hot. They flourish in early summer as well as early fall, so expect to see cucumber quality and quantity taper off in late July and August. But if you're surrounded by farmers who know what's up, expect a nice early-fall showing.

I actually find that fall is a great time to make cucumber pickles. The urgency of summer's sexiest produce has worn off, offering me the bandwidth to focus on these guys.

Big N's Sour Pickles

Makes 9 quarts

MY FRIEND NANCY SYLVESTER'S PARENTS were known among our wild bunch of high-school and college companions as warm, welcoming, tolerant people who always had good food around. Her father, whom we affectionately called Big N, was known for his sour pickles, barbecue sauce, and no-nonsense approach to everything. He did not approve of our shenanigans but he handled them like a seasoned pro.

Big N died this year from cancer. When I learned he was sick, I knew I wanted to film him making his pickles for *A Chef's Life*. I treasure the scenes with my family members from the show like invaluable gifts, and I wanted to give a similar one to the Sylvesters. After the shoot, during which nervous Nancy nearly blew up the stove, I asked Big N if I could publish his pickle recipe in my book. He looked at me knowingly and said sure. A few days later I got this e-mail:

Mother's Pickle Recipe

One peck of cucumbers
½ box of salt or more
Pour boiling water over them
Make sure water covers pickles
Put plates on top of pickles
Let them soak for thirty hours
Rinse pickles and put in quart jar
Turn jars upside down so they can drain

Put one pod of hot pepper in each jar
Two tea spoons of sugar in each jar
Put jars in pan on the stove in boiling water
Fill each jar with boiling cider vinegar
Process the jars by leaving them in a cannery for ten minutes
For one peck one gallon of vinegar and nine quart jars

Big N believed there was one right way to do everything, so he took it for granted I would use the smallest cucumbers I could find and that I'd pack those cucumbers into that jar like it was the last one on earth. He assumed I knew cucumbers longer than three inches would need to be halved to help facilitate the extremely tight pack-in. He also guessed I'd be using a two-pound box of pickling salt and that I knew the plates were meant to weigh the cucumbers down in the brine. And he couldn't have been more wrong with this one, but he

felt sure I'd be smart enough to fill the jars with the hot vinegar once I had already loaded them in the canner basket. I never would have done that without instruction, as I'm the type of cook who learns how not to do something the hard way. Big N also guessed I knew what a peck was. It's about eight quarts.

Big N ate these pickles alongside chocolate cake, and I've tried that. It's an interesting combination. Where they really shine is in chicken salad. Nancy's mom, Jane, grates them on a box grater and uses them as well as their tart pickle juice instead of sweet relish to round out her simple but famous rendition of the classic.

Fancy Sandwiches

Makes roughly 1 loaf of sandwiches

IN A WORLD WHERE WHITE BREAD is about as well regarded as high-fructose corn syrup, it would seem strange to call these sandwiches fancy. But not so long ago, dainty sandwiches made from soft white bread, cucumbers, and something creamy were the kind of fancy that called for doilies and an elevated pinkie finger.

In today's white-bread-hating world (of which I'm a multigrain card-carrying member), I deem these pillowy cucumber purses even fancier. They are a special-occasion or Saturday-afternoon food, meant to be smiled at and savored.

Ground-up radishes add a colorful kick to a combination of butter, cream cheese, and mayo, a trifecta I like to call the temple of fat. Don't feel bad, though. A trip to the land where white bread and mayonnaise rule is worthwhile every now and then.

---

3 medium or 2 large cucumbers, peeled and sliced into ⅛-inch-thick rings

2 teaspoons salt

1 tablespoon lemon juice

1 loaf white bread

½ teaspoon white pepper

Radish Spread

1 cup radishes of your choice, washed and quartered

8 tablespoons (1 stick) unsalted butter, at room temperature

½ cup cream cheese, at room temperature

¼ cup mayonnaise

½ teaspoon salt

¼ cup radish greens, minced

Make the spread: Using a food processor, pulse the radishes till they are finely minced but not pureed. In a separate bowl, cream the butter, cream cheese, mayo, and salt using a spatula. Stir in the radishes and their greens. Set the spread aside till you're ready to get fancy. It'll keep covered in the refrigerator for one week.

Make the sandwiches: Toss the cucumbers with the salt and drain them in a colander for 10 minutes. Pat the cucumbers dry. Then toss them with the lemon juice. Smear 2 tablespoons radish spread over each slice of bread and top one side of each with an overlapping layer of cucumber slices. Sprinkle the slices with white pepper. Top that with another radish-smeared slice of bread. Continue with the remaining sandwiches.

Cut the crusts off the sandwiches. Discard the trim or run in a corner, make sure no one's looking, and stuff it in your face, 'cause they're gonna stop making white bread soon enough. Then cut the sandwiches into triangles.

Cover the sandwiches tightly with plastic wrap and refrigerate for at least 15 minutes and up to 2 hours before serving. They benefit from a short firm-up in the fridge but will taste stale after a while.

Everyday Cucumbers

Serves 4

THIS SALAD MADE A daily appearance on Mom's summer table. Sometimes it was just cucumbers. Sometimes there was red onion sliced in, or the leftover ends of tomatoes. It was an easy way to round out a table with a dish you could prepare far in advance. The cucumbers improved with time, and flies were turned off by the vinegar.

The chef in me now knows that these cucumbers act as balance, as acid. Vinegary cucumbers gave corn permission to be sweet. They offered squash and onions room to be a mouthful. They built fried pork chops a house in which to play rich. Today I throw into this basic recipe all sorts of things that show up at the same time as cucumbers, like blueberries, peaches, squash, watermelon, and herbs.

- 2 medium cucumbers, peeled and sliced into ¼-inch circles
- 1 medium red onion, peeled and sliced thin
- 2 teaspoons granulated sugar
- 1 teaspoon salt
- ½ teaspoon black pepper
- 1 medium tomato, cut horizontally into ½-inch slices, then quartered
- ½ cup apple cider vinegar

Toss the cucumber, onion, sugar, salt, and pepper in a medium bowl. Let it hang out for about 15 minutes. Add the tomatoes and vinegar, and allow it all to marry at least 20 minutes and up to 4 hours. Serve at room temperature every day you can.

Cucumber Ginger Limeade

Makes 4 cups

THE SUBTLE HEATING QUALITIES OF GINGER swirled together with cool cucumber juice make this the perfect summertime mocktail. Of course, if it's a buzz you're chasing, add gin, vodka, or tequila for a relaxing afternoon in the sun.

1½ cups peeled and roughly chopped cucumber

1½ cups water

1⅓ cups Ginger Lime Syrup

1 cup lime juice

Sliced cucumber for garnish

Ginger Lime Syrup
Makes 3 cups syrup

3 limes

1 cup peeled and roughly chopped ginger

1½ cups granulated sugar

2 cups water

Make the syrup: Remove the zest from the limes with a Microplane, taking care not to include the white pith. Combine the ginger, sugar, and zest in a food processor and process for about 15 seconds. The sugar will begin to liquefy, but that's okay. Transfer contents to a small saucepan and add the water. Over medium heat, stir to dissolve and allow the syrup to heat at a low simmer for about 5 minutes. Remove from the heat and steep another 10 to 15 minutes. Strain the syrup through a fine-mesh sieve and discard the solids.

Assemble and serve: Combine cucumber and water in a blender and liquefy. Transfer the cucumber water to a small pitcher and stir in the remaining ingredients. Chill thoroughly to prevent diluting it down when you serve it over crushed ice garnished with cucumber slices.

Wedge You Like a Salad with That Ranch?

Serves 4

IT HURTS THE CHLOROPHYLL-LOVING, bitter-green chewer inside me to say it, but I could mow down a good wedge salad any day of the week. Yes, iceberg lettuce has little flavor or nutritional value, but it sure does make a fine canvas for ranch dressing, smoky bacon, tomato, and red onion. This ranch dressing is infused with both the flavor and crunch of cucumber, making it a prince among its peers.

We had a wedge salad on the menu for years at Chef and the Farmer. I kept it on the menu to make people happy, but it didn't add to the story we were trying to tell and took prime menu real estate away from something that could. I eventually took it off and upset a lot of people—many of them my family members. Here it is again.

Don't pigeonhole this dressing as something suitable only for an iceberg wedge. Instead, shower it over tomatoes garnished with crispy croutons, spoon it over roasted beets, or choose it to dress grilled Romaine. You'll find lots of possibilities.

Cucumber Ranch
Makes 4 cups

- 3 medium slicing cukes or 2 English cukes
- 1½ teaspoons salt
- 1 cup full-fat sour cream
- ⅔ cup mayonnaise
- ¼ cup buttermilk
- 3 tablespoons minced chives
- 3 tablespoons chopped parsley
- 2 teaspoons onion powder
- 2 teaspoons garlic powder
- 2 teaspoons lemon juice
- 1 teaspoon Worcestershire sauce

Salad
Serves 4

- ½ medium red onion, peeled, halved, and sliced thin with the grain
- 8 ounces slab bacon
- 1 head iceberg lettuce
- 3 cups Cucumber Ranch (I know it sounds like a lot, but there *are* cucumbers in there)
- ½ teaspoon salt
- 2 medium tomatoes cut into 1-inch dice
- ½ teaspoon black pepper

Note: *I recommend slab bacon here but recognize it's not available everywhere. If you can't find unsliced bacon, use the thickest-cut slices you can and cut them into 1-inch squares.*

Make the dressing: Peel and split the cucumbers lengthwise. Remove the seeds with a small spoon. Slice them into very thin half-moons. Toss the cucumber slices with 1½ teaspoons salt and place over a colander to drain for about 30 minutes. Once all the liquid has leached out, you should end up with about 2 cups of cucumber slices.

you stir well just before serving.

Make the salad: Soak the red onion slices in a little ice water for about 10 minutes to make them less offensive. Slice the slab bacon into ½-inch-wide long slices. Then cut the slices into ½ x 1-inch batons. In a 10-inch skillet, begin rendering the bacon over medium heat. Cook the bacon until most of the fat has rendered out and the bacon is brown and slightly crispy. Set the bacon aside.

Slice the head of iceberg in half from root end to tip. Slice the halves in half. Chill the iceberg till you're ready to serve.

To serve, spoon some dressing on the bottom of a plate. Position a wedge of lettuce on top of the dressing, leafy exposed side up. Sprinkle the iceberg with a little salt. Spoon more dressing on top of the lettuce, allowing it to creep down into the crevices of the iceberg. Finish each salad with diced tomato, a nice helping of bacon, red onion to your liking, and black pepper.

Whisk the remaining ingredients together and stir in the drained cucumbers. Allow the dressing to marry for a minimum of 1 hour before serving.

The dressing will keep for up to 5 days covered in the refrigerator. Make sure

Cool Cucumber Crab Dip

Serves 6

MY GOOD FRIEND Eleanor Johnston appreciates the art of dipping. She, her cousin Kari, and her mom, Mary Drake, have hosted many evenings designed for her friends to catch up. These events always shared three things: lots of head-back, chin-in-the-air laughing, too many cocktails, and loads of dip—pimento dip, onion dip, blue cheese chutney dip, chicken salad dip, and, my favorite, crab dip.

My family hates dip. Johna's and Currie's distaste for mayonnaise is so strong they won't touch anything that's white and creamy for fear it might hide a trace of mayo. The first time I spent a weekend at Eleanor's with a cocktail in hand and crab dip and crackers in my lap, I knew I had found my tribe.

I remember reading in one of my favorite cookbooks of all time, *The Elements of Taste,* by Gray Kunz, that after you touch crab, your hands often smell like cucumber. I haven't experienced that myself, but because of it, I've always paired the two ingredients with success. The cucumber here adds freshness and texture and makes this a lighter, "wetter" crab dip than most. It's perfect with plain Jane salt-seasoned crackers and a crisp cool glass of white wine. Let's hope Eleanor agrees.

2 medium cucumbers or 1 large English cucumber	1 tablespoon Greek yogurt, sour cream, or crème fraîche	2 tablespoons prepared horseradish
1½ teaspoons salt, divided	1 pound picked crabmeat (anything but claw will work fine)	½ teaspoon hot sauce
1 cup cream cheese, at room temperature	¼ cup lemon juice	¼ cup finely chopped scallion
		3 tablespoons chopped mint

Peel, halve, and seed 1½ medium cucumbers or ⅔ of a large English cucumber. Using a mandoline, slice the halves into 1/16-inch half-moons. Toss the slices with ½ teaspoon salt and set them over a colander to drain while you put together the rest of your dip. You should end up with roughly 1 cup of limp cucumber slices.

Using a Microplane, grate the remaining cucumber. You'll be left with cucumber pulp and the water that leaches off of the pulp. Strain the pulp from the water and discard the pulp. Set aside up to ⅓ cup of the water for this dip and shoot the remaining like tequila…or with tequila, for that matter.

In the bowl of a mixer fitted with the paddle attachment, beat the cream cheese, yogurt, and cucumber water until it's lightened and smooth. Add the crab, the remaining salt, lemon juice, horseradish, hot sauce, scallion, and mint. Paddle this up till it looks like dip. Stir in the cucumber slices by hand, and serve chilled with crackers, crudités, or chips.

Spice-Rubbed Flank Steak with Cucumber and Charred Onion Relish

Serves 6

OH, HOW I LOVE THE RELISHES. They're easy to make, and because they're full of vinegar, they keep and improve over time. This relish is a chunky play on the Argentinean condiment chimichurri that gets additional depth of flavor from charred red onions.

Think of this relish more as a room-temperature salad when you're portioning it out. You'll want some of it with every bite. Also consider it as a companion to lamb, chicken, beans, or a full-flavored fish like trout.

Cucumber and Charred Onion Relish

- 5 medium slicing cucumbers or 3 English cukes
- 1 tablespoon plus 1 teaspoon kosher salt
- 2 medium red onions
- ½ cup plus 1 tablespoon extra-virgin olive oil
- 5 cloves of garlic, grated on a Microplane
- ½ cup chopped mint
- ¼ cup chopped parsley
- ¼ cup chopped oregano
- 2 teaspoons red chili flakes
- 1 tablespoon granulated sugar
- ⅓ cup sherry vinegar
- 2 tablespoons lemon juice

Spice-Rubbed Flank Steak

- 3 tablespoons salt
- 2 tablespoons granulated sugar
- 1 tablespoon paprika
- 1 tablespoon ground cumin
- 1 tablespoon granulated garlic
- 20 grinds of the pepper mill or 1 teaspoon black pepper
- 2 flank steaks, roughly 3 pounds total
- 2 tablespoons vegetable oil
- 6 cups cucumber relish

Make the relish: Peel and cut the flesh from the seeds on all four sides of your cucumbers in long strips. Dice the strips into ½-inch cubes. Toss those cubes with 1 tablespoon salt and set them in a colander to drain for no less than 30 minutes. Do not rinse.

Peel and slice the red onions into rings that are ¼ inch thick. Try to keep the disk of onion rings intact for now. They will be easier to manage on the grill. Brush them with 1 tablespoon olive oil and the remaining salt, and grill on both sides until the onions are nicely charred and limp. Allow the onions to cool and combine the cucumber and onions with the remaining ingredients. Let the relish sit a minimum of 2 hours before serving. It will keep tightly covered for up to one month in the refrigerator.

Make the flank steak: Mix together the salt, sugar, paprika, cumin, garlic, and black pepper. Rub it all over both sides of the flank steaks. Let them sit covered in the rub at room temperature for at least 30 minutes and up to 1 hour before cooking. Alternatively, you could rub the flank steaks the night before you plan to cook them.

Either way, 30 minutes before you plan to cook the steaks, take them and your relish out of the refrigerator and bring them up to room temperature. Preheat your grill to high. Just before grilling, brush the steaks with the vegetable oil. Lay the steaks down over direct heat and cook for 3 minutes on each side. Move the steaks to a cooler part of the grill and cook for an additional 5 minutes, flipping once, for medium rare.

Transfer the meat to a cutting board and allow it to rest for 10 minutes before slicing. Slice the flank steak thinly against the grain and serve with plenty of the relish.

Miso Flounder with Cucumber Noodles
and Gingered Collards

Serves 4

THIS COMPOSED, CRAZY-DELICIOUS plate was inspired by my first trip to Andrea Reusing's restaurant, Lantern, in Chapel Hill. It was early in my "chef-ing" career, and a lot of what Ben and I experienced that night left an impression on us. I was most enchanted by the way Andrea was able to take North Carolina's most classic ingredients and swap them in for their brothers from another mother in Asia.

One dish we had that evening, red snapper with a miso sake butter, made me start to see many connections between Asia's way of eating and our own. I locked the silky, rich profile of that sauce up in my memory's trap and took it home to Deep Run, where I promptly started serving my version with gingered collards and cucumbers marinated in vinegar—much like the ones that sat on my family's table almost every day when I was growing up.

Almost any fish would shine in this application, and simple rice is a nice way to sop up the sauce. But for me, what makes the dish come to life is when the soft miso honey drips down and takes a swim with the bracing cucumber noodles.

4 6-ounce pieces skinless flounder (but any fish, mild or strong, works here)

1 teaspoon salt

½ teaspoon cayenne

3 tablespoons vegetable oil

1 cup miso honey sauce

4 cups cucumber noodles

2 cups Gingered Collards *(page 433)*

Cucumber Noodles

4 to 5 medium cucumbers

2 teaspoons salt

1 teaspoon granulated sugar

2 small scallions or 1 large, sliced thin

3 tablespoons sherry vinegar

2 teaspoons chopped mint

1 teaspoon sesame oil

½ teaspoon hot sauce

1 tablespoon lime juice

2 teaspoons sesame or benne seeds

Miso Sauce

Makes 1 cup

2 teaspoons plus 8 tablespoons (1 stick) cold unsalted butter

2 tablespoons minced red onion

⅓ cup sake

3 tablespoons red miso paste

¼ cup water

¼ cup honey

2 tablespoons mirin

1 teaspoon hot sauce

Make the Cucumber Noodles: Ideally you would do this with a Japanese mandoline fitted with midsize teeth, slicing each of four sides of the cucumber just down to the seeds. Often I will discard the first slice from each side in an effort to get rid of the tough skin portion. If you don't have a mandoline, just use the technique provided on page 348 to make ribbons with a vegetable peeler. They will work equally well.

In a medium bowl, toss together the cucumber noodles, salt, and sugar. Allow this to sit about 10 minutes as you get your other components together.

Whisk together the scallion, sherry vinegar, chopped mint, sesame oil, hot sauce, and lime juice. Pour this mixture over the cucumber and let it sit a minimum of 30 minutes and up to 3 hours before serving. Sprinkle the sesame or benne seeds over top.

Make the sauce: In a small sauté or saucepan, melt 2 teaspoons butter. Add the red onion and sweat for about 3 minutes or until the onions are translucent. Add the sake and reduce the liquid by half. Whisk in the miso paste, water, honey, mirin, and hot sauce. Simmer for about five minutes. The sauce should be a dark caramel brown and quite thick. Remove the miso honey from the heat until you are just about ready to serve.

Cook the fish and serve: Preheat your oven to 200°F. Season each side of your fish with salt and a little cayenne. In a large, heavy-bottomed sauté pan or cast-iron skillet, heat the vegetable oil until almost smoking. Lay the fish with the prettiest side facing down. Do not crowd the pan. If you do, the fish will be white and flabby rather than brown and crispy.

As the fish is cooking, return the miso sauce to low heat, and, 1 tablespoon at a time, whisk in cold butter until it's emulsified and fully incorporated. Once all the butter has been whisked in, remove the sauce from the heat and set aside.

Let the fish develop a nice brown crust on the first side. This could take up to 3 minutes. Flip the fish and cook for 1 minute on the opposite side (if using a thin fish like flounder). Transfer the fish to your warm oven until you're ready to serve.

Sit each piece of fish on a bed of about ½ cup of cucumber noodles and gild it all with roughly ¼ cup miso honey sauce. Serve alongside Gingered Collards (*page 433*) and Perfect Rice (*page 292*) without the butter.

TOMATOES

N 2012, CHEF AND THE FARMER appeared to be a raging success. We had survived the financial crash of 2008 and the restaurant filled up every night with customers sniffing wine and enjoying food we were proud of.

Behind the pretty plates and the servers' smiles, though, the scene was starkly different. Ben and I struggled to get along at work. We found ourselves on opposite sides of every issue and were fatigued by running a business that was busy but not making money. We went to work every day desperate to hire support staff, but solid applicants were scarce.

Kinston didn't have a restaurant community flush with aspiring chefs and managers looking for the next step up. Instead, Kinston housed a lot of folks in need of jobs but with no relevant experience. When we opened, our prospects had not been promising, though we did find a few folks who are now trusted partners. I wasn't looking for cooks with finesse, technique, or creative ability. I was looking them in the eye to see if they had crack habits.

If we couldn't generate interest in our restaurant outside Eastern North Carolina, Ben and I would never attract the employees who would help us have lives outside of Chef and the Farmer—and we'd never stop fighting.

I knew down deep that if I could get food writers or chefs to eat with us, word would begin to spread. Then, in the spring of 2013, I got my wish. The Southern Foodways Alliance, an organization that examines the food culture of the South, planned a trip to Eastern North Carolina to study barbecue. As part of the weekend and as a respite from smoked meat, they hoped to have lunch at Chef and the Farmer.

A fear-laced thrill shot out of every hair follicle on my body at the thought of it. Dozens of food enthusiasts, writers, and chefs would be my captive audience. John T. Edge himself, the director of the SFA and an influential journalist, would eat what

I wanted him to eat—a chef's dream. The focus of the trip was barbecue, so I decided to make vegetables a counterpoint. But I didn't want to serve a bunch of sides. I needed a centerpiece.

My favorite food of all time is a tomato sandwich on white bread with Duke's mayo and a blanket of salt and black pepper. I ate so many of these this past summer that I broke out in a rash. I know the rash was from the tomatoes because I broke out in the same rash last year, and the year before. But no rash or burning-belly indigestion is enough to make me put down that sandwich. I can't stop.

Still, I couldn't serve a Wonder Bread sandwich to this group. I had to somehow improve on an already perfect original. I decided to focus first on what, aside from the tomatoes, made the tomato sandwich magnificent—the mayo—and work on my rendition of white bread later.

In a jerry-rigged stovetop smoker, I smoked ears of corn and used the kernels as the flavor base for my mayo. I thought this would evoke the sweet umami flavor of bacon, and I was right! This was quite possibly the best mayo I'd ever tasted, and coming from a girl whose version of PB&J as a kid was a banana mayonnaise sandwich, that's saying something. The smoke made it ultra-savory, like whipped tangy bacon, so I also pickled some red onions to point up the flavors.

There was no way I could wait till our local tomatoes came into season to test the combination. I rushed out to buy a few of the sad, hard, reddish-pink things the stores pass off as tomatoes when there are no real ones to be had. Back at the restaurant, I realized I had forgotten bread, so I waited for our pastry chef, Kim, to finish baking our sweet potato onion loaves for service. Meanwhile, I sliced and seasoned the

RECIPES

Elbow-Lick Tomato Sandwich

Tomatoes in Jars

Tomato Chicken Macaroni

Tomatoes and Rice

Stewed Tomatoes

Roasted and Fresh Tomato Pie

Cherry Tomatoes in Basil Vinegar

BLT Dip

*Chilled Sun Gold Tomato Soup
with Lots of Summer Stuff*

*Cocktail Tomatoes
with Brown-Butter Scallops*

tomatoes, hoping time and salt would make them taste like their summer-ripe relatives.

When I had all the parts to build my dream, I split one of our warm loaves and slathered both sides with the mayo. I layered tomatoes and pickled onions on the bottom and covered them with the mayo-dressed top. I wanted to try it in peace, so I grabbed the beast with both hands and hurried toward my office. Then I heard Ben's voice. He would want a bite—nope! I turned and sped to a stairwell, shut the door, and took a huge bite out of my creation before even sitting down on the steps.

I knew this was it—the bread, the mayo, even the halfhearted tomatoes. I scarfed that sandwich down like a wild animal. Tomato juice mingled with smoked mayo and vinegary onions dripped down my arm all the way to my elbow. I licked my arms and did my best to lick my elbow. Licked the palm of my hand and imagined how unimaginable it would be with juicy, ripe Cherokee Purples. *Yes!*

The SFA luncheon was perfect. To say it like a chef would say it, "We killed it!" A month later, John T. called to tell me that he had named my tomato sandwich one of the top ten things he'd eaten that year in *Garden & Gun* magazine. I said thank you and acted like it wasn't a big deal. Then I ran into Ben's office and squealed. My greatest hopes had been exceeded. I could imagine cooks, butchers, dishwashers, and bakers lining up to work at the restaurant that made the best tomato sandwich in the world. We'd finally be able to hire enough people to take a break ourselves.

When the issue came out there was a full-page close-up of me chomping down on the drippy wonder. It made my family proud and the recognition validated our work. But cooks didn't suddenly grab their knife rolls and come running to Kinston. What did happen was probably more powerful. The story sent a ripple of pride through our staff. Locals had always said our restaurant was good…for Kinston. John T. said it was good for anywhere. His words and our tomato sandwich did what seemed impossible: it inspired us and made us all work harder.

TOMATO WISDOM

Heirloom versus Hybrid

LIKE *FARM TO TABLE,* the term *heirloom* means almost nothing and everything at this point. There are heirloom varieties of all fruits and vegetables, but I will stick my neck out and say more people share opinions about heirloom tomatoes than anything else.

Heirloom tomatoes are varieties whose seeds have been handed down for at least fifty years and for that period the plant has kept basically the same characteristics. Heirlooms of all kinds are open-pollinated, which means that insects and wind pollinate them. That part sounds obvious, but it's not the norm in modern agriculture.

Hybrids, the other, more mainstream type of tomatoes on the market today, come from farmers intentionally cross-breeding different varieties to achieve qualities valued in the modern marketplace. They naturally select tomatoes that are easy to grow, disease- and pest-resistant, and prolific. They look for varieties that have a long shelf life, don't bruise easily, and make good travelers. Then they make them parents in a very controlled environment, often by hand. Because of this, you can't save seeds from hybrids. If you did, the plant you grew may or may not resemble its parent. Hybrids are the tomatoes we see in our average grocery store, and, really, they are not demons. Many of them, like my favorite cherry tomato, Sun Gold, actually taste very good.

It's complicated and polarizing, but people on both sides seem to agree on two things: heirloom-tomato harvests are unpredictable, but they often have superior eating qualities.

Grow Your Own or Buy at a Farmers' Market

IF YOU CAN'T GROW YOUR OWN, try your absolute best to buy tomatoes, heirloom or not, from a farmers' market. Shipping and storing tomatoes generally calls for refrigeration and temperatures below fifty degrees for long periods. This is the point at which the tomato flavor and texture suffer. Tomatoes that have been stored below fifty degrees for more than two hours will have a mealy texture when served raw.

When you get your farmers' market tomatoes home, store them with their stem sides down in a single layer in a cool dark place if possible. The little stem eye is the most vulnerable spot on the tomato, and exposing it to light will speed up decay.

Our restaurant is closed on Sunday and Monday, so if we have tomatoes that won't make it at room temperature till Tuesday without spoiling, we refrigerate those and use them in cooked applications.

Elbow-Lick Tomato Sandwich

Makes 6 big sandwiches

"Thank you for the wonderful sandwich I just ate. Bread, tomatoes, onion, corn and dressing were all so good! No dishes to wash, just my face." —Scarlett Howard

YOU MAY NOT BE UP for making the bread or the mayo just for this sandwich, but both recipes are suited for so many other things. The mayo is perfect with sweet potato fries, on a burger, or thinned out a little with buttermilk and mixed with fresh corn to make a dip. The bread is just a strong suggestion and recipe for those of you who are into making bread. What I *really* want you to do is eat tomato sandwiches as often as you can when tomatoes are juicy and at their best.

1	tablespoon granulated sugar
½	cup red wine vinegar
⅓	cup warm water
1	large red onion, peeled and sliced into ¼-inch-thick rings
1	loaf Sweet Potato Onion Bread *(page 321)*
1½	cups Smoked Corn Mayo

4	Cherokee Purple tomatoes, cut from north to south in ¼-inch-thick slices
1	tablespoon salt
40	turns of a pepper mill, or 2 teaspoons black pepper

Smoked Corn Mayo
Makes a scant 2 cups

3	ears of corn, blanched *(page 220)*

2	egg yolks
¼	cup lemon juice
1	clove of garlic, minced
1	teaspoon Dijon mustard
1	teaspoon honey
1	teaspoon salt
¼	teaspoon cayenne
1	cup grapeseed or sunflower oil

Make the mayo: Smoke whole ears of blanched corn for about 15 minutes over apple, cherry, or peach wood. You could do this on a low grill or using a stovetop smoker. You're looking for the corn to take on honey color in places; not all over, but in spots.

Cut it off the cob and transfer half of it to a blender. Add the yolks, lemon juice, garlic, Dijon, honey, salt, and cayenne. Blend till smooth. Slowly stream in the oil to emulsify. Transfer the mayo to a bowl and stir in the remaining corn. Refrigerate in a sealed container for up to 5 days till you're ready to use.

Make the sandwich: At least 2 hours before you want to eat your sandwich, dissolve the sugar in the vinegar and water. Stir in the onions and let them pickle.

Preheat the oven to 350°F and drain the onions. Slice the loaf of bread through its equator and slide it, cut-side up, into the oven to toast. Bring it out and slather the cut sides with Smoked Corn Mayo. Then put down your first layer of tomatoes. Season those with salt and pepper and follow up with 2 more layers of the same. Top with a layer of the red onion, and cap that sandwich with its top. Slice it into individual portions and serve with lots of napkins.

Tomatoes in Jars

Makes 9 pints or 4½ quarts

I CALL THESE TOMATOES IN JARS because to equate them with tomatoes preserved in aluminum cans would be misleading. "Canning" tomatoes, as we call preserving them here, is just about the most rewarding and useful thing you can do all summer. I'm obsessed with it. The way home-canned tomatoes taste next to those that have been sitting in a can for God knows how long is motivating all on its own. Tomatoes you preserve yourself also have less sodium and fewer preservatives and none of the scary stuff that leaches out of aluminum cans.

There are two schools of thought when it comes to canning tomatoes. A lot of people recommend paste tomatoes. These are varieties like Roma, Amish Paste, and San Marzano. They are obvious candidates because they are meaty, not juicy, and have a high acid content. But I'm a fan of including tomatoes I enjoy eating raw. Yes, you will end up with jars that have a lot of tomato juice in them, but I like that. It tastes good. So for what it's worth my favorite combination is half Amish Paste, half Cherokee Purple. If you're able to put these together, it'll feel spiritual.

The recipe here is for preserving moderately seasoned, barely cooked tomatoes in a sealed glass jar. That's the way the country cooks of Eastern Carolina did it. Those jars rarely turned into spaghetti sauce. Instead, they became the base recipes for things like Tomato Chicken Macaroni (*page 268*) and Tomatoes and Rice (*page 269*).

10 pounds tomatoes of your choice	½ cup plus 1 tablespoon lemon juice	3 tablespoons salt
		3 tablespoons granulated sugar

Note: *You can use whatever size jar you like here, but I recommend wide-mouthed jars over their narrow-mouthed brethren for just about everything but storing toothbrushes.*

Bring a large pot of water up to a rolling boil and set up an ice bath nearby. Make a slit in the bottom of each tomato with a knife, and drop about 5 tomatoes at a time in the boiling water. Let the water come back to a boil and cook the tomatoes for about 45 seconds, or until you see their skins start to split. Using a slotted spoon or spider, transfer the tomatoes to the ice bath. Follow up with the other remaining tomatoes.

Peel the tomatoes and discard the skins. Cut each tomato into quarters and cut out the white, starchy core. Transfer the cored and quartered tomatoes to an 8- to 10-quart heavy-bottomed pot. Bring the tomatoes up to a boil and skim off any scum that rises to the surface.

Meanwhile, sterilize your jars according to the instructions on page 16, and put 1 tablespoon of lemon juice, 1 teaspoon of salt, and 1 teaspoon of sugar per 1 pint of tomatoes in the bottom of each jar. If you are using quart jars, you'll need to double those amounts.

Once the tomatoes have been at a rolling boil for about 3 minutes, fill the hot jars with hot tomatoes. Put the lids on and process in a hot-water bath (*page 16*) for 10 minutes.

Tomatoes and Rice

Tomato Chicken
Macaroni

Tomato Chicken Macaroni

Serves 5

ALTHOUGH IT'S SIMPLE TO MAKE, this does take a little time, so plan ahead. And yes, if you must you can use leftover meat from a roast chicken and both broth and canned tomatoes from the supermarket. But I beg you, if at all possible, go the distance and make it the way I suggest. The end result is a window into what we miss when we rely on the grocery store to do our prep work.

1 young chicken, 2½ to 3 pounds	1 quart Tomatoes in Jars (*page 264*)	½ pound uncooked macaroni (1¾ cups)
1 yellow onion, peeled and split in half	2½ teaspoons salt	1 tablespoon butter
	¼ teaspoon chili flakes	

Rinse your chicken and remove the giblets and liver. Place the neck and the bird, breast-side up, in a 6- to 8-quart Dutch oven along with the onion. Barely cover the bird with cool water, and bring it up to a boil. Cover and reduce to a simmer. Cook the chicken till it's falling to pieces. This could take anywhere from 45 minutes to 1½ hours. Remove it from the heat and let it sit in the broth for 30 minutes.

Discard the cooked onion. Take the chicken out and strain the broth. Return the broth to the pot and reduce the liquid to 1 quart. Pick all the chicken from the carcass. You'll end up with about 2½ cups, but you'll need only 1½ cups for this recipe. Reserve the rest for something else.

Add the tomatoes (juice and all) and chicken to the broth and season it with the salt and chili flakes. Bring it up to a boil and add the macaroni. Cook for 7 minutes. Remove it from the heat. Stir in the butter and serve right away.

It's going to be slightly brothy, so if you don't go ahead and serve it, the pasta will swell to absorb the remaining liquid. It will still taste good, but you'll have some very soft noodles.

Tomatoes and Rice

Makes 5 cups

I COULD RHAPSODIZE ABOUT THIS DISH forever. It's great cooking that anyone can manage. Mom made this once a week to serve alongside hamburger patties browned in a cast-iron skillet.

Unlike the red rice on page 302, the rice and tomatoes here should be distinct from one another. It's not rice cooked in tomato juice; it's cooked rice mingled with tomatoes and their juice. There's a big difference.

1 cup rice (either white or brown is fine)	2 teaspoons salt, divided
2 cups water	1 quart canned tomatoes
	1 teaspoon granulated sugar
	10 turns of the pepper mill or ¼ teaspoon black pepper

Combine the rice, the water, and 1 teaspoon salt in a 3- to 4-quart saucepan. Bring it up to a simmer and cook, stirring occasionally to make sure the rice doesn't stick to the bottom, for about 15 minutes or until the rice is just barely tender. Add the tomatoes, remaining salt, sugar, and black pepper. Cover and cook 3 more minutes. Serve within 10 minutes. You could wait longer but the consistency of the rice may change.

Stewed Tomatoes

Makes a generous 5 cups

I CAN'T THINK OF ANYTHING MORE versatile and delicious than these tomatoes. I eat them by themselves. I eat them over rice, tossed with pasta, as a friend for fish, underneath steak, baked with eggs (*page 55*), and spooned next to squash (*page 346*). They are my ketchup, my marinara.

Stewed tomatoes balance a lot of my plates and are a component for several recipes in this book. Make them with fresh tomatoes if possible, but canned will work in the wintertime. If gluten is a problem for you, try whisking in a third of a cup of cornmeal to thicken it up instead of using bread crumbs, or leave the starch out altogether for a slightly looser end result.

2 tablespoons butter	1 tablespoon red wine vinegar
2 yellow onions, small-diced	¼ teaspoon chili flakes
3 teaspoons salt, divided	1 large stem fresh basil (about ¼ cup of leaves, packed)
8 tomatoes, diced, with all the juice	½ cup bread crumbs, preferably homemade
4 garlic cloves, sliced	
2 tablespoons light brown sugar	

In a 4- to 6-quart heavy-bottomed saucepan or Dutch oven, melt 2 tablespoons of butter. Add the onions and 1 teaspoon of salt. Cook the onions over medium heat for about 10 minutes until they have caramelized slightly. Add the tomatoes, remaining salt, garlic, sugar, vinegar, chili flakes, and basil. Cover and bring it up to a boil. Cook for 30 minutes. Uncover. Add the bread crumbs and cook an additional 5 minutes. The bread will cause the tomatoes to thicken up slightly. Serve warm, but be aware these are even better the next day.

Roasted and Fresh Tomato Pie

Makes a 10-inch pie

AS SOON AS THE FIRST TOMATO BLOSSOM turns into a tiny green orb, people start calling Chef and the Farmer to find out if tomato pie is on the menu. In a restaurant where we sell more big hunks of meat than I'd like to admit, tomato pie outsells everything all summer. If you have access to two different colors of tomatoes, combine them here—one for the roasted portion and another for the fresh. It's a nice visual touch.

And if you're up for making the filling but not the crust, buy a store-bought crust and know that I've done it too.

1	tablespoon butter	2	tablespoons extra-virgin olive oil
1	large yellow onion, halved and cut into julienne with the grain	10	turns of the pepper mill or ¼ teaspoon black pepper
2	teaspoons salt, divided	⅓	cup picked basil leaves
3½	pounds tomatoes cut into ½-inch dice, divided	½	cup mayonnaise
1	teaspoon granulated sugar, divided	⅓	cup grated Fontina
1	teaspoon picked thyme	⅓	cup grated Parmigiano-Reggiano

Pie Crust

1¼	cups all-purpose flour
2½	teaspoons granulated sugar
½	teaspoon salt
6	tablespoons cold butter cut into ½-inch cubes
2	tablespoons ice-cold water
½	teaspoon white vinegar

Make the crust: Place the flour, sugar, and salt in the bowl of a mixer fitted with the paddle attachment. Mix on medium for a few seconds. Then begin adding the butter one cube at a time. Continue until the flour is speckled and crumbly. With the mixer still running, add the water and vinegar until just combined. Do not overmix. Lay roughly a 10 x 10-inch square of plastic wrap on the counter in front of you and turn the dough out onto it. Wrap the dough tightly in the plastic wrap and chill in the refrigerator overnight.

Bring the crust to room temperature. Dust your counter and rolling pin lightly with flour and roll the crust slightly larger than your pie pan. Lay the crust in the pan and press gently into its edges. Cut off the edges that hang over and discard. Freeze the crust in the pie pan for at least 15 minutes or until you're ready to blind-bake.

Preheat the oven to 400°F. Lay foil or parchment paper on top of the crust and weight that down with dried beans or rice. Blind-bake for 30 minutes.

Make the filling and topping: Preheat your oven to 375°F. In a medium sauté pan or skillet, melt the butter and add the onions and ½ teaspoon salt. Cook the onions over

medium-low heat till they are deeply caramelized. This will take about 40 minutes. If your onions get away from you and burn a little, add ¼ cup of water to the pan, scrape up the overbrowned bits, and keep going. In the end, you'll have a scant ⅔ cup caramelized onions.

Toss half the tomatoes with ½ teaspoon salt and ½ teaspoon sugar. Set them over a colander and let them drain while you get everything else ready, at least 30 minutes.

Toss the remaining tomatoes with ½ teaspoon salt, the thyme, and the olive oil. Spread them out in a single layer on a sheet tray with as much room separating the individual pieces as possible. Slide the

tray onto the middle rack of your oven and roast for 20 to 30 minutes. You're looking for the tomatoes to dry out and brown slightly.

Once all the individual components are done, stir together the onions, the fresh tomatoes, the roasted tomatoes, the remaining salt and sugar, black pepper, and basil. In a separate, smaller bowl, stir together the mayonnaise, Fontina, and Parm.

Spoon the filling into your blind-baked crust and crown it with the mayo-and-cheese topping. Bake in the middle rack of your oven for 30 minutes. You can serve this warm or at room temperature. Both have their virtues.

Cherry Tomatoes in Basil Vinegar

Makes 4 cups

I'M DOING EVERYTHING I CAN in this book to avoid seeming precious or "chef-y," because I really want you to make this food I love so much. But please forgive me when I recommend something fussy: peeling tomatoes. In the right place, the simple act of taking the thin, somewhat distracting skin off a tomato elevates what's already worship-worthy. Plus, my grandma did it. She just took a sharp knife to the outside of large slicing tomatoes and gently worked away the skin. She'd season peeled tomatoes with salt, pepper, and a little sugar and serve them on a summer buffet just like that.

I like peeling all kinds of tomatoes and particularly enjoy eating skinless cherry tomatoes in salads. These take a little planning and time to execute, but they aren't forgettable. The resulting vinegar, which all on its own is useful in vinaigrettes, takes advantage of an oversupply of flowering basil, which I always seem to have when tomatoes are at their peak.

Use these little guys as part of a pickle plate, to balance simple Stewed Fresh Butterbeans (*page 153*), Slow-Cooked Limas (*page 166*), or Corn and Snap Bean Succotash (*page 229*). Or set them out with something creamy like Buttermilk Blue Cheese Dressing (*page 514*) or Smoked Corn Mayo (*page 262*) as an hors d'oeuvre. And if there's someone who just tricks your trigger, give him or her these as a gift. I know I'd be pleased.

2 **cups basil leaves**	2 **teaspoons salt**	4 **cups cherry tomatoes (different shapes and colors would be ideal)**
4 **black peppercorns**	2½ **cups rice wine vinegar**	
⅓ **cup granulated sugar**		3 **large sprigs basil**

Make the vinegar: Cram a glass quart jar with about 2 cups basil leaves. A few stems and flowers are okay. Drop in the peppercorns, sugar, and salt. Pour the vinegar over top. Screw a lid on and shake to dissolve the sugar and salt. Let it sit for at least 3 days and up to 2 weeks in a dark spot before using. Strain out basil and peppercorns before you add the tomatoes, and add a few sprigs of fresh basil for a visual cue.

Peel and marinate the tomatoes: Bring a 4- to 6-quart pot of water to a boil and make a shallow *X* on the bottom of each tomato. Drop half of the tomatoes in the boiling water and cook for about 15 seconds, until the skins start to split. Remove the tomatoes and drop them into an ice bath. Once they are well chilled, peel away their skins and drop them into the basil vinegar. Repeat with the rest of the tomatoes.

Let them sit in the vinegar at least 2 days before using. They will keep refrigerated and improve slightly for up to 2 weeks. Do not can in a hot-water bath. The additional heat will damage the texture of the tomatoes.

BLT Dip

Serves 6

HOLLEY PEARCE, MY COORDINATOR OF CHAOS and close friend, loves food but doesn't do much cooking. We met because she dined in one of our restaurants four nights a week. When Holley, who's from Mississippi, started working with me, her lack of cooking skills became a running joke. One weekend, we had a little gathering at my office, and Pearce (as her friends call her) brought something she called BLT dip. She said it was just something her family had always taken to the beach. Unable to stop myself, I stood by it snacking till all that was left of the dip was a puddle of pink mayonnaise-y bliss.

This is not Holley's version but it is inspired by her spirit and the most majestic combination of flavors out there. I like to go retro and make white-bread triangle toast to serve this on, but you could use any type of crostini or chip.

Green Goddess
Makes 1 cup

- ½ cup mayonnaise
- ½ cup sour cream
- ½ cup picked basil leaves
- 2 tablespoons picked tarragon leaves
- 2 tablespoons lemon juice
- 2 anchovy fillets or 1 teaspoon anchovy paste
- 1 garlic clove, sliced
- ½ teaspoon granulated sugar
- ¼ teaspoon salt

Dip

- 3 medium tomatoes, small-diced
- 1 teaspoon salt, divided
- ½ teaspoon granulated sugar
- ½ head heart of Romaine
- 10 turns of the pepper mill or ¼ teaspoon black pepper
- 1 pound smoked bacon, cooked till crisp, then crumbled
- ⅓ cup thinly sliced scallions, green part only

Make the dressing: Combine everything in the blender and blend until completely smooth and green. Refrigerate till you're ready to use.

Make and assemble the dip: Toss the tomatoes together with ½ teaspoon of salt and the sugar. Set that over a colander to drain for about 30 minutes.

To prep the Romaine, cut off all but ¼ inch of the leafy portion of each piece of lettuce on either side of the stem and reserve that for another use. Chop the Romaine stems into ⅓-inch pieces. You should have about 1 cup Romaine stems.

Set aside about 2 tablespoons sliced scallions and ¼ cup Romaine stems for garnish. Then in a medium bowl, stir the tomatoes, black pepper, remaining salt, Romaine, and scallions together with the Green Goddess.

To serve, spoon the tomato mixture into a serving bowl. Top with the reserved Romaine stems followed by the bacon. Garnish with the scallions. Serve at room temperature.

Chilled Sun Gold Tomato Soup with Lots of Summer Stuff

Makes 7 cups

THIS IS NOT A GAZPACHO. It's a chilled soup we sometimes treat like a sauce (Rice-Crusted Catfish, *page 304*). Soup or sauce, its flavor triggers my taste memory of Campbell's from a can (in a very good way). Little Sun Gold cherry tomatoes are my favorite here, but not having them shouldn't be a deal breaker. Any sweet cherry, teardrop, or grape tomato variety will suffice.

I recommend passing the soup through a fine-mesh strainer to give it an ultrasmooth texture, but you can skip that if you like.

2 yellow onions, diced

4 garlic cloves, smashed

2 teaspoons salt, divided

2 tablespoons extra-virgin olive oil

8 cups Sun Gold cherry tomatoes

1 bay leaf

¼ teaspoon chili flakes

5 cups water

⅔ cup buttermilk

¼ cup heavy cream

1 tablespoon sherry vinegar

Summer Garnish

1 cup sweet corn, cut off the cob

1 cup of your favorite tomatoes, small-diced or quartered if they are cherry or grape

1 cup diced peaches or cantaloupe

1 cup diced cucumber

2 tablespoons chopped or torn soft herbs; basil, tarragon, chervil, mint, and cilantro are all good choices

1 tablespoon minced chives

1 teaspoon salt

1 tablespoon lemon juice

2 tablespoons olive oil for finishing

Make the soup: In a 4- to 6-quart saucepan or Dutch oven, sweat the onion, garlic, and ½ teaspoon of the salt in the olive oil for about 10 minutes. Add the cherry tomatoes, bay leaf, chili flakes, and water just to cover. Bring it up to boil and cook at a steady simmer, uncovered, till the liquid has reduced by half, about 30 minutes.

Remove the bay leaf and allow the tomato mixture to cool slightly. Transfer it, along with the buttermilk, heavy cream, sherry vinegar, and remaining 1½ teaspoons salt to a blender. Blend it up till smooth. I recommend doing this in batches to prevent a massive hot kitchen mess.

Pass the blended soup through a fine-mesh sieve and give it a good stir to make sure everything is incorporated evenly. Chill it down completely and taste for seasoning. Because all tomatoes are a little different, you may need to adjust the seasoning with salt, sugar, vinegar, or cream.

Make the garnish and serve: In a medium bowl, stir everything together and let it hang out, refrigerated, for about 10 minutes while the flavors marry. Serve the chilled summer stuff on top of the chilled soup on a hot day.

Cocktail Tomatoes with Brown-Butter Scallops

Serves 4

TO CALL THESE TOMATOES A STAPLE in our restaurant's kitchen is shortchanging their impact.

Infused with the flavors of cocktail sauce, these tomatoes show up alongside many things that come from the sea. We also blend or chop them into sauces, use them as a garnish for bloody Marys, put them on top of deviled eggs, slice them onto pimento cheese sandwiches, and plop them on top of a burger. Even the liquid by-product is distinctive when used as a marinade for shrimp or as a base for vinaigrettes.

Let the tomatoes cure for one week before you use them and make sure they are completely submerged in the liquid. Kept that way, refrigerated, they'll last for up to three months.

Cocktail Tomatoes
Makes 4 quarts

- 5 pounds Roma or other firm meaty tomatoes, quartered
- 1 bunch scallions, white and green parts, sliced thin
- 4 jalapeños, sliced thin
- Zest of 3 lemons, removed with a vegetable peeler
- 1 cup lemon juice
- 1 cup white wine vinegar
- ½ cup prepared horseradish
- ⅓ cup Worcestershire sauce
- 2 tablespoons salt
- ⅔ cup granulated sugar
- ⅓ cup molasses
- 2 cups extra-virgin olive oil
- ⅓ cup chopped garlic
- 3 tablespoons ground coriander
- 2 tablespoons ground cumin
- 1 tablespoon ground celery seeds
- 1 tablespoon cayenne

Brown-Butter Scallops
Serves 4

- 1 pound dry-packed scallops (about 12)
- 2 teaspoons salt
- ½ teaspoon cayenne
- 2 teaspoons vegetable oil, divided
- 3 tablespoons butter, divided
- 2 cups Cocktail Tomatoes plus ½ cup reserved liquid

Make the tomatoes: Place the quartered tomatoes in a 6- to 8-quart glass or heatproof plastic container and set aside. Bring the remaining ingredients up to a bare boil in a 4-quart saucepan or Dutch oven. Carefully pour the hot liquid over the tomatoes. Let them cool at room temperature overnight. Then transfer them, covered, to the refrigerator and let them cure for a minimum of 1 week before using.

Cook and serve the scallops: Remove and discard the connector muscle from the scallops and dry them well with a paper towel. Preheat your oven to 200°F and

high heat. Add half the scallops, making sure they do not touch one another, and cook on the first side for 2 minutes. They should be nicely caramelized around the edges at the very least. With any luck they'll be picture-quality seared all over the top. Flip and cook on the other side for 30 seconds. Transfer the first round to the oven and quickly wipe out the pan.

Add the remaining oil and 1 more teaspoon butter. Brown the final batch of scallops on 1 side for 2 minutes. Flip them over and add the remaining butter to the pan. Let it sizzle and foam while the scallops cook on that other side for 30 seconds. Remove the scallops from the pan and transfer them to the oven. Continue to heat the butter till it smells nutty and has browned slightly, about 1 minute. Stir in the

season the scallops on both sides with the salt and cayenne.

In a 10-inch cast-iron skillet, heat 1 teaspoon oil and 1 teaspoon butter over

tomatoes and their liquid. Watch it come up to a quick bubble.

Serve immediately under the scallops with Foolproof Grits (*page 31*).

Carolina Gold

Brown

Uncle Ben's

Black

Rice Grits

MY MOM'S LIFELONG BOUT with rheumatoid arthritis has included many difficult surgeries and experimental treatments. Through it all, Mom raised four girls, taught school, and bred Doberman pinschers for spending money. As you might imagine (or have read in this book), meals were simple at my house. Mom didn't fry chicken, can pickles, or roll out biscuits. Instead, when Scarlett geared up to make a soul-warming meal for our family, it was almost always a pot of chicken and rice. This was our comfort food, *the* dish of my childhood, and probably the only thing my sisters and I all prepare for our children.

As a chef (and arrogant daughter), I felt I could improve on my mom's chicken and rice. I had watched her do it so many times, and each time I just *knew* she was cooking that chicken way too long. I believed the addition of a few aromatics like onion, garlic, and thyme would make what was already very tasty start to blow people's minds. So when my frail seventy-year-old mom went under the knife for her second shoulder replacement, I decided to make her individual portions of chicken and rice for her recovery. Although never the nurturing kind, I was pregnant with the twins at the time and was starting to look at all my relationships a little differently. For me, a big bowl of chicken and rice glistening with fat and thick as porridge was exactly what I craved when I was nursing a cold, a broken heart, or a hangover. Surely my gesture would nourish Mom in the same way.

Two days prior to her return from the Mayo Clinic, I made a rich, roasted chicken stock using backs, necks, feet, garlic, bay leaves, and mirepoix. I chilled the stock overnight and scooped off the fat the following day. Then I covered three whole chickens with the gelatinous, brown culinary wonder and brought it up to a simmer. I simmered the chickens for 10 minutes, turned off the heat, covered the pot, and let it sit for an hour. At this point I was feeling like a genius and had started to daydream

about improving the preparation of several other iconic Southern dishes. Generations to come would thank me.

Next I removed the chickens and tasted the broth.

"Hmmm. It tastes like onions, garlic, and roasted bones? Well, I'll add some salt and black pepper." Black pepper was, after all, the one spice my mom used in excess.

"Oh, and maybe I should add some herbs, some thyme and rosemary, just to round out that oniony aroma?"

I always felt like mom's chicken and rice would have been better if it were just a little more soupy, so I forwent her measurement of one part rice to three parts broth and poured in one cup rice for every four cups of liquid. I covered the pot, turned on the heat, and went about picking the chicken from the carcass. These were some perfectly poached chickens. The juice and fat running between my fingers pleased me;

patted me on the back, even. I was going to make her proud.

In fifteen minutes I removed the lid and stared into what looked like dark stock with some rice floating in it. It was definitely too soupy, so I decided to just let it go a little longer. I'm not sure what I thought this would do, and actually I knew it was a bad idea, but all of a sudden I felt desperate and had forgotten how to cook. Five minutes later, my rice had burst, broken its shape (the cardinal sin of rice cooking), *and* it was still floating in cups of broth. This was not at all what I had intended. In minutes I would have a nasty country congee Scarlett would most definitely not eat.

"Okay, so I'll add all the chicken really fast with the heat off, cool down the broth, and stop the rice from bursting any further. I can save it!"

I most certainly could not save it. I did add all the chicken back to the pot, seasoned the hell out of the mess, and got the flavor to at least an acceptable place...for

RECIPES

Scarlett's Chicken and Rice

Perfect Rice with Herb Butter

Buttermilk Orange Rice Pudding with Pistachio

Crispy Ginger Rice with Leeks, Shiitakes, and a Fried Egg

Sprouted Hoppin' John Salad with Hot Bacon Vinaigrette

Country Ham and Celery Creamed Rice

Cast-Iron-Cooked Red Rice and Softshell Scampi

Rice-Crusted Catfish with Cilantro-Lime Sweet Corn and Sun Gold Sauce

my misguided palate. After chilling it down, I vacuum-sealed twenty small portions for my mom, drove them over to her house, and nestled them in her freezer.

When Mom got home, she was scary-thin, weak, and a little bit crazy-acting. I was seven months pregnant with two babies, scary-big, and also crazy-acting. I told Mom I had made chicken and rice for her to have through her recovery, and she rolled her eyes. I did my best to overlook the reaction and carried on. A week later I walked over to my mom's to check her reserves and found that only one bag was missing.

"Mom, don't forget about that chicken and rice in the freezer. You have a lot of it," I called from her stocked freezer to where she lay on the sofa, covered in blankets.

"Ugh. It's not good. You can't make it. Take it with you. I don't want it," Mom complained with a grimace, eyes still closed.

Okay, so I knew my chicken and rice didn't top the charts, but my mom was actually pissed off about the heartfelt gesture I had made. Enough was enough—if she wouldn't receive my gift graciously, then yeah, I'd take it back. I reached in the freezer, inverted my maternity shirt to reveal my stretched-to-the-limit belly, and shoveled the remaining nineteen packets into my top. I waddled across the yard to my house, flung frozen packets of chicken and rice all over the living room, threw myself onto the sofa, and cried.

Perhaps I overreacted. I was hurt that my mom didn't just eat my chicken and rice and say thank you. I'm guessing she was hurt that I'd felt I could make it better. Once my mom recovered and I'd had my babies, I asked to watch her make chicken and rice her way and took an honest interest in the food of my mother's kitchen. I learned that simplicity is very hard to pull off, and there are some recipes you just don't mess with.

Two years later, I cooked a career-defining meal for the Southern Foodways Alliance Symposium in Oxford, Mississippi. I literally worked for months to make the meal stand out in terms of technique, flavor, and emotion, and I designed each course to honor the women who made me the woman I am. The tables were set with feminine china, doilies, and ornate iced-tea glasses. Small photo albums populated by pictures of my family dotted every table. My parents traveled from North Carolina for the lunch and looked proud and frightened and out of place.

I cooked vegetables to honor my grandma Hill, Tom Thumb for Grandmother Iris, and chicken and rice for my mom. This event is known among food enthusiasts as a big deal, but I was most nervous about what Mom would think of the chicken and rice. I boiled twenty-five laying hens till they were "falling to pieces" and relied on salt, pepper, rice, water, and my mom's instructions for the rest. When all was said and done, Mom told me the chicken and rice was "very good" and that she ate the whole bowl. Once again, she made me cry.

RICE WISDOM

What Type of Rice Will Work?

I TESTED ALL THE RECIPES in this chapter using long-grain rice, or rice that is three times as long as it is fat. Carolina, jasmine, Uncle Ben's, and basmati all work here, and I prefer them in that order.

Weighing Uncle Ben's Against Carolina Gold (Gasp!)

I MAKE A LOT OF FUSS over Carolina Gold rice. It's like comparing a Cherokee Purple tomato to a commonplace Better Boy. The Better Boy is a tomato, the Uncle Ben's of rice. It does the trick, and one right out of the field even suits me on a tomato sandwich. They are easy to grow, easier to store, and have a firmer texture than their heirloom cousins. Cherokee Purples, by contrast, are finicky in the field and fussy after harvest. Even with all that, you'd be hard-pressed to find a person

with a mouth who prefers the eating experience of Better Boys over that of Cherokee Purples.

For the home cook, Carolina Gold is harder to source, harder to store, and arguably harder to cook than Uncle Ben's. But the texture, fragrance, color, mouthfeel, and flavor of this heirloom grain are worth it. My mom disagrees. She's a huge fan of Uncle Ben's. I too respect its ease of use now that I have kids.

Cooking in Advance

WHEN WE SERVE RICE in the restaurant, we often cook it ahead of time and chill it down quickly on sheet trays. I like this method at home as well. It allows me to get a step that requires attention out of the way before guests arrive. Uncooked rice makes a nifty pie weight. As crusts blind-bake, the rice toasts and takes on another dimension of flavor.

Scarlett's Chicken and Rice

Makes 4 quarts

ALSO CALLED A "BOG" in parts of the South, chicken and rice was a stand-alone meal at my house. Nowadays, I like to serve it with a bright salad of Romaine, thinly sliced celery, herbs like parsley and chives, and a mustard vinaigrette. Mom is fine with it.

Note: *Today most people make this with a young chicken from the store. If you were to run across a laying hen past her egg-dropping prime, beg for her and make a pot of chicken and rice. That hen will take up to four hours to "cook to pieces," but the broth she'll offer up will be well worth the time.*

- 1 large chicken and its neck left whole, gizzards removed
- 3 quarts cool water, or just enough to cover the bird
- 1½ to 2 tablespoons salt
- 40 to 60 grinds of the pepper mill, or 2 to 3 teaspoons black pepper
- 2 cups white rice
- 2 tablespoons lemon juice

Put your bird breast up in a 6- to 8-quart heavy-bottomed pot or Dutch oven. Cover the bird, just barely, with cool water. Add the salt and 2 teaspoons pepper. Cover and bring it all up to a simmer. Cook for about an hour or until the bird is, in my mom's words, "falling to pieces."

If you're working with a typical young chicken this should not take any longer than an hour and a half. If it is a laying hen, it could take up to 5 hours. I know that sounds crazy, but a hen will provide a much better broth.

Once the bird is falling to pieces turn off the heat and let it rest in the broth for 30 minutes. Take the chicken out of the broth and tear the meat into medium pieces. Discard the skin and bones. Put the meat back into the pot. Bring the broth and the chicken up to a simmer. Add the rice. If you are a rice rinser, resist the urge here, as the starch helps make the broth homey and rich. Cook the rice for about 12 minutes; depending on the variety or brand, the time may vary. The rice should be just cooked through and should absolutely hold its shape. Turn off the heat. Add the lemon juice and the remaining teaspoon black pepper if you wish.

Perfect Rice with Herb Butter

Makes 3 cups rice

PERFECT IS A STRONG WORD. I use it here because this method allows you to cook rice like pasta till it's done to your liking. It also gives you the ability to reheat the rice without worrying over whether or not it will get all gummy and gross.

Rice

- 3 quarts water
- 1 tablespoon salt
- 1 cup long-grain rice

Herb Butter

Makes ⅔ cup butter

- 8 tablespoons (1 stick) butter
- ⅓ cup packed basil leaves

- 2 tablespoons packed mint leaves
- 2 tablespoons packed parsley leaves
- Zest and juice of 1 lemon
- ½ teaspoon salt

Make the herb butter: Bring your butter to room temperature. If it's truly room temperature, your finger will make an indentation by the pressure of its weight. Okay?

Once you've got soft butter, dump the basil, mint, and parsley into the bowl of a food processor. Process for about 15 seconds, just to get things broken down a bit. Add the butter, lemon zest and juice, and salt, and process until the butter is nice and green and the herbs are finely minced.

If you're going to use the butter right away, do not refrigerate. If you plan on using the butter later, it will keep, covered, in the fridge for up to a week. But make sure it's room temperature before you pop a dollop on the rice.

Cook the rice: Bring the water and the salt to a boil in a 4-quart saucepan. Add your rice and give it a stir. Cook the rice at a gentle boil till it's just tender. Depending on the variety you've chosen, this will take between 10 and 20 minutes.

If you plan to serve the rice right away, drain it in a colander, turn it out into serving bowls, and top each serving with 2 teaspoons herb butter.

If you want to serve your rice later, drain it in a colander and run cool water over it briefly. Transfer the rice to a cookie sheet. Spread it out into a single layer and pop it in the fridge. Once it's completely cooled, cover it with foil. When you're ready to serve the rice, heat it covered in a 350°F oven for 20 minutes. It should be warm, fluffy, and primed to melt some butter.

Buttermilk Orange Rice Pudding with Pistachio

Makes about 3 cups

MY RESEARCH ON THE SUBJECT shows you either grew up on rice pudding and can't imagine a more transcendent sweet or you grew up looking at the congealed cups of it in the cafeteria and can't imagine eating it. Until recently I was a member of the latter group. But winter and an absence of fresh fruit will make a chef do desperate things. Several Februarys ago, I made rice pudding that, to my surprise, was the type of dessert I wanted to eat while curled up on the couch under a blanket.

I very much like this warm, but some people think that's strange. You choose.

- ½ cup long-grain rice
- ½ cup granulated sugar
- 4 cups whole milk
- Half a vanilla bean, split and scraped
- 1 whole star anise
- 1 3-inch cinnamon stick
- Zest of ½ orange, removed with a Microplane
- ⅛ teaspoon freshly grated nutmeg
- ⅛ teaspoon salt
- ½ cup buttermilk
- ½ cup chopped pistachios

In a 2-quart sauté pan or saucepan, stir together the rice, sugar, milk, vanilla bean, star anise, cinnamon stick, orange zest, nutmeg, and salt. Slowly bring it up to a simmer over medium heat. Stir it every 2 minutes or so, watching to make sure the bottom of the pan doesn't scorch and that the milk doesn't boil over. Lower the heat a touch and cook the pudding for 30 minutes, stirring frequently. It will begin to thicken after about 8 minutes. After 30 minutes the rice will still be a little soupy, but remove it from the heat and let it sit for 10 minutes. Once you're ready to serve, stir in the buttermilk, sprinkle with chopped pistachios, and go for it.

Crispy Ginger Rice with Leeks, Shiitakes, and a Fried Egg

Serves 2

MY MOM GENERALLY MADE a pot of rice for supper. What we didn't eat, she left in the pot overnight. The next morning she heated a little bacon grease in a small pan and crisped up that rice for breakfast. We usually ate it with sausage and eggs. This is my homage to rice for breakfast.

It's really a game plan for transforming leftover rice into something new and special. You can go wild using anything you have in your refrigerator. Just know so much of the success of this dish is tied to letting the rice sit undisturbed in the hot fat. Resist the urge to stir!

- ½ cup long-grain rice
- 3 tablespoons butter, divided
- 1 tablespoon vegetable oil
- 1 cup diced shiitake mushrooms (you can substitute any mushroom you like)
- 1 heaping tablespoon minced ginger
- 1 teaspoon minced garlic
- 1 cup leeks, white part only, sliced ¼ inch thick
- ¼ teaspoon chili flakes
- 1 teaspoon salt, divided
- 2 large eggs
- 2 tablespoons picked cilantro

Cook the rice according to the instructions on page 292, and let it sit uncovered in the refrigerator a minimum of an hour and up to overnight. This allows the rice to dehydrate slightly and will make it crispier in the end.

In a 10- to 12-inch sauté pan, heat 1 tablespoon butter and the vegetable oil over medium heat until foaming. Add the shiitakes. Shake the pan once and let the mushrooms sit and caramelize for 2 minutes. Drop in the ginger. Then add 1 tablespoon butter followed by the cooked rice. Press it into a thin layer over the surface area of the entire pan. Once you've pressed the rice out, leave it there, resisting the urge to shake or stir. To the top of the rice, add the garlic, leeks, chili flakes, and ½ teaspoon salt. After about 3 minutes,

turn up a little rice on the edge of the pan with a spatula. Assuming it's started to take on a slight golden color and crispy texture, stir in the ingredients that were sitting on top and press the rice down again into a homogenous layer. Let it go another 2 minutes before removing it from the heat.

Cook the eggs and serve: In a 10-inch cast-iron skillet or whatever pan you prefer for cooking eggs, heat the remaining butter over medium heat until foaming. Crack the eggs on opposite sides of the pan. Cook gently about 2 minutes, until the whites are set. Sprinkle the eggs with the remaining ½ teaspoon salt.

Fluff the rice and serve under a runny egg. Garnish with cilantro.

Sprouted Hoppin' John Salad with Hot Bacon Vinaigrette

Serves 4

MY MENTOR SCOTT BARTON told me during a lesson on the subject that Hoppin' John was fundamentally rice and peas with some sort of smoked-pork product. I took some liberties with this salad, but according to Scott's rule, it's still Hoppin' John. It's also a riff on fresh spinach with hot bacon vinaigrette—the salad that turned me on to salad.

1 cup Perfect Rice *(page 292)*

1 cup field pea sprouts *(page 165)*

1 cup baby arugula

½ red bell pepper, julienned

½ teaspoon salt

6 turns of the pepper mill or ⅛ teaspoon black pepper

Hot Bacon Vinaigrette

8 ounces sliced bacon

¼ cup thinly sliced scallion, white part only

1 garlic clove, grated on a mandoline

2 tablespoons sherry vinegar

1 teaspoon lemon juice

1 teaspoon honey

1 teaspoon smooth Dijon mustard

¼ teaspoon salt

In a medium bowl, toss the rice, sprouted peas, arugula, red bell pepper, salt, and the black pepper together. Set aside

In a 10- to 12-inch sauté pan, cook the bacon till crisp. Transfer the bacon to a plate. Crumble it up and reserve. Pour off the bacon fat and reserve 2 tablespoons for the dressing.

Add those 2 tablespoons of fat back to the pan. Over medium heat, stir in the scallion and let it sizzle for 10 seconds.

Then quickly add the garlic followed by the vinegar, lemon juice, honey, Dijon, and salt. With a wooden spoon scrape all the little bacon bits, or fond, from the bottom of the pan. Once the dressing begins bubbling furiously, pour it over the salad. Stir it up and serve with the crumbled bacon on top. The arugula will wilt, and that's the point.

Country Ham and Celery Creamed Rice

Makes 4 cups

In 2010, Ashley Christensen, of Poole's Diner, invited me to be one of five chefs to cook at a festival in Asheville, North Carolina. This doesn't sound like a big deal now, but at the time I didn't have any chef friends and wasn't part of a culinary community…and I wanted to be. I wasn't even sure how I might relate to or stack up against my peers. I was working in a bubble.

I didn't know it, but an invitation to cook on an intimate level with other chefs is a powerful thing. At events, you make friends, you talk shop, and as a result you end up spreading the word about your new friend who's doing really cool stuff.

The first event of the festival was a risotto competition. I had put all my creative energy into the next event's dish, and risotto is not my specialty, so my goal was to avoid embarrassing myself. Playing it safe, I put some flavors together I knew would work and used a rice I was familiar with (Carolina Gold).

I'll be damned if there weren't tears shed over my country ham and celery creamed rice. The other chefs were high-fiving me and dreaming up the next time we could cook together. Here's a streamlined version of the dish that earned me many more invitations to cook.

Note: *Ask the butcher at your grocery store to shave country ham as thin as possible. If country ham is not an option for you, prosciutto or serrano ham will work fine. Just make sure the slices are so thin they are nearly transparent.*

This recipe calls for pot liquor. If you follow the directions for Stewed Collard Greens with Ham Hock (page 426), the salt level will be right on. If you go rogue and use your own, taste it beforehand and adjust.

Creamed Rice

- **2** tablespoons butter, divided
- **1** small yellow onion, small-diced
- **1** teaspoon salt, divided
- **2** stalks celery, small-diced
- **2** garlic cloves, sliced thin
- **1** cup long-grain rice
- **20** turns of the pepper mill or ½ teaspoon black pepper
- **¼** cup white wine
- **2** cups pot liquor, reserved from cooking greens with pork as seasoning
- **1** cup water
- **2** ounces country ham or prosciutto, shaved very thin and cut into ribbons
- **¼** cup heavy cream, whipped to medium-stiff peaks

Celery Herb Salad

- Zest of ½ orange
- **¼** teaspoon salt
- **2** tablespoons lemon juice
- **⅓** cup celery leaves, picked
- **⅓** cup parsley leaves, picked
- **⅓** cup chervil or watercress leaves, picked

As the rice cooks, mix the salad. In a medium bowl whisk the orange zest, salt, and lemon juice. Throw in the celery leaves and the herbs and toss gently to coat. Set aside.

Once nearly all the liquid has evaporated from the rice, add the remaining pot liquor and continue stirring frequently. Finally, add 1 cup water and the country ham. Cook and stir until the rice absorbs the water. The rice should be cooked through but not mushy. If it requires more cooking, add a little additional water. Once the rice is done, remove the pan from the heat and stir in the remaining butter. As you stir, the rice should spread and seem relaxed, not stiff. If you need to add a quarter cup more water to loosen it up, do so.

Just before putting the rice on the plate, stir in the whipped cream. The cream will wrap a fluffy pillow around every grain of rice for a short 5 minutes, so get the rice to the plates fast. Top with the salad.

Melt 1 tablespoon butter in a 10 to 12 inch sauté pan or brazier over medium heat. Add the onion and ½ teaspoon salt and sweat until translucent, about 5 minutes. Stir in the celery and garlic and cook another 2 minutes. Add the rice, the remaining salt, and the black pepper. Stir it around and let the rice toast for about 30 seconds. In one batch, add the white wine and ½ cup of the pot liquor. Keep stirring, making sure you scrape up any rice that's sticking to the bottom of the pan.

Cast Iron-Cooked Red Rice
and Softshell Scampi

Cast-Iron-Cooked Red Rice and Softshell Scampi

Serves 4

PEOPLE STRAIGHT UP LOSE THEIR MINDS when softshell crabs come into season. I like them too, but my favorite part of this dish is the complex flavor of this rice cooked with shrimp stock in the persistent heat of a cast-iron pan.

Note: *If you don't have shrimp shells lying around, just ask your fish market to save them for you, then make the stock in a large batch and freeze it so you don't have to go through the process again for a while.*

Shrimp Stock
Makes 2 quarts

- 1 yellow onion, large-diced
- 2 stalks celery
- 2 medium carrots
- 5 garlic cloves
- 1 tablespoon vegetable oil
- 1 pound raw shrimp shells
- 2 tablespoons tomato paste
- 2 bay leaves
- 2½ quarts water

Red Rice
Makes 4 cups

- 2 tablespoons butter
- 1 yellow onion, small-diced

- 1½ teaspoons salt, divided
- 3 garlic cloves, sliced
- 1 cup long-grain rice
- 1 teaspoon granulated sugar
- ½ teaspoon ancho chili powder
- ¼ teaspoon cayenne
- 2 bay leaves
- 2½ cups shrimp stock
- 1 fresh tomato, peeled and blended in the food processor

Softshell Scampi
Makes 4 crabs

- 1 cup Wondra flour (you can substitute all-purpose flour if needed)

- 1¼ teaspoons salt, divided
- ¼ teaspoon cayenne
- 4 live or frozen softshell crabs (any size is okay; I like jumbo)
- 8 tablespoons (1 stick) butter, divided
- 6 garlic cloves, grated on a Microplane
- ¼ teaspoon chili flakes
- Zest of 3 lemons
- ½ cup lemon juice
- 1 heaping cup picked basil leaves

Make the stock: In your food processor, grate the onion, celery, carrot, and garlic. If you don't have a food processor have lost the attachments, roughly chop the vegetables very small. Set them aside.

In a 4-quart heavy-bottomed pot or Dutch oven, heat the oil over medium heat until shimmering. Add the shrimp shells and cook, stirring, until they turn a deep crustacean pink and are lightly browned in spots. Add the grated vegetables and

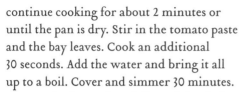

continue cooking for about 2 minutes or until the pan is dry. Stir in the tomato paste and the bay leaves. Cook an additional 30 seconds. Add the water and bring it all up to a boil. Cover and simmer 30 minutes.

Strain the stock and discard the shells. This makes more than you need for the recipe, so store it in the freezer for up to 3 months. If a seafood recipe calls for water, consider substituting this shrimp stock. It's a great way to add depth of sea flavor to all sorts of fish and shellfish dishes.

Make the rice: Melt the butter over medium heat in a 10-inch cast-iron pan. Add the onions, ½ teaspoon salt, and the garlic. Sweat for about 5 minutes. Stir in the rice and toast for 30 seconds. Add the sugar, chili powder, cayenne, bay leaves, stock, and blended tomato. Give it all a stir to incorporate fully and reduce the heat to low.

Step away and leave this guy alone. I know that's going to be hard, but please try. It will come up to a simmer slowly and should cook, uncovered, a scant 25 minutes. When the rice is done, all the liquid will be gone and the rice around the sides of the pan will begin to crisp.

Clean and cook the crabs: Start by stirring together the Wondra, 1 teaspoon salt, and cayenne. Pour the breader in a dish large enough to hold and dredge all 4 crabs. I like a 10 x 14-inch casserole dish.

Preparing live softshells is not for everyone. But it's important to start with a live crab or a frozen one from a reputable source. Frozen crabs will be cleaned when you buy them. They should be thawed quickly under cold running water and cooked shortly after.

To clean a softy, use kitchen shears and cut just behind its eyes to remove the face. Then lift up the shell flaps on either side and pull away and discard the feathery gills. Last, turn the crab over and cut away the apron. The apron looks different for male and female crabs. Just follow the outline and cut it away.

The crab will be quite wet at this point, making it perfect for dredging. Drag each crab through the seasoned flour and shake off any excess.

Heat 4 tablespoons of the butter in a 12-inch heavy-bottomed sauté pan or skillet. Once the butter is foaming, add the crabs, belly-side down. Cook over medium heat for 3 minutes. Flip the crabs and cook an additional 3 to 4 minutes until nicely browned on that side. Transfer the crabs to a paper-towel-lined plate while you build the sauce.

Throw the garlic and chili flakes into the pan and cook until they become fragrant. Add the lemon zest, juice, remaining salt, remaining butter, and basil. Cook till it bubbles briefly.

Serve the crabs over a big spoonful of the rice. Ladle the buttery sauce over top.

Rice-Crusted Catfish with
Cilantro-Lime Sweet Corn and Sun Gold Sauce

Serves 4

THIS CATFISH IS SPECIAL. I cooked it at the James Beard House in New York, and the experience was a nightmare. The fryer went out just as we dropped in our first fillet, so we had to panfry eighty orders of fish without warning. Thank God, because we learned that panfrying this piece of fish, breaded in this way, makes a tastier dinner.

I know ground rice sounds the same as rice flour, but it's not. What sets this apart is the coarseness of the grind. It creates a shatteringly crisp exterior without the clunky cake-y feeling of a traditional breading. You could pair this catfish with any number of items in this book…I have. But my favorite pairing is this one. I call it summer on a plate.

3 cups Cilantro-Lime Sweet Corn *(page 228)*	1 garlic clove, grated on a Microplane	½ cup long-grain rice
	Zest of 1 lemon	½ cup cornmeal
3 cups Sun Gold Tomato Soup *(page 279)*	2 teaspoons salt, divided	⅛ teaspoon cayenne
		½ teaspoon paprika
1½ cups buttermilk	4 6-ounce pieces catfish, cut in half	½ cup vegetable oil or lard

In a dish large enough to hold all the fish, whisk together the buttermilk, garlic, zest, and 1 teaspoon salt. Lay the catfish fillets in the buttermilk, making sure they are completely submerged. Refrigerate a minimum of 1 hour or up to overnight.

Meanwhile, grind the rice in a spice mill or high-powered blender until it is the texture of coarse cornmeal. Transfer it to a plate and stir in the cornmeal, remaining salt, cayenne, and paprika.

Remove the catfish fillets from the buttermilk and let any additional liquid drip off. Dredge each piece in the ground rice, knocking off the excess. Lay the fillets on a rack and refrigerate for a minimum of 1 hour. This step is not optional. If you skip it, the breading may flake off while frying.

Once you're ready to cook, heat the oil over medium heat in a 12-inch cast-iron skillet or heavy-bottomed sauté pan. Test the oil by dropping a little piece of the breader into it. If it sizzles right away, go ahead and lay 4 pieces of fish carefully in the oil. Adjust the heat so that things gently sizzle. The oil should not be smoking and it should take about a minute and a half for you to start seeing the sides begin to brown. Turn the fillets after 3 minutes. They should be chicken-nugget brown. Season the top with a little salt and cook an additional 3 minutes on the underside to give them the same color.

Drain on paper towels. Serve warm over Cilantro-Lime Sweet Corn (*page 228*) surrounded by Chilled Sun Gold Tomato Soup (*page 279*).

SWEET POTATOES

AT A CERTAIN POINT, Eastern Carolina itself, the flat part of the state called the coastal plain, became an ingredient in my pantry. If Szechuan dishes are defined by tongue-numbing peppercorns and the Provençal diet boasts bundles of herbs and olives, then Eastern Carolina's cuisine is at least partially shaped by sweet potatoes. No doubt we depend on a lot of other ingredients, like muscadines and butterbeans, but for the past century and a half, people have relied on a holy trinity of pork, cornbread, and sweet potatoes for everyday sustenance and flavor.

Historically, much of the rural South survived on ground corn and pork products, so that's not unique, but the sweet potato piece seems unusual till you look around and see that we grow more sweet potatoes in Eastern Carolina than anywhere else in the country. Over 50 percent of the nation's supply comes from our little region. Sweet potatoes, like tobacco, love our long, hot, humid summer as well as our sandy soil. And our pragmatic people love sweet potatoes.

My uncle Redding, who lived to be a hundred, ate a sweet potato every day of his life and made sure everybody he met knew it. My granddaddy Currin left for work in the fields with a roasted sweet potato in his pocket to ward off a midafternoon slump. All the women on both sides of my family had what they called a sweet potato pan, a round metal pan that stayed in the oven pretty much all the time. Rarely washed, it was lined with a brown paper bag in lieu of foil for each new batch of potatoes.

Sweet potatoes, at least in our kitchen, never saw the refrigerator. I'm not going to take on modern health codes here, but Mom took sweet potatoes from the porch potato bin and stuck them straight in the oven, where they sat after they'd been

roasted for up to two days. She preferred their flavor at room temperature and said their skin, which we never ate, protected them from spoiling.

Often my forays into Eastern Carolina's culinary fabric force me to look closer at some mundane part of my youth and question the how and why of it. It's odd that sweet potatoes were such a staple for us, but we only ate them one of two ways—roasted in their jackets or dolled up for yams. Why couldn't we have been like Bubba Gump, who lived on the bayou and ate shrimp a thousand different ways? When Grandma Hill made our candied yams, she made them only one way.

The youngest of ten children, Lorraine Hill began life as a farmer's daughter in Duplin County, North Carolina. Over time she became a farmer's wife, a mother, and eventually a grandmother. She moved and loved like someone whose work was never done and rarely noticed by anyone. Grandma Hill was strong, always digging in the yard under a white-brimmed hat or making work in her kitchen look easy. She was matter-of-fact, not warm and fuzzy. My mom always looked up to her, and my grandma always protected my mom.

I have this vision of Grandma Hill swinging open our glass porch door with her backside, two casserole dishes in hand and a red wool pencil skirt brushing

her stockinged calves. Her husband, Buck (Granddaddy Hill), died from Alzheimer's in his early sixties, so Grandma forged a life without him and was a fixture at most Sunday lunches and certainly every holiday in our house. Among other things, she always brought yams. Her yams weren't yams at all; that's just what we called sweet potatoes baked with brown sugar, butter, and spices.

I've tried hard not to compare people to food in this book, but I have no choice here. Everything about Grandma's candied yams personified the woman who made them. When lots of home cooks took to flourishes like toasted marshmallows or pecan streusel, Lorraine's work showed restraint. She'd been shaped by the Great Depression and lived every day like she was going to have less tomorrow. With just a touch of sugar, a dab of butter, and spare spices, her candied yams preached moderation too. Grandma's version of the classic reflected the degree to which she was a realist, a truth talker, and a pragmatic farmer's wife. Too much sugar was a bad thing, and she warned me on many occasions with a stern look and a swat to the hand that I was "plump enough."

Even without all the extra flair of whole cinnamon sticks or orange slices, Grandma Hill's candied yams were always the first thing finished at family gatherings. Like her, they were reliable and good. And although I never curled up in the marshmallowy warm cradle of Grandma's arms, and she never led me to believe I was the best or the brightest kid out there, I knew she was my family. I knew she was the way she was for a reason, and I knew what to expect when I rolled back the foil on her not-so-candied candied yams.

SWEET POTATO WISDOM

Sweet Potatoes Are Better

I LOVE THE TASTE AND TEXTURE of French fries, potato chips, baked potatoes, and mashed potatoes, but hate the guilt I feel when I eat them. The white potato offers little more than calories and carbohydrates, so I run from it like it's actual fat trying to attach itself to my thighs. That's why I try sweet potatoes and their super nutrition anywhere a white potato might be used.

Potatoes and Yams

WHEN I THINK OF A SWEET POTATO, I think of an elongated root with rose skin and orange, mildly sweet, creamy flesh. This is only one of two major types of true sweet potatoes. The others are a little harder and have a paler skin and yellow flesh. Both hail from South America. Although we throw the word *yam* around all the time, yams are not sweet potatoes. Yams are edible roots, but their skin is thicker and kind of scaly. Their flesh is dry, starchy, fibrous, and often stark white.

Even if I call them candied yams, I'm using the orange-fleshed sweet potatoes abundant in North Carolina, such as Covington, Beauregard, and Jewel.

Mashing and Blending

SWEET POTATOES have much less starch than white potatoes. There's no need to worry about throwing roasted sweet potato flesh in the food processor. You can blend it all day long and it won't become gluey.

Size and Sweetness

SOME PEOPLE BELIEVE small sweet potatoes are sweeter than big ones. Not all sweet potatoes taste the same, but I don't believe size is the determining factor. Small ones are ideal for roasting whole in their jackets, and we like big ones for peeling and cutting into shapes.

Sweet potatoes need to cure in a humid spot for four to seven days. Curing extends their shelf life and improves their flavor by transforming some of the starches into sugar.

Fat Makes Them Healthier!

SWEET POTATOES are naturally high in vitamin K, which is a fat-soluble vitamin. To absorb everything the root has in store for you, eat it with a little butter or oil.

Eat the Skin

I NEVER DREAMED of eating a sweet potato's skin till recently. For some reason it seemed off-limits. No more! Coated in a little oil, seasoned, and roasted, sweet potatoes with the skin left on are a new trend in our kitchen.

Roasted Sweet Potatoes in Their Jackets

Preheat your oven to 400°F. To make cleanup easier, line a baking pan with a paper bag or foil. Select sweet potatoes that are similar in size. You want them all to be done at about the same time, and this will help make that happen.

Place your potatoes on the baking sheet, and make sure they're not touching. Roast them on the middle rack of your oven. Once you start to smell them, probably after about 45 minutes, give the potatoes a look. My mom always looked for a little of their juice to have leached out and caramelized, but that is more romantic than necessary. When the potatoes are done, their skins should have separated slightly from their flesh and they should pierce easily with a knife or fork.

Grandma Hill's Candied Yams

Serves 6

IF YOU'RE LOOKING for syrup-sweet, marshmallow-crowned yams, this is not the recipe for you. If you're interested in sweet potatoes that taste like sweet potatoes with a little extra, then consider Grandma Hill's approach. I like the fact that you can assemble them ahead of time and bake the yams off just before you want to serve them.

2 **pounds roasted sweet potatoes (about 3 medium potatoes)**	½ **teaspoon salt**
	¼ **teaspoon grated nutmeg**
¼ **cup dark brown sugar**	4 **tablespoons cold butter, cut into cubes (1 cube per round of potato)**
½ **teaspoon ground cinnamon**	**Zest of 1 orange**

Preheat your oven to 350°F. Slip the skins off the roasted sweet potatoes and slice them into 1½-inch-thick rounds. Lay the rounds flat on the bottom of a baking dish just large enough to hold them in a single layer with about half an inch separating each round.

In a small bowl, stir together the sugar, cinnamon, salt, and nutmeg. Sprinkle each round with equal parts of the sugar mixture and dot the top of each round with cold butter. Grate the orange zest right over the sweet potatoes. Cover with foil and bake for 30 minutes. Remove the foil and bake another 10 minutes so things caramelize a little.

Common sense tells you to serve these warm, but I actually prefer them room temperature. Do whatever works for you.

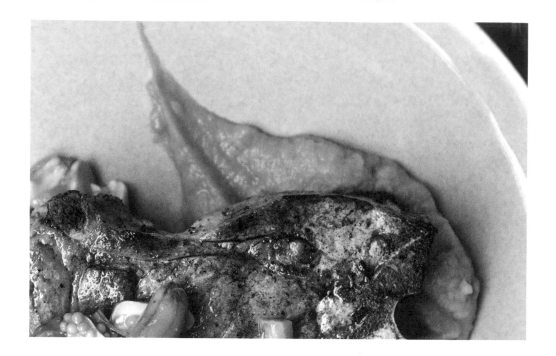

Citrus Sweet Potato Butter

Serves 6

WHEN WE OPENED THE RESTAURANT, I said I would never serve a buffet. Now I know if you want to do something, just say that's the thing you'll never do. We have a party room upstairs, and despite valiant efforts to pass hors d'oeuvres, the party we host most often and execute best is the buffet.

Nine times out of ten, Citrus Sweet Potato Butter finds its way into one of our chafing dishes. It's a crowd-pleaser and a concise way to articulate fall on a plate. Serve it with Butter-Baked Turkey with Pecan Cranberry Relish and Warm Sorghum Vinaigrette (*page 144*) or the Big Bone-In Pork Chops with Pickled Peanut Salad (*page 394*).

1½ pounds roasted sweet potatoes (about 3 medium sweet potatoes), peeled

Zest of ½ orange, removed with a Microplane

Zest of ½ lime, removed with a Microplane

Zest of ½ lemon, removed with a Microplane

½ cup orange juice

¼ cup light brown sugar

⅓ cup butter, melted

1 teaspoon salt

2 dashes hot sauce

Blend the potatoes: Combine all the ingredients in the bowl of a food processor and blend until smooth like baby food.
To heat and serve, put a little water in the bottom of a saucepan and add the potatoes. Heat over low heat, stirring often to make sure they don't burn.

Sweet Potato Mostarda

Makes 4 cups

MOSTARDA IS A SWEET AND TANGY Italian condiment made from fruit, sugar, and powdered mustard. I've tweaked it here and switched fruit out for sweet potatoes. Like traditional *mostarda,* it's meant to sit on top or next to rich meats and cheeses. Chopped up and treated like a pickle, it is an unexpected but happy addition to egg salad, hot dogs, and hamburgers.

- 1½ **pounds sweet potatoes, about 2 medium**
- 3 **cups granulated sugar**
- 2 **cups cider vinegar**

- 1 **cinnamon stick**
- 2 **lemons, sliced**
- 4 **allspice berries**
- 10 **cloves**
- 2 **tablespoons mustard seeds**

- 3 **teaspoons Colman's Mustard Powder**
- 2 **teaspoons salt**
- 1 **teaspoon ground turmeric**

Peel the sweet potatoes, and slice them in half lengthwise. Put the flat side down on your cutting board and slice the potato into half-moons that are ⅛ of an inch thick.

In a medium nonreactive saucepan, combine the remaining ingredients and bring them up to a simmer. Stir in the potato slices and simmer for 2 minutes. At first you'll have a little trouble getting all the slices submerged, but after about a minute it shouldn't be a problem. Stand over this the entire time it's cooking and stir frequently so that the potatoes cook evenly. We're looking for them to wilt slightly but remain crisp.

After 2 minutes, remove the pan from the heat and let the potatoes and their syrup cool to room temperature. Let the Mostarda cure for 1 week before using. It will keep, covered in the refrigerator, for 3 months.

Sweet Potato and Turkey Shepherd's Pie

Makes a 9x13-inch casserole

I WAS ONE OF THOSE MOMS who made all of their kids' baby food. Normally I'd be annoyed by someone who bragged about that, but I worked a lot and felt like making their food was the one way my work could be meaningful for them.

I used the baby-food aisle at the grocery store as my guide, mimicking the textures and combinations that coincided with their increasing age. Oddly enough, this combination of sweet potato, turkey, and spinach is something I started out blending up when they were eight or nine months old, and I just developed the same healthful ingredients over time into something we all like to eat.

Sweet Potato Parmesan Topping

- 4 to 5 medium sweet potatoes
- ¼ cup brown sugar
- 4 tablespoons butter
- ½ teaspoon salt
- ⅔ cup grated Parmigiano-Reggiano

Turkey Filling

- 3 tablespoons extra-virgin olive oil, divided
- 2 medium yellow onions, diced
- 2 teaspoons salt, divided
- 3 cups quartered button mushrooms
- 2 pounds ground turkey
- 1 tablespoon minced garlic
- 1 teaspoon ground chipotle powder
- 2 teaspoons smoked paprika
- 2 teaspoons turmeric
- 2 teaspoons ground cumin
- 8 ounces tomato sauce
- 8 ounces water
- 10 ounces frozen spinach

Make the topping: Peel the sweet potatoes, and cut them into rough 2-inch chunks. Place the potatoes in a medium saucepan and cover them with water. Bring them up to a boil, reduce to a simmer, and cook until the potatoes are very tender.

Drain the potatoes and return them to the pan. Place the pan over low heat and add the brown sugar, butter, and salt. Using a fork or device of your choice, mash the potatoes so that they are nearly smooth and the butter and sugar are fully incorporated. Set aside.

Make the filling: In a 12-inch sauté pan or Dutch oven, heat 1 tablespoon of olive oil over medium heat. Add the onion and 1 teaspoon of salt. Sweat for about five minutes, or until the onions are translucent. Push the onions to the edge of the pan and force them into a tight mound.

Add the remaining olive oil and the mushrooms. Allow them to sit and caramelize in the hot pan for about one minute. Resist the urge to shake the mushrooms around, as you are trying to develop flavor by letting them brown. After 2 minutes, stir together the onions and

the turkey and begin breaking it up with a spatula. Season the turkey with the remaining salt, garlic, chipotle powder, paprika, turmeric, and cumin. Allow the turkey to brown and the spices to toast. This will take about 4 minutes.

Stir in the onion mixture, tomato sauce, water, and spinach. Let this all cook down until it's very thick and saucy. Remove from the heat.

Assemble and bake: Preheat your oven to 350°F. Spread the turkey mixture onto the bottom of a 9 x 13-inch baking dish, a 12-inch cast iron skillet, or 8-ounce ramekins. Spoon the sweet potato over the top so that it's in an even layer. Sprinkle the sweet potato with the Parmigiano-Reggiano cheese.

Bake for 1 hour uncovered. Allow it to cool for about 10 minutes before serving. My kids like this on its own, but I generally eat it with a green salad on the side for balance.

the mushrooms, making sure you scrape up any browned bits from the bottom of the pan.

Transfer the onion and mushroom mixture to a plate, and add the final tablespoon of olive oil to the pan. Add

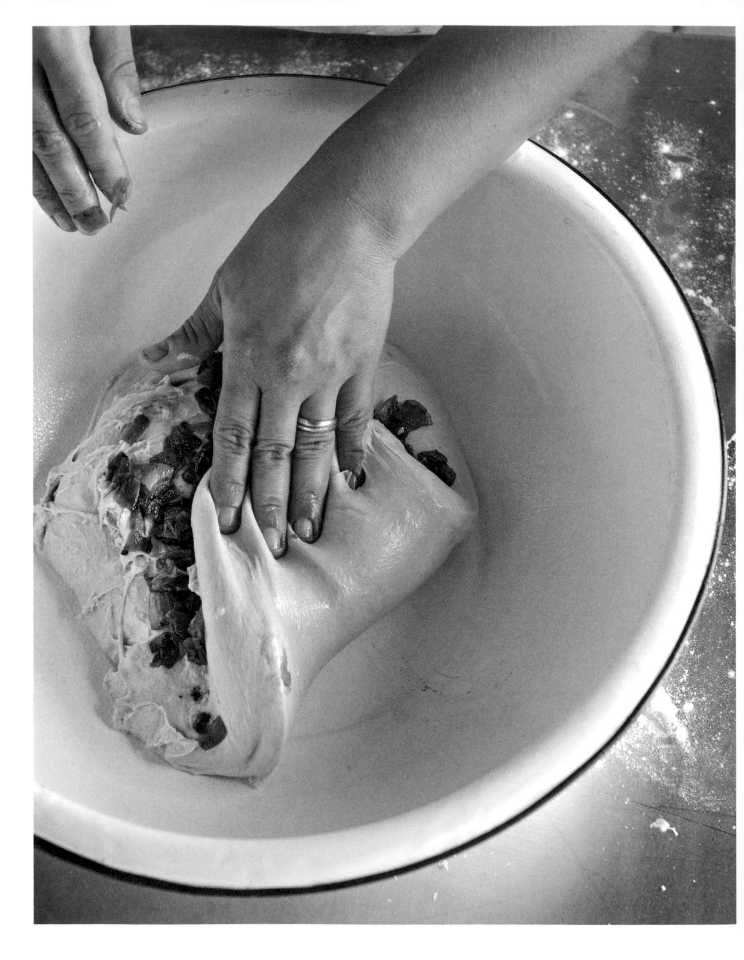

Sweet Potato Onion Bread

Makes 2 doughnut-shaped loaves

SERVING QUALITY BREAD at Chef and the Farmer was a priority from the beginning. But Kim Adams, our pastry chef, who's been with us since day one, had no experience making bread and neither did I. We set out to master at least one style of loaf, and we did. We served rosemary ciabatta for four years to every diner whose butt landed in our seats. It bothered me that our bread service didn't match the regional focus of our other food, but I didn't want to serve biscuits or cornbread either.

In 2010 Ben and I ate dinner at Dan Barber's Blue Hill at Stone Barns for his sister's college graduation. As part of a vegetable-focused dinner, we had the most amazing potato and onion bread. Over that bread and some wine, I hatched the idea to do something similar with sweet potatoes, an ingredient inextricably tied to Eastern North Carolina.

This stuff is special—chewy with deep flavor and a dark crust. If you want a sandwich that will make you cry tears of joy, make the Elbow-Lick Tomato Sandwich on page 262, and get a tissue.

Starter

- ¼ teaspoon dry active yeast
- ½ cup warm water, 105°F to 115°F
- ⅔ cup bread flour

Bread Dough

- 5 onions, large-diced
- 1 tablespoon vegetable oil
- 1 tablespoon plus 1 teaspoon salt, divided
- 3¾ cups bread flour plus extra for dusting
- 1¾ cups plus 3 teaspoons lukewarm water

Starter

- 2 teaspoons honey
- 1 cup roasted sweet potato puree

Make the starter: The night before you want to bake the bread, combine the yeast and the water in a small bowl. Let it sit for 10 minutes. In another bowl, whisk together the flour and ⅓ cup of the yeast water to make a very sticky starter. Discard the remaining water.

Cover with plastic wrap and let it sit out at room temperature overnight or up to 12 hours. You are looking for lots of big bubbles.

Make the dough: In a large sauté pan or skillet, combine the onions, oil, and 1 teaspoon salt. Over medium heat, cook the onions till they caramelize and are golden brown, 30 to 40 minutes. Set the onions aside to cool.

In the bowl of a mixer, stir together the flour and water with your hands or a wooden spoon to produce a wet rough dough. Cover the dough with plastic and let it rest for 10 to 20 minutes.

Sweet Potato Onion Bread

Continued from the previous page

Fit the mixer with the dough hook. Add the starter, honey, sweet potato puree, and remaining salt. Mix on medium high. It will be very rough in the beginning and won't look like it's coming together until about 10 minutes into it. Just be patient and don't add flour even though you'll think you should. The dough is ready after 15 to 20 minutes when it is uniformly smooth, silky, and wraps around the hook. Again, resist your urge to add flour to make the wrapping happen. Just give it mixing time. It's a very sticky and wet dough.

Coat a large bowl (at least 3 times the size of the dough ball) with pan spray. Turn the dough into this bowl. Cover the

bowl with oil-sprayed plastic wrap. The dough will go through a bulk rise for 4 hours as it doubles in size and swells with lots of air bubbles. During this rise you will be adding the onions and turning the dough.

First, let the dough rest in the bowl for 20 minutes. Then uncover the dough and top with a quarter of the onions. In the bowl turn the dough by pulling up each corner and folding it into the center. Flip the dough over so that it sits on its seams. Let the dough rest for 20 minutes. Add the second batch of onions and turn the dough again. Let it rest another 20 minutes. Do this two more times. The last addition of the onions will be a bit messy and the onions will begin to slide out of the

dough. Try your best to keep the onions incorporated, but don't continue to fold or knead the dough.

Once all the onions are incorporated and you've turned the dough 4 times, let it sit covered and undisturbed for 2 hours and 40 minutes.

Turn the dough out onto the floured work surface once again and divide it in half. Shape each half into a round. Let them rest for 10 minutes.

Meanwhile, get out two baking sheets. Line them with parchment and dust them with flour. Stick your finger through the center of one of the dough balls. Stretch it slightly to form a little hole. Transfer that dough round to the baking sheet and continue to carefully stretch the center

into a 3-inch hole. Your bread round at this point will look like a giant flat doughnut. Do the same thing to the second ball of dough. Dust the tops of the stretched rounds with a little flour and cover them gently with plastic wrap. Set them aside, ideally in a warm part of your kitchen, to proof for an hour and a half.

Preheat your oven to 450°F and position 2 racks in the upper third and the lower third of your oven. Remove the plastic and slide both baking sheets onto the racks. Bake for 15 minutes, then rotate the loaves of bread from top to bottom and vice versa. Bake an additional 15 minutes. Remove them from the oven and let them cool at least 15 minutes before serving.

Sweet Potato Pie Ice Cream Sundae

Makes 4 sundaes

IN THE BEGINNING, our dessert program relied on good ideas and not honed techniques, so we worked with what we did well: ice cream. This whimsical dessert reminds people of a cross between sweet potato casseroles with marshmallow and sweet potato pie, but in the fun form of a sundae.

Note: *You're going to need a blowtorch and a candy thermometer for this one—two things every aspirational home kitchen should have, but not many do.*

4 cups Sweet Potato Ice Cream

1 cup Salted Orange Caramel

1 cup Salt-and-Butter-Roasted Pecans *(page 134)*, roughly chopped

1½ cups Toasted Meringue

Sweet Potato Ice Cream

3 tablespoons butter

1 teaspoon lime zest, removed with a Microplane

½ teaspoon cinnamon

¼ teaspoon nutmeg

¼ teaspoon salt

1 can sweetened condensed milk

1 can evaporated milk

1 pound roasted sweet potatoes (about 2 cups)

¼ cup light brown sugar

¼ cup maple syrup

2 teaspoons vanilla bean paste or the insides of 1 vanilla bean, scraped

Make the ice cream: In a small heavy-bottomed skillet or saucepan, heat the butter till it's melted and foaming. At this point, start watching it closely and swirling it around. The foam will subside and you'll start to see little brown bits at the bottom of your pan. Once you notice that beginning to happen and the butter starts to smell nutty, let it go just a little longer, maybe 10 seconds. Remove it from the heat and immediately add the zest, cinnamon, and nutmeg.

In a powerful blender, combine all the ingredients and blend everything till it's

super-smooth. Transfer the mixture to the refrigerator and chill overnight.

The next day, freeze it in your ice cream machine and transfer it to your freezer for 2 hours to firm up. Then make the caramel and the meringue.

Assemble and serve: In a sundae glass or a bowl, drop a giant 8-ounce scoop of ice cream. Drizzle caramel over top and sprinkle with roasted pecans. Spoon a big dollop of the meringue on top of that and toast with a blowtorch. Finish with a few more pecans if you like. Serve immediately.

Salted Orange Caramel

Makes 1 cup

½ cup heavy cream	1 cup granulated sugar
Zest of 2 oranges, removed with a Microplane	½ cup orange juice
	½ teaspoon salt

Heat the cream and the zest in a small saucepan to just below a boil. Remove it from the heat and let it steep for 15 minutes.

In a 2-quart saucepan, combine the sugar and orange juice. Dissolve the sugar before it comes to a boil. Once it boils, don't continue to stir it, as that can make your caramel grainy. Keep your eye on it. Once the sugar starts to turn amber, swirl the pan so the amber begins to spread.

Watch this closely and swirl till all the sugar is amber. Remove it from the heat and whisk in the warm heavy cream. Be careful because it will bubble up quite a bit. Stir in the salt and let it cool to room temperature. This will keep refrigerated for up to 2 weeks.

Toasted Meringue

Makes 2 cups

⅓ cup plus 1½ teaspoons granulated sugar, divided	3 tablespoons water
	1 egg white, at room temperature

In a small saucepan, combine ⅓ cup sugar and the water. Bring it up to a boil and cook until your candy thermometer reads 220°F.

Meanwhile in a mixer fitted with the whisk attachment, beat the egg white on medium-high speed until foamy. Slowly add the remaining 1½ teaspoons sugar and whisk until you achieve soft peaks. With the mixer running, slowly add the hot sugar syrup. The whites will get glossy. Continue whisking until stiff peaks form. This will keep refrigerated for 12 hours.

Fried Yams with Five-Spice
Maple Bacon Candy

Serves 4

WHEN MY GRANDMA HILL was living her last years, a woman by the name of Charlotte Jenkins helped care for her. I was cooking in New York at the time, and when I came home for vacation, my aunt Linda suggested I spend the afternoon with Charlotte in the kitchen.

Even though at the time I worked in kitchens teaming with cooks at the top of their game, two things Charlotte did that day stuck with me. She butchered a chicken in the sink in forty-five seconds, and she made sweet potatoes that she boiled and then fried.

These are a three-way cross between what Ms. Charlotte did, candied yams, and tostones, or twice-fried plantains. You could eat these anytime of day, but I think they make a lot of sense for brunch.

1½ pounds sweet potatoes, peeled	*Maple Bacon Candy*	1 teaspoon Chinese five-spice powder
⅔ cup vegetable oil	8 ounces thick-cut smoked bacon cut into 1-inch pieces	1 cup maple syrup
1 teaspoon salt	2 tablespoons thinly sliced ginger	2 tablespoons lemon juice

For the yams: Bring a 4- to 6-quart pot of water up to a boil. While that's working, slice the sweet potatoes into 1-inch-thick rings. Drop the potato disks into the boiling water and cover. Boil for a good 8 minutes. Remove one of the smaller rings and see if the center is at all tender. You do not want these potatoes to be cooked all the way through. Rather, you are looking for firm potatoes with a little give. There is a short window you're trying to isolate. At 8 minutes, the smallest potatoes should be ready. At 10 minutes, they should all be just right.

Transfer the potato disks to a baking sheet and line them up in a single layer. Once they are cool enough to handle, press them between two sheets of parchment paper or foil. If they are overcooked, the disks will break apart. If they are in that perfect window, they will give slightly and smoosh out around the edges. You want something that is only slightly thinner than what you started with, maybe ⅔ of an inch after smooshing. Refrigerate the disks till you're ready to fry them. Cold disks will hold up better when dropped into the oil.

Make the syrup: In a 10-inch sauté pan or skillet, fry off the bacon till almost crispy. Set it aside and pour off (and save) all but 2 tablespoons of bacon fat. Add the ginger to the 2 tablespoons bacon fat left in the pan and let it sizzle for about 30 seconds over medium heat. Add the five-spice powder

and toast till it becomes quite fragrant,
about 10 seconds. Stir in the maple syrup
and bring it up to a boil. Let the syrup cook
down by a third and thicken slightly. Stir
in the bacon and the lemon juice. Bring it
back to a simmer just before serving.

Fry the yams: In a 12-inch, heavy-bottomed
skillet or sauté pan, heat the oil over
medium heat. Pinch off a tiny bit of sweet
potato and drop it in the oil. If it starts
sizzling immediately, go ahead and gently
place the disks in the oil. Do not crowd

them and make sure they are in a single
layer. Fry until the cracks and crevices on
the bottom are caramelized crispy brown,
about 6 minutes. Gently flip the potatoes
over and do the same on the other side.

When both sides are browned, drain
the disks on paper towels and season both
sides with salt. To serve, stack the yams on
top of one another and spoon the bacon
syrup over top. Serve like hotcakes.

Braised Pork Shoulder and Sweet Potato Free-Form Lasagna

Makes 8 individual-serving lasagnas

THIS FREE-FORM LASAGNA is one of Chef and the Farmer's only signature dishes. By *free-form* I mean that we roll fresh pasta into 16-inch-long-by-5-inch-wide noodles. Then, one by one, we cook the noodles briefly in boiling water, spread the slippery hot suckers out on a baking sheet, and fold three layers around the cooled thick filling. People either think it's genius or look at it and wonder where their saucy lasagna is.

Despite the occasional complaint from red-sauce lasagna lovers, we bring this back year after year because I'm hardheaded and I love its crispy edges and cheesy barbecue flavor.

If rolling out fresh pasta doesn't appeal to you, just layer this with store-bought noodles as you would a traditional lasagna.

Note: *Pasta is not my specialty, but this recipe, adapted from Patrick O'Connell's* Inn at Little Washington Cookbook, *is reliable and works for all sorts of noodles.*

Braised Pork Shoulder and Sweet Potato Free-Form Lasagna

Continued from the previous page

8 lasagna noodles

6 cups braised pork shoulder

6 cups sweet potato ricotta filling

2 cups diced fresh mozzarella

1 cup diced smoked mozzarella

Braised Pork Shoulder

1 tablespoon vegetable oil

2½ pounds Boston butt, cut into 1-inch cubes

20 turns of the pepper mill or ½ teaspoon black pepper

3 teaspoons salt, divided

1 medium yellow onion, small-diced

1 medium carrot, small-diced

1 stalk celery, small-diced

4 garlic cloves, thinly sliced

⅓ cup bourbon

1 cup white wine

⅓ cup cider vinegar

2 tablespoons molasses

2 cups chicken stock

2 bay leaves

3 sprigs thyme

½ teaspoon chili flakes

Sweet Potato Ricotta Filling

3 cups roasted and peeled sweet potatoes

2½ cups ricotta

⅔ cup grated Parmigiano-Reggiano

½ teaspoon salt

¼ teaspoon nutmeg

Pasta Dough

4 eggs

2 yolks

1½ teaspoons salt

3 tablespoons olive oil, plus more for drizzling

3 cups all-purpose flour, plus more for dusting

Braise the pork: If you haven't roasted your sweet potatoes for the filling, do it now (*page 312*). Heat the vegetable oil in a 4-quart Dutch oven over medium heat. Toss the pork with the pepper and 2½ teaspoons of the salt. Brown it on all sides in two batches, taking care not to get the oil too hot. The brown bits stuck to the bottom of the pan build flavor in your sauce, so don't burn them.

Remove the pork from the pan and set aside. Drain off all but 2 tablespoons of the fat and add the onions, carrots, celery, garlic, and remaining salt. Sweat the vegetables for 5 minutes over medium heat, stirring occasionally to scrape up the browned bits.

Add the pork, the liquids, and the herbs and spices to the pan. Bring up to a simmer and cover. Cook for 1 hour, checking frequently to make sure the pork continues to be just barely submerged by liquid. If too much liquid evaporates, add a little water.

After an hour, remove the lid and let simmer for 30 minutes. The liquid will cook down and thicken slightly, but the pork should continue to be barely submerged. The pork is done when it's very tender and flakes apart under the pressure of a spoon.

Let it cool. Pluck out the bay leaves and the thyme, then transfer the pork and the vegetables to a mixer fitted with the paddle. Mix on low till it's a homogenous meat and vegetable mixture. Chill the pork thoroughly.

Make the sweet potato filling: In a medium bowl, break up the sweet potatoes with a fork. Fold in the ricotta, Parmigiano-Reggiano, salt, and nutmeg.

Make the pasta: In a medium bowl, whisk together the eggs, yolks, salt, and 3 tablespoons olive oil. Put the flour in the bowl of a mixer fitted with the dough hook. Make a well in the center of the flour and gently add the egg mixture. On low, mix the dough for about 3 minutes. It should come together, form a ball, and start to pull away from the sides. If it's crumbly and dry, add a tablespoon or two of water. Continue kneading the dough till it's smooth and perfect like a baby's bottom. This may take 10 minutes.

Transfer the dough to the counter, cover with plastic wrap, and let it rest for about 30 minutes.

Take a third of the dough and, using a rolling pin, roll it into a flat rectangle. Open your pasta roller to the largest setting and feed the rectangle through it two times. Dial the setting back one notch and do it again. Feed the pasta twice through each setting till you reach number three. Cut the sheets into 18 x 5-inch rectangles. Dust them with flour and set aside while you roll out the remaining sheets.

Build the lasagnas: Bring a large pot of water to a boil and line 2 baking sheets with parchment paper. Drizzle the parchment paper with a little olive oil. Drop 4 lasagna sheets into the boiling water and let them cook for about 30 seconds. Using tongs, lift the noodles out of the water and transfer them to the baking sheets. Spread the noodles out so they are flat. Boil the remaining noodles and lay them out.

About an inch from the bottom of each noodle, scoop ¼ cup chilled pork shoulder. Top that with an equal amount of sweet potato filling and about 2 tablespoons of the diced mozzarella cheeses. Fold the noodle over the top of that layer. Press the pasta down gently to stabilize, and build a second, equal layer on the semiflat surface you just made. Fold the noodle back over, covering that layer. Flatten it again, and build the top of the lasagna. Finish this exposed layer with additional diced mozzarella. If you have extra pasta hanging over the side, just trim it off. You can refrigerate covered lasagnas for up to 2 days before baking.

Bake the lasagnas: Preheat your oven to 400°F. If the lasagnas have been refrigerated, let them warm up to room temperature for 30 minutes before baking. Drizzle the lasagnas with olive oil before you slide them into the upper and lower third of your oven. Bake them for 15 minutes, then rotate the baking sheets and bake an additional 15 minutes. The cheese should be melted and the edges should be brown and crispy. Serve warm, perhaps with wilted greens.

SUMMER SQUASH

WALK DOWN THE NEATLY TILLED ROWS of any summer garden in Eastern Carolina, and you'll likely find all the same vegetables. Until recently, people here never really messed around with experiments like eggplant or fancy peppers. Herbs were something we bought dried and, aside from sage, rarely used. Cherry tomatoes would have been too small to do anything with, and asparagus grew out of a can. We never raised sugar snaps or snow peas because they were "foreign." And greens of all kinds were reserved for a fall harvest. So from yard to yard, all our gardens looked the same, revealing no hint of the eccentric folks tending them.

Early summer meant three things: cucumbers, onions, and squash—not zucchini, not squash blossoms, not pattypans, just yellow squash, and lots of it. In a modest garden, people would set out five to ten squash plants and harvest the abundance largely for the same preparation. Some people made squash relish or pickled it with their cucumbers, and I'm sure there was a crazy in every fire district who threw thick slices on the grill. But for the most part, people here made squash and onions.

Unfortunately, its name doesn't whisper to you in the way succotash, tomato pie, and fried okra do. But in the coastal plain of North Carolina, squash and onions remains a staple, with variations based on how long your matriarch let it cook down.

Every cook started with a high-sided cast-iron pan—the largest one in her repertoire—bacon grease stockpiled from breakfasts past, and a pile of sliced squash and sweet onions so tall and round it barely fit in her well-seasoned vessel. She would hit the (at this point unmanageable) pile of veggies with salt and pepper from above and gentle heat from below, prompting a period of shrinking and stirring that could go on for over an hour, depending on the original girth. Once it had shrunk down and dried out, some grandmas, my dad's mom included, called it done. My dad grew up eating pale squash that were both mushy and squeaky. He hated them, and for a man I've watched belly up to a room-temperature can of Vienna sausages, that's saying something.

Other grandmas—my mother's mother fell into this category—pushed through the dried-out stage, allowing their squash to stick a bit. Slowly and under controlled heat, Grandma Hill allowed the pale pulp to caramelize, scraping up the browned bits and stirring them back into the mix, until the whole thing had taken on a golden hue and a toasted-onion aroma. This is the squash and onions I grew up on. I neither loved nor hated them, finishing my bowl when I was hungry, pushing it aside when I wasn't.

Other women behind the Southern stove take their squash and onions to another level. Grandma Magdalene, grandmother of my friend Cynthia Hill (who directs *A Chef's Life*), shrunk, stuck, and stirred them for hours, switching out the pan when size deemed it "fittin'," and she turned off the heat only when the results were chestnut brown, sweet, pungent, and wildly fragrant. She served her squash and onions at room temperature as part of an impressive spread. On a table of platters heaped with fried chicken, banana sandwiches, corn, butterbeans, cucumbers, and tomatoes, a tiny bowl of squash and onions sat near the edge, full of flavor, prepared with attention and brimming with love.

SQUASH WISDOM

More than the Crookneck

GROWING UP, I thought squash were always yellow with a long neck and a swollen bottom. I didn't learn until much later that there was a world of summer squash out there beyond those crooknecks. Zucchini, straight necks, pattypans, and eight-ball squash round out the varieties and can stand in for each other in nearly every recipe.

Squash are beautiful. Combining a range of yellows, greens, and whites in one preparation can be memorable. So take advantage of all the crazy varieties and be confident enough to blend them together.

Pattypans

I'D BE DOING the squash family an injustice if I didn't speak specifically about the squatty sister called pattypan. To me, she's modern and about to take the world by storm.

Pattypans, even at their largest, have a greater flesh-to-seed ratio than any other member of the squash family. Truthfully, all squash make a fine

showing when subjected to the unique heat of the grill, but the pattypan stands firm, its middle section softening more slowly than that of the zucchini, its more popular brother.

Treat Them Right

NEVER, EVER, EVER peel a summer squash. The beauty, integrity, and flavor sit in the skin.

While corn, tomatoes, okra, and cucumbers are the most quintessential, in-your-face-Southern summer vegetables, I consider squash, when treated in the proper way, the most elegant and understated. Squash is feminine. She plays well with others and leaves a little to the imagination.

Bigger Is Bad

I LIKE SMALL to medium summer squash, and if I'm trying to be really precious, I use tiny ones that still have a blossom attached. Stay away from very large squash. They have tough, flavorless flesh and big seed sections that are hard to work around.

Squash and Onions

Squash and Onions

Serves 6

THIS IS THE WAY Cynthia's grandma would have cooked her squash and onions, down to almost nothing. I like serving these next to things that are bright, like very simple Everyday Cucumbers (*page 246*) or the Raw Corn and Cantaloupe Salad (*page 233*). If you have some left over, save it to make the Squash and Onion Smother, a more refined variation that I serve in my restaurant.

¼	cup bacon fat		sliced into half-moons
3	large yellow onions, halved and sliced thin with the grain	15	turns of the pepper mill or a scant ½ teaspoon black pepper
6	medium yellow squash,	1½	teaspoons salt

In a Dutch oven or 12-inch cast-iron pan, melt the bacon fat and add the onions, squash, pepper, and salt. Let it cook down over medium heat for about 10 minutes. The squash will release a whole lot of liquid and things will begin to shrink. Once it's reduced by about half, lower the heat slightly and start stirring every few minutes. You are looking for a little caramelization on the bottom of the pan, so it's okay if the vegetables stick a bit. Using a wooden spoon, scrape it all up and stir it in. The mix will continue to shrink and develop color and flavor over a period of about an hour. It's done when it's chestnut color and looks like a chunky apple butter. You'll have between 3 and 4 cups.

Squash and Onion Smother

Makes a scant 2 cups

I'M ALWAYS LOOKING for ways to share traditional preparations with the diners in my restaurant. Problem is...there ain't nothing uglier than Grandma's squash and onions. Before we could put those cooked-down and scraped-up flavors on the plate, we needed to tweak the presentation. The result is something I'm calling a smother. It offers up all the complex character of squash and onions but will remind you of hummus.

Spread it on Romaine and make it the beginning of a lettuce wrap, treat it like you would a bean dip, or have it as a complement to Okra Oven Fries (*page 405*).

1	cup Squash and Onions	¼	cup olive oil for finishing
5	cloves Garlic Confit (*page 156*)	¼	cup lemon juice
1	tablespoon tahini	½	teaspoon salt
¼	teaspoon cumin	5	turns of the pepper mill or a scant ⅛ teaspoon black pepper
¼	cup Greek yogurt		

Combine all the ingredients in a high-powered blender. Blend until smooth. Serve at room temperature. This spread really loves to be coupled with the Assorted Squash Pickle Salad (*page 343*).

Squash and Onion Smother

Assorted Squash Pickle Salad

Makes 1 quart

THIS IS IN THE STYLE OF A PICKLE but is not meant to be canned in a hot-water bath. That process will change the texture and vibrant color of the "salad." These are a match made in fried-fish heaven, as well as something I would serve next to sausage, on sandwiches, or with roast chicken. It's also an apt foil for purees like Squash and Onion Smother (*page 340*) or Butterbean Hummus (*page 156*).

It's best to use a mandoline here, as well as more than one variety of summer squash. A combination of colors and sizes will leave you with a fresh-looking, shockingly beautiful, quick pickle.

- 1 medium red onion, halved and thinly sliced
- 3 medium squash, sliced to ⅛ of an inch on a mandoline
- 1 teaspoon salt
- 2 sprigs basil
- 2 sprigs mint
- 2 teaspoons whole coriander seeds
- 1 teaspoon whole cumin seeds
- 1 cup rice wine vinegar
- ¼ cup distilled white vinegar
- ½ cup water
- ⅔ cup granulated sugar
- ¼ teaspoon chili flakes

In a large bowl, toss together the onion, squash, and salt. Allow this to sit for about an hour. Drain, rinse, and toss the squash with the basil and mint.

In a medium saucepan, toast the coriander and cumin seeds just until they become fragrant. Add the vinegars, water, sugar, and chili flakes. Bring it up to a boil and pour the brine over the squash, herb, and onion mix. Allow it to cool slightly and, using a plate or something similar, weigh down your pickles so they are completely submerged in the warm brine.

Refrigerate the pickles overnight, at a minimum, before using. These will keep refrigerated and submerged in the brine for up to 6 months. Make sure you remove the herbs before serving. They are for flavor, not for looks, as you'll see.

Grilled Squash, Basil Pesto,
and Stewed Tomatoes

Squash and Fontina
Casserole Pudding

Grilled Squash, Basil Pesto, and Stewed Tomatoes

Serves 4

THIS RECIPE SHOULD BE A TEMPLATE for you to experiment with grilled vegetables in general. I've taken the Italian lexicon and made a mockery of it here, combining a Southern-style tomato sauce with basil pesto. Mario Batali would probably spank me if he saw it. But I promise, it does taste good.

I generally serve this whole thing at room temperature. I think it allows the flavors to pop and makes the host's job easier.

Squash

6 to 8 medium pattypans cut into sixths, or 3 medium squash or zucchini cut into 1-inch-thick rounds

2 tablespoons extra-virgin olive oil

2 teaspoons salt

20 turns of the pepper mill or a scant ½ teaspoon black pepper

3 tablespoons Basil Pesto

2 cups Stewed Tomatoes *(page 270)*

⅓ cup shaved Parmigiano-Reggiano (use a vegetable peeler)

2 tablespoons aged balsamic vinegar

Basil Pesto

Makes 1 cup

2 cups basil leaves

⅓ cup mint leaves

3 tablespoons pine nuts

¼ cup grated Parmigiano-Reggiano

1 teaspoon salt

1 teaspoon honey

Juice and zest of 2 lemons

⅓ cup olive oil for finishing

Make the pesto: In a food processor, combine the basil, mint, pine nuts, Parm, and salt. Pulse it a few times. Then add the honey, juice, zest, and, finally, the olive oil. Blend it all, about 30 seconds, but not long enough for friction to warm the pesto up.

Transfer the pesto to an airtight container and store it for up to a month in the refrigerator. Make sure the pesto itself sits under a thin layer of olive oil to keep it from turning brown.

Grill the squash: Preheat your grill or cast-iron skillet to medium-high. In a medium bowl, toss the squash with the olive oil, salt, and black pepper. Using tongs, grill

or sear them about 3 minutes on each side. You're looking for the squash to be nicely marked up from the grill or skillet but still firm to your tongs' touch.

Cool the squash on a platter or baking sheet. Place them in a single layer, ideally on a rack, to prevent them from turning soggy.

To serve: Serve family-style by spooning a large puddle of the stewed tomatoes over the bottom of a serving dish. Then toss the squash with the pesto, drop them on top of the tomatoes, and shower the whole thing with shaved Parm. Drizzle with aged balsamic and serve.

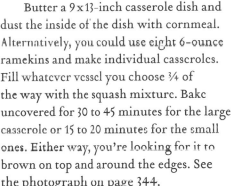

Squash and Fontina Casserole Pudding

Makes one 9 x 13-inch casserole

SQUASH CASSEROLES ARE a dime a dozen. In my opinion too many of them are the side to push aside when they share a plate with summer peers like sweet corn, cucumber, or tomatoes. This one is different, I promise. It gets a creamy texture and cooked-down flavor from an extended period on the stove and a funky richness from Fontina.

Crowned in Cucumber Noodles (*page 254*), then nestled on a throne of Cilantro-Lime Sweet Corn (*page 228*), this casserole becomes queen of the vegetable plate.

- 4 medium yellow onions, halved and sliced thin
- 2 tablespoons minced garlic
- 2 tablespoons bacon fat (butter is a fine substitute)
- 8 to 10 medium squash or zucchini, sliced ¼ inch thick (about 2½ quarts)
- 3 teaspoons finely chopped fresh sage
- 1 teaspoon picked and finely chopped rosemary
- 3 teaspoons salt
- 20 turns of the pepper mill or a scant 1 teaspoon ground black pepper
- 2 cups grated Fontina cheese (you could substitute Swiss or white American)
- 1 large egg
- 2 tablespoons butter
- ¼ cup cornmeal

Preheat your oven to 350°F.

In a 6-quart Dutch oven sweat the onions and garlic in the bacon fat until translucent. Add the squash, sage, rosemary, salt, and black pepper. Stir it all to combine and cook over medium heat for about 40 minutes, stirring periodically to make sure the bottom of the pot doesn't burn. You are looking for the squash to release all its liquid, dry out, and take on a deep golden hue.

Remove the pan from the heat. While things are still steamy, stir in the Fontina. Allow the mixture to cool slightly. Then stir in the egg.

Butter a 9 x 13-inch casserole dish and dust the inside of the dish with cornmeal. Alternatively, you could use eight 6-ounce ramekins and make individual casseroles. Fill whatever vessel you choose ¾ of the way with the squash mixture. Bake uncovered for 30 to 45 minutes for the large casserole or 15 to 20 minutes for the small ones. Either way, you're looking for it to brown on top and around the edges. See the photograph on page 344.

Serve warm.

Squash Noodles with Crab and Jalapeño

Serves 4

THIS IS THE TYPE OF LOW-CARB, high-flavor food I cook at home. Just enough prep work for a glass of wine and then the dish comes together in one pan in 3 minutes. If you don't have crab, pulled chicken works just as well.

- 5 or 6 large and long zucchini and summer squash
- 5 tablespoons butter, divided
- 2 teaspoons salt
- 1 cup lump crab, picked through for shells
- ⅓ of a jalapeño, sliced very thin
- ⅓ cup lemon juice
- 8 large sprigs mint, torn, plus more for garnish
- 15 to 20 large leaves basil

Start by making long ribbons of the zucchini and squash using a vegetable peeler. To do this, hold the squash in one hand while peeling the full length of the vegetable with the other. Do this on all four sides, peeling down till you reach the seeded core of the squash. You will end up with long, thick noodles of squash and zucchini without seeds. Discard the cores.

In a 12-inch sauté pan, melt 1 tablespoon of the butter. Add the noodles and the salt. Once the squash starts to wilt down, add the crab and jalapeño. Continue to wilt the squash as you toss and heat the crab. Once the mix barely warms through, add the lemon juice and the remaining butter. Think of this like pasta. You are building the sauce and allowing it to tighten up. At the last minute, add the herbs and toss once more. Serve immediately. Garnish with more mint if you like.

Squash and Pistachio Crumble

Makes one 9 x 13-inch crumble

I WENT THROUGH a vegetable-as-dessert phase. Luckily, my sister Johna pulled me aside one day and pointed out that four out of the five sweets on our menu focused on a root or a shoot. Not all of those vegetal desserts were keepers, but the one we come back to year after year is this Squash and Pistachio Crumble.

It's a favorite of mine because it tastes like apple pie, and it's a crafty way to shrink the abundance of squash in early summer. Try this recipe and you'll see that it's not a gimmick.

Squash Filling

- 6 cups yellow squash or zucchini, sliced into ⅛-inch half-moons
- ¾ cup lemon juice
- ½ cup water
- ¾ cup granulated sugar
- ½ teaspoon salt
- Zest of 1 lemon
- ¼ teaspoon cinnamon
- ⅛ teaspoon nutmeg

Crumble

- 1½ cups all-purpose flour
- ½ cup cornmeal
- 1 cup granulated sugar
- ½ teaspoon salt
- 1½ cups (3 sticks) cold butter, cut into cubes
- 1 cup chopped pistachios
- 2 cups roughly chopped pistachios

Make the filling: Put the squash in a Dutch oven or 12-inch cast-iron pan. Add the lemon juice, water, sugar, and salt. Bring it up to a simmer and cook down until the squash is tender and the liquid is reduced by half.

Add the zest, cinnamon, and nutmeg. Cook briefly, about 2 minutes, to incorporate. Set aside.

Make the crumble: In the bowl of a food processor, combine the flour, cornmeal, sugar, and salt. Pulse to combine. Add the butter, a few pieces at a time, and pulse till crumbly. At the last second, throw in the pistachios and pulse once or twice more just to combine.

Assemble and bake: Preheat your oven to 350°F. Press a ½-inch layer of crumble over the bottom of a 9 x 13-inch baking dish or six 6-ounce ovenproof ramekins and bake for 15 minutes in the center of your oven. Remove the blind-baked crust from the oven and spoon the squash filling over the top. Layer the remaining crumble on top of the squash and return it to the oven to bake for 30 minutes. Serve warm. I like it with vanilla ice cream.

Twin Muffins

Makes 24 muffins

CHILDREN SHOW YOU AT AN EARLY AGE what they like and don't like. My twins told us with tummy rubbing and yummy smiles by age one and a half that they were carb-craving sugar hounds. They love cupcakes, chocolate, and cookies. I want them to love nuts, grains, and vegetables. This muffin is my attempt to combine both our desires. The twins eat them up, as does everyone else in my house.

If you don't have flax meal, you can use all whole wheat flour. Feel free to substitute in the nuts or dried fruit of your choosing.

1 cup unrefined coconut oil	2 cups grated squash	1 teaspoon baking powder
3 large eggs, separated	2 cups whole wheat flour	⅛ teaspoon nutmeg
¾ cup brown sugar	1 cup flax meal	½ cup chopped walnuts
2 teaspoons vanilla extract or paste	3 teaspoons cinnamon	1 cup chocolate chips
1 cup crushed pineapple	1 teaspoon baking soda	⅔ cup dried cranberries
	1 teaspoon salt	

Preheat your oven to 400°F and line two muffin trays (for 24 muffins total) with liners. Melt the coconut oil in the microwave until just liquid, about 45 seconds.

In a medium bowl or in a mixer fitted with the whisk attachment, beat the egg whites till they form stiff peaks.

In a bowl large enough to eventually hold all the ingredients, whisk together the coconut oil, egg yolks, sugar, and vanilla. Stir in the pineapple and the squash.

In another bowl, stir together the flour, flax meal, cinnamon, baking soda, salt, baking powder, nutmeg, walnuts, chocolate chips, and cranberries. Gently fold in the egg whites. Add this into the wet mix and stir to just incorporate. A few lumps are fine and better than overmixing.

Spoon the batter into the muffin cups, filling them about ⅔ of the way up. Bake the muffins for 18 minutes.

SAUSAGE

Fresh Bulk

NEESE'S
~ Southern Style ~
COUNTRY SAUSAGE

Tom Thumb

Fresh Link

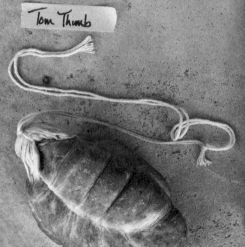

Air-dried

AIR DRIED COUNTRY SAUSAGE

HOT

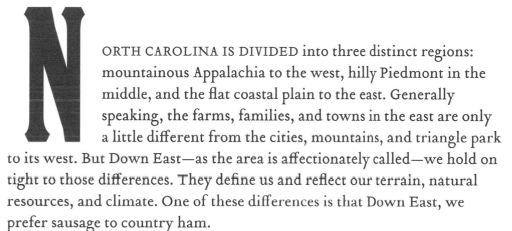
N ORTH CAROLINA IS DIVIDED into three distinct regions: mountainous Appalachia to the west, hilly Piedmont in the middle, and the flat coastal plain to the east. Generally speaking, the farms, families, and towns in the east are only a little different from the cities, mountains, and triangle park to its west. But Down East—as the area is affectionately called—we hold on tight to those differences. They define us and reflect our terrain, natural resources, and climate. One of these differences is that Down East, we prefer sausage to country ham.

That's not to say we don't cure hams here. Pork in all forms has long been a big, big part of our diet, but force Eastern North Carolinians to choose one thing to nestle inside their biscuits for eternity, and they'd call for a fatty link of country-style sausage.

My children will likely not feel the same tug toward sausage that I do, but until about forty years ago, making sausage was part of the yearly ritual of putting up meat for winter—part of a hog-killing day. I'm too young to remember the spectacle, but I grew up hearing my sisters tell stories so detailed, so fresh, I feel like I was there.

Every fall, just after the first cold snap, both sides of my dad's family, the Tyndalls and the Howards, took off work or stayed home from school and came together to sacrifice and process several hogs for winter.

Part celebration, part hard-as-hell physical labor, hog killings demanded days of preparation. My great-aunts, mom, and grandmother deviled eggs, made potato salad, and iced layer cakes. My dad, uncles, cousins, and grandfather stocked firewood, sharpened knives, and rounded up the long list of players who made meat preservation without refrigeration a reality. Lard stands and presses, pounds and pounds of salt, earthenware crocks, pine bowls, crackling paddles, meat grinders, and sausage stuffers

came out of storage and took their marks. Hog killings were huge two-day productions. Every person, every tool, played a part.

On day one, the men slaughtered and scalded the pigs. Using the sharp side of a tin-can lid, sets of hands scraped off the coarse hair, exposing pink, human-like skin and body-temperature, flabby flesh. A tractor or pulley lifted the pigs by their hind legs to hang. Here, in the outdoor refrigerator that was November in North Carolina, the pigs started to cool down. With the quick, educated jab of a knife, the most skilled person in the group, my granddaddy Currin, punctured the jugulars and the pigs bled out. Then things got dirty. Granddaddy Currin split open the belly, releasing an odor and a torrent of innards that spilled into a tub on the ground.

While the modern wasteful eye might see this as a tangle of disgusting garbage, frugal country folk smiled down in wonder at their pile of shiny treasures. The lungs, called lights, would be fried up that night in something called hog hash and served in a gravy over rice. The brains would be scrambled the next morning with eggs, and the intestines, rinsed and washed, would house the star of the event, sausage.

On day two, all the participants woke with their particular missions in mind. The men prepared to cure hams, pickle feet, render lard, and press cracklins. The women gathered to make sausage.

The Dixie bell, a ten-foot-by-ten-foot wooden shack named for the woodstove that defined the space, had a metal roof and no windows. This is where the Tyndall women ground, mixed, and stuffed their sausage. It was cold outside, but the stove made it so hot inside that the walls glistened with rendered fat.

My grandmother Iris and her sisters Bertha, Carrie, and Zinnie lumbered around a square table. They were big women; all of the Tyndall women were. Faded aprons stretched to cover their bellies, and thick stockings encased what our family affectionately referred to as the "Tyndall trunks." Some of the women sat; some of them stood. All of them huddled around a pile of fresh pork. Bertha worked the knife, sculpting cubes the perfect size to fit through the grinder. Carrie dropped and pressed the pork through the die. Iris, my grandmother, mixed the ground pork with sage, chili flakes, black pepper, and salt, making sure the ratio of fat to lean was a consistent seventy to thirty. And Zinnie, the most petite aunt, fed mixed sausage into casings with the ease of a concert pianist at her instrument. The women worked and chattered around a symphony of flesh and fat forced through a die, metal turning against metal, and a crackling fire.

Although they followed only one recipe, the Tyndall women made three distinct sausages. Fresh bulk sausage was loose. It never met a casing and got pattied up and

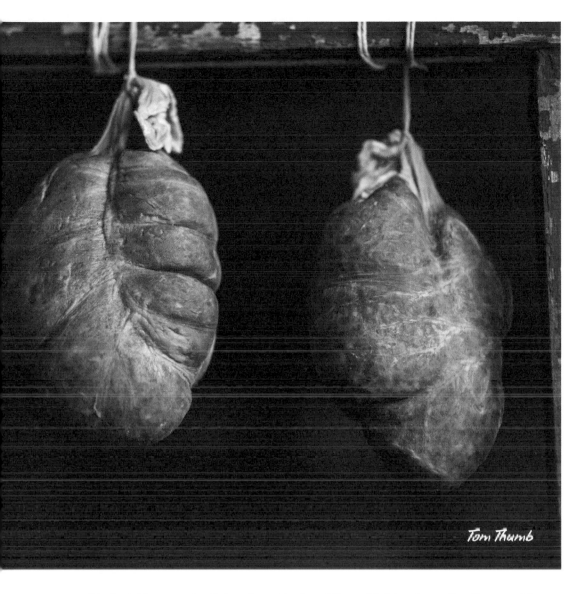

Tom Thumb

panfried within a week of slaughter. For breakfast with biscuits or for dinner with Tomatoes and Rice (*page 269*), this sausage tasted fresh and smelled of sage as its fat rendered quickly in a hot pan.

Most of the sausage, though, got stuffed into traditional pork casings and hung in a salt- or smokehouse to cure. Here the links had plenty of space to breathe, dry, and develop flavor. Sausage that hung for extended periods of time dried a bit, darkened in color, and developed a certain funkiness that the women in my family coined "tang." We called and continue to call these links country-style sausage. Aged for roughly two weeks, this semidry sausage still worked as stuffing for a biscuit or panfried as the meat for supper. Hung longer, it proved too dry to eat on its own. Instead shriveled links like these were best as seasoning for turnip salad, rutabagas, or collard greens.

But for Zinnie, Iris, Bertha, and Carrie, the king of all sausages was the Tom Thumb. It's hard to imagine this stone-faced pragmatic crew celebrating, but when they did, it was around a Tom Thumb. A by-product of my people's inability to

SAUSAGE WISDOM

Country Sausage

THERE'S A LOT TO SAY about sausage, but this chapter is about only one microdot on the sausage spectrum: country-style sausage.

People here make a fresh sausage heavily seasoned with sage and pepper. They eat it fresh or age it in a traditional pork casing or in the pig's appendix. We never age our sausage like salami, which is sliced up and eaten as is. Instead, our aging is just a step toward developing flavor before it's cooked. These air-dried sausages are our most popular agent for seasoning greens and beans.

Browning and Crumbling

A LOT OF PEOPLE think they're browning sausage and they're not. Here's how to do it right. Heat a heavy-bottomed skillet, sauté pan, or Dutch oven over medium-high heat. Add one teaspoon vegetable oil and swirl it around to coat the pan. Just before the oil starts to smoke, pinch the sausage off into pieces and add it to the pan. Spread it out in a single but compact layer. Once it's in the pan, do not move it around for about two minutes. You'll see fat rendering off and the

sausage itself shrinking. You should also see some caramelization around the edges of the crumbles. At that point, swoop in with your spatula and turn the sausage over. Brown on the other side. Drain the sausage on paper towels.

Saving the Fat

LIKE BACON FAT, rendered sausage fat is flavorful. It's also more perishable. Store rendered sausage fat in a sealed container (I use a glass jar) in your refrigerator for up to one week. Break it out when you sauté greens, scramble eggs, or sweat onions.

Substitutions

SOME OF YOU MAY SAY, "Well, what about turkey sausage—can I use that?" My answer is to sigh and say, "Sure. Just don't go writing bad reviews of my book when you've called on a turkey instead of a pig."

If you don't want to go to the trouble to make your own fresh sausage, I get it. Here are some basic grocery-store brands that work: Neese's Extra Sage or Hot, Jimmy Dean Sage, Pender, Purnell's Old Folks Country Sausage, Tennessee Pride.

understand waste, the Tom Thumb was made by stuffing the family's sausage mix into the cleaned and rinsed cavity of a pig's appendix.

A pig's appendix is not like a human appendix. It's sometimes called a middle cap and is actually a sac that hangs off the lower intestine and aids in digestion. If you know what a chitterling is, making a Tom Thumb is basically like stuffing a giant chitterling and letting it cure. If three families came together for a hog killing, they slaughtered three hogs, and every household got one of these. If the weather was cold

My Sausage Soapbox

THIS TRADITION IS ALIVE but under hospice care. When I say a few people still make country sausage in all its forms, I mean a few old people. You don't walk into butcher shops and pork centers here and see a twenty-year-old behind the meat counter stuffing casings and working the band saw. It's sad but true.

I could go on a rant, but here's the abridged version. We've got very few indigenous charcuterie traditions in our country. This is one of them. If stuffing and hanging sausage is not your thing, support the tradition by ordering some air-dried sausage or a Tom Thumb from the Country Butcher Shop or Nahunta in North Carolina or Edwards in Surry, Virginia. Cook it, eat it, and think about all the planning our forefathers went to just to put food on the table. Next think about how they were so desperate not to waste anything remotely edible that they decided to stuff a shit sack with sausage and hang it to cure till it tasted good. Then think about that food you just threw in the trash.

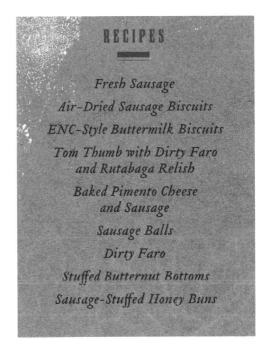

RECIPES

Fresh Sausage

Air-Dried Sausage Biscuits

ENC-Style Buttermilk Biscuits

Tom Thumb with Dirty Faro and Rutabaga Relish

Baked Pimento Cheese and Sausage

Sausage Balls

Dirty Faro

Stuffed Butternut Bottoms

Sausage-Stuffed Honey Buns

enough to have the hog killing before Christmas, the Tommy T (as it's been called) hung in the smokehouse till New Year's. It shrank and developed flavor from the loss of moisture and from the fragrant, thick casing. A fresh Tom Thumb weighed about three pounds; a ripe, cured one about two.

Instead of cooking a skinny bird on New Year's, the Tyndall women boiled this alien-shaped sausage and used the resulting broth to cook cabbage, turnips, or collards. Then they sliced Tommy into one-inch-thick rounds, panfried them, and splayed them out on a platter around the cooked greens.

The idea that this was the way the Howard women used to ring in the New Year became an obsession for me. I wanted to do the same, so I sought out the handful of people in Eastern Carolina who still made Tom Thumbs, asked them questions, and made my own. I hung it. Let it cure. Boiled it. Cooked the greens. Panfried the slices. Fanned them out on a platter and celebrated family, memory, and work.

Fresh Sausage

Makes 3 pounds

THIS IS MY VERSION of the fresh bulk sausage my family made. It calls for fresh herbs, garlic, and ginger when the Tyndall women would have used dried. If you'd like to substitute dried garlic powder, ginger, or sage, you can with great effect here. Just decrease the measurement by half.

Use this sausage whenever a recipe calls for crumbled, browned sausage or patty it up and panfry it like a hamburger. If you'd like to try your hand at links either fresh or semidried, follow the instructions on page 364 and stuff it into pork casings.

Don't be deterred if you don't have a meat grinder. Making fresh bulk sausage is incredibly easy if you ask your butcher to grind the pork for you. You may want to do that even if you do have a meat grinder.

2 pounds pork shoulder, cut into 1-inch cubes	1½ tablespoons salt
1 pound fresh pork fat, cut into 1-inch cubes	1½ teaspoons red chili flakes
3 tablespoons fresh sage, finely minced	20 turns of the pepper mill or a scant 1 teaspoon black pepper
2 tablespoons fresh ginger, grated on a Microplane	½ teaspoon cayenne
2 tablespoons fresh garlic, roughly 5 cloves, grated on a Microplane	⅓ cup cold water

Toss the pork cubes together with everything but the water. Put the seasoned pork, the grinder attachments, and the bowl of your mixer in the freezer 30 minutes before you're ready to grind. Using the medium die of your meat grinder, grind the pork into the chilled mixing bowl.

Add the water. Using the paddle attachment, mix the pork on medium speed for 1 minute. The seasoning will be evenly distributed and the mixture will seem sticky. Cook off a small patty in a frying pan to taste for seasoning. If the salt and spice level is good for you, transfer the pork to a sealed container and refrigerate overnight before using. You could use it right away, but the flavor will improve with a little time. Use or freeze within 5 days.

Air-Dried Sausage Biscuits

Serves 5

THE ONLY HOLIDAY or family gathering where the Howards know without question what they'll be eating is Christmas morning. Convening over sausage biscuits while we open presents is the singular long-standing tradition we share. It's the morning and the meal I look forward to more than any other all year.

The week before Christmas, my dad goes to all his favorite butcher shops and grocery stores to buy fresh, semidry, air-dried, hot, and mild country-style sausages. For a total of fifteen people, many of them children, he'll buy thirty pounds of links.

Christmas morning, he wakes before dawn to grill the sausage. Ben gets up nowdays too because Dad tends to burn a lot in hopes of cooking it fast and eating it faster.

When the rest of us are up, we start baking biscuits. Traditionally we made canned biscuits only and loved every individual layer of them. But in recent years, I've also been baking homemade biscuits the way my friend Lillie Hardy taught me. The homemade ones, always gone first, are gilded with a touch of Dijon and a dollop of muscadine preserves (*page 533*)...and a link of sausage, of course.

Note: *This recipe is to make the sausage. Turn the page for the biscuits.*

Air-Dried Sausage Makes a 10-foot coil	10 to 12 feet of hog casings	4 grams InstaCure #2 or 1 scant teaspoon
	3 pounds Fresh Sausage (*page 363*)	

Soak the pork casings in warm water for about 30 minutes before using. When you grind and mix the sausage, add 4 grams InstaCure #2 at the same time you add all the other spices. They would not have done this in the old days, but we are going to play it safe in *Deep Run Roots*.

Put the mixed sausage and the stuffer in the freezer for 20 minutes. Run warm water through the casings. This opens them up and lets you know if you've got any big holes in there. Bring the sausage out and slide the casing onto the stuffing tube, leaving 6 inches hanging off the end. Stuff the sausage in the stuffer and begin filling the casings. Fill the sausage in one long coil. Inspect the coil for air pockets and use a sterilized needle to puncture those spots. Tie off each end. At this point a lot of cultures twist the coil into individual links, but we keep it whole and slice the coil into portions before cooking. If you want to age it some, hang the sausage on a rack in your refrigerator, making sure the sides of the sausage are not touching

each other at any point and there's plenty of room for airflow. If possible, secure a little fan inside your refrigerator's door to encourage drying. After about a week the sausage should have darkened slightly in color and shrunken a little. At any point after that, slice off a hunk and use it in Turnip Roots and Greens (*page 68*) or Slow-Cooked Limas (*page 166*).

To cook the sausage for biscuits, preheat your grill to medium or preheat an oven to 375°F. Slice the sausage into 2-inch pieces. Grill the sausages for 10 minutes on each side or until just cooked through. In the oven, roast the sausages for 25 minutes. Serve, split lengthwise, inside a warm biscuit.

ENC-Style Buttermilk Biscuits

Makes 10 biscuits

TRADITIONAL EASTERN NORTH CAROLINA BISCUITS are different. Not poofed up in a zillion layers or bready, they're flat under a timid dome, crispy on the bottom, and porky-smelling. Because my mom baked high-rising canned biscuits, I thought the squat biscuits I ate at Byrd's diner, the B&S Café, the Tyndall Family Restaurant, and Pleasant Hill Grocery were baked only in restaurants...till I met Lillie Hardy, my friend and home-cook mentor.

Lillie gave me a lesson on biscuit making, and beforehand I thought she was going to show me something I already knew—how to measure, gently knead, roll out, and cut big fluffy biscuits. Instead, she showed me how to fashion the biscuits that I had thought only a scowling magician toiling hunchbacked behind a swinging kitchen door could craft.

Because these are flat, they don't make great bookends for stout combinations like bacon, egg, and cheese or the very popular fried-chicken biscuits with pickles I keep seeing on menus. This is a one-stuffing kind of biscuit, a happy home for a link of sausage split lengthwise or a naturally slight slice of country ham. Lillie and most people around, though, eat them just as often right out of the oven with molasses.

The instructions make them seem easier than they actually are. Don't think you're gonna wake up hungry Saturday morning and whip out a perfect batch of these biscuits the first time you try; you'd better have a plan B. It takes practice. At least it did for me.

½ cup lard plus more for greasing the pan	4 teaspoons baking powder	1 cup buttermilk
2½ cups all-purpose flour	⅔ teaspoon salt	

Preheat your oven to 375°F. Using your hand as both a scoop and spatula, grease a baking sheet liberally with lard.

Sift the flour, salt, and baking powder into a large bowl and make a deep and wide well in the center. Add ½ cup lard followed by the buttermilk, taking care to keep both contained in the well for now. If you're right-handed, take your right hand down into the lard-buttermilk goop and start bringing that together with your fingers. You want to make that as much of a homogenous mixture as you can without bringing too much flour into the fold just yet. Once you get it together, start moving the wet mixture back and forth, to and fro in the flour. Turn it over and do the same. Turn it over again and introduce more flour with each movement. Once I get it

until the dough is not sticky but still very soft and tender. You will have about ½ cup flour left in the bowl. I could give you an exact measurement for flour, but there are a lot of factors in play here, so I've chosen to do it as Lillie would.

Pull off a large golfball-size piece of dough and roll it up with your hand, pinching the bottom together. Put it in the corner of the greased baking sheet and press it down to ½ inch thick. Follow with the next biscuit. All sides of every biscuit should be touching other biscuits. It's okay if you don't fill the entire tray; it's more important that they be crowded.

Slide the tray onto the rack in the lower third of your oven and bake for 18 minutes. Rotate the tray to the top rack and bake an additional 7 minutes.

going, I like to do a little motion that feels like a one-handed knead, using my thumb as if it were the other hand. It's all real gentle, but it pushes new flour in with each movement. Continue introducing flour

The biscuits should be golden brown and crisp on the bottom, a little less brown on top. Let them cool if you can for 2 minutes before eating.

Tom Thumb with Dirty Faro and Rutabaga Relish

Makes 1 or 2 Tommy Ts, depending on the size of the casing

SOMETIMES CALLED DAN DOODLE, this sausage scares a lot of people when they hear what he is. They get even more freaked out when they see it. Don't be scared! Celebrate instead.

- **1 or 2 pig appendixes**
- 2 tablespoons baking soda (optional)
- **Fresh Sausage (page 363)**
- 4 grams InstaCure #2 or 1 scant teaspoon

- 1 yellow onion, peeled and split
- 1 large carrot, split
- 2 stalks celery, halved
- 1 teaspoon salt
- 2 teaspoons light brown sugar

- 2 tablespoons vegetable oil
- 5 cups Dirty Faro (page 373)
- 2 cups Rutabaga Relish (page 471)

Stuff and cure the Tom Thumb: The appendix will likely be packed in a salt cure and will smell awful. Rinse it several times in cool water inside and out, changing the water around it as you go. If you just can't get past the smell, turn the casing inside out, cover it with water, and stir in 1 tablespoon of the baking soda to dissolve. Refrigerate overnight in the water. Drain the next day and do it again with the remaining baking soda. I've done this both ways and have decided I enjoy the funk the casing imparts to the sausage. You're gonna get some of that no matter what, but a double-day soak in baking soda water should cut it a bit.

Mix your sausage as instructed (*page 363*), adding in the InstaCure #2. Make sure it is well distributed throughout the sausage mixture. Using clean hands, stuff the sausage mix into the cavity of the appendix. Press down firmly, filling every crevice of the casing. The appendix is much stronger than a traditional hog casing, so don't worry about ripping it. It's more important to focus on packing as much sausage in as tightly as possible. Once it's stuffed, it will look like an alien whoopee cushion.

Tie the top of the sac tightly with twine and make a loop to hang it with. Hang Tommy in your fridge for at least a week and up to 15 days. Make sure nothing is touching Tommy and that there is airflow around him.

He will darken in color and shrink slightly. You're not really hanging him long enough for mold to grow, but if you do see any black spots, throw him away.

Cook: Rinse Tommy off and put him in the bottom of a 6-quart Dutch oven. Add the onion, carrot, and celery and enough water to just barely cover. Bring it up to a boil

over medium heat. Cover and cook for 45 minutes. Take Tommy out and let him cool in the fridge for at least 15 minutes.

Bring Tommy out and slice him into 1-inch rounds. The rounds should be firm and cooked through. In a 10- to 12-inch cast-iron skillet, heat the oil over medium heat. Add half the slices and cook on the first side till it's caramelized brown. Flip and brown the other side. Follow up with the remaining Tommy rounds.

To serve, mound the Dirty Faro on a platter and fan the browned sausage slices all around. Garnish with the Rutabaga Relish.

Baked Pimento Cheese and Sausage

Serves 1 to 8 (depending on whom you're serving)

JUST AFTER I HAPPENED into making blueberry barbecue sauce (*page 198*) and found my voice, I started thinking about appetizers that spoke of the region. Pimento cheese and crackers came to mind. And although other chefs have done pimento cheese to accolades, I just didn't think it fully reflected the dip culture Down East. Then I thought of the artery cement my sister Leraine serves on Christmas Eve. Cream cheese, sausage, and Ro-Tel heated in a crockpot till somebody spoons it into a Frito Scoop. (I can't believe I just wrote *Frito Scoop* in my book.)

Since its debut at Chef and the Farmer, baked pimento cheese and sausage has never gone away. We've taken it off the menu, but those in the know have always ordered it, and we've obliged them. Now its home is at the Boiler Room, where it's their number-one seller. They serve the cheese with our homemade saltines.

Note: *Using high-quality cheese makes a big difference here. At the very least, do not use pre-shredded cheese food from a bag. That stuff is often coated with a powdery substance that keeps it from clumping, but it also keeps it from tasting like cheese.*

---

3 cups pimento cheese

1 pound fresh sausage, cooked and crumbled (about 1½ cups)

⅔ cup panko bread crumbs

Pimento Cheese
Makes 3 cups

2 cups grated sharp yellow cheddar (about 10 ounces)

2 cups grated aged white cheddar (about 10 ounces)

½ cup finely diced roasted red peppers or pimentos

⅓ cup crushed canned tomatoes or fresh tomatoes pulsed in a food processor

¼ cup of your favorite mayonnaise

2 tablespoons sour cream

¼ teaspoon hot sauce

½ teaspoon salt (optional)

Make the pimento cheese: Combine everything but the salt in the bowl of a mixer fitted with the paddle attachment. Process for about 30 seconds on low till you have a slightly creamy cheese spread. Taste, add the salt if you wish, and paddle 10 seconds more. Chill till you're ready to use.

Preheat your oven to 350°F. Stir together the cold pimento cheese and the cooked, very well drained, and cooled sausage.

Press it down into a 1-quart baking dish or 8-inch cast-iron skillet and top with the panko crumbs. Bake uncovered for 20 minutes. The bread crumbs will not necessarily brown; they are there more to provide texture and to soak up some of the grease that rises to the top. When the baked cheese is done, it will be bubbling around all the edges.

Serve this with saltines, Ritz crackers, or toast. I like some pickles on the side.

Sausage Balls

Makes 40 1-ounce balls

SAUSAGE BALLS rank up there with cheese balls as our country's most clichéd and beloved party foods. The difference between the two is that most sausage balls are made with a little cheese and a little sausage bound by a whole lot of Bisquick. They taste like dry, porky balls of flour, and every time I take a bite of one I'm disappointed.

These sausage balls are more like meatballs bound by a little starch and punctuated by cheddar. To me that's what something called a sausage ball should be.

It doesn't matter whether you make your own sausage for this recipe or not. What does matter is the cheese. A sharp-aged cheddar is best and absolutely must arrive at your house in block form; the pre-shredded, dusty stuff will not melt well.

1 cup cornmeal	8 ounces sharp cheddar, grated on the medium holes of a box grater (1⅔ cups)	1 small yellow onion, grated
1 tablespoon light brown sugar		2 ounces cream cheese
½ teaspoon salt		
1½ teaspoons baking powder	1 pound fresh sausage	

Preheat your oven to 375°F and line a baking sheet with parchment or waxed paper. Spray the parchment with nonstick spray.

In a medium bowl, stir together the cornmeal, sugar, salt, and baking powder. Toss that together with the cheese to evenly coat. In another medium bowl, use your hands to combine the sausage, onion, and cream cheese.

Once the sausage mixture is homogenous, add it to the cheddar cheese mixture. Get in there with your hands to combine the two. You're looking for a slightly dry dough. Pinch off 1-ounce pieces and roll them into balls. Place them 1 inch apart on a baking sheet and bake for 20 minutes.

I prefer to serve these warm with Apple Mustard (*page 502*), but room-temperature sausage balls are totally acceptable. The mix freezes well too.

Dirty Faro

Makes 5 cups

MY ONLY EXPOSURE to dirty rice is from Bojangles', the fried-chicken fast-food chain that people here worship like a religion. For me to say I've improved on their version is heresy of some kind. But I have.

When you look at these ingredients, it's hard to believe they come together to make the toothsome, earthy side dish that they do. But because of its complexity and ability to complement pork and poultry of any kind, this faro graces our menu fall through winter. I eat it at home with wilted greens and roasted beets. See the photograph on page 369, under Tom Thumb.

- 2 teaspoons extra-virgin olive oil, divided
- 1 cup faro
- 1½ teaspoons salt, divided
- ½ pound sausage
- ¼ cup chicken livers, finely chopped

- 1 onion, small-diced
- ⅔ cup small-diced celery
- 2 teaspoons minced garlic
- 1 teaspoon ground cumin
- ¼ teaspoon cayenne

- ¾ cup water
- ⅓ cup thinly sliced scallion, green part only
- ½ cup celery leaves, picked

Cook the faro: In a 3-quart saucepan, heat 1 teaspoon olive oil over medium heat. Stir in the faro and toast for 1 minute. Add 2½ cups water. Cover and cook 10 minutes. Uncover, add 1 teaspoon salt, and cook an additional 2 to 3 minutes or just until al dente. Drain and cool.

Make it dirty: In a 12-inch skillet or cast-iron pan, brown the sausage over medium-high heat in the remaining 1 teaspoon olive oil. Once it's nicely browned on one side, add the livers and cook 30 seconds.

Stir in the onion, celery, garlic, spices, and remaining ½ teaspoon salt. Sauté for 2 minutes. Add the water, and simmer, uncovered, for about 2 minutes or until a little over half the liquid has evaporated. Stir in the faro and continue cooking until all the liquid has evaporated. Just before serving, stir in the sliced scallions. Garnish with the celery leaves.

Stuffed Butternut Bottoms

Serves 4

SWEET BUTTERNUT SQUASH, bitter greens, and spicy sausage are meant to be together. We served the trio for a long time as a take on a casserole, and nobody could believe how much one ingredient helped the others be their best selves. I like the stuffed squash bottom because when nature gives you bowls, you should fill them.

2 butternut squash	½ pound sausage	¼ teaspoon chili flakes
1½ tablespoons dark brown sugar, divided	1 cup leeks, white and pale green part only, sliced into ¼-inch half-moons	¼ cup apple cider
1¼ teaspoons salt, divided		½ cup grated Fontina cheese
8 turns of the pepper mill or scant ¼ teaspoon black pepper	2 cloves minced garlic (about 1 teaspoon)	¼ cup grated Parmigiano-Reggiano
2 tablespoons vegetable oil, divided	5 cups chopped turnip greens or kale	2 tablespoons panko bread crumbs

Preheat your oven to 375°F and line a baking sheet with foil or parchment paper. Cut the necks off your butternuts and split them and their bottoms down the middle. Save 1 of the 4 neck pieces for this recipe. Use the remaining 3 for something else. Scoop the seeds out of the bottoms. Rub the reserved half neck and the 4 half bottoms with 1 tablespoon dark brown sugar, ½ teaspoon salt, and the black pepper. Drizzle with 1 tablespoon vegetable oil and place, flesh-side up, on the baking sheet. Roast for 50 minutes. The squash will brown a little but shouldn't be mushy. You'll still see a little puddle of accumulated cooking juices inside the cavity. That's good. Scoop the flesh out of the neck. Chop it up and set it aside.

In a 10- to 12-inch skillet or sauté pan, heat 1 teaspoon oil and add the sausage. Brown it well, working it into crumbles as you go. Remove the sausage from the pan

and reserve. Lower the heat and sweat the leeks with ¼ teaspoon salt for 2 minutes. Add the garlic. Stir in the greens, ½ teaspoon salt, and the chili flakes and wilt 30 seconds. Add the apple cider. Let the liquid cook away till the pan is dry. The greens should have darkened in color and lost a bit of structure, but they should not be totally limp. Take them off the heat and stir in the reserved butternut flesh, the Fontina, and the remaining 2 teaspoons dark brown sugar.

Raise the heat in your oven to 400°F and stir together the Parm, panko, and remaining 2 teaspoons vegetable oil. Stuff the sausage filling into each squash bottom. The liquid sitting in the bottom of each squash will fill in around the greens. Top the filling with the panko mixture. Slide the baking sheet onto the middle rack of your oven and bake for 15 minutes. Serve warm.

Sausage-Stuffed Honey Buns

Makes 20 buns

MY MOM SPENT MOST OF MY CHILDHOOD trying to make sure I didn't get fat while my dad stuffed a honey bun and a sausage biscuit in my backpack on my way to the bus. Clearly they were not on the same page.

These pull-apart yeast buns look normal enough on the outside, but an investigation into their coiled interior uncovers little caramelized bits of sausage melted together with honey and brown sugar. Eating them reminds me of having a side of sausage with my pancakes.

Honey Glaze

- 1½ cups (3 sticks) butter
- 2 cups honey
- ⅔ cup light corn syrup
- ¼ cup granulated sugar
- Zest and juice of 2 oranges, zest removed with a Microplane
- 4 sprigs thyme

Sausage Filling

- 1 pound fresh sausage
- 8 tablespoons (1 stick) room-temperature butter
- ½ cup honey
- ¼ cup dark brown sugar

Bun Dough

- 1¼ cups milk
- 2¼ teaspoons dry active yeast
- ¼ cup warm water
- 5 cups all-purpose flour, sifted and divided
- 1½ teaspoons salt
- 1 tablespoon granulated sugar
- ½ cup shortening
- ⅔ cup honey
- 2 eggs

Make the glaze: Over medium heat, melt the butter in a 2- to 3-quart saucepan. Add the honey, corn syrup, sugar, orange zest, juice, and the thyme. Bring it up to a low boil and cook for 1 minute. Remove the glaze from the heat and set aside. Pluck out the thyme and discard. The glaze will keep refrigerated for up to 1 week.

Make the filling: Cook the sausage briefly in a 10-inch skillet. You want to render some of its fat but you don't want to cook it all the way through. Drain and set aside.

In a mixer fitted with the paddle attachment, work together the soft butter, honey, and brown sugar. Add the sausage and paddle briefly till you have a

homogenous mix. Set aside. This will keep for up to 3 days in the fridge but must be brought to room temperature before you smear it on the buns.

Make the buns: In a 2- to 3-quart saucepan, heat the milk till bubbles form around the edges. Take it off the heat. Meanwhile, in a small bowl, dissolve the yeast in the warm water. Let that sit for 10 minutes while the milk cools to lukewarm. Add the yeasty water to the milk and whisk. Stir in 2 cups flour, salt, and sugar. Mix with a spatula till relatively smooth. (A few little lumps are not a problem.) Put this in a warm place for 10 to 15 minutes until it's bubbly and you can tell the yeast is acting up.

Preheat your oven to 375°F. Fill 2 round cake pans ¼ of the way full with the honey glaze. You should have a little of the glaze left over to drizzle on the buns just before serving. Once the dough has doubled, punch it down with your fist. Then flour your work surface and divide the dough in half. Roll each half into an 8 × 10-inch rectangle. Spread the sausage filling evenly over each rectangle, leaving a 1-inch border around the edges. Starting at the long edge closest to you, roll the rectangles up into a jelly roll cylinders. Rest the jelly rolls on their seams and slice about an inch off the ends of each and discard. Cut the rolls in half and divide those halves into 5 buns each. Put the buns cut side down in the pans with the honey glaze, starting in the middle and working out like a flower. Leave about ¹/₃ inch space between the buns if you can.

Put the buns in a warm place to proof for 30 minutes. They should rise and plump up to meet one another. Cover the pans with foil and slide them onto the middle rack of your oven. Bake for 30 minutes. Remove the foil and continue baking 15 minutes.

Take the buns out of the oven and invert the pans onto a platter. Serve warm or at room temperature, drizzled with more honey glaze if you like.

While you're waiting, paddle the shortening in your mixer till it's fluffy. Add ²/₃ cup honey and 1 egg at a time, mixing in between each addition to make sure things are fully incorporated.

Once you've got a bubbly yeast mixture, with the mixer on low, gradually add it to the shortening. When you've incorporated all of that, add the remaining flour in 4 batches. Pull the paddle off and attach the dough hook. Raise the speed to medium and knead for 10 minutes. The dough should pull away from the sides and become smooth. If at the end of 10 minutes it's not smooth, let it go another 3 minutes.

Turn the dough out onto a floured work surface and knead for about 2 minutes more with your hands. Your dough should be smooth as a baby's bottom. Transfer the dough to a lightly oiled bowl and cover with plastic wrap. Put the bowl in a warm place and let it sit till the dough doubles in bulk. This will take about an hour.

PEANUTS

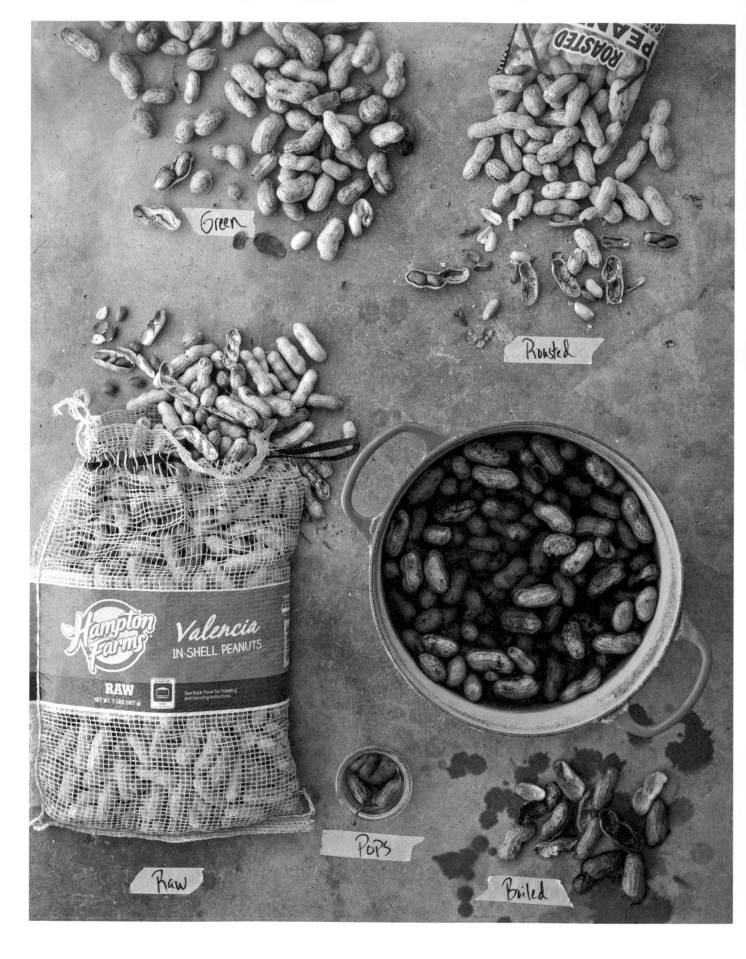

Green

Roasted

Valencia
IN-SHELL PEANUTS

Hampton Farms

RAW
NET WT. 2 LBS (907 g)

See Back Panel for Roasting
and Handling Instructions.

Pops

Raw

Boiled

FOR BETTER OR WORSE, much of North Carolina prospered on the tobacco trade for close to a hundred and fifty years. Almost every person who lived here between 1860 and 1970 had some connection to what we call the "golden leaf."

Unlike cotton or corn, tobacco was not a crop you just set out, tended in the field, harvested, and sold; its cultivation and transformation into a smokable leaf was tedious work that demanded many hands. The nuances and timing of that work shaped our culture.

For instance, because "barning baccar" called on the labor of not only men but all the women and children around, schools here didn't start each fall till the tobacco season had wrapped. And since this work was hot-as-hell summer work, our days began before dawn, and our biggest, most fortifying meal became midday dinner. Times have changed, but the cultural adaptation I want to live on beyond cigarettes and early mornings is the tradition of Pepsi and peanuts.

The worst job in the tobacco business is topping and suckering. A day of it began before seven in the morning and required the people doing it to walk up and down sun-soaked rows plucking every pink flower they found from the tops of tall tobacco plants. Tobacco as most people know it is cured, brittle, gold, and aromatic. But for the ones toiling in those rows, the golden leaf was green, sticky, itchy like okra, and riddled with squishy pale worms the size of an index finger. The morning break was a welcome reprieve.

At around ten o'clock, a dusty pickup turned slowly off the road and lumbered down the dirt path that lined the tobacco field. The pickup's driver, usually the farm manager, didn't top and sucker anymore, but he had definitely done it in the past and understood his current role, which allowed him to sit in the cabin of a truck

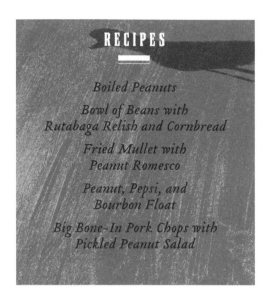

RECIPES

Boiled Peanuts

*Bowl of Beans with
Rutabaga Relish and Cornbread*

*Fried Mullet with
Peanut Romesco*

*Peanut, Pepsi, and
Bourbon Float*

*Big Bone-In Pork Chops with
Pickled Peanut Salad*

with a radio and rolled-down windows, was a privilege. He brought with him a cooler of cold bottles of Pepsi and a box of Lance peanuts in thin sleeves.

Hot, hungry workers, many of them children, knew their break began once they'd topped and suckered to the end of the row where the pickup sat. They worked fast and gathered under a shade tree. Sticky tobacco gum covered every hand and arm, so despite the urge to sit down and throw back handfuls of salty peanuts, they took to dumping the slender sleeve into the glass bottle of Pepsi and turning up the bottle for a salty, sweet, and crunchy swig. The combination offered energy and made the snack last longer than if they had tipped the bag of nuts or the bottle of soda back separately.

Pepsi was "born" in New Bern, just an hour east of Deep Run, and the same sandy, loamy soil that loves tobacco and sweet potatoes also loves the peanut plant. In many cases, the family farms of our region once lived off a small tobacco crop, a big garden, some chickens, a peanut patch, and a few pigs. Peanuts, a low-maintenance plant harvested well after the tobacco frenzy, rounded out a practical diet. And the peanut vines, comparable to alfalfa in nutrition, became convenient feed for the pigs. The model sounds like a study in modern sustainable-farming practices, but then it was just a way of life.

Over time other people in Eastern Carolina took to dumping their peanuts in their Pepsi, not because their hands were sticky but because the combination tasted good. For generations, old men rocked in chairs at country stores as they smoked cigarettes, watched cars go by, and took swigs of Pepsi dotted with peanuts. Housewives ironed clothes, watched their "stories," and sipped on the needed pick-me-up before their young'uns got off the school bus. Things are different now. Our world, thankfully, doesn't revolve around tobacco, and snacks come pre-assembled with every flavor sensation the manufacturer thinks you might want. Still, for palates that get wound up about salted-caramel anything and seven-dollar chocolate bars adorned with sea salt, the combination of Pepsi and peanuts works. Give it a try.

PEANUT WISDOM

Two Types

THERE ARE TWO BASIC types of peanuts grown in the United States. Virginia-style peanuts are the large, ballpark peanuts you generally think about popping in your mouth. Runner peanuts are much smaller, and, while some folks prefer these for eating out of hand, they are generally chopped or ground into peanut butter.

Green Peanuts

GREEN PEANUTS have just come out of the ground. Their hulls are moist and much softer than the in-shell peanuts we are accustomed to seeing in the grocery store. At this point, both the hull and the peanut are most similar to a fresh field pea and just about as perishable. These are what you want for perfect boiled peanuts. If you don't grow peanuts yourself or live in peanut country though, it's going to be next to impossible to get your hands on true green peanuts.

Raw Peanuts

RAW PEANUTS have been harvested and dried slightly to prevent them from getting moldy. They're versatile, acting more like the dried legumes they are than their green or roasted counterparts do. Try to find raw peanuts that have already been shelled to save time, and don't mistake roasted peanuts for raw. They will not perform the same in recipes. All of the raw-peanut recipes in this chapter call for boiling the "beans" first. In this case, you always want to salt after the peanuts are cooked through. Peanuts, like all other legumes, will develop a tough outer layer if salt is added too early in the cooking process.

Bowl of Beans *(page 386)* and the Big Bone-In Pork Chops with Pickled Peanut Salad *(page 394)* call for raw peanuts.

Roasted Peanuts

ROASTED PEANUTS are what most people think of when they think of peanuts. They are cooked and cannot be boiled or rehydrated.

Fried Mullet with Peanut Romesco *(page 388)*, and the Peanut, Pepsi, and Bourbon Float *(page 391)* rely on roasted peanuts.

Shelling

I'D LIKE TO OFFER you a mind-blowing method for shelling peanuts and removing their paper-thin brown husks, but nothing I've done works well enough to merit a mention. My best piece of advice is to source already-shelled raw peanuts. They come without the shell or the husk.

Boiled Peanuts

Makes 3 quarts

IT WASN'T UNTIL MY SENIOR YEAR of college that I ate my first boiled peanut. It came from a can and was a comfort snack for my roommate, Amanda Branch. I wasn't into cooking yet, but I was already suspicious of the can. Oddly enough, the peanuts were pretty good. I'm not saying Amanda ever worried about me stealing from her stash, but I did enjoy sharing a few with her from time to time—usually late at night under clouded judgment.

While the hardest part of this recipe is finding green, in-shell peanuts, there are a few things you should know before boiling your first batch.

First, most mature peanuts are harvested around October 1, but the most ideal candidates for boiling are pulled from the earth about three weeks earlier. Slightly immature peanuts with tender shells are the absolute best to boil.

Second, if you find this is something you love, consider boiling a very big batch in early fall when green peanuts are around. Then freeze them with a little of their liquid in plastic bags. Thaw them gently on the stove and serve warm to astounded, smiling folks who were expecting a mediocre nut mix.

Third, some people say you can soak raw (not green) peanuts overnight and boil them the next day to good effect, but I recommend the can over that.

Last, but in my estimation most important, make sure you don't overlook or discard the underdeveloped peanuts, called pops. Peanut farmers call pops trash, but boiled-peanut connoisseurs ferret them out. Some even eat the shells. Because they have softer husks and underdeveloped beans, they trap a lot of salty brine in with the immature soft peanuts. You should look for the pops—trust me.

| 1½ | pounds green, in-shell peanuts | 1½ | gallons water | 1 | cup salt |

In an 8-quart pot, combine the peanuts, water, and salt. Bring it up to a low boil and cover. If the peanuts are perfectly green and immature, boiling them could take as little as an hour. If they are older, be prepared to boil away for up to 4 hours.

It's important that all through the process the peanuts have plenty of water to bob around in, so feel comfortable adding more water as you need it. In the end you are looking for pliable shells and anywhere from al dente to soft peanuts—your preference.

Serve warm. Store leftover peanuts in their brine. They'll keep, refrigerated in a sealed container, for up to a week and in the freezer for up to a year.

Bowl of Beans with Rutabaga Relish and Cornbread

Serves 6

I WAS REALLY PROUD OF MYSELF when I came up with this one. With my clever hat on, I treat raw peanuts like the beans they are and boil them with aromatics. They're served just like a bowl of pintos would be, with Mom's Cornpone (*page 28*) and a tangy condiment. I've chosen my Rutabaga Relish (*page 471*), but something like chowchow or even salsa would work in its place.

2 tablespoons extra-virgin olive oil	1 teaspoon picked thyme, divided	½ teaspoon salt
5 ounces country ham	½ teaspoon chili flakes	Mom's Cornpone (*page 28*)
1 large yellow onion, small-diced	1 bay leaf	1½ cups Rutabaga Relish (*page 471*)
6 cloves of garlic, sliced	4 cups raw, shelled peanuts	
	3 quarts water, divided	

In a 6-quart saucepan or Dutch oven, heat your olive oil till shimmering. Add the country ham and brown on both sides. Remove and reserve the ham. Lower the heat and add the onions. Allow them to sweat about 8 minutes, or until they are translucent and fragrant. Add the reserved ham, garlic, ½ teaspoon of the thyme, the chili flakes, bay leaf, peanuts, and 2 quarts of the water. Cover and bring up to a gentle boil. Cook the peanuts, covered, for 2 hours or until they are quite tender and without that crunch you associate with a nut. They will not become mushy like regular beans, so don't worry about overcooking them. As they boil you may have to add additional water to keep all the peanuts just barely submerged in water.

When they are done cooking, stir in the remaining thyme and the salt. Remove the bay leaf as well as the ham. Transfer 2 cups of the beans plus a little liquid to the blender. Blend until totally smooth and transfer every bit of that back to the pot, stirring to combine. What you have should be the consistency of a pot of pinto beans at their stewy prime. If it's too loose, blend a few more peanuts. If it's too thick, add a little water.

To serve, spoon about a cup of beans into a bowl and top each serving with about a half a cup of relish and a wedge of cornbread. The relish is key here, as these are some rich beans. If you don't have the Rutabaga Relish substitute your favorite chowchow.

Fried Mullet with Peanut Romesco

Serves 4

ROMESCO IS A SPANISH SAUCE typically made with ground nuts, like almonds, hazelnuts, or pine nuts, and roasted red peppers. I use roasted peanuts in my version and omit the bread traditionally used as a thickener. Often a companion for fish, romesco is set off at our restaurant with panfried sea mullet and a bright arugula salad. If you don't have sea mullet, a mild white fish like flounder or catfish will work just as well.

Often I grab a little container of this romesco and take it home. For breakfast I smear it on toast under a fried egg. It's also a convenient way to enliven pasta salad, warm rice, or vegetable soup. Basically, it's good to have on hand.

Panfried Mullet

- 1 cup fine cornmeal
- 2 teaspoons salt, divided
- 1½ pounds sea mullet fillets
- ½ teaspoon cayenne
- ⅔ cup vegetable oil for frying

Half a lemon

Peanut Romesco

Makes 2 cups

- ⅓ cup roughly chopped sun-dried tomatoes
- 2½ tablespoons sherry or red wine vinegar
- ⅔ cup roasted unsalted peanuts
- 1 large roasted red pepper, roughly chopped (about ⅔ cup)

- 2 garlic cloves, smashed
- 1 tablespoon chopped mint
- 1 tablespoon chopped parsley
- 2 teaspoons smoked paprika
- 1 teaspoon salt
- 1 teaspoon honey
- ½ teaspoon chipotle powder
- ½ cup extra-virgin olive oil

Make the romesco: In a small bowl, stir together the sun-dried tomatoes and the vinegar. Let that hang out a minimum of 15 minutes. You want the tomatoes to plump up with the vinegar.

To the bowl of your food processor, add the peanuts, roasted red peppers, garlic cloves, mint, parsley, paprika, salt, honey, chipotle powder, and the sun-dried tomato–vinegar mixture. Process for 10 seconds, then stream in your olive oil. I like to see a little of the peanuts, so I blend the romesco till it's the texture of chunky peanut butter, but if you prefer a smoother sauce, blend it further.

You can eat this right away, but I prefer to let it mellow in the refrigerator overnight. The romesco will keep, covered in the fridge, for up to 1 week.

Fry the fish: In a small bowl, stir together the cornmeal and 1 teaspoon of the salt. Season the fish on both sides with the remaining salt and the cayenne. Dredge the fillets in the cornmeal and shake off any excess.

Heat the oil in a 12-inch cast-iron skillet over moderately high heat till it shimmers but before it smokes. Carefully lay the fish in a single layer and cook on the first side for about 2 minutes, or until it's golden brown. Flip the fish and cook on the other side an additional 2 minutes.

Drain the fish on a paper-towel-lined plate and squirt with lemon juice. Serve the fish immediately on top of the romesco.

Peanut, Pepsi, and Bourbon Float

Serves 4

FROM THE TOBACCO FIELD to a swanky dining room, our region's work snack is now a tall glass of fabulous. This foaming spectacle of sweet, salty, creamy, crunchy, and boozy is the gold standard of ice cream floats.

2 cups Peanut Ice Cream

16 ounces Pepsi

4 ounces bourbon (optional)

Peanut Ice Cream
Makes 1 quart

1 cup milk

2 cups heavy cream

3 cups salt-roasted peanuts, divided

8 egg yolks

A tiny pinch salt

1 cup granulated sugar

1 teaspoon vanilla extract

In a 1-quart container with a lid, stir together the milk, heavy cream, and 1½ cups of the peanuts. Tuck this in the refrigerator overnight. Roughly chop the remaining peanuts and set aside.

The next day, whisk together the egg yolks, salt, sugar, and vanilla extract in a medium bowl. In a 2-quart saucepan, heat the heavy cream and peanut mixture to just under a boil. Slowly whisk half of this mixture into the yolks, taking care not to scramble them. Transfer the tempered yolks to the saucepan, and, stirring the whole time, cook until the mixture thickens slightly and coats the back of a spoon.

Strain it all through a fine-mesh sieve and discard the tired peanuts. Chill the ice cream base thoroughly—ideally overnight. Freeze the ice cream in your ice cream machine according to the manufacturer's instructions. During the last few minutes of freezing, pour in the chopped peanuts. Let this ice cream spend at least 3 hours in your freezer before serving.

To serve, chill 4 glasses. Drop a nice scoop of Peanut Ice Cream in the bottom of the glass, top with roughly ½ cup Pepsi, and finish with bourbon to your liking.

Big Bone–In Pork Chops with
Pickled Peanut Salad

Big Bone-In Pork Chops with Pickled Peanut Salad

Serves 4

IF I WROTE A COOKBOOK and didn't include the recipe for Chef and the Farmer's pork chops, someone would try to take my life. Problem is, over the years we've paired our pork chops with every sweet, tangy, and savory combination out there, so narrowing down how best to reproduce it is tough.

This pickled peanut salad combines the heft of a bean salad with the pop of a relish, and on its very own, it's worthy of a try. Be ready, though; this is not something you decide you're going to make for dinner and two hours later, voilà, it's surrounded by smiles at your family table. It's not hard, but it does require time. My advice is to make a large batch of the pickled mustard seeds and keep them around for things that need a bright burst. They are a staple in chefs' kitchens and should be in yours.

This combination of pork and peanuts gets even better alongside Citrus Sweet Potato Butter *(page 316)*, and that's how I like to serue it.

Note: *If you want to brine your pork chops, and you do, make sure the chops you buy haven't been pumped with a sodium solution to facilitate moist meat. Much of the pork in an average grocery store has been, so check labels and ask questions; otherwise you may end up with super-salty chops.*

Brined Pork Chops
Makes 4 chops

- 2 quarts water
- ¾ cup brown sugar
- ⅔ cup plus 1 teaspoon salt, divided
- ¼ cup smooth Dijon mustard
- 1 tablespoon black peppercorns
- 3 sprigs rosemary
- 4 sprigs sage
- 6 garlic cloves, smashed
- 4 bone-in, 16-ounce pork chops

Black pepper
- 2 tablespoons vegetable oil

Pickled Peanut Salad
Makes 1 quart

- 2 cups raw peanuts
- 2 teaspoons salt, divided
- ½ cup Pickled Mustard Seeds
- ⅔ cup mustard-seed pickling liquid
- ⅔ cup celery, thinly sliced on a bias
- 1 red bell pepper, cored and sliced into 1½-inch julienne
- ⅓ cup thinly sliced scallion
- ⅓ cup picked parsley, leaves torn into 3 pieces each
- 2 tablespoons lemon juice

Pickled Mustard Seeds
Makes ½ cup

- ¼ cup yellow mustard seeds
- ¼ cup white wine vinegar
- 1 clove smashed garlic
- ¼ teaspoon turmeric

Pinch chili flakes
- 1 tablespoon granulated sugar
- ⅛ teaspoon salt

Pickle the mustard seeds: Pour the mustard seeds in a 2-quart, heavy-bottomed saucepan and cover them with cool water. Over medium heat, bring them up to a boil and immediately drain and rinse them under cool water. Repeat this process 2 more times. Boiling and rinsing the mustard seeds numerous times cooks away their bitter tannins.

Meanwhile, bring the vinegar, ½ cup water, the garlic, turmeric, chili flakes, sugar, and salt up to a boil. After you rinse the mustard seeds the third time, place them in a nonreactive container and pour the pickling brine over the top. Let the seeds sit overnight before using.

Make the salad: Combine the peanuts and 2 quarts of water in a 4-quart saucepan. Bring them up to a boil. Reduce to a simmer and cook, covered, for 2 hours. Remove them from the heat and stir in 1½ teaspoons salt. Let the peanuts sit in the salty liquid a minimum of 15 minutes before draining them. Discard the liquid.

In a medium bowl, stir together the peanuts, mustard seeds, and the pickling liquid. Marinate, covered and refrigerated, a minimum of overnight or up to 1 week. About an hour before serving, stir in the remaining ingredients. Serve at room temperature.

For the pork chops: In a 4-quart saucepan, combine the water, sugar, ⅔ cup salt, Dijon, peppercorns, rosemary, sage, and garlic cloves. Bring that up to a boil and let it boil 1 minute. Remove it from the heat and cool to room temperature. Once it's cool, put the pork chops in a container large enough to hold them and the brine. Pour the brine over the top, making sure they are completely submerged. Brine them for 3 hours in the refrigerator. Remove the chops from the brine. Pat them dry and let them rest in the fridge a minimum of 1 hour before cooking.

Take the chops out of the fridge 30 minutes before you plan to cook them and preheat your oven to 350°F. Season the chops on both sides with the remaining salt and a couple turns of the pepper mill. Meanwhile, in a 12-inch heavy skillet, heat the vegetable oil until just smoking. Brown the chops, two at a time, on both sides, making sure that the hot oil also kisses the fatty lips of each chop.

Squeeze all the chops in a single layer in the skillet and slide that skillet in the oven. Cook until an instant-read thermometer reads 130°F, about 12 minutes for chops that are 1½ inches thick. Let the chops rest 10 minutes before serving.

To serve, spoon ½ cup Citrus Sweet Potato Butter, if using, on the bottom of a plate. Nestle the pork chop on top of that, and spoon the Pickled Peanut Salad over the pork.

OKRA

IF THE SOUTH HAD A MASCOT, it would be okra. Loved, hated, misunderstood, defended, and worn like a badge that defines you, both okra and my region's people go out into the world pridefully carrying the same baggage.

You love, hate, or have an unfounded fear of okra—and the same is true of the South. There's no vegetable more polarizing than this poor little pod. You'd think people would save such malice for more ostentatious, scene-stealing produce like tomatoes and watermelon, but no. Haters want to hate on a little green phallic thing the size of your index finger. And it's only one part of okra that tends to bother people: the slimy seeds.

People who hate okra pluck it out of soup and demand an extra plate for fear the goopy goo might ruin the whole bowl. They tell exaggerated stories about the childhood encounters that scarred them for life. Okra's reputation is so bad, some people won't even try it.

Same goes for people's disdain for the South. Parts of our region's history are incredibly shameful, and some people who currently call themselves Southerners make me want to stick a pencil in my eye. But couldn't you say the same of just about any place and its people? Hands down, the Southeastern United States is the butt of more jokes and the subject of more ignorant prejudice than any other place in the Land of the Free. (New Jersey is second.)

I'll argue that people who profess an unconditional love of okra and the South are equally irrational. When I started testing the recipes for this chapter, I asked my assistant Holley if she liked okra. "Oh yeah," she declared with enthusiasm. "It's my favorite vegetable!"

Oh really? Holley's response sounded like a rehearsed line she'd been practicing

her whole life. You mean to tell me you enjoy okra more than sweet corn, tomatoes, or potatoes? Next time someone goes on and on about how much he loves okra, ask him his favorite way to prepare it. The answer will probably be sliced, dropped in something wet, dropped in something dry, then dropped in hot oil, where it's fried into something that's as close to a hushpuppy as it is to okra.

Vocal lovers of the South are the same. Ask those Confederate flag–toting Rebels what makes their hearts sing for the South, and you'll hear, "People are nicer below the Mason-Dixon Line," or "We live a slower-paced life here." That sounds great, but I don't know where those nicer, slower-paced people live. It's not near me.

The vegetable and the region reflect each other in other ways too. Until my job forced it on me, I rarely ate okra. I also feared slime, fuzz, and green things growing in my mouth. But when summer became September and the local produce staring at me was eggplant, muscadines, peppers, and okra, I had to go work on some okra. What I found is that the maligned slime is actually very useful when harnessed and celebrated. I tasted crisp okra pods by themselves and learned that okra has a sweet, green, pleasing flavor distinct from everything else, but it isn't too demanding—not a show stealer. I also discovered all sorts of ways to work around that infamous slime and how to find more and less of it.

Now I seek okra out. I want to cook with it. I want to change people's minds about it. I'm not going to print myself an I LOVE OKRA T-shirt or name my next child after it, but I understand and respect it just as much as I do every other vegetable.

It's the same way with the South. Actually, I think it's the same way with any region, religion, way of life, fruit, or vegetable. If you don't know it, it's easy to hate it. People in other regions look at the South from their couches and see racism, fried food, slow talkers, and Honey Boo Boo. But when those people come here, when they eat our food, drive through our country, and spend time talking to the region's residents, they realize that Southern people are just people, and the South is just a place, some of it slimy, some of it shiny.

OKRA WISDOM

One Size Doesn't Fit All

WHEN SELECTING OKRA, I think about how I'll use it before I determine what size to look for. Small to medium pods with barely defined ridges are good for grilling, charring, or frying whole. I prefer small underdeveloped pods for pickling.

Pods that are longer than four inches tend to get tough and stringy, so they're not great for eating whole. The more mature the pod, the more developed the seeds inside. It's these seeds that produce the slime people either despise or seek, so choose accordingly. I like big mature okra when I'm trying to thicken something, like Gumbo Sauce *(page 412)* or Summer Vegetable Scallion Pancake batter *(page 406).*

Smooth or Furry

THERE ARE BASICALLY two types of okra: pods with smooth skin and pods with downy or furry skin. Some people choose to scrub furry okra with a vegetable brush or dish towel, but I worry with this step only when I'm making okra pickles.

Although there are a slew of okra varieties, Red Burgundy is one I'm a big fan of. It has a rust-red smooth skin and long slender pods that stay tender as they grow longer. Red Burgundy is even good raw. Unfortunately, like purple beans and red carrots, they do lose their unique color when cooked or pickled.

Storage

STORE OKRA in a paper bag in the refrigerator and don't wash it till you plan to use it. If you see okra with brown spots, it means it was picked a while ago or washed and stored damp.

Okra blossoms are beautiful and edible but incredibly perishable. If you plan on garnishing your plates with some of these butter-yellow blossoms, pick them no more than three hours prior to using them.

The Caps Are Edible

FOR SOME REASON, people feel like they need to trim the caps off okra. If I'm slicing pods to fry or using it in a stew for substance and girth, I do slice off the cap. But if I'm cooking okra whole, I like it to look like okra, so I leave the cute cap intact. It's edible!

Fried Okra Hash

Serves 2

MY MOM DIDN'T FRY much of anything. She was always worried about her children's level of plump, and she believed frying was fattening as well as messy. This meant that the two things most people associate directly with the South, fried chicken and fried okra, I never ate at home. I did eat them at other places, and the most memorable was the okra I had at my friend Jessica Howard's house.

Jessica had it all. Two big wheels, three *real* Cabbage Patch Dolls, and all the newfangled junk food you could hope for. Cheetos, Doritos, Oreos, Combos, Ho Hos, Easy Cheese, and Mountain Dew—the desirables I never saw at my own house—were by far my favorite part of hers. But Jessica's mom, Ms. Linda, browned chicken in a skillet, whipped mashed potatoes with lots of margarine, and fried okra. Her okra wasn't like the okra completely encapsulated in a clean wall of crisp breading we ate at school; Ms. Linda's was a mix of textures and degrees of doneness I never got enough of. She sliced them into little rounds. Some were completely shrouded in salty cornmeal and perfectly crisp; other pieces were slightly too dark and kind of nutty. And a little bit of every serving was naked, kissed only by cast-iron, oil, and salt. There was also part of her fried okra that wasn't okra at all—it was just cornmeal crisped in oil that had drifted off the pods. I'm guessing the okra's slime held it together.

All three of those distinct okra iterations come together in something that I'm calling hash, for lack of a better word. Whatever its proper name, this is magic draining on a paper-towel-lined plate.

½ cup cornmeal	¼ teaspoon cayenne	⅔ cup vegetable oil
1 teaspoon salt, divided	2 cups of okra sliced ⅓ inch thick (about 15 medium okra)	

Combine the cornmeal, ½ teaspoon salt, and cayenne in a medium bowl. Rinse the okra well with water and toss the damp okra with the cornmeal mixture. Set aside.

In a 12-inch cast-iron skillet, heat the oil over medium-high heat. Once the oil starts to shimmer, add a piece of okra. If it starts to sizzle right away, add the remaining okra, making sure you spread it out in a single layer. All of the okra needs to be touching oil. Lower the heat slightly and sizzle on 1 side undisturbed for 4 minutes. Toss the okra around with a spatula and cook an additional 3 to 4 minutes. Some of the okra will be honey brown, some will be more chestnut, and some will be blond. Using a slotted spoon, transfer the okra to a paper-towel-lined plate to drain. Season with the remaining ½ teaspoon salt. Serve warm.

Okra Oven Fries

Serves 4

OKRA COOKED IN THE OVEN like this are a revelation. The first time I did it, I planned on having them as a side with dinner, but I ate every single piece before we sat down and concluded they were more appropriate as a snack.

In the spirit of kale chips, but way tastier and more substantial, these fries *will* cook unevenly, so expect some crispy spots mingled with more chewy bites. If you're using large, fat okra, slice them into quarters. If you've got immature pods, split them in half.

1 **pound okra (20 to 25), split or quartered lengthwise**	2 **tablespoons extra-virgin olive oil**	10 **turns of the pepper mill or ¼ teaspoon black pepper**
	2 **teaspoons ground coriander**	
	1 **teaspoon salt**	

Preheat your oven to 400°F. In a medium bowl, toss the okra with the olive oil, coriander, salt, and black pepper. Spread the okra onto your largest baking pan or two pans if necessary. What's important is that the okra have plenty of room to spread out. If they are all piled on top of one another, they will steam, not roast.

Slide the pan onto the middle rack of your oven. After 10 minutes, toss the okra gently with a spatula and rotate your pans if you are using two. Cook an additional 10 to 15 minutes. When the okra is done, it will be brown and crispy in a lot of places but shouldn't smell burned. Serve warm or at room temperature as a snack. Sometimes I like to have a dip for these; Cilantro Buttermilk (*page 474*) works well, as does Kitchen-Sink Mayo (*page 120*).

Summer Vegetable Scallion Pancakes

Serves 4

THESE FRITTERS CAPITALIZE on okra's slime like nothing else. They're sort of a cross between a scallion pancake and fried okra, and their pillowy texture and vegetal flavor, coupled with the sweet pop of corn, is pleasing and addictive.

Choose large mature pods, and use only their fat midsections. The swollen seeds hiding in there will actually do a lot to hold the fritter batter together. I like to eat these right out of the frying pan over Stewed Tomatoes (*page 270*), but they're also nice at room temperature as a scoop for Butterbean Hummus (*page 156*).

1 cup okra, caps and tips removed, midsections minced	3 tablespoons minced scallion	1 egg
	1 teaspoon salt, divided	¼ teaspoon hot sauce
½ cup fresh corn, cut off the cob	2 tablespoons cornmeal	¼ to ⅓ cup vegetable oil
¼ cup squash or zucchini, grated on a box grater or in a food processor	2 tablespoons all-purpose flour	
	2 tablespoons buttermilk	

Preheat your oven to 200°F. In a medium bowl, stir together the minced okra, corn, squash, scallion, and ½ teaspoon of the salt. Let that sit for about 5 minutes. The salt will leach out the moisture in the squash. That moisture will activate the slime in the okra and bring the veggies together in kind of a gooey-looking mass.

Stir in the cornmeal and flour to incorporate. Whisk together the buttermilk, egg, and hot sauce, and stir it into the dry, slimy mass. Mix this up a few times and let it sit at least 3 minutes and up to 1 hour before you get ready to cook the fritters.

In a 10- to 12-inch skillet or cast-iron pan, add the oil over medium heat. If you want larger fritters, spoon about 2 tablespoons of the batter into the preheated oil and press down on each dollop to flatten it slightly. The fritters should be about ¼ inch thick. If you'd like smaller fritters, start with 1 tablespoon of batter.

Carefully continue dropping dollops of batter into the hot oil, making sure the fritters don't touch. Cook the fritters over medium heat on each side till they are chestnut-colored in some spots and golden in others. Transfer the fritters to a paper-towel-lined plate to drain and season them while hot with the remaining salt. Keep them warm in your oven while you fry the next batch. Serve warm with stewed tomatoes.

A Pickle Plate for Everyone

Makes 4 quarts pickles

THE PICKLE PLATE IS MAKING A COMEBACK. Just about everybody used to put out a plate of pickles when guests came over. That tradition lost favor for a while, but nowadays we once again view pickles as a great way to get started.

This combination pays homage to earthenware crocks of mixed fermenting vegetables from the summer garden. For a long time, fermentation was the way many people preserved vegetables. It just so happens to be all the rage these days.

I pair okra and corn because I want my pickle plate to appeal to everybody, and everybody likes corn. You could add green beans, green tomatoes, or any type of pepper. I've thrown a couple of jalapeños in there for heat and because somebody always wants to show off.

If a plate of pickles is not your thing, cut the corn off the cob. Toss it with the okra and serve as a condiment with steaks or lamb.

2 pounds whole okra, washed, pods kept whole	5 ears of corn, shucked and cut into 2-inch rounds	2 jalapeños
	4 garlic cloves, smashed	2 teaspoons black peppercorns
		⅔ cup salt

If you have furry okra, you may want to scrub the pods using a cloth or vegetable brush. The pickling liquid that gets trapped between the okra's down and its skin can look suspicious, so beware.

In a 2- to 3-gallon sterilized pot or earthenware fermentation crock, lay down half the okra. Top it with half the corn, the garlic cloves, jalapeños, and peppercorns. Finish with the remaining okra followed by the final layer of the other ingredients. Dissolve the salt in 1 gallon of water and pour that water over the vegetables.

It's of the utmost importance that the vegetables are submerged under close to 2 inches of water. Any okra or corn that bobs up and sees air will spoil, so find a plate or cake pan to sit on top of the vegetables, then put a weight on top of that plate. I use

a plate weighted down by a Tupperware container full of the same salt brine I'm using for the pickle. Cover the whole setup with cheesecloth or a clean dish towel and store it in a dark spot for 4 days.

Don't freak out when you see a little scum rise on top of the brine. That's normal. Just skim it off. On the fourth day, check an okra. If you like its tang, skim all the remaining funk from the top of the liquid and transfer the pickles in their brine to the refrigerator. This will stop the fermentation process. If you want a little more pucker, let them go for another day or two outside the fridge.

The pickles will keep in your refrigerator, submerged in their brine in a glass or heavy plastic container with a tight-fitting lid, for 2 months.

Tempura-Fried Okra with Ranch Ice Cream

Serves 4

I WAS BEING SNARKY when I put this on the restaurant menu. After three summers of okra dishes that garnered half-smiles, I decided I'd just give the people what they wanted—ranch dressing—but frozen like ice cream.

Although I knew the combination would sell, I misjudged why. I thought people would order it because we were in Eastern Carolina and I was selling fried something with ranch. I'm pretty sure that's why a lot of people ordered it the first time. The second time they ordered it, they called its name with a drop of drool pooling at the corner of their mouths because the memory of the hot, slender pod of okra and the little dab of the frozen ranch sang loud and clear and fine. That memory and the subsequent bite of cold fat on hot fat mingled with salt, tang, and crispy batter was something they wanted again.

Note: *It's important that your okra is at room temperature before you fry it. If it's cold, the batter will not adhere as well.*

½ cup Cucumber Ranch, minus the cucumber *(page 248)*	1 egg yolk	1 teaspoon salt, divided
	1 cup club soda	
2 quarts peanut or canola oil	½ cup Wondra or rice flour	½ teaspoon granulated sugar
	¼ cup cornmeal	8 ounces whole okra (about 4 cups)

Up to 3 hours before you'd like to serve the okra, process the ranch dressing in your ice cream machine. Then transfer it to your freezer. I like this ice cream pretty soft, so serve it directly from the machine or bring it out of your freezer a few minutes before you pair it with the okra. You'll only need ½ cup for this recipe, but you'll probably need to freeze at least 2 cups to satisfy the machine. You can melt the ranch and reuse it as regular dressing, or just fry more okra or other similar vegetables.

Heat the oil to 350°F in a 4- to 6-quart Dutch oven and preheat the oven to 200°F. Set up a rack on top of a baking sheet nearby. Just before frying, whisk together the yolk and club soda. Then whisk in the flour, cornmeal, ½ teaspoon salt, and sugar. The batter will look and feel like watery pancake batter and will seem too thin to cling to the okra. Please test fry an okra before adding any more flour or cornmeal to the batter.

Completely submerge the test okra in the batter, and drop it into the hot oil. If it adheres and doesn't completely flake off, you're good. What you're looking for is a transparent, crispy coating. You should actually be able to see the oil bubbling between the okra and the batter. A few holes in the crispy exterior is acceptable. Whole sides washed away are not. If the batter flies off, add another tablespoon of cornmeal.

Fry the rest of the okra in 2 batches for about 4 minutes each. Two minutes in, roll the okra over in the oil carefully to make sure it's frying evenly. Transfer the first batch of okra to the rack and season it with half the salt. Slide that okra into the warm oven while you fry the second batch in the same fashion. Serve the okra hot with the Ranch Ice Cream.

Shrimp and Grits with Gumbo Sauce

Serves 6

I DIDN'T HAVE SHRIMP AND GRITS till I was at least twenty years old, so saying it was a hallmark of my upbringing would be a complete lie. I can claim the dish as a prominent feature in my career, though. Before we opened, all the naysayers and hopeful fans seemed ready for us to hang our hat (or our necks) on the quality of our shrimp and grits...and I hardly knew what that was. I figured it out fast.

We had shrimp and grits on our menu for more than six years. At that point, we were all so sick of the dish we were thrilled to see it go. Our customers...not so thrilled. Now we try to do a shrimp and grits that reflects the season. And because shrimp and grits represents a culinary tradition that I have no real connection to, I chose to go full poser and brought cajun flavors into the mix. A true Cajun or Creole will grimace at my interpretation, but it's fresh, light, and flavorful.

I serve about the same amount of sauce as I do grits because I'm an American and I like sauce. If you like less, change the ratio and bake eggs for breakfast in the leftover sauce.

5	cups Gumbo Sauce
2	tablespoons butter
1½	pounds shrimp, 21/25 count, peeled and deveined (reserve the shells for your shrimp stock)
1	teaspoon salt
⅛	teaspoon cayenne
1	tablespoon lemon juice
6	cups Foolproof Grits *(page 31)*

Gumbo Sauce
Makes 6 cups

2	teaspoons vegetable oil
12	ounces smoked sausage or andouille, sliced into ⅓-inch rounds
1½	medium yellow onions, halved and sliced thinly with the grain
1	large green bell pepper, julienned
1	teaspoon salt

3	cloves of garlic, thinly sliced
1	cup white wine
2	cups okra sliced into ¼-inch rounds
4	cups Tomatoes in Jars *(page 264)* (canned work too)
3	cups Shrimp Stock *(page 302)*
¼	teaspoon chili flakes
2	tablespoons sherry vinegar
1	tablespoon butter

Make the gumbo sauce: In a Dutch oven, add the oil and brown the sausage over medium heat. Transfer the sausage to a plate and pour off all but 2 tablespoons of the oil in the pan. If your sausage was lean and you don't have 2 tablespoons of fat left over, add enough vegetable oil to make it right.

Stir in the onion, peppers, and salt and continue to cook over medium heat for about 15 minutes or until they are nicely browned and shrunken by half. Stir frequently to prevent them from burning.

With the heat on, add the garlic and wine. Let the wine boil down till there is about ¼ cup of liquid left in the pan. Stir in the browned sausage, okra, tomatoes,

shrimp stock, and chili flakes. Simmer uncovered for 20 to 25 minutes to reduce the sauce by nearly half. Stir in the vinegar and butter and keep warm.

Cook the shrimp and serve: In a 12-inch sauté pan or cast-iron skillet, heat the butter over high heat. Pat the shrimp dry and add them to the screaming-hot pan. Cook the shrimp, without shaking, for 3 minutes on one side. Season with salt, cayenne, and lemon juice. Toss and scrape up any stragglers from the bottom of the pan.

Take them off the heat and serve the shrimp on top of the gumbo on top of warm grits.

COLLARDS

*CHEF'S LIFE* started with an anonymous zip-lock bag of smelly collard kraut.

In 2009, Ben and I still lived in the river house in the tiny rural community of Pleasant Hill, North Carolina. Pleasant Hill sits on the edge of Jones County and is about a ten-minute drive from our current home in Deep Run. It's defined by a rundown country store that sells gas and biscuits but doesn't take credit cards. If you'd call Deep Run rural, you'd consider Pleasant Hill podunk.

One morning a few days before Christmas, I woke up to let our dog Gracie out. Usually in a hurry to sniff the yard, Gracie paused in the doorway, looked down, and whined. On our doorstep sat a zip-lock bag plump with milky liquid and dark green, almost brown, leaves. It smelled like rank feet and rotten roughage. I assumed someone was trying to teach me a lesson. At the time, our neighbors didn't consider Ben and me champions of Eastern Carolina. Instead, we were interlopers from New York City who didn't go to church and owned the fancy restaurant in Kinston. Leaving the jiggly bag right where Gracie found it, I turned on my heel and did what I always do when Eastern North Carolina asks me a question that I can't answer: I called my dad.

"Vivyen," my dad said, chuckling, a parent who knew things his grown children still didn't, "that's not a prank, it's a gift. It's collard kraut. It stinks like hell, but some people like it. Don't take it to the restaurant. They'll think you've got rotten food in the kitchen. The Mills boys probably gave it to you. They make kraut every year."

Collard kraut! This zip-lock and its contents suddenly became the object of my obsession. Sandor Katz's book *The Art of Fermentation* was the hottest text among

chefs at the time. I hadn't yet read it, but I knew kraut was a fermentation gateway, and I knew this smelly bag contained something cool. Unfortunately, I had no idea what to do with collard kraut, or with traditional sauerkraut, for that matter. For a moment I considered putting it on a hot dog. Instead, I took it to the restaurant and by lunch I had projected enough mental energy at the kraut to cook it with brainwaves.

The Internet gave me nothing and no one answered the phone at the Mills house, so I decided to just go for it. The kraut *had* to taste better than it smelled. I rinsed a leaf, cut it into ribbons, and set it aside—way aside. We had a creamed-collard toast on the menu at the time, so I heated some of that up and panfried a few crostini in bacon fat, then topped those with creamed collards and finished it all with kraut. The combination was better than the actual dish on our menu. The kraut brought acidity, funk, and a fresh texture. It didn't taste at all like it smelled while swimming in the brine.

How could this be? How could some old people down the road from me be making something my chef peers would see as cutting-edge? And why did they make it? Was Eastern North Carolina and our food a melting pot of other cultures, like the rest of the United States? I had to find out what else I didn't know.

The next morning I rushed to Pleasant Hill grocery. Pete Mills ran the store, and although I'd probably said two words to him since I'd lived there, I knew where I'd find him.

"Mr. Mills! Thank you so much for the collard kraut! I love it! I can't believe I've never even heard of it before!"

"You're welcome."

I waited a moment, sure he'd offer up an explanation. How could he have so little to say about something so amazing?

"How do you eat it?" I asked.

"Well, we just cook it."

Clearly I was more enthusiastic than he was. A man in his late sixties, Mr. Mills sat there on his stool chewing on something I couldn't identify.

"Can I make some with you? I'd really like to see how you do it."

"Well, we won't make it again till next year."

"What do you mean, next year?"

"Well, everything's got to be just right, and we only make it once't a year."

My enthusiasm easily fizzles, but I carried the collard kraut thing with me all year. I halfheartedly attempted a batch on my own, but something went dreadfully wrong, and I had to throw it, as well as the container it was in, away in the middle of the night. I got pregnant and sidetracked in August, but as soon as summer turned into fall, I started pestering Mr. Mills again.

The Monday before Thanksgiving, Pete told me they'd be making kraut at their aunt Pat's house the next day. The signs were right, he said. I could come if I wanted.

"Signs? What do you mean, signs?"

"You can't make kraut when the almanac tells you the signs are in the bowels. It'll rot. They're in the head right now, so we better get to it."

When I pulled up to Aunt Pat's early the next morning, the Mills brothers— Pete, Van, and Fred—and a first cousin, Charles (aka Pee Wee), were already at work in a small square shed out back. The men were amused by my presence and asked straightaway why I wanted to watch what they were doing. When I answered that I thought their time-honored tradition might give me insight into who I was and where

COLLARD WISDOM

Collards Are a Symbol

IF THE SOUTHEAST'S IDENTITY is a pie, collards are a slice of it. There's this misconception that Southern food is an endless buffet of fried chicken, whole-hog barbecue, and macaroni and cheese. But historically, that's just not the case. The region's everyday foods relied on meat as a condiment far more than meat as the main attraction. Nothing exemplifies that more than a pot of collards.

Collards are non-heading cabbages, sometimes called tree cabbages. They became popular in the South because they thrive in loamy soil and grow pretty much all year in mild climates. Although the plant itself arrived on ships from Europe, the tradition of cooking them down slowly and drinking their pot liquor is from Africa.

Classic collard cookery took a cheap, fringe cut of cured and often smoked pork and stretched it over a large, fortifying pot of stewed collard greens. In many cases, those greens became dinner, fortified with just a little meat and cornbread. It was dinner and supper so many times, in fact, that collards' slice of Southern pie remains relevant in an age where more Southerners eat fast food than slow-stewed greens.

The Collard Chopper

IF YOU SNOOPED through the cupboards of any Southern kitchen even fifteen years ago, you'd find a few staples in each one: a cast-iron skillet, a large pot for greens, a jar of bacon grease, and a collard chopper (see photo, page 427). Even though my mom cooked turnips, we had a collard chopper, and we called it that. Its primary function was to cut up greens after they'd been cooked, but we used it to chop berries for shortcake and nuts for pies. I often wonder why they've faded from the limelight. They're a heck of a lot easier to clean than a food processor.

Collards Like It Cold

COLLARDS GROW just about all year here in the Carolinas, but we think of them as a fall and winter crop because they taste better after a frost. When cold air hits a collard leaf, it changes some of its starch into sugar. This balances the bitterness collards are notorious for. It's not folklore—collards *are* better after a frost.

There's two ways to harvest collards. If you're frugal-minded and want to keep your collards producing through the winter and into early spring, cut the bottom outer leaves off all your plants to produce your first round

I came from, I got blank stares in return. So I just smiled, cupped my pregnant belly, and watched.

The men worked quietly and everybody knew their roles. Pete took the collards out of a small pickup that was backed against the shed and made quick work of trimming the root end from each sprawling green bunch.

of greens. These are the oldest leaves and should be eaten first if you choose to harvest in batches. Continue to pluck leaves around the outside of the plant for subsequent harvests. If this is the method you choose, come December your plants will look like little palm trees, but they will still be producing.

If you're in it for the best-tasting pot of collards possible, harvest an entire plant. That will give you a mix of bitter, hunter-green outer leaves and sweet, Kermit-green inner leaves that will result in a balanced bite. Whole heads like this are often available at farmers' markets around Thanksgiving and Christmas.

If you've never seen that but know a farmer who sells collard leaves in bunches, request a whole head. You'll pay for it, but it's worth the experience.

Varieties

EASTERN NORTH CAROLINA takes collards seriously. Ayden, a small town about twenty minutes from me, is the self-proclaimed collard capital of the world. They have a collard queen, a collard festival, and their very own variety of collards.

Most collards you see are the Georgia variety. They have dark green, sometimes purplish-blue, leaves and a deep, often bitter taste. In Eastern Carolina we favor a variety called the cabbage collard. Until recently, your only chance of growing these sweet, light green, quick-cooking leaves was if you knew someone with a stash of seeds or if you bought baby plants from the Collard Shack in Ayden, North Carolina. But because of interest in heirloom vegetables and Southern cuisine, the cabbage collard has crossed state lines. Several seed companies online now offer cabbage collard seeds.

Prepping

PREPARING COLLARDS for the pot seems overwhelming, given how bulky they are, but it's actually not a tedious process. I like to wash my collards in a stopped-up sink with two changes of water, similar to how my mom washes her turnips (page 66). Then I strip the leaf from the stem, starting at the bottom and working up, reserving some of the fat stem ends for pickling.

In some cases, like with Collard Kraut (page 425) or Stewed Collard Greens (page 426), I remove only the stem that extends beyond the leaf.

"You can't do this till there's been a frost. Collards ain't sweet enough till then. These come from seed our family saved for a hundred years. They're sturdier than the cabbage collards everybody eats around here, but they *are* sweet." I gobbled up Pete's words, and to let him know I wanted more, I asked another question.

"Where's Aunt Pat?"

RECISE

Collard Kraut

Stewed Collard Greens with Ham Hock

Creamed Collards with Pickled Collard Stems

Twice-Baked Collard Potatoes

Collard, Carrot, and Raisin Salad

Gingered Collards

Healthy Soup

Collard Dolmades with Sweet Potato Yogurt

"Oh, she's in the house. Women don't help with the kraut."

"What do you mean?"

"They just don't. It's men's work."

Inside the shed, Fred and Pee Wee washed each collard bunch in two changes of water then dropped the bundles into a plastic fifty-gallon trash can. The trash can confused me, and it must have shown on my face, because Pete chimed in.

"We used to use one of those big crocks, but it cracked. This is easier."

After Pee Wee dropped several layers of collards in, Van pounded the leaves with a four-foot-long wooden club similar to the one Bamm-Bamm carried around in *The Flintstones*. Then he poured a layer of pickling salt straight from the box and topped it with more collards.

"What's the pounding all about?"

"It breaks it up—lets you fit more in the can and gets the collards ready for the salt."

Once the trash can was three-quarters full of collards, the men filled it with water and weighed the leaves down with smooth blocks of oak. Pete stuck his finger in and tasted the water. He looked at me close and then pointed his finger. I think he finally understood I wanted to know everything.

"It needs to taste like the Atlantic Ocean. Too salty and the kraut won't make. Not enough salt and it'll spoil. And the water has got to be from a well. None of that city water. It don't work. And don't go weighing it down with hickory or pecan or pine. That'll give the kraut an off taste."

I scribbled furiously in my mental notebook and started to see Pete Mills in a different light. He, all these men, and maybe all the older people around me were planets of wisdom orbiting around a bunch of young people who didn't even know enough to ask the right questions. What would happen to all these traditions when Pete and his brothers and cousin were gone?

Van covered the trash can with a towel and tied a rope around the can's rim.

"That'll keep the bugs out. If the weather stays like it is now, we'll check it in about three weeks. I'll bring you some when it's ready."

"Can I ask y'all a few more questions?"

"Sure."

"Why do you do this?"

"I guess 'cause we like it. But Mama and Daddy did it so they had greens to eat in the winter."

"Will your children continue to make it after y'all stop?"

"No. I reckon not."

I left Aunt Pat's house that day on a mission. I wanted to seek out more collard krauts and spread the gospel. I wanted to write a blog about it, make a movie about it, have a festival around it. I blabbered and blabbered to Ben. I had my babies and kept blabbering. Finally, Ben convinced me to call my friend Cynthia Hill, a documentary film producer. And the rest is *A Chef's Life*.

Collard Kraut

I'M GIVING YOU a shrunken version of the Mills brothers' recipe. Because I can't just tell you to sprinkle "enough" salt between layers of collards, I recommend a mixed brine. Other than that and the omission of folklore, this is the way they do it.

This recipe calls for four pounds of collards, weighed after the large end stems have been removed. You can make as much or as little kraut as you like as long as you measure one-third cup of kosher salt for every two quarts of water. The method, not the size of the batch, is important here.

To make the kraut, you're going to need a very clean vessel, a weight, and a lid. The Millses used a fifty-gallon plastic trash can. I often ferment in an old-school earthenware crock. In this recipe I use a stockpot, its lid, and a zip-lock bag full of brine as a weight.

4	pounds collard leaves, harvested preferably after a frost, large end stems removed	2	gallons distilled water	1⅓ cups kosher salt

Begin by washing your collards and your vessel very well. Pack the collard leaves down into the bottom of your pot a few leaves at a time. Press them firmly with a potato masher or pestle after every layer. The goal is to bruise the leaves but also to pack them as tightly in the vessel as possible. Once you've packed all the collard leaves in there, mix the water and the salt and pour the brine over the top. The collards should be submerged by 2 inches.

From this point forward, it's incredibly important that no collards see the light of day. They must be submerged in the brine throughout the entire fermentation process. To do this, pour the remaining brine into a gallon zip-lock bag and put that bag on top of the collards. The weight of the bag should keep the collard greens below the surface of the brine. If not, fill another bag with brine and place it on top of the first bag. Cover the vessel with a cheesecloth or a towel, and secure that cover so it doesn't fall off or in. Then cover your stockpot loosely with its lid.

Store the kraut at room temperature (70°F is ideal) away from direct sunlight for about 3 weeks. The Millses make their kraut outside in November. You could do that too, but the cooler the temperature the longer it takes. Check it periodically and skim off any scum that rises to the top. It will begin to smell and bubble and, well, ferment after about 5 days. At the end of a month, transfer the kraut to a refrigerator, where it should keep for up to 6 months submerged in its brine.

The Mills brothers rinse the kraut well and cook it just as they would any pot of collards (*page 426*). But I like to eat it rinsed and raw on burgers on avocado toast or with barbecue. Consider stirring Collard Kraut into Lentil Apple Soup (*page 494*) as a tangy garnish or finishing the Oyster and Clam Pan Roast (*page 122*) with a spoonful of it for contrast. Believe it or not, it's quite versatile.

Stewed Collard Greens with Ham Hock

Serves 4

EVEN THOUGH I GREW UP in a turnip-eating house, I understand the weight collards carry in Carolina kitchens. Every restaurant in the country-cooking genre and most households here claim them as their patron green, and I cook with them in a variety of ways at the restaurant. I'll chalk up my mom's affinity for turnips over collards to the way she saw my grandma Iris prepare the South's most revered green.

Mom likes to point out the defining difference between the way her mother cooked and the way my dad's mother cooked was how they approached fat. Grandma Hill, my mom's mom, skimmed fat away and used less than recipes called for. My grandma Iris did the opposite. She believed fat equaled flavor, and her pot of collards proved it.

After Grandma Iris simmered the collards for two hours, she scooped them out of their pot liquor and put them in a bowl. To that she added the meat the collards cooked with, sugar, and salt and went at it all with the collard chopper till the mixture was spoonable. Then she turned back to her pot and skimmed off the white cap that had risen to the top of the pot liquor. Now, I know you think I'm gonna say she threw the white foamy fat out. She didn't. She threw it in. This is not an uncommon practice. The white stuff has a name. It's called shine, and it's prized among collard cooks who know.

Aware that a proper pot of collards is a loaded topic, I'm giving you the way my grandma Iris would have done it.

- 1 ham hock or 8 to 10 ounces other pork seasoning meat
- 3 quarts of water
- 1 medium yellow onion, diced
- ½ teaspoon red chili flakes
- 10 turns of the pepper mill or ¼ teaspoon black pepper
- 2 pounds or 1 whole head collards, large stems

removed
- 1 teaspoon salt
- 1 tablespoon granulated sugar (optional)

In a 6- to 8-quart Dutch oven or pot, combine the ham hock or seasoning meat, water, onion, chili flakes, and black pepper. Cover. Bring it up to a boil and cook, covered, for 30 minutes. Add the collards. Lower the heat to a heavy simmer. Cover

and cook for an hour and a half. Take the lid off and test the greens for doneness. They should have taken on some of the porky goodness from the broth and have a silky-soft texture.

Scoop the greens into a bowl, leaving the pot liquor behind. Pick the smoked morsels from the hock or chop the

seasoning meat into rough pieces and add them to the greens. Using a collard chopper or a knife, roughly chop the greens and the meat together. You can go as far as you like here, but I prefer a little texture. Stir in up to 1 teaspoon salt and 1 tablespoon sugar if you deem it necessary. Finally, skim the shine off the top of the pot liquor and stir it in.

Serve the greens warm with hot sauce or hot pepper vinegar. Reserve the pot liquor for another use or drink it up for good health.

Creamed Collards
with Pickled Collard Stems

Serves 4

EARLY ON IN MY COLLARD STUDIES I became fixated on how I could encourage more consumption of pot liquor. It's considered a cure-all by a lot of old-timers—the South's chicken soup, if you will—and it tastes wonderfully rich and bitter and sweet. But only a certain type of person is going to drink the by-product of stewing greens and pork, so that was a problem. Then the possibility of creaming collards like spinach came up, and I had an idea.

Instead of adding cheese and cream to my collards, which just makes the collards taste like cheese and cream, I'd make a velouté—a roux-thickened broth—using pot liquor. The result was like eating a bowl of collards in pot-liquor-flavored gravy. It's sinful but you kind of don't feel bad about it.

Because this is one rich bowl of collards, we typically treat it like a warm dip or a spread. Mom's Cornpone (*page 28*) works perfectly as a vehicle, and pickled collard stems finish it off in lieu of hot pepper vinegar.

Pickled Stems

Makes 1 cup

- ½ cup cider vinegar
- ½ cup water
- ¼ cup granulated sugar
- 4 garlic cloves, smashed
- 2 bay leaves
- 1 teaspoon red chili flakes
- ¼ teaspoon salt
- 1 cup collard stems, trimmed of leaves and cut into ¼-inch rounds

Creamed Collards

Makes 3 cups

- 2 tablespoons butter
- 2 tablespoons all-purpose flour
- 2 cups Stewed Collard Greens (*page 426*), 1 cup pot liquor reserved
- ¼ cup heavy cream

Pickle the stems: Combine the vinegar, water, sugar, garlic, bay leaves, chili flakes, and salt in a small saucepan. Bring it up to a boil and add the stems. Cook for 2 minutes. Remove from the heat and let it cool to room temperature. You can eat these right away, but they'll be better the next day. The pickles will keep in the fridge for up to a month.

Cream the collards: In a 10-inch skillet, melt the butter over medium heat. Whisk in the flour and cook for 1 minute. Pour in the pot liquor and whisk while it comes up to a boil and thickens.

Stir in the collards and the cream and heat through. Serve warm, sprinkled with the pickled stems.

Twice-Baked Collard Potatoes

Serves 4

IF I BURNED A CALORIE every time someone asked me to put a baked potato on Chef and the Farmer's menu, I'd be skinny. After eight years of running the restaurant, I finally relented, but on my terms. Creamed collards stirred into baked-potato flesh are a wink toward the classic steak-house combination of baked potato and creamed spinach. More than gimmick, though, these potatoes improve on the typical twice-baked with a sweet bitterness and textural contrast you don't usually find. Coming across a little seasoning meat treasure in there is pretty nice too.

This is an easy thing to do for a party. Stuff and sear the potatoes beforehand and just heat them through in the oven before you eat. And, for the love of God, eat the skin.

2	large russet potatoes, washed
1	teaspoon extra-virgin olive oil
1½	teaspoons salt, divided
1	cup Creamed Collards *(page 429)*, warm
10	turns of the pepper mill or ¼ teaspoon black pepper
2	tablespoons crème fraîche or sour cream
2	teaspoons butter
1	teaspoon vegetable oil
½	cup Pickled Collard Stems *(page 429)*

Note: *2 large russet potatoes should provide roughly 2 cups of cooked potato flesh. If you have significantly more or less, adjust the other ingredients to reflect the difference.*

Preheat your oven to 400°F. Rub the outside of the potatoes with the olive oil and season them with 1 teaspoon salt. Roast the potatoes on a baking sheet on the middle rack of your oven for 1 hour. Let the potatoes cool just till you're able to handle them. Their flesh will pass much easier through the ricer if it's warm.

Split the potatoes in half horizontally and cut the rounded tip off the bottom of each half so the potatoes will stand up. You could split them in half through their equator, but you'll turn more heads if you do it my way. Scoop out all but the ¼ inch of potato that clings to the skin and pass the flesh through a potato ricer or food mill. If you don't have one of these, you could improvise by mashing the potato with a fork, but do not by any means put that potato flesh in the food processor. You'll make glue.

Stir together the riced potato flesh, warm Creamed Collards, the remaining

½ teaspoon salt, the black pepper, and the crème fraîche. Mix well.

Stuff the potato skins with the filling and make sure it's flush with the top of the skin. You're going to sear the tops of these in a pan, so the filling cannot finish in a mound. At this point you could refrigerate the stuffed potatoes for up to 2 days before searing and heating them through. If you do that, however, please bring them to room temperature beforehand or let them spend 5 more minutes in the oven than the recipe recommends.

To serve, preheat your oven to 400°F. Melt the butter and oil over medium heat in a 12-inch cast-iron pan or skillet. Once the butter is foaming, brown the large, flat stuffed end of the potatoes first for about 4 minutes. Turn one over and check its color. You want it brown and crispy. If you've got that, flip the remaining potatoes over and slide the pan into your oven. Cook for 8 minutes more. Sprinkle the potatoes with Pickled Collard Stems and serve warm.

Collard, Carrot, and Raisin Salad

Serves 4

I LIKE KALE, but the massaged-kale cult is a little out of hand. In this bowl of tasty health food, I retaliate with collard greens and salty peanuts married with sweet carrots and raisins. It's a great thing for entertaining or for lunch at work because it's better the next day.

- 3 cups collard leaves (about 8 ounces), stems removed, leaves cut into 1-inch dice
- 1 cup shredded carrots
- 2 tablespoons extra-virgin olive oil
- ½ shallot (3 tablespoons), sliced into ⅛-inch rounds
- ¼ teaspoon chili flakes
- ¼ cup raisins
- ½ cup crushed pineapple
- ¼ cup orange juice
- 3 tablespoons cider vinegar
- 1 teaspoon smooth Dijon mustard
- 1 teaspoon honey
- ¾ teaspoon salt
- ⅓ cup salt-roasted peanuts

In a medium bowl, combine the collards and the carrots. Set aside. In an 8- to 10-inch saucepan or skillet, heat the olive oil, shallots, and chili flakes over medium heat until they really start to sizzle. Just before they begin to brown, add the raisins, pineapple, orange juice, vinegar, Dijon, honey, and salt. Bring that thick mixture up to a boil and pour it over the collards. Toss together and refrigerate for at least 30 minutes and up to overnight. Just before serving, stir in the peanuts.

Gingered Collards

Serves 4

UNFORTUNATELY, collards have been typecast as a stewing green. We don't think of them as something we can sauté up quickly, like spinach or chard, but they are that too. The end result is going to have more texture than some limp wilting greens, but texture isn't always a bad thing. Instead of moving the greens around constantly in the pan, let them sit for 2 minutes at a time. They'll take on some color and additional flavor.

Use this recipe as a template and add components you have on hand, like raisins, dried cranberries, pine nuts, or pecans. Serve these with Miso Flounder with Cucumber Noodles (*page 254*), or cook the greens just like this and toss them with rice or quinoa for a healthy lunch. See the photograph on page 255 under the flounder.

- 2 teaspoons butter
- 1 teaspoon vegetable oil
- 2 tablespoons minced ginger
- 1 pound collards, stems removed, leaves cut into 1-inch squares
- 4 garlic cloves, sliced thin
- 1 teaspoon salt
- ¼ teaspoon red chili flakes
- 1 cup water
- 2 teaspoons light brown sugar
- ½ cup orange juice

Heat a 12-inch cast-iron skillet or sauté pan over medium heat. Add the butter and oil. Once it begins to foam, throw in the ginger, followed by the collards. Hit the cabbage with the garlic, salt, and chili flakes. Do not shake the pan. Please push against the magnetic force drawing you to the handle of the pan for at least 3 minutes, as you need to let things snap and sizzle until the collards begin to brown around the edges.

Once you start to see some caramelization, shake the pan with joy and toss the collards to and fro. Then spread them out in the pan again and let them sit and caramelize another 3 to 4 minutes. Once the collards are brown in spots, aromatic with ginger, and wilted, add the water, brown sugar, and orange juice. Cook until the liquid has evaporated. Serve warm.

Healthy Soup

Makes 3 quarts

DON'T LET THE NAME DETER YOU. Ben coined it because I make pot after pot of this during the winter, and I intentionally leave out carbs and bacon and cream and other stuff he thinks should appear in it because I am, in fact, trying to achieve a leaner state. The idea of this started with the cabbage-soup-diet fad from the 1990s. I actually made that sad soup, and even back then, before I was a chef, I couldn't understand why it had to taste so bland.

The approach for making soup is a little unorthodox. It builds on my mom's technique for chicken and rice and produces a much more flavorful broth than adding pieces of chicken to chicken stock. I save my Parmigiano-Reggiano rinds in the freezer for moments like this. You should do the same, whether or not you make this soup; they add a lot of background flavor to broths. The idea is to use what you have, but collards are my favorite green for this because they retain more texture than anything else. Sub in any greens or herbs you like.

Note: *Because we eat this at home a lot, I always have cooked lentils, potatoes, barley, or brown rice on hand so that Ben can add heft to his bowl.*

- 1 2 ½- to 3 ½-pound chicken
- 1 yellow onion, peeled and split
- 10 garlic cloves
- 8 sprigs thyme
- 2 teaspoons dried oregano
- ½ teaspoon chili flakes
- 3 bay leaves
- 3 quarts water
- 2 tablespoons extra-virgin olive oil
- 2 small yellow onions, diced
- 1 cup diced celery (2 large stalks)
- 1 cup diced carrots (2 medium)
- 2 teaspoons salt, divided
- 2 cups Tomatoes in Jars *(page 264)* or canned tomatoes
- 5 ounces Parmigiano-Reggiano rinds (about 3 square inches)
- 1 pound collards, large stems removed, leaves cut into 1-inch squares
- 2 tablespoons light brown sugar
- 10 turns of the pepper mill or ¼ teaspoon black pepper
- 1 cup Basil Pesto *(page 346)*, optional

Rinse the chicken and place it, breast-side up, in a 6- to 8-quart Dutch oven. Add the peeled onion, garlic, herbs, chili flakes, bay leaves, and water. Cover and bring it up to a boil. Reduce to a simmer and cook for 1 hour or until the chicken is, as my mother would say, "falling to pieces." Let the chicken cool in the broth for 30 minutes. Transfer the chicken to a rimmed plate. Pluck out the herbs, bay leaves, and onion (but feel free to leave the garlic) and pour the broth into a bowl.

Wipe the same Dutch oven dry and add the olive oil. Over medium heat, sweat the diced onion, celery, and carrots with 1 teaspoon salt for 5 minutes. Add the broth, tomatoes, and Parm rinds to the pot. Cover and bring it up to a boil. Reduce to a simmer and cook for 20 minutes. Meanwhile, pick the meat off the chicken and get the collards ready. You want these collards spoon-friendly so make sure you cut them into squares, not ribbons.

After 20 minutes, remove the Parm rinds and add the chicken, collards, remaining 1 teaspoon salt, 2 tablespoons sugar, and the black pepper. Cook for 20 minutes more.

Serve warm as is or with a dollop of pesto.

Collard Dolmades Prep

Collard Dolmades with Sweet Potato Yogurt

Makes 15 dolmades

I'M AN AWKWARD ENTERTAINER: overzealous, nervous, all over myself, one might say. So I love an hors d'oeuvre that people can talk about, a snack that's capable of lifting some of the pressure off me to be charismatic and fabulous. If you take the time to make these, you won't have to say a word when your guests arrive. These dolmades are cute and taste like Thanksgiving wrapped up in a collard leaf.

⅓ cup apple cider

¼ cup dried cranberries

10 to 15 large, intact collard leaves

1½ cups Fresh Sausage *(page 363)*

1 tablespoon fresh ginger (grated on a Microplane)

1 tablespoon brown sugar

½ teaspoon salt

15 turns of the pepper mill or scant ½ teaspoon black pepper

⅓ cup roughly chopped, toasted pecans

Sweet Potato Yogurt

Makes 1 cup

½ cup Roasted Sweet Potatoes *(page 312)*

½ cup plain Greek yogurt

Zest of 1 lemon (removed with a Microplane)

2 tablespoons lemon juice

1 tablespoon honey

½ teaspoon salt

¼ teaspoon cayenne

Make the dolmades: In a small saucepan or in the microwave, bring the apple cider up to a simmer and pour it over the cranberries to rehydrate them. While the cranberries are cooling, bring a large pot of heavily salted water to a boil and set up an ice bath nearby.

Once the water is at a rolling boil, drop in the collard leaves, two at a time, blanching each set for about 45 seconds. Using tongs, transfer the blanched, now bright green leaves to an ice bath. Continue this process with the remaining leaves.

Once you've blanched and shocked all the collards, dry them thoroughly between paper towels and remove the large stem with a knife, taking care to make sure both sides of the leaf stay intact.

In the bowl of a mixer fitted with the paddle attachment, combine the (uncooked) sausage, the drained cranberries, ginger, brown sugar, salt, and black pepper. Paddle on low until the mixture is homogenous. Then stir in the pecans.

To assemble the dolmades, cut the collard leaves into roughly 4 x 6-inch rectangles. Spoon 2 tablespoons of the sausage mix onto the lower center portion of the collard rectangle. Using your fingers, shape the filling into a short cigar. Fold the side edges in over the filling. Fold the bottom over, and roll it up much like an egg roll.

Continue cutting, filling, tucking, and rolling until you've used up all of your filling. Store the assembled dolmades,

seam-side down, in the refrigerator for up to 2 days until you're ready to cook them.

Make the yogurt: Combine all the ingredients in a blender and process until super-smooth.

Cook and serve: When I do this at home, I call on a steamer basket like the one you would use to steam broccoli. A bamboo dumpling steamer works great as well. Just make sure the dolmades don't touch

the bottom of the pan or the water. Whatever your steamer situation is, set it up and bring the water up to a boil. Place the dolmades in the basket on a rack in a single layer, taking care that they are not touching. Cover and steam hard for 10 minutes.

If you need to cook these in batches, they will keep warm in a bowl covered with plastic wrap. Serve the dolmades with a swoosh of Sweet Potato Yogurt.

IN OUR BACKYARD WHEN I was very young, we had a sad peach orchard, about four trees that never produced fruit. I remember the orchard not for its nonexistent yield but for its role in maintaining household order—Mom or Dad saying, "If you don't straighten up, I'm gonna need you to go out there and get a peach-tree switch, Vivyen."

I forgot about those stinging switches for a long time, but then we decided to do a peach episode for the show. Peach season had become one of the seasons I watched the clock for every year. Peaches, like tomatoes and figs, are no good until they're really good. Ingredients with a clearly defined season like that are what I cook for.

In more than just the obvious ways, *A Chef's Life* helped shape the person I strive to be today. The act of digging deeper into the food of my region for the story's sake introduced me to unlikely teachers, friends, and a means of connecting to my heritage I would never have been open to if I weren't on assignment. I grew up looking for differences between me and the other people here. Our show allowed me to see the ways we're the same.

Every episode of *A Chef's Life* takes a featured ingredient and weaves three storylines around it: one about a producer or grower of it, one about the traditional application of it, and one about our modern use of the ingredient at the restaurants. Over the years, I developed a deep understanding of how to incorporate peaches into savory dishes at Chef and the Farmer, so I had that part down. And just outside of town, there was a peach orchard, so I had the producing-and-growing part too. What I didn't have was a connection to a traditional preparation. My family had always just eaten peaches out of hand, and that was that.

Surprised by the memory of peach trees with no peaches, I asked my mom why she manicured an orchard year after year that produced no fruit.

She told me a story I had heard before but never really listened to. She and my dad met on a school trip to New York. She was a senior at B. F. Grady High School and he was a junior at Pink Hill, but because John was a cocky guy who followed his own rules, he went on her senior trip. She had a serious boyfriend at the time, but Dad impressed her, and they agreed to go out on a date.

Duplin County, where Mom grew up, and Deep Run, where Dad lived, were twenty miles apart. But when a family had one car and one telephone, communities that close together seemed oddly distant. Dad stood Mom up on their first date—calling hours later to say he was stuck in a hurricane she didn't know about. Despite the dubious start, my parents married before they turned twenty-one.

When Mom was a young girl, they had a peach orchard on their farm, and for days and days every July, her family canned peaches.

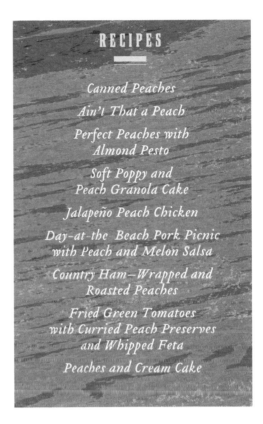

Mom's job was to take the sealed jars from the kitchen and slide them under the house, where they stored all their summer put-ups. Then every Sunday after church, she'd slide back under the house to mine a jar for her favorite meal of the week: fried chicken, canned peaches, and whipped cream from their cows. Mom's dad plowed over the peach orchard when she was around ten in favor of hog pens, and Mom had always missed the trees, the peaches, and the Sunday ritual. When she and my dad built a house in Deep Run, she wanted to tie it to her childhood. The peach trees were her attempt.

I was dumbfounded by the story. I had matured beyond the idea that my parents existed only to birth and nurture me, but just barely. To think of them as teenagers on school trips with crushes and butterflies, then as young adults trying to build a home that made them feel at home, helped me see my parents as people—more like me than not.

PEACH WISDOM

If You Must Peel, Here's How

A LOT OF PEOPLE are bothered by the skin of a peach. Know that once you peel a peach, it starts to oxidize. Even if you toss it with a little lemon juice, it will eventually turn brown. Nevertheless, there's almost nothing more shiny and beautiful than a just-peeled peach.

To peel them with ease, bring a large pot of water to a boil and set up an ice bath nearby. Make a shallow *X* in the bottom of each peach with a paring knife. Drop the peaches, a few at a time, into the water and let them stay there for up to one minute. Be careful not to cook them, but make sure the skin starts to split and peel away from the flesh. Remove them from the boiling water and drop into the ice bath. Peel them using the *X* as a guide.

A Peach Pit Has a Pit

PEACHES ARE STONE FRUITS. Inside every peach is a hard stonelike pit or seed, and inside that seed is something called a bitter almond or *noyaux*. This stark white kernel is used to flavor amaretto but isn't necessarily tasty to eat on its own like its cousin the almond.

Does It Smell Ripe?

I'VE HAD MY HAND SWATTED more than once at a farmers' market for squeezing the peaches. True, pressing a peach gently to see if its flesh gives is one way to tell how ripe the fruit is, but I like to rely on smell. If it's fragrant, it's probably not only ripe, but right.

Peaches ripen at room temperature in two to three days; refrigerated, they remain slightly unripe for about two weeks without lessening terribly in quality. Farmers almost never sell ripe peaches to vendors because they bruise easily, so don't feel cheated if you have to go home and set your peach out on the counter for a day or two.

Varieties

PEACHES ARE EITHER CLINGSTONE or freestone varieties. We get clingstones first, and they are a pain to work with because the flesh clings to the pit. A little later in the season, we see freestone varieties. Their pits separate easily from the flesh, and they are a pleasure.

For most of these recipes you can muddle through a batch of clingstones, but if you plan on canning, make sure you find freestones. The end product will look better, and you'll enjoy the process.

In the United States, most peaches are yellow-fleshed, but peaches can have white or red flesh too. And nectarines are actually just peaches with a genetic mutation for smooth skin.

Canned Peaches

Makes 8 pints

THERE ARE LOTS OF WAYS to can a peach. I've used all kinds of stuff, including vanilla bean pods, nutmeg, cinnamon, and star anise, to flavor the syrup, but after a few medicine-flavored jars of peaches, I decided I prefer the simple, unmistakable flavor of the peach all by itself. If you add anything, throw in the *noyaux* from inside the pits.

Two things to keep in mind here: It's important to can peaches that are ripe, but not soft. You're going to manhandle a pretty delicate fruit, so start with a peach that has a shot at holding up as you ram it into a jar. Also, if you choose to double this recipe, do so in batches. If you peel and quarter too many peaches before canning them, they'll turn brown.

They may not sound like much, but these peaches with a big dollop of whipped cream are my kind of dessert—easy and satisfying.

4 quart jars or 8 pint jars	20 medium barely ripe, firm peaches	6 cups water
	3 cups granulated sugar	

Begin by peeling the peaches (*page 444*), removing their pits, and quartering them. Sterilize your jars (*page 16*), add any flavoring elements you wish, and start stuffing the quartered peaches in the jars, cavity-side down. This is harder than it looks but very important. If the cavity is facing down, you'll be able to fit more peaches in the jar. The idea is to get as many peaches in as you can, then try to add one more.

As you fill the jars, heat the sugar and water to make the syrup. I like to do this in a teakettle. It makes pouring the syrup into the jars easier. Once the jars are stuffed with peaches, pour the hot syrup slowly over the top, allowing the syrup to creep its way through all the peaches. Cover the peaches by ½ inch with syrup. Process the jars (*page 16*) immediately in a hot-water bath for 30 minutes.

Ain't That a Peach

Makes 4 cocktails

MY MOM AND GRANDMA would never have done this, but if you take a little of that peach syrup from the jar and mix it with a little bourbon and lemon juice, you've got something pretty darn special.

8	ounces bourbon
½	cup syrup from canned peaches
1 tablespoon plus 1 teaspoon lemon juice	
Peach slices for garnish (optional)	

Stir the first three ingredients together and serve over ice. Garnish with peach slices.

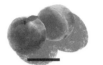

Perfect Peaches with Almond Pesto

Serves 4

TO COMPOSE A DISH, I generally select a cast of characters whose qualities complement one another in a way that makes the sum greater than its parts. Take a steak dish, for instance. I believe the vegetable side is just as important as the piece of meat and the sauce. They all come together to make one another better. That's not the case here. The peach is the star of this show, and all her underlings are there to make her taste her best. Because these peaches have only a few nuts to hide behind, don't make this if you don't have fragrant, ripe, perfect peaches.

Stir leftover pesto into rice or toss it with spaghetti and finish with more Parm and fried sage.

⅓ cup extra-virgin olive oil

20 to 24 fresh sage leaves

½ teaspoon salt

3 medium or 2 large perfectly ripe peaches

¼ cup amaretto

1⅓ cups Almond Pesto

Almond Pesto
Makes 2 cups

⅔ cup raw, whole almonds

Zest of ½ orange, removed with a Microplane (about 1 teaspoon)

¼ cup Parmigiano-Reggiano, cut into small, rough pieces

¼ teaspoon chili flakes

¼ teaspoon nutmeg

¼ teaspoon salt

2 teaspoons honey

½ cup orange juice, divided

½ cup extra-virgin olive oil, divided

1 tablespoon lemon juice

Make the pesto: Gently toast the almonds in a 10-inch skillet over medium heat till they are fragrant, about 2 to 3 minutes. Let the almonds cool to room temperature and transfer them, the orange zest, Parm, chili flakes, nutmeg, and salt to the bowl of a food processor. Pulse until they are coarsely chopped.

With the motor running, quickly stream in the honey, half the orange juice, half the olive oil, and all the lemon juice.

Transfer the almond mixture to a medium bowl and stir in the remaining orange juice and olive oil. Let the flavors marry a minimum of 1 hour before serving, and store in the refrigerator for up to 1 week. Make sure you bring it to room temperature before pairing it with the peaches. As you might imagine, this makes lots of other things, like apples, arugula, and chicken, look like stars too.

Make and serve the peaches: In a 6-inch skillet or sauté pan, bring the olive oil to a shimmer over medium heat. Add the sage leaves and fry them about 10 seconds. They should stay a silver green and curl up slightly. Drain the leaves on paper towels and sprinkle with the salt.

Just before you plan to serve the salad, wash the peaches, making an effort to brush away fuzz if you've got it. Cut the peaches into ½-inch wedges and transfer them to a medium bowl. Gently toss them together with the amaretto.

Spoon a puddle of the pesto on the bottom of your plates. Don't be afraid. You want a teaspoon of almond in every bite, so puddle accordingly. Stack the peaches on top of the pesto and drizzle more on half of your tower. Scatter fried sage around like rose petals and serve.

Soft Poppy and Peach Granola Cake

Makes 12 slices

CRISPY IN PLACES, soft on the inside, crunchy with lots of healthful seeds, and slightly sweet from peach, this breakfast cake is like a granola bar and a bowl of oatmeal had a chewy baby.

Although it's easy, there's a lot of waiting around in this process, so think of this as something you make on a Saturday or Sunday to have on hand as a quick breakfast or snack during the week.

Use this recipe as a flexible guide to reflect what's in your pantry. Fruits like strawberries, apples, or figs work here, and you can substitute any range of nuts, seeds, or milk. But do try to incorporate the poppy seeds. I think they really make it.

1½ cups peaches, cut into ½-inch dice (with skin is fine)	2 cups water
	½ teaspoon salt
3 tablespoons light brown sugar	1 cup rolled oats
	2 tablespoons sliced almonds
½ vanilla bean, split and scraped	3 tablespoons sunflower seeds
⅛ teaspoon nutmeg	1 tablespoon poppy seeds

- 1 tablespoon flaxseeds
- 2 tablespoons coconut oil, divided
- ¼ cup almond milk

Stir together the peaches, sugar, vanilla bean, and nutmeg. Cover and set aside for at least 3 hours and up to overnight. Just before you use the peaches, pluck out the vanilla pod and discard.

In a 2- to 3-quart saucepan, bring the water and salt up to a boil and stir in the rolled oats. Cook it over medium heat for 10 minutes, stirring frequently. Add the peaches as well as all their liquid. Cook an additional 2 minutes. Remove the pan from the heat and stir in the nuts, seeds, 1 tablespoon of the coconut oil, and the milk.

At this point you could refrigerate the oatmeal for up to 3 days, but if you choose to go ahead and bake it off, cool the oatmeal for at least 30 minutes. It will become gluey and quite thick.

Preheat your oven to 350°F and grease a 12-inch cast-iron skillet or a 9x13-inch baking dish with the remaining coconut oil. Spread the oatmeal mixture in an even layer over the bottom of your greased vessel. Slide it onto the middle rack of your oven and bake for about 1 hour and 15 minutes. It should be crispy and lightly browned around all the edges and will have a slightly crisp top. Remove it from the oven and let it cool. Cut or tear it into squares or triangles or whatever works for you. Serve at room temperature.

Jalapeño Peach Chicken

Serves 3 or 4

FIND A MEAT EATER who doesn't love gnawing on a chicken bone and bring that person to me. I'll have some questions. These wings (or drums) are roasted and finished in the oven with the glaze, but you could just as easily cook them on the grill and apply the sauce at the same time to achieve caramelization.

The glaze is hot pepper jelly's baby sister and the family's favorite. (I have some experience with this dynamic, so I call it as I see it.) It's also a punchy base for vinaigrettes, a sauce for any type of poultry or pork, and a companion for creamy cheeses. Make a big batch and store it in the refrigerator for up to three months or jar and process in a hot-water bath canner for ten minutes (*page 16*).

12 to 14	**chicken wings or 10 drumsticks**
1	**tablespoon vegetable oil**
1	**tablespoon salt**
⅔	**cup Jalapeño Peach Glaze**

Jalapeño Peach Glaze

Makes 5 cups

3	**cups chopped peach, about 4–5 medium peaches**
1	**pound jalapeños, stemmed and seeded**
½	**onion, roughly chopped**
2	**tablespoons ginger, peeled and roughly chopped**
1¼	**cups cider vinegar**
2¼	**cups granulated sugar**
1	**teaspoon salt**

Make the glaze: Combine the peaches, jalapeños, onion, and ginger in the bowl of a food processor. Pulse until everything is shredded and juicy, but not fully pureed.

Transfer the chunky mess to a 4- to 6-quart Dutch oven and add the vinegar, sugar, and salt. Over medium heat, bring it up to a boil, skimming the foam that finds its way to the top as often as you can. Less foam boiled down into the sauce means a more pristine clear glaze. Cook the sauce at a medium simmer for about 30 minutes. It should thicken slightly but not appear to be darkening in color. After 30 minutes, test the viscosity of the sauce by pouring a little on a chilled plate and sliding that plate into the fridge for 5 minutes. If it runs like heavy cream when you tilt the plate, cook it longer. If it pools up in a drip like loose honey, it's ready.

Cook the chicken: Preheat your oven to 400°F and let the chicken come to room temperature. Toss it with the oil and salt and spread the chicken in a single layer onto a baking sheet. Make sure the pieces are not touching one another so they will brown evenly.

Slide the tray onto the middle rack of your oven and roast undisturbed for 10 minutes. Take the chicken out of the oven. Stir the pieces around in the pan and cook an additional 10 minutes. Take them out again, pour off any fat that has accumulated, and toss them with the sauce. Put the tray back in the oven and let them roast an additional 15 minutes. They should be caramelized in places and shiny in others.

Day-at-the-Beach Pork Picnic with Peach and Melon Salsa

Serves 8

THE ENTIRE HOWARD CLAN goes to the beach for one week every year. We rent a house big enough to sleep all twenty of us. I cook a lot, and instead of soaking up the sun, most of us sit inside and talk. I treat the week like a long-drawn-out catering event, planning snacks, breakfasts, and supper and packing all the ingredients that say summer to me.

I make this one-pot pleaser toward the end of the week when we've decided we've sat inside and looked at one another long enough and it's time to actually spend a day on the beach. It's usually everyone's favorite meal.

2 tablespoons salt

2 tablespoons brown sugar

2 tablespoons ground cumin

5- or 6-pound pork picnic or Boston butt

Peach and Melon Salsa
Makes 5 cups

4 to 5 medium peaches cut into ½-inch dice (about 3 cups)

2 cups watermelon, cut into ½-inch dice

⅓ cup thinly sliced scallion (about 4 whole)

1 tablespoon chipotle in adobo, minced

Zest of 2 limes

3 tablespoons lime juice

½ teaspoon salt

3 tablespoons chopped cilantro

2 tablespoons chopped mint

Cook the pork: Preheat your oven to 300°F. Stir together the salt, sugar, and cumin and rub the pork like it's your job, making sure to use all of it. Place the roast, skin-side up or fat-cap up, in the bottom of a Dutch oven. Put the lid on and slide it onto the middle rack of your oven.

Cook it for 4 hours, covered. Raise the heat to 400°F and remove the lid. Cook an additional hour uncovered. Let the meat rest for about 20 minutes before slicing or pulling.

Make the salsa and serve: Stir everything together and let the flavors marry for about 30 minutes before serving. You could put this together up to a day in advance, but I like to do it the evening we eat it. This creates a cocktail hour and keeps the colors in the salsa vibrant.

The salsa is both a salad and a sauce, so be generous with it and serve with about 8 ounces of pork.

Country Ham–Wrapped and Roasted Peaches

Serves 4

I WANTED TO BRING THE ITALIAN tradition of prosciutto and melon Down East, so I wrapped some country ham around peaches. Then I felt like the sugars needed to be coaxed out of the peaches, and the ham would be better if it were a little crispy, so I sent them to the oven. After that, I knew they needed something creamy to round them out and a bright note to punctuate, so I added goat cheese and honey vinegar. Now that they had everything else, the peaches cried out for something crunchy like pecans.

I guess the tradition is more demanding here.

3 large, ripe freestone peaches

12 to 14 slices smoked country ham or prosciutto, ¹⁄₁₀ of an inch thick

3 tablespoons extra-virgin olive oil

⅔ cup Gingered Goat Cheese

¼ cup Balsamic Honey

½ cup Viv's Addiction (page 133), roughly chopped

Balsamic Honey
Makes a heaping ¼ cup

3 tablespoons honey

3 tablespoons aged balsamic vinegar

Gingered Goat Cheese
Makes 1 cup

⅔ cup fresh goat cheese

⅓ cup buttermilk

2 tablespoons fresh ginger, grated on the Microplane

¼ teaspoon salt

Make the goat cheese: Combine all the ingredients in the bowl of a food processor and blend till smooth. It should be soft, creamy, and spreadable—not runny. If it's too loose, thicken it with a little more goat cheese.

For the honey: Whisk the ingredients together and set aside at room temperature till you're ready to use.

Wrap and roast the peaches: Preheat your oven to 500°F. Cut the peaches into wedges that are 1½ inches thick at their widest point. Wrap each peach with 1 full slice of country ham. It should go around roughly 1½ times. Lay the peaches ham-seam-side down on a baking sheet.

Five minutes before you're ready to cook the peaches, slide a 9 x 12-inch baking sheet into the oven to preheat. Take it out and drizzle the bottom with 1 tablespoon of the olive oil. Carefully place the peaches in a single row, making sure none of them are touching, and drizzle their tops with the remaining oil.

Roast the peaches on the middle rack of your oven for about 10 minutes. The ham should crisp up slightly, and the peaches will start to shrink.

Serve them on a puddle of goat cheese. Drizzle with the balsamic honey and top with the pecans.

Fried Green Tomatoes with Curried Peach Preserves and Whipped Feta

Serves 4

SOMEWHERE BETWEEN AN APPETIZER and a dessert, this is a wacky take on a cheese plate. Even if the idea of peach preserves and fried green tomatoes together freaks you out, you should still make these Curried Peach Preserves. They perfectly sum up my culinary point of view: old-school technique meets a modern palate. Serve them with pork, chicken, duck, or creamy cheeses.

- 1 cup buttermilk
- 1 teaspoon salt
- 3 medium green tomatoes
- 1 cup Sesame Breader
- 1½ cups vegetable oil
- 1¼ cups Curried Peach Preserves
- 1 cup Whipped Feta

Curried Peach Preserves
Makes 2 quarts

- 2 pounds granulated sugar
- 1 tablespoon Madras curry powder

Zest of 1 lime, removed with a vegetable peeler

Zest of 1 orange, removed with a vegetable peeler

- 2-inch piece fresh ginger, peeled and sliced super-thin
- 3 whole star anise
- 3 pounds ripe whole peaches, peeled
- ½ teaspoon salt
- ¼ cup lime juice
- 2 tablespoons orange juice

Whipped Feta
- 1 cup feta
- ¼ cup buttermilk

Sesame Breader
Makes 1 cup

- 1 tablespoon extra-virgin olive oil
- ¼ cup stale rustic-style bread, crusts cut off and cut into ½-inch cubes
- ¼ cup sesame seeds or benne seeds
- ¼ cup all-purpose flour
- ¼ cup potato starch
- 1 teaspoon salt
- 2 teaspoons ground coriander
- 1 teaspoon smoked paprika
- ½ teaspoon cayenne

Make the preserves: In a 4- to 6-quart bowl, stir together the sugar, curry powder, zests, ginger, and star anise. Cut the peaches into ½-inch wedges and drop them into the bowl with the curried sugar. Once you've wedged all the peaches, toss them carefully with the sugar mixture, making sure all the peaches are coated in sugar. Cover the bowl with plastic wrap and let it sit at room temperature overnight.

The next day the peaches will have released quite a bit of juice. Transfer all the contents of the bowl to a 4- to 6-quart Dutch oven or heavy-bottomed pot. Over medium heat, bring the peach mixture up to a simmer and cook gently for about 30 minutes. Whole pieces of peach will be swimming in syrup.

Spoon a little of the preserves onto a cold plate. Transfer the plate to the refrigerator for a minute or two and test the viscosity of the preserves. Ideally you want something that's the consistency of

molasses. If you're there, stir in the salt and the citrus juices. If you're not, cook 10 minutes more, then stir in the salt and juices.

These will keep, covered in the refrigerator, for up to 6 months. Alternatively, you could process them in jars in a hot-water bath for 10 minutes according to the instructions on page 16.

Whip the feta: Combine the feta and the buttermilk in the bowl of a food processor and blend it up till smooth. This can be done up to 3 days in advance. About 30 minutes before serving, bring the feta out and allow it to warm to room temperature.

Make the tomatoes: In a medium bowl, whisk together the buttermilk and 1 teaspoon salt. Peel the tomatoes using a knife and slice them into ½-inch-thick rounds or wedges. Marinate them, refrigerated, a minimum of 3 and up to 24 hours in the buttermilk.

Make the breader. In a 6-inch skillet, heat the olive oil over medium heat and add the bread cubes. Stir them around and toast till quite crispy. Drain and cool the toast on a paper towel.

Transfer the bread cubes to the bowl of a food processor and blend them into small crumbs. Turn the crumbs out into a bowl and stir in all the other dry ingredients.

Fry and serve: Preheat your oven to 200°F. In a 10-inch skillet, heat half the oil over medium heat. Take the tomatoes out of the buttermilk and dredge them in the breader. Fry them in batches in a single layer for about 4 minutes on each side. When they are crisp and brown on both sides, nestle them in the oven to stay warm while you fry the others. Add more oil as you see fit.

Serve the warm tomatoes on top of the whipped feta and next to a heaping spoonful of preserves.

Peaches and Cream Cake

Serves 12 to 16

WHAT I LOVE ABOUT THIS CAKE is how subtle, light, and elegant it is. Peach is in every part of it, but the end result plays more than one note. What I don't love about this cake is how much work it is. Plan ahead and make sure there are people around to eat every last crumb of your labor.

Peach Puree and Syrup

2¼ pounds peaches

½ cup packed light brown sugar

Finely grated zest of 1 large lemon

¼ cup fresh lemon juice

½ cup peach schnapps, plus more as needed

Pastry Cream

½ cup cold water

2 (.25-ounce) packets unflavored gelatin powder

½ cup granulated sugar

3 tablespoons cornstarch

2 large eggs, at room temperature

2 cups whole milk

1 vanilla bean

¼ teaspoon salt

4 tablespoons butter, cut into 4 equal pieces and chilled

1¼ cups reserved peach puree

Peach Caramel

1 cup granulated sugar

½ cup water

4 tablespoons butter, cut into 4 equal pieces and chilled

2 tablespoons cream

¾ cup reserved peach puree

½ teaspoon salt

½ teaspoon freshly grated nutmeg

Chiffon Cake

8 large eggs, separated, at room temperature

1 teaspoon fresh lemon juice

1½ cups granulated sugar, divided

2 cups all-purpose flour

2½ teaspoons baking powder

¾ teaspoon salt

½ teaspoon freshly grated nutmeg

½ cup vegetable oil

¾ cup almond milk or whole milk

1 teaspoon vanilla extract

2 teaspoons almond extract

For the peach puree and syrup: Peel and pit the peaches and cut the fruit into thin wedges. Place in a medium bowl. Stir in the brown sugar, lemon zest, and lemon juice. Cover and let stand at room temperature for at least 2 hours and up to overnight, stirring occasionally.

Strain the peaches and pour the liquid into a measuring cup. Add peach schnapps to total 1 cup. Set aside until needed.

Reserve 1 cup of the peach slices to garnish the cake. Cover and refrigerate until needed.

Puree the rest of the peaches in a food processor or blender to yield about 2 cups of puree.

Continued on page 462

Peaches and Cream Cake

Continued from the previous page

For the pastry cream: Pour the water into a small bowl. Sprinkle the gelatin over the water and stir gently until smooth. Set aside until needed. The gelatin will absorb the water as it sits.

Whisk together the sugar, cornstarch, and eggs in a large bowl.

Pour the milk into a large saucepan. Split the vanilla bean lengthwise. Scrape out the seeds with the tip of a knife and add them, along with the salt, to the milk, and then drop in the split pod. Bring the milk to a simmer over medium heat. As soon as bubbles form around the edge of the milk, remove the pan from the heat and pour it slowly into the sugar mixture, whisking constantly.

Return the milk mixture to the saucepan and cook, stirring constantly with a heatproof rubber spatula, until the mixture thickens and begins to bubble, about 5 minutes. Remove the pan from the heat and whisk in the cold butter one piece at a time; let each piece melt before adding the next. Discard the vanilla bean pod. Strain through a fine-mesh sieve into a clean bowl.

Heat the gelatin mixture in the microwave for a few seconds or in a small saucepan over low heat until it melts, then whisk it into the hot pastry cream.

Whisk in the reserved 1 cup peach puree. Press a piece of plastic wrap directly onto the surface of the pastry cream and refrigerate until chilled and firm, at least 4 hours and up to overnight.

For the peach caramel: Stir together the sugar and water in a medium heavy saucepan. Cover and cook over high heat for 4 minutes. Uncover and cook without stirring until the mixture thickens and turns the color of medium amber, about 10 minutes. While it is cooking, brush the sides of the pan several times with a pastry brush dipped into cold water to prevent crystals from forming.

Remove the pan from the heat and drop in all of the butter. The mixture will bubble and foam vigorously. Whisk until smooth.

Add the cream. The mixture will again bubble and foam vigorously. Whisk until smooth.

Whisk in the remaining ¼ cup peach puree, salt, and nutmeg. Pour into a clean bowl. Let stand at room temperature until cool. The caramel will continue to thicken as it cools.

For the chiffon cake: Preheat the oven to 325°F. Line six 9-inch cake pans with parchment paper. Do not grease or spray the pans. (If baking the cake layers in batches, use fresh parchment paper each time.)

In the bowl of your mixer fitted with the whisk attachment, beat the egg whites and lemon juice on low speed until the whites look opaque and begin to thicken. Increase the speed to high and gradually add ½ cup of the sugar. Whisk until the whites are glossy and hold medium peaks. Transfer the egg whites to another bowl and set aside.

In the bowl of your mixer, sift together the flour, baking powder, salt, nutmeg, and remaining 1 cup of sugar.

In a medium bowl, whisk together the egg yolks, oil, milk, and vanilla and almond extracts until well combined.

Form a well in the center of the flour mixture and pour in the yolk mixture. Using the paddle attachment, mix on low speed until blended and smooth. Increase the speed to medium and beat for 2 minutes. Using a spatula, gently fold in the egg whites.

Spoon 1 heaping cup (7 ounces by weight) of batter into each prepared pan. Gently tilt and rotate the pan so that the batter spreads to the edges. The batter will be very shallow.

Bake until the cake layers are golden brown on top, 30 to 35 minutes. The tops should spring back without leaving a fingerprint when gently pressed in the center.

Turn the pans upside down on wire racks to cool completely. Run a knife around the inside of the pan to release the layers. Peel off the parchment.

When all of the layers are baked and cooled, brush the top of each with 2¼ tablespoons of the peach schnapps mixture.

To assemble the cake: Place a cake layer on a serving platter or cake plate. Spread 1¼ cups of pastry cream over the layer. Repeat until all six layers are stacked and filled, leaving the top layer bare. Cover with plastic wrap and refrigerate at least 6 hours and up to overnight.

Slowly pour the room-temperature caramel over the center of the cake, letting it spread over the top and drip down the sides. Garnish the top with the reserved peach slices.

RUTABAGAS

LILLIE HARDY AND I met the day her mother, Mary Vaughn, taught me how to can tomatoes. Ms. Mary was very quiet, answering all my questions with "Yes" or "No." Lillie was even quieter; she sat perched on a metal chair, arms crossed, in the corner of the room.

I got the impression Lillie was there to make sure her mom was comfortable and to figure out what exactly was going on. We had just started filming *A Chef's Life* and everybody we met with our cameras thought the chances of this thing being successful were slim. The way Lillie looked me up and down let me know she was skeptical as well.

I slowly won Ms. Mary's trust over jars of hot tomatoes, lemon juice, sugar, and salt that July afternoon. She opened up, laughed, and shared stories from her time as the Bryan family cook. Lillie sat in her chair, silent most of the day. But just as we were wrapping up, she walked over to help and asked if I was ever going to learn how to make biscuits. Quick like a bunny, I answered, "I'm ready when you are!"

My biscuit class with Lillie was our first and probably most infamous lesson. I waltzed in confident, the professional chef who thought she knew more than any home cook could, and Ms. Lillie schooled me. At one point I had made such a mess, she actually told me to get my hand out of the biscuit bowl. By the end of it we had some pretty biscuits (hers) and some ugly biscuits (mine). I was covered in flour and feeling humble. And I wanted to learn more from my new teacher.

Following several other lectures on subjects like fishing off a pier, fried cornbread, and turnips, Lillie agreed to show me how she stewed rutabagas.

"I don't need no cutting board. I needs that there knife and this here han'," Lillie announced, holding up her right hand, each fingertip crowned by a long nail whose

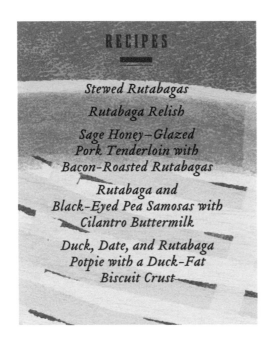

RECIPES

Stewed Rutabagas

Rutabaga Relish

*Sage Honey–Glazed
Pork Tenderloin with
Bacon-Roasted Rutabagas*

*Rutabaga and
Black-Eyed Pea Samosas with
Cilantro Buttermilk*

*Duck, Date, and Rutabaga
Potpie with a Duck-Fat
Biscuit Crust*

red polish was chipped from fieldwork.

"Now, look here." She grabbed a paring knife with her right hand and a softball-size rutabaga with her left. Starting at the top, she peeled away the gnarly ridges around its neck. Lillie, barely five feet tall, worked deftly, led by muscle memory and nearly seventy years of practice. After her knife rounded the rutabaga's final curve, she dropped the naked root on the counter and held up its entire rough skin in one long curvy piece. She was showing off. I was impressed.

Like biscuits, stewed rutabagas are a regional recipe I had dismissed in favor of fancy knifework like *brunoise* of rutabaga. Watching her peel the rough roots using only a dull knife and the torque of her hand, I marveled at how I hadn't taken the skin off anything without my Y-shaped peeler since culinary school. Of course, with Lillie holding court, I got the chance to try my hand at it again. I worked slowly. My rutabaga skin didn't unravel in one long piece like hers, but I didn't cut myself, so it wasn't a total fail.

When it came time to cut the roots down to stewing size, I told Lillie I was gonna need a cutting board.

"What you want with a cutting board?" Lillie scrunched up her brow and held out a pale, peachy-fleshed rutabaga. Once again she took her knife and sliced down about an inch into the top center of the root. Lillie curved the knife in, then flicked her wrist back, and off popped a rough cube of rutabaga flesh, ready for the stewing.

Rutabagas are hard, the hardest edible roots I know of. I often have trouble getting my knife through them even with the help of a cutting board. So when I tried to chip away at the tough tuber using only my hand and a knife, I struggled. My teacher enjoyed that part.

While I fantasized about the smooth brown cutting board and yellow curvy peeler sitting idle back at home, Lillie and I chipped away at enough rutabagas to fill a pot of water simmering with smoked bacon.

"No sausage, huh?" I questioned and peered down into the boiling pot. "I thought you liked sausage for seasoning meat?"

"Most times I do, but I like rutabagas with something that's got that...you know—smoke."

"Why?" I pressed.

"I don't know." She looked up at me, her lips rounded up in an amused smile. "It's just what we do. Why you do what you do?"

RUTABAGA WISDOM

Rutabagas Are Not Turnips

RUTABAGAS AND TURNIP ROOTS are similar but different. That being said, most of the time they can be substituted for each other in recipes, with slight tweaks. Rutabagas generally take longer to cook and are more difficult to peel. They are sweeter than turnips and smell like cabbage. That sweetness likes to be punched up a little with additional sugar. Try dark brown sugar, sorghum, or maple syrup.

Although you don't normally see rutabaga greens, you can and should eat them if you happen upon them. They remind me of a cross between a cabbage and a collard green.

Waxing on Size and Freshness

WHEN MOST ROOT VEGETABLES get big, it's a bad sign in terms of their flavor and texture. The size doesn't seem to matter for the rutabaga. Big is okay here.

If you're lucky enough to buy rutabagas not covered in wax, you're working with a very fresh product. The wax is applied to preserve the roots and is the only reason you can find rutabagas in the grocery store year-round, so don't hate on it. I do find, though, that super-fresh rutabagas taste more like cabbage than turnips and cook faster than the waxed versions.

Season

RUTABAGAS ARE a cold-weather crop and the only root I know that can withstand the frozen ground without suffering.

Stewed Rutabagas

Makes 5 cups

I'M WITH LILLIE: I think a seasoning meat that's smoked, like bacon, brings out the best in "bagars," but I've also tried Parmigiano rind and was impressed by that marriage. If you're lucky enough to find rutabagas with the greens attached, throw them right in with the roots.

- 2 quarts water
- 8 ounces smoked bacon, preferably slab, but slices will work too
- 2 pounds rutabagas, peeled and cut into 1-inch dice (about 8 cups)
- 2 tablespoons dark brown sugar
- 1 teaspoon salt
- 10 turns of the pepper mill or scant ¼ teaspoon black pepper

Combine the water and the bacon in a 4-quart saucepan or Dutch oven. Cover and bring it up to a boil. Reduce the heat to a simmer and cook for 15 minutes. Add the rutabagas and continue at a simmer, covered, for about an hour, checking the water level periodically to make sure the roots are mostly submerged.

The amount of time it takes for the rutabagas to soften up really depends on the age of the roots. I've cooked them in as little as 30 minutes and as much as an hour and a half, so you should test for doneness along the way. Once the roots are very tender, drain off all but ½ cup of the cooking liquid and pluck out the bacon.

Add the sugar, salt, and pepper. Take the collard chopper, a potato masher, or a large fork to the bagars like a boss. You're looking for a chunky, rustic texture. Taste and add a little more cooking liquid or sugar if you like.

Rutabaga Relish

Makes 2 quarts

I GAVE JARS OF THIS AWAY for Christmas a few years back, and I've never been more proud of a gift. Several things make this relish stand out. Most notably because rutabagas are so darn hard, they stay crunchy even when pickled.

I love to eat this relish with roasted meats, sausages, beans, and greens.

Note: *I'm about to offer some very specific directions on how to cut the rutabagas, but it's purely for appearance's sake. If these freak you out or you're not up to the task, shred the roots, onions, and bell pepper using the dicing blade on your food processor.*

1½	pounds rutabagas
2	quarts plus 2 cups water, divided
⅔	cup salt, divided
2	large red bell peppers
1	medium yellow onion
1¼	cups granulated sugar
¼	cup dark brown sugar
3	cups cider vinegar
2	garlic cloves, sliced
1	tablespoon coriander seeds
1	tablespoon mustard seeds
1	teaspoon chili flakes
1	tablespoon turmeric

Peel and halve the rutabagas through the stem end. Lay the flat surface of each rutabaga half on a cutting board and slice into 1-inch wedges. Holding the wedges together for ease of work, slice them into 1/16-inch-thick triangles.

Using a whisk, dissolve ½ cup of salt in 2 quarts of water. Stir in the rutabaga triangles and let that sit overnight or a minimum of 6 hours.

Slice the top and bottom off the peppers, then cut through one side to open up the peppers so you can remove core and membranes. Cut along the equator of each pepper to create 2 long strips 1 to 2 inches wide. Then cut across into julienne. Peel and halve the onion through its stem end and again crosswise. Slice with the grain into a thin julienne. Stir together the peppers, onion, and remaining salt and water. Let that sit an hour. Drain and rinse the onions and rutabagas. Combine all the vegetables in a heatproof, nonreactive container.

Bring the sugars, vinegar, garlic, and spices up to a boil and cook for 1 minute. Pour the boiling vinegar over the vegetables and stir, making sure all the veggies are submerged.

To preserve, pack the hot relish in sterilized jars, and cover it by ½ inch with pickling liquid. Process the jars in a hot-water bath for 10 minutes (*page 16*). Alternatively, store the relish in a sealed container in the refrigerator for up to 6 months. The relish is best after 1 week.

Sage Honey–Glazed Pork Tenderloin with Bacon-Roasted Rutabagas

Serves 5

PORK TENDERLOIN IS NOT SOMETHING we ever cook at the restaurant, but I've noticed my girlfriends whip it out all the time for their families and dinner parties. This recipe is for you girls…you know who you are. Stop overcooking that pork.

1 large pork tenderloin

2 teaspoons salt

20 turns of the pepper mill or scant 1 teaspoon black pepper

2 tablespoons vegetable oil

Sage Honey

2 teaspoons dried sage

⅓ cup honey

½ cup cider vinegar

2 garlic cloves, smashed

2 teaspoons mustard seeds

½ teaspoon chili flakes

Roasted Rutabagas

4 cups rutabagas, peeled and cut into 1-inch dice

2 cups slab bacon (8 ounces), cut into ¾-inch dice (sliced bacon will not work here)

2 teaspoons light brown sugar

1 teaspoon salt

6 turns of the pepper mill or ⅛ teaspoon black pepper

1 tablespoon vegetable oil

Make the sage honey: Combine all the ingredients in the smallest pot you have. Bring it up to a simmer and cook about 5 minutes. Watch this closely because it can get away from you in an instant. Reduce the liquid by a little less than half. Before serving, pluck out the garlic and discard.

Roast the rutabagas: Preheat your oven to 375°F. Season the rutabagas and bacon with the sugar, salt, and pepper. Toss in the oil and spread it all out in a single layer on a baking sheet. Do not crowd the ingredients; they need room to breathe and roast. Slide the tray onto the middle rack of your oven and roast for 30 minutes. Remove the roots and gently toss with a spatula. Return to the oven and cook 30 minutes more. They should be caramelized on 2 sides and fragrant. If they are blond and boring-looking, keep roasting.

Cook the pork: Keep your oven at 375°F and season the pork on all sides with salt and pepper. In a 10-inch sauté pan or cast-iron skillet, heat the oil until almost smoking. Add the pork, lower the heat slightly, and brown about 3 minutes on each of the tenderloin's 4 sides. Once it's nice and caramelized, transfer the pork and the pan to the middle rack of your oven and cook for an additional 6 minutes. Transfer the pork to a rack to cool and let it rest about 5 minutes before slicing. It will be a pale pink in the middle and feel squishy, but that's because it's *tender*loin. Don't freak out.

To serve, slice the tenderloin into ½-inch slices and drizzle with the sage honey. Plate it on a bed of the roasted roots.

Rutabaga and Black-Eyed Pea Samosas with Cilantro Buttermilk

Makes 32 samosas

MY FIRST HIGH-VOLUME restaurant job was as a steam cook at Jean-Georges Vongerichten's Spice Market in New York. I worked next to the fry station and snacked all night on misfired orders of chicken samosas. Knowing that traditional Indian samosas are made of potato and chickpeas and remembering how much I loved Spice Market's, I decided to make my own version using ingredients from Carolina's pantry.

Although the samosas seem a world away, rutabagas, black-eyed peas, and buttermilk tie the fried snacks to Eastern Carolina. At the end of February, when we're fresh out of ideas for how to reinvent the root, I chime in with "What about our samosas?" They are great for restaurants or home entertaining because you can make a big batch, freeze them, and fry straight from frozen.

1 tablespoon plus 1 teaspoon salt, divided

4 cups peeled and diced rutabaga (1 pound)

1 cup cooked black-eyed peas

1 medium onion, small-diced

1 tablespoon minced ginger

1 tablespoon minced garlic

2 tablespoons vegetable oil

2 tablespoons coriander seeds, toasted and ground

1 tablespoon cumin seeds, toasted and ground

½ teaspoon turmeric

¼ teaspoon cayenne

1 large tomato, diced, with its juice

1 tablespoon tamarind puree, optional

Egg wash

1 pack spring roll shells, not wonton wrappers (These are paper-thin. I like Wei-Chuan brand.)

2 quarts vegetable oil for frying

Cilantro Buttermilk
Makes a scant 1 cup

½ cup nice, thick, full-fat buttermilk

½ cup packed cilantro, stems and leaves

2 tablespoons mint leaves

1 tablespoon lemon juice

¼ teaspoon salt

¼ cup plain Greek yogurt

For the filling: In a 4-quart saucepan or Dutch oven, bring 2½ quarts water and 1 tablespoon salt up to a boil. Add the rutabagas and boil for 30 to 35 minutes, or until the roots are very tender. Add the cooked black-eyed peas during the last 5

minute of cooking. When all is said and done, you want both the rutabagas and the peas soft. Strain and set aside.

In a 12-inch sauté pan, sweat the onion, ginger, garlic, and ½ teaspoon salt in 2 tablespoons vegetable oil for 10 minutes over medium heat. Do not

lower-left-hand corner of the triangle and fold it flush with the right side. Continue to fold the filling up into a triangle. This is the same process as folding a flag. Egg wash the last fold and place the samosa, seam-side down, on your cookie sheet. Cover the finished samosas with the damp towel to prevent them from drying out.

The samosas can be stored in the freezer for up to 1 month and fried from frozen or refrigerated for up to 24 hours.

Make the cilantro buttermilk:
Combine everything but the yogurt in the blender. Blend until smooth and green. Transfer it to a bowl and whisk in the yogurt. It should slightly thicken the mixture.

To fry: Preheat your oven to 200°F. In a 4- to 6-quart Dutch oven, heat the oil to 350°F.

Carefully drop a few samosas into the oil using a slotted metal spoon. If they are not frozen, they will be brown and crispy in about 2 minutes. If frozen, they will take about 4 minutes. Fry the samosas in batches, making sure you don't add more than 5 to the oil at one time.

Drain the samosas on paper towels and hold them in a warm oven till you're done frying all of them off. Serve warm with the Cilantro Buttermilk for dipping.

allow it to color. Add all the spices and cook another minute. Stir in the tomato, tamarind purée (if using), rutabagas, peas, ½ cup water, and ½ teaspoon salt. Cook for about 5 minutes or until the mixture is thick and both the rutabagas and the peas have broken down a little. Taste the slightly lumpy, full-flavored mess and add more salt if you feel it needs it.

Allow the filling to cool completely. Set up a station with egg wash, a cookie sheet, a clean, damp dish towel, your samosa filling, and a spoon. Split the wrappers in half lengthwise into two long rectangles and brush the short side of one rectangle with egg wash. Connect two rectangles using the egg-washed side, creating a long thin rectangle. Spoon approximately 2 tablespoons of the filling onto the lower-left-hand side of the rectangle. Take the

Rutabaga and Black-Eyed Pea Samosas with Cilantro Buttermilk

Duck, Date, and Rutabaga
Potpie with a Duck-Fat Biscuit Crust

Serves 6

THIS IS MY ODE TO DUCK AND COMFORT: Cold-weather food without a doubt. Rutabaga and dates give this more than just the savory dimension we expect from a potpie. The crust…well, that little number is Lillie's biscuit made with duck fat instead of lard, then rolled out into a disk. Yep, you wanna try that.

Note: *If you can't find duck fat, lard works well in the crust.*

Duck and Date Filling

- 3 duck leg quarters, 10 to 12 ounces each
- 3 teaspoons salt, divided
- 1½ teaspoons black pepper, divided
- 1 tablespoon vegetable oil
- 2 large yellow onions, diced
- 2 medium carrots, peeled and diced
- 2 ribs celery, diced
- 3 cloves garlic, smashed
- 2 cups red wine
- 2 cups chicken stock
- 1½ pounds rutabaga, cut into 1-inch dice (4 cups)
- ⅔ cup dried dates, cut into eighths (Do not buy pre-chopped dates. *Ever.*)
- 4 sprigs rosemary
- 4 sprigs thyme
- 2 bay leaves
- 3 star anise
- ¼ teaspoon nutmeg
- 2 tablespoons butter
- 2 tablespoons all-purpose flour

Biscuit Crust

- 1¼ cups all-purpose flour
- 2 teaspoons baking powder
- ¾ teaspoon salt, divided
- ¼ cup duck fat or lard
- ½ cup buttermilk

Make the filling: Season the duck with 2 teaspoons salt and 1 teaspoon black pepper. In a 4- to 6-quart Dutch oven or brazier heat the vegetable oil over medium-low and brown the duck legs, skin-side down, for about 7 to 10 minutes. You want to do this slowly so that you render out as much fat as possible. When they're nicely browned, flip them over and do the same on the flesh side.

Take the duck legs out and set them aside. Pour off all but about 1 tablespoon of the duck fat, and add the onion, carrot, celery, garlic, 1 teaspoon salt, and ½

teaspoon black pepper. Raise the heat to medium and cook for about 15 minutes. You want to brown the vegetables a little. If this seems to be a struggle, raise your heat a bit.

Once your vegetables are caramelized, add the wine. Bring it up to a boil and cook for 2 to 3 minutes. Stir in the stock, rutabagas, dates, herbs, star anise, and nutmeg. Add the duck legs and any juices that accumulated while they were resting and bring it up to a simmer. The liquid should come about ¾ of the way up the sides of the duck legs. They should not be submerged. Adjust the liquid level with stock or water. Lower the heat and cover. Cook the duck over medium-low heat for 1 hour at a brisk simmer.

After an hour, uncover and cook 10 minutes more. Remove the pan from the heat and let the duck rest in the braising liquid for 20 minutes.

Transfer the duck to a plate. Once it's cool enough to handle, pull the meat off the bone in nice, fork-friendly pieces. Meanwhile, strain the braising liquid. Reserve the vegetables and the broth. Discard the herbs and spices. Skim any fat you can from the top of the braising liquid. If you're a freak about that, chill the liquid so all the fat floats to the top and scoop it off. If you're in a hurry to eat, do the best you can.

In a 10-inch cast-iron skillet, melt 2 tablespoons butter over medium heat till foaming. Add the flour and cook for 1 to 2 minutes. Whisk in 2½ cups of the reserved braising liquid, and bring it up to a boil. It should thicken up and coat the back of a spoon like thin gravy. Stir in the reserved duck and the vegetables.

Make the crust: Sift the flour, baking powder, and ½ teaspoon salt into the bottom of a large bowl and make a deep and wide well in the center. Add the duck fat followed by the buttermilk, taking care to keep both contained in the well for now. If you're right-handed, take your right hand down into the fat and buttermilk goop and start bringing that together with your fingers. You want to make that as much of a homogenous mixture as you can

without bringing too much flour into the fold just yet. Once you get it together, start moving the wet mixture back and forth, to and fro in the flour. Turn it over and do the same. Turn it over and introduce more flour with each movement. I like to do a little motion once I get it going that feels like a one-handed knead, using my thumb as if it were the other hand. It's all real gentle, but it pushes new flour in with each movement. Continue introducing flour until the dough is not sticky but still very soft and tender. You will have about ¼ cup flour left in the bowl. Chill the dough for about 30 minutes.

Lay a 10-inch square of parchment or waxed paper on your counter. Dust it with flour and turn the dough onto it. Form it into a ball and roll it out into ¼ inch thickness.

Assemble and bake: Preheat your oven to 375°F. Make sure the filling is warm. It doesn't need to be hot, but it can't be cold throughout or it won't heat through.

Pick up the parchment by the edges and gently flip the pastry on top of the skillet. Trim the edges with a knife or crimp, as you like. Cut a 1-inch slit on top of the biscuit and sprinkle with ¼ teaspoon salt.

Put the skillet on a baking sheet and slide it onto the middle rack of your oven. Bake for 30 minutes. The crust should be golden brown, the filling should have started to bubble up the sides, and your kitchen should smell like duck perfume.

Serve warm.

APPLES

DEEP RUN USED TO be a tiny bit more bustling than it is now. There was a grocery store called Teachey's #2, a body shop, and a restaurant called the B&S Café. We call a lot of things here cafés that are not actually cafés in the French sense of the word. In Deep Run, any casual restaurant open for breakfast and lunch is a café, and some of us (my mom) pronounce it "calf."

The B&S "calf" specialized in barbecue and made a sandwich by splitting chewy cornbread through its equator and filling it with sweet slaw and smoked, chopped, vinegar-sauced pork shoulder. They did that every day. But on Saturdays they made applejacks, and applejacks are why I remember the B&S.

They sat to the left of the cash register inside a large glass box with wood trim. Each one, wrapped in white grease paper, was a fried half-moon stuffed modestly with a mild apple filling. More snack than dessert, applejacks at the B&S toed the line between savory and sweet with faint porkiness wrapped around chewy apple slices that held their shape and tasted like the floral essence of the fruit. I understood the B&S applejacks to be special—a treat someone made in limited quantity only once a week.

The B&S closed for business when I was about ten years old, marking the end of my weekly rendezvous with the crescent-shaped treat. I've tried to replicate those applejacks countless times at the restaurant, but my dough was always different and my filling was mushy, more like a fried apple pie from McDonald's than the delicate applejack of my memory. Still, I came back to it year after year during apple season to make adjustments. But I never got it right.

I asked my dad if he knew anybody who had worked at the B&S, because I wanted to tell the story of the applejack on *A Chef's Life* and I hadn't been able to figure it out on my own. My dad helps connect me with a lot of the people I call on for stories, and in this case

he told me Claire Merrell Barwick, the owner of the B&S, was my neighbor.

While our crew set up in Ms. Barwick's kitchen, I sat in the car. Our policy is that I don't say hello, wave, or make eye contact with the person I'm interviewing till the camera is rolling. That's because, as Oprah says, "the first time is the best time." The nervous energy that fuels the beginning of an interaction is good for TV.

As I sat there cataloging Ms. Barwick's impressive collection of lawn trinkets, I marveled that I had driven past her house hundreds of times and never considered it or the person who lived there for longer than a moment. Had I known the applejack whisperer rolled out dough in the brick house with the white gazebo out front, I might be a hand-pie mogul right now.

When I got my cue to come inside, I met Ms. Barwick, a short, plump lady with white hair, a round face, and a broad smile. She hugged me like we were family and led me to the kitchen. Her living room was filled with knickknacks curated from a lifetime of road trips. The centerpiece was a china cabinet packed with hundreds of salt- and pepper shakers from every state and tourist attraction in the nation. Ms. Barwick saw me gawking and said: "Yeah...that's my thing."

During our cooking lesson, Ms. Barwick told me the B&S made about a hundred applejacks every Saturday at fifty cents apiece, and they almost always sold out.

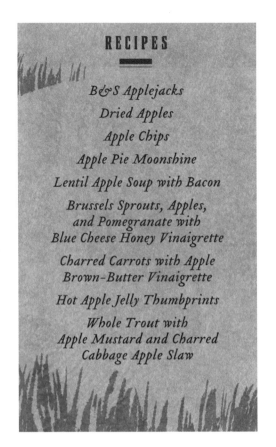

RECIPES

B&S Applejacks

Dried Apples

Apple Chips

Apple Pie Moonshine

Lentil Apple Soup with Bacon

*Brussels Sprouts, Apples,
and Pomegranate with
Blue Cheese Honey Vinaigrette*

*Charred Carrots with Apple
Brown-Butter Vinaigrette*

Hot Apple Jelly Thumbprints

*Whole Trout with
Apple Mustard and Charred
Cabbage Apple Slaw*

I learned that my attempts at applejacks disappointed because I'd made them with fresh apples instead of dried.

Ms. Barwick rehydrated dried apples in water and sugar and mixed a simple dough of flour, lard, and hot water. She rolled circles so thin I could see my hand through them. As she dropped judicious tablespoons of apple filling over each round, she talked about the B&S, about how much she'd loved her work there, and about how sad they were when they had to close. And she told me about my granddaddy Currin and what a good man and good customer he was.

When it was all over and I had eaten two applejacks, Ms. Barwick walked me outside. We passed through a glassed-in porch crawling with succulents, aloe, and cacti. Impressed by her collection, I commented that I loved houseplants too and tended a pretty impressive roster of succulents up the road. Pointing to an unruly jade plant, she confided to me that her son had died in a car accident when he was seventeen and the plant had been a condolence gift. She said she treated that jade like it was her son, coddling it and giving it everything she had to make it thrive. Then she reached down, plucked up one of her aloe plants, and told me to take it home.

Out in the carport Ms. Barwick said she wanted to give me something else. Around the corner sat a 16 x 16-inch glass box with wood trim, a hinged lid, and a scarred wooden base. She said it was originally a cheese box that sat on the counter at a country store. The glass protected the cheese from flies but let customers see the wheel and point out what size wedge they wanted. The B&S had used the same box to hold applejacks.

I left Ms. Barwick's that day with an aloe plant, a rare antique, and four white enamel butterbean pans to add to my collection. Just before I pulled away, Ms. Barwick flagged me down to give me one last hug. She said she had been so nervous

APPLE WISDOM

Varieties That Work

HERE'S WHAT MY EXPERIENCE tells me about apple varieties and their characteristics.

When I'm looking for a surefire easy-to-source winner, an apple that works in salads, for preserves, for drying, or for cooking, I select a Fuji or Honeycrisp. I like the level of sweetness and have almost never come across a mealy, soft specimen.

When I want an apple that's tart, sturdy under heat, and hard to bruise, I choose a Granny Smith.

The apples I grew up eating, Yellow and Red Delicious, are disappointing to me these days. Yellow Delicious bruise easily, are rarely crisp, and have a flat flavor. Red Delicious skin is thick and tannic. Maybe it's just me, but they look better than they taste.

If I can find Cortland apples, I buy them. They are slow to brown, so they make an excellent choice for raw preparations that may sit awhile. (To keep a sliced apple from browning, mix a solution of half lemon juice and half water. Store the apples in this for up to three hours.) Cortlands are also good for drying.

Please Wash Your Apples

IT'S IMPORTANT TO WASH all your fruits and vegetables but especially important to wash apples. Apple trees are threatened by a host of insects, disease, and fungi, and many farmers take measures to protect their orchards—chemical measures that mean you should wash your apples well.

before we started and that this had been the best day she could remember. She said the experience had made her feel valuable again.

On my way home, I cried (you already know that, I'm sure). In her, I saw an older version of myself—a collector, a mother, a restaurateur, and a cook who's happiest in her kitchen. But Ms. Barwick's contributions had been marginalized by her age. We place so much emphasis on the new and the young that everyone else just gets put in a box we access only when it's comfortable.

Our culture, it seems, no longer values the wisdom of older folks. We don't seek it out, ask questions, or spend quality time with our elders. I don't expect I'll be able to change that in a big way by doing it on my little show. But making someone like Ms. Barwick feel valuable makes me feel valuable. Thanks, Ms. Barwick.

B&S Applejacks

Makes 12 hand pies

THE HARDEST PART about making these is rolling out the dough. We recently started using a tortilla press to make the job easier. It does require a few more strokes from the rolling pin after it's been pressed, but overall the gadget helps.

The other thing I see people struggle with is the urge to overfill the pies. Two tablespoons of filling just doesn't look like that much when it's laid out on the dough. That's because it's not that much. This hand pie is just as much about the thin, blistered brown crust as it is about the filling. Let it be.

The rosemary sugar is not a traditional garnish, but I like it. Your call.

Filling
- 2½ cups roughly chopped dried apple slices
- 2½ cups apple cider
- 2¼ cups water
- ⅓ cup granulated sugar
- ½ teaspoon salt
- Zest of 1 lemon, removed with a Microplane
- 3 tablespoons lemon juice

Dough
- 2 cups all-purpose flour, plus more for rolling out the dough
- ⅓ cup lard or shortening, plus 2 cups for frying
- ⅔ cup hot water

Rosemary Sugar
- 2 teaspoons finely chopped rosemary
- ⅓ cup granulated sugar
- 1 teaspoon salt

Make the filling: In a 10-inch sauté pan or skillet, combine everything but the lemon juice over medium heat. Bring it up to a boil and cook until the pan is nearly dry. Stir in the lemon juice and cool down the filling before assembling. The filling can be made up to 5 days in advance.

Make the dough: Mound the flour in the center of a large bowl. Make a little well in the center and drop the lard in the well. Pour about ½ cup of the hot water over the lard and, using your hand, work together the lard and the water until it's all sludgy and homogenous.

Pour the remaining water into the lard and begin working in the flour by moving the lard mass around, accumulating flour as you go. Continue until a soft, tender dough forms. You will use nearly all the flour in the bowl. The dough will be quite pliable and tender, but it should not be sticky. Cover the dough with a damp paper towel until you're ready to make the pies.

Make the pies: Pinch off a golf-ball-size round of dough. Flour your work surface, a tortilla press if using, the dough ball, and your rolling pin. Place the ball in the center of the press and flatten it, or roll the dough into a thin circle with your rolling pin. Each round should be so thin you can see colors through it. Spoon 2 tablespoons

edges with a fork. Trim the edges with a knife and transfer the pies to a floured baking sheet till you're ready to fry.

Make the sugar: Combine the rosemary, sugar, and salt in a food processor. Pulse a few times. Transfer the sugar to a bowl and set aside.

Fry and serve: Heat 1 cup of the lard in a 12-inch cast-iron skillet over medium heat. Ms. Barwick tests the heat by dropping a pinch of flour in it. If it sizzles right away, she starts frying the jacks.

In a 12-inch skillet you should be able to fry 4 or 5 jacks at a time. The lard should come a little over halfway up the jacks. They should not be completely submerged. Cook till they are golden brown on one side and carefully turn them over and brown on the other

filling in the center of each round. Using the back of your spoon, flatten the filling slightly so the delicate dough doesn't have to do it when you fold it over.

Using your finger, dampen half the circle's edge with water. Fold the dough over to make a crescent and crimp the

side. Drain the cooked jacks on paper towels and sprinkle with the rosemary sugar on both sides while they're still hot. Follow up with the remaining jacks, adding more lard if you need it.

Serve warm or at room temperature.

Dried Apples

Makes 2 quarts

LEE CALHOUN KNOWS WAY MORE ABOUT SOUTHERN heirloom apples than anyone else. He wrote the definitive book on the subject, but when I met him all I could think about was how I wished he were my grandfather. Mild-mannered and funny, Lee retired from a long career in the military, then went on a quest to discover and document all the existing Southern heirloom apple varieties. How does one do this, you ask? They drive around and peek into people's backyards.

Lee told me that although today we think of apples in terms of eating them fresh or cooking them, our forefathers often planted varieties that were particularly good for drying. Apple trees make apples only once a year, and drying apples is the most efficient way to preserve them. Most methods for fruit preservation call for added sugar and spices, but drying apples relies on the opposite. Time and oxygen leach out moisture and shrink the apple down to its essence. The end product is chewy, easily stored, and perfect for baking.

The absolute easiest way to do this is in a dehydrator, but for the sake of history and for those of us who don't have a dehydrator, here's the old-fashioned way.

Note: *When selecting your apples for drying, consider that the flavor of the apple will be amplified when dried. Tart apples will be very tart and sweet apples will be sweeter.*

1 cup lemon juice	4 cups water	3 pounds apples

In a large bowl, whisk the lemon juice and water together. If you wish, peel your apples. I don't here because the skin of an apple is pretty and full of fiber. Remove the cores from your apples with an apple corer and slice the apples on a mandoline. You want them to be about ⅛ of an inch thick.

Submerge the apple rings in the lemon water for 15 minutes. Pat them dry and string the apples onto a 5-foot piece of butcher's twine. Tie the twine till it's taut between two posts either in your house or on a screened-in porch, and spread the apple slices out so they are not touching one another. Let the apples dry for 4 days. They will brown slightly and shrivel.

Store the dried apples in a sealed container or plastic bag at room temperature for up to 3 months.

Apple Chips

Makes 3 quarts

I OFFER A NUMBER OF RECIPES for fruit preserves in this book, but this is my favorite. First introduced to me by Annette Brothers, my farmer friend Warren's mother, these get their name because they stay crisp through macerating and cooking that goes on over the course of two days.

The main problem people have with fruit preserves, and the reason I feel like I need to apologize for my enthusiasm, is that nobody knows what to do with them. They think their options end at spooning preserves over a biscuit or eating them with a bite of cheese. But fruit preserves have much more potential.

I mix these apples chips, for instance, with a touch of Dijon mustard and some sherry vinegar and slather them on pork chops, baked hams, and roast chicken. Add a little more acidity to that mix, like lemon juice, some salt, and olive oil, and you've got a salad dressing packed with fruity flavor you can't get from a fresh apple.

Note: *Although I almost never recommend peeling apples, peel these. Slow-cooking them with sugar makes the skin tough.*

5 pounds crisp eating apples, such as Fuji or Honeycrisp	5 pounds granulated sugar	2 lemons sliced thin, seeds removed
	5 cloves	1 teaspoon salt
	4 whole star anise	1 cup apple cider (if needed)

Peel the apples and cut the flesh from the core in 4 pieces. Reserve the peelings and cores for Hot Apple Jelly (*page 500*). Using a mandoline, cut the apple quarters into slices that are roughly ⅛ of an inch thick. Toss the slices with the sugar, cloves, star anise, and lemon slices, making sure to coat all the apples. Cover with plastic wrap and leave out at room temperature overnight.

The next day, transfer the contents of the bowl to a 6- to 8-quart Dutch oven and add the salt. Cook the preserves gently over medium low heat, covered, until the slices become translucent and are swimming in

a golden syrup. Stir periodically and skim any scum that rises to the surface as the preserves cook. This should take about an hour. If after 45 minutes the apples are not beginning to turn clear and the syrup is starting to darken, add 1 cup apple cider and keep cooking.

Store the preserves in a sealed container in the refrigerator for up to 3 months or funnel them into jars and process in a hot-water bath for 10 minutes according to the instructions on page 16.

Apple Pie Moonshine

Makes 1½ gallons

THIS IS OUR version of a classic cocktail. When boot leggers had to hide their shine, they'd mix it with apple cider and store it in the cider jug. The juice-colored camouflage quelled suspicion and made white lightning easier to drink. Eventually apple pie moonshine, also called applejack, became a concoction moonshiners hung their hat on. My dad still gets several mason jars of the stuff every Christmas. I don't think he's ever consumed any, but I have—and I like it.

If you can, put this together a week in advance. It benefits from mellowing time. The moonshine is appropriate to add to a punch bowl at a fall or winter party, perhaps along with some apples bobbing around for looks. Apple Pie Moonshine makes a thoughtful gift for the right person.

1	gallon apple cider	3	cinnamon sticks
1½	cups light brown sugar	3	star anise
4	lemons, halved	2	2-inch pieces of ginger, peeled
2	oranges, halved	4	cups moonshine
4	cloves	4	apples, quartered

In a 2-gallon pot, bring the cider, sugar, citrus, and spices up to a low boil. Cook for 5 minutes. Take it off the heat and let it cool completely. Stir in the moonshine and the apples. Cover and let it sit overnight at room temperature.

The next day, take out the citrus and transfer the Apple Pie Moonshine to jars with lids wide enough to house the apples. Store in the refrigerator till you're ready to serve. Serve chilled over ice.

Lentil Apple Soup with Bacon

Makes 8 cups

THE FIRST TIME I had lentil soup I was at a coworker's apartment in Bushwick, Brooklyn. He lived in a converted factory full of artists who were having a group show in the hallways of their building. His name was Ben and I had a deep, secret crush on him.

Already smitten, I was taken with the fact that Ben had cooked something for the evening. Although I was not sure what that suspect pot of brown stuff was, I accepted a coffee mug full of it (I would have taken anything he'd offered me). I'm not sure if Ben's lentil soup was really good or if I was just taste-blind from adoration, but I devoured it and asked for a second helping. I've been a lentil lover ever since.

As much as I love traditional lentil soup, it's a little flat for me. The apples in my version add fruity sweetness, and the buttermilk a punch of creamy acidity. And the bacon—you know what the bacon does.

- 1 teaspoon vegetable oil
- 8 ounces sliced bacon, cut into 1-inch pieces
- 1½ cups thinly sliced leeks
- 1 cup diced celery
- ½ cup diced carrots
- 2 tablespoons minced ginger
- 2 cloves minced garlic (2 teaspoons)
- 1 teaspoon ground cumin
- 15 turns of the pepper mill or scant ½ teaspoon black pepper
- 1 cup green lentils
- 5 cups chicken stock or water
- 1 cup apple cider
- 2 cups ½-inch-diced Granny Smith apples
- 1 teaspoon salt
- 1 teaspoon minced rosemary
- ½ cup buttermilk

Heat the vegetable oil over medium heat in a 4-quart Dutch oven or saucepan. Add the bacon and cook till it's almost crispy. Drain the bacon on paper towels and pour off all but 2 tablespoons bacon fat.

Lower the heat slightly and add the leeks, celery, carrots, ginger, and garlic. Sweat for 10 minutes. Stir in the cumin and black pepper. Cook for 30 seconds more, till you can smell the spices. Add the lentils, stock, and cider. Cover. Bring it up to a boil. Reduce to a simmer and cook for 30 minutes. Stir in the apples, salt, and rosemary and cook an additional 3 minutes.

Taste for seasoning. If you used homemade chicken stock or water, you may need to add up to 1 teaspoon salt. If the soup is too thick for your taste, add more liquid.

Serve warm in bowls with a dollop of buttermilk and a sprinkle of reserved bacon.

Brussels Sprouts, Apples, and Pomegranate with Blue Cheese Honey Vinaigrette

Serves 6

I LOVE BLUE CHEESE so much I ignore the way my lips itch when I eat it. Whisking it up with honey and coaxing it over crisp apples and Brussels sprouts turns a cheese that people are sometimes daunted by into a dressing it's hard to dislike.

This salad is especially convenient for entertaining because, unlike lettuces that wilt and wane once they're dressed, the Brussels sprouts benefit from a short soak.

12 to 16 large Brussels sprouts

3 medium Fuji or other crisp, sweet eating apples

Juice of 1 lemon

4 radishes, cut into eighths

3 tablespoons thinly sliced scallion

1½ teaspoons salt

1 cup Blue Cheese Honey Vinaigrette

2 tablespoons torn mint leaves

½ cup pomegranate seeds

Blue Cheese Honey Vinaigrette

½ cup high-quality blue cheese such as Maytag, broken into crumbles

3 tablespoons lemon juice

3 tablespoons cider vinegar

3 tablespoons honey

1 teaspoon salt

10 turns of the pepper mill or ¼ teaspoon black pepper

¼ cup grapeseed or sunflower oil

Make the vinaigrette: In a medium bowl whisk together the cheese, lemon juice, vinegar, honey, salt, and pepper until the blue cheese is broken up and the liquid appears creamy. Then slowly whisk in the oil and set aside. Just before pouring the dressing over the salad, give it another whisk. This dressing will keep in a sealed container in the fridge for up to 5 days.

Assemble the salad: Slice the stem end off the Brussels sprouts and separate the sprouts into individual leaves. Set aside. Just before building the salad, dice the apples and toss them with the lemon juice. To the apples add the radishes, Brussels sprouts, scallion, salt, and ¼ cup vinaigrette.

Let the salad sit for at least 10 minutes and up to 30 minutes before serving. Just before you do, top with the mint, pomegranate seeds, and another drizzle of dressing.

Charred Carrots with
Apple Brown-Butter Vinaigrette

Serves 5

IF IT'S A VEGETABLE, I've charred it. Browning fruits or vegetables over high heat develops both bitter and sweet notes and creates texture. Charring is kind of like building an oversize grill mark on the surface of a vegetable or fruit. For the carrots in this dish, it's the first step toward transforming a mundane root into something meaty. I might even call the whole thing seductive once it's bathed in browned butter, apples, pine nuts, and thyme.

1 tablespoon vegetable oil	1 pound medium carrots, washed and scrubbed	2 sprigs thyme, picked
1 teaspoon salt, divided	3 tablespoons butter	¼ teaspoon chili flakes
½ teaspoon ground coriander	2 tablespoons pine nuts	1 large crisp eating apple, cut into ½-inch dice
½ teaspoon ground fennel	2 scallion bottoms, white part only, sliced into ⅛-inch-thick rounds	3 tablespoons lemon juice

Preheat your oven to 300°F. In a 12-inch cast-iron skillet, heat the vegetable oil over medium-high heat. In a small bowl, mix ½ teaspoon salt, coriander, and fennel. Toss the mixture together with the carrots. Place the carrots in a single layer in your preheated pan and begin charring them on all sides. This will take about 8 minutes.

Transfer the pan to your oven and roast for 50 minutes. The carrots should be a dark caramelized brown on all sides and should pierce easily with a knife when they're done.

Just before you bring the carrots out of the oven, heat the butter in an 8- to 10-inch sauté pan till it starts to take on a little color. Add the pine nuts, scallions, thyme, and chili flakes and continue cooking till the pine nuts are toasted and the butter is brown and nutty-smelling. Add the apples, remaining ½ teaspoon salt, and the lemon juice and cook an additional 45 seconds. The apples will absorb most of the liquid, but you should have a tablespoon or two of vinaigrette visible in the pan.

Spoon the apples, pine nuts, and all their liquid over the carrots. Serve warm.

Hot Apple Jelly Thumbprints

Makes 2 dozen cheese wafers

A BIT OF A MIND-BENDER, these look like traditional jam thumbprint cookies, but they're a riff on cheese straws with their own built-in, assertive garnish. I first made the little devils when charged with developing a creative, portable Tabasco-containing snack for hungover people. I'd say I hit the mark hard.

The cheese-straw part of this is pretty standard and freezes well. I use Gouda, but sharp cheddar works too. The apple jelly, however, requires a little more attention. Apple jelly is the easiest way to use up the peelings and cores from Apple Chips (*page 490*) or anything else you happen to do with skinless apple flesh.

Because the skin and the core have more pectin than the rest of the apple, it's a resourceful way to use them.

Note: *You can make these cookies without actually making the jelly. Just heat 1 cup store-bought apple jelly until it's liquid and stir in 2 tablespoons hot sauce and 1 teaspoon lemon juice. Let it cool and set up again. Then you're ready to go.*

Hot Apple Jelly
Makes 1 cup

Peels and cores from 5 pounds of apples (about 1¾ pounds)

¾ **cup granulated sugar**

2 **tablespoons hot sauce such as Tabasco or Texas Pete**

1 **teaspoon lemon juice**

Gouda Thumbprint Cookies

1 **cup all-purpose flour**

¼ **teaspoon salt**

⅛ **teaspoon baking powder**

8 **tablespoons (1 stick) room-temperature butter**

1½ **cups shredded smoked Gouda**

Make the jelly: Put the peels and cores in a 4-quart saucepan and add enough water to almost reach the top of the trimmings. but don't submerge them in liquid. Bring it up to a boil, cover and cook at a quick simmer, keeping watch to make sure the apples are at this point shrunken and submerged in water.

Put a small plate or bowl in the freezer to test the viscosity of your jelly later. After 30 minutes, strain the trimmings and transfer the slightly thickened liquid back to your saucepan. Over medium heat, reduce the liquid to 1 cup. Add ¾ cup sugar. Bring it up to a boil and cook for 5 minutes. Take the plate out of the freezer and spoon a little apple jelly onto its cold surface. If it pools up and jells, it's ready. If not, cook another 3 minutes.

Once it's at the right consistency, stir in the hot sauce and lemon juice. Let the jelly cool to room temperature before you use it. It will keep in a sealed container in the fridge for up to 3 months.

Make the cookies: In a medium bowl, sift the flour, salt, and baking powder. In a mixer fitted with the paddle attachment, cream the butter and cheese at medium speed for 2 minutes. Then reduce the speed of your mixer and add the flour mixture. Continue to paddle for 2 minutes, longer than you expect, until the dough is nice and fluffy.

Preheat your oven to 350°F. Load a piping bag with the cookie dough and pipe 2-teaspoon-size rounds onto a Silpat or parchment-lined baking pan. Using your thumb, make a small indentation in the center of each round. Spoon 1 teaspoon apple jelly into each indentation. Bake for about 12 minutes or until lightly browned on the bottom.

The cookies should keep at room temperature in a sealed container for up to a week.

Whole Trout with Apple Mustard and Charred Cabbage Apple Slaw

Serves 4

FAMILY VACATIONS AS A KID looked like this: Howards wake up at three in the morning and get in the yellow station wagon. Howards drive to the mountains, eat breakfast at the Daniel Boone Inn, go to Tweetsie Railroad, stop at a roadside stand to buy fresh apples, apple butter, and cider. Howards get back in the wagon and drive home.

Today Chef and the Farmer serves marvelous rainbow trout from those same mountains. And because I associate that place with apples, I've put them together here.

This apple mustard is like apple butter with an edge. It's not meant for toast or biscuits, but it's a great counterpoint to chicken, pork, or a full-flavored fish like trout or salmon.

4 whole rainbow trout	½ small orange sliced thin, seeds removed	1 small head green, purple, or savoy cabbage
⅓ cup extra-virgin olive oil, divided	1 cup apple cider	1 tablespoon extra-virgin olive oil
20 turns of the pepper mill or scant 1 teaspoon black pepper	1 cup water	1½ teaspoons salt, divided
	1½ cups dark brown sugar	
1 tablespoon salt	⅓ cup smooth Dijon mustard	1 large Fuji or other crisp eating apple
1 lemon, sliced thin	⅓ cup cider vinegar	2 ribs celery, sliced into ⅛-inch slices on the bias
4 sprigs sage	½ teaspoon cayenne	
4 sprigs rosemary	½ teaspoon salt	
⅔ cup Apple Mustard	1 star anise	10 turns of the pepper mill or scant ¼ teaspoon black pepper
Charred Cabbage Apple Slaw	4 cloves	
	3 sprigs thyme	
		¼ cup lemon juice
Apple Mustard	*Charred Cabbage Apple Slaw*	2 teaspoons chopped fresh dill
Makes 4 cups	Makes 5 cups	½ cup Salt-and-Butter-Roasted Pecans (*page 134*) (walnuts or hazelnuts work here too)
1½ pounds apples, diced, skin and core intact (6 cups)	¼ cup apple cider vinegar	
2 yellow onions, diced	2 tablespoons honey	
	1 small red onion, peeled and sliced into ⅛-inch rounds	

Make the slaw: In a small bowl, whisk the vinegar, ¼ cup water, and the honey together till the honey dissolves. Add the red onion. Set aside.

Cut the cabbage into twelve wedges, leaving the core attached. Heat a 12-inch cast-iron skillet or sauté pan over medium-high heat, and add 1 tablespoon olive oil. Sear the cabbage on the cut sides till they are charred, not golden brown—dark and charred. Season the cabbage with 1 teaspoon salt and set aside to cool.

Just before you assemble your slaw, cut the 4 sides of the apple off its core. Then slice the apple into ⅛-inch-thick slices.

In a medium bowl, toss together the cabbage, the onions with their liquid, celery, apple, black pepper, lemon juice, dill, and remaining salt. Let this mingle while you cook the fish. Just before serving, stir in the pecans.

Make the apple mustard: In a 4-quart Dutch oven or saucepan, combine the apples and their cores, onions, orange slices, cider, water, sugar, mustard, vinegar, cayenne, and salt. Put the star anise, cloves and thyme in a sachet and drop it in. Bring it up to a boil, cover, and cook for 10 minutes. Reduce the heat to a very low simmer and cook for an hour, checking periodically to make sure the pan is not dry.

Remove the sachet and transfer the contents of the pot to a blender and blend till totally smooth. Put the apple butter back in the Dutch oven and cook uncovered on low heat another 20 minutes. Adjust the seasoning with salt or brown sugar to your liking.

Cook the trout: Season each fish, inside and out, with olive oil, black pepper, and salt. Stuff the cavity of each fish with lemon slices, 1 sprig sage, and 1 sprig rosemary.

Preheat your oven to 325°F. In a 12-inch cast-iron skillet, heat 1 tablespoon of the remaining olive oil over medium high heat. Once it's shimmering, add 2 trout and brown them on both sides. If your pan is nice and hot, it should take about 3 minutes per side. Transfer them to a baking sheet. Add another tablespoon oil and brown the remaining trout. Slide all 4 trout onto the middle rack of your oven and roast for 15 minutes.

Serve warm with the slaw and apple mustard.

BEETS

MY CHILDREN ARE GROWING UP literally across
the road from my childhood home, but they see North
Carolina from a wildly different vantage point than I did.
From the foods they eat to the places they've been, Theo
and Flo have been exposed to both more and less than I
was as a child. Take beets, for instance.

The most terrifying vegetable of my youth, beets swam in a suspicious
liquid with a sharp smell. They sat at the beginning, the middle, and
the end of the table at Bethel Baptist's covered-dish lunches in petite crystal
dishes flanked by flamboyant forks. I never understood why something
so alien, so off-putting, got the royal treatment when the deviled eggs
it took my mom all morning to make rode to church in a lime-green
Tupperware tray.

Theo and Flo are not otherwise spectacular eaters, but they like beets.
With the understanding that beets are among the healthiest vegetables you
can eat, I trained the twins, with deep purple baby food purees, to enjoy
them. I'm sure they'd hate the pickled beets of Bethel Baptist as much as
I did, but because fresh beets are available in grocery stores year-round,
pickled beets are not what they know.

I approached the beet with my kids' finicky palates in mind. What could I do to
this healthy root to make my kids like it? How could I accentuate the beet's natural
sweetness without highlighting its distinctive earthiness? Maybe a little honey?
Orange juice? Salt and olive oil?

Imagining my mom caressing a beet and pondering the same question is comical.
In fact, imagining my mom designing any meal, aside from my birthday feast maybe,

RECIPES

Pickled Beets

Basic Roasted Beets

Hot Pink Lemonade

My Favorite Beet Salad

*Grilled Lamb Kebabs with
Beet Tzatziki*

*Chocolate Orange Beet Cake with
Cream Cheese Walnut Icing*

*Cumin-Crusted Pork Belly
with Sweet and Sour
Beet Bottoms and Tops*

with my personal preferences in mind is funny. That's not a criticism. It's the way it was for most women of her generation and the generations before her. They cooked what they had access to, what they understood, and if you were hungry, you ate it. Even though we shopped at a grocery store, our plates reflected our place precisely. We had a historical connection to just about everything we ate. Even the canned biscuits, instant grits, and store-bought pickled beets represented our traditions coupled with our place in time.

When I'm at home acting as a short-order cook, swapping out PB&J for the chicken potpie my kids won't eat because of the peas I sneaked in there, or when I'm bartering dessert for bites of broccoli, I admire the way I was brought up. I ate what my parents ate, and that was it.

I wonder what my children's relationship to Eastern Carolina and its food will be. I don't expect their experience to mirror mine, and I'm an unusual case anyway, having boomeranged on the subject of this region's value as I reached adulthood. I do want to instill in them a respect for where they come from, for the people who came before them, and for the foods that defined that place. I want them to eat both pickled beets and roasted beets. I want them to know beets were pickled because they were harvested once or twice a year and that the sharp-smelling brine is what preserved them.

In a world where they're more likely to eat hummus than cornbread, I've got my work cut out for me. My penchant for nostalgia is not unique, nor is it blind. I'm not at all claiming that the way people used to parent or cook was better than the way people do those things today. I'm simply looking for balance, respect, and an understanding of our past. It's my wish that they know more about where they grew up than what that place is like right now. I hope they feel a connection to Deep Run, its people, and our food. I want Theo and Flo, no matter where they choose to live as adults, to feel rooted by their history. That relationship started with beets. I can't wait to see how it grows.

BEET WISDOM

Beets Are Beautiful

THERE'S NOTHING in the edible world more beautiful than the cross-section of a raw beet. Golden, Red, and Chioggia (or Candy Stripe) are the most popular varieties, and each of them has distinct visual appeal. Sliced horizontally, Bull's Blood and Golden beets show off concentric circles of different shades of the same hue, while the Chioggia beet boasts a magenta and white round pattern that looks like it came straight off the set of *Charlie and the Chocolate Factory.*

The disappointing news is that when you cook a Chioggia beet, it loses its stripes and the entire root turns a muted pink. Bull's Blood and Golden beets also lose their pattern but remain the same color. Golden beets have a more muted flavor and a thinner skin than red varieties.

To showcase raw beets' psyche-delic appearance, slice them super-thin with a mandoline. Separate the different colors of beets into different containers and cover each variety with cool water. Drain and rinse them a few times to wash off the colored starch. They will keep, refrigerated in the water, for up to two days.

Season and Storage

BEETS ARE AN EARLY-FALL and early-spring crop that doesn't like hot weather at all. Greenless roots can hold up in a cool dark place for a month. And larger beets store better than baby ones and become sweeter over time.

I Like Babies

ANY FARMER I work with will tell you I like baby vegetables. Little beets are among my favorites because they make for a great presentation.

Often farmers harvest the immature beets to make room for other beets to grow larger, so it works for us both.

Beet Greens Are the Bomb

LET IT BE KNOWN: Beet greens are the bomb. They are a cooking green I rank up with chard and kale.

I trim about two-thirds of the tough stem away and sauté with garlic, ginger, and chilies. They cook up fast and have a little of that distinctively earthy thing about beets on the back end.

Peeling Made Easy-Ish

PEELING ROASTED or boiled beets is a stain-making mess. I work over the sink and use paper towels to gently rub away their skin. If they're cooked till you can pierce them with a knife but not too much more, the skins will peel away easily.

Pickled Beets

Makes 6 pints

WE DIDN'T INVENT pickled beets in Eastern Carolina, but we have our own style. I'd argue our brine is sweeter than most. In fact, some of the most addictive beet pickles I've tried sat in a thick syrup of two parts granulated sugar to one part vinegar. That's sweet! My version has a lot less sugar, but I call on spices like clove and star anise to step up the perceived sweetness. Try these on a turkey or veggie sandwich or toss them with oregano, parsley, and chopped garlic to make a pickled beet chimichurri for roast meats.

3 pounds beets (any kind or color will work)	1 cup granulated sugar	2 teaspoons dried thyme
3 cups cider vinegar	½ cup light brown sugar	1 teaspoon chili flakes
2 cups water	3 cloves	3 star anise
	3 bay leaves	

Place washed, skin-on beets in the bottom of a 6-quart Dutch oven or saucepan. Cover the beets with water by 2 inches, and bring them up to a boil. Boil, covered, for

20 minutes. Check to see if they are done by sliding a knife into the center. The beet should give just a little resistance. If they are not done, continue cooking just until they are. Drain off the water and set the beets aside to cool.

Once they are cool enough to handle, peel and slice the beets into ½-inch rounds. Position the rounds in wide-mouthed canning jars or a similar heatproof container. If you have rounds that are too wide to fit, cut them into half-moons or quarters or whatever you have to do to get them in there.

Combine the remaining ingredients in a nonreactive, 3-quart saucepan and bring it up to a boil. Carefully pour the brine over the beets, making sure the beets are completely submerged in the liquid. At this point you could refrigerate the beets for up to 3 months without processing in a hot-water bath. If you'd like to store them at room temperature and keep them longer, follow the directions on canning (*page 16*) and process the jars for 5 minutes.

Basic Roasted Beets

Makes about 3 cups

THERE ARE TWO SCHOOLS OF THOUGHT when it comes to basic beet cookery: you can boil or you can roast. For most preparations, I prefer roasting. I believe it intensifies the earthy sweet flavor of the beet instead of watering it down.

As soon as the beets are cool enough to handle, I peel one and taste it. All beets are not created equal, and when they are warm and vulnerable, you have the unique opportunity to improve their flavor with a scattering of salt, sugar, and lemon juice.

1 pound beets, skin on	2 tablespoons extra-virgin olive oil	2 teaspoons lemon juice
½ cup water	1½ teaspoons granulated sugar	1 teaspoon salt

Preheat your oven to 375°F. Wash the beets thoroughly and place them and the water in a casserole dish. Drizzle the beets with olive oil and cover the dish tightly with foil. Bake on the center rack of your oven for 40 minutes to 1½ hours, depending on the size of your beets. The kitchen should be fragrant and the beets should be tender when pierced with a knife. Remove the beets from the oven and let them sit covered for 5 minutes.

Once they are just cool enough to handle, peel and cut into wedges or slices. Toss with the sugar, lemon juice, and salt. Adjust with slightly more of any of these items for your taste.

Hot Pink Lemonade

Makes 4 cups

I GET ON KICKS like everybody else. My juice kick lasted about six months and will be remembered by the dingy red stains on our kitchen counter. My affinity for beet juice outlasted the kick only because I like its distinctive taste and trust that anything that color has got to be astoundingly good for you. Juicing apostles preach that beets detoxify your blood, clean out your liver, and lower your blood pressure. And because I believe everything I read on the Internet, drinking beet juice makes me feel better. This is a beet drink even my kids gulp. Flo likes it because it's pink.

½ cup granulated sugar

3 cups water, divided

¾ cup fresh lemon juice

2 medium beets, peeled and juiced (about ½ cup beet juice)

Dissolve ½ cup sugar into ½ cup very hot water to make a simple syrup. In a pitcher, stir together the lemon juice, simple syrup, remaining water, and beet juice. Serve chilled over ice.

My Favorite Beet Salad

Serves 4

IT'S TOUGH FOR ME to recommend just one roasted beet salad because beet salads are by far my favorite salads to eat. But just the thought of beets bathed in tart-sweet oranges makes my mouth water, and blue cheese is one of my greatest pleasures in life. So I guess that's it.

2 cups roasted beets, peeled and sliced into ¼-inch rounds or small wedges *(page 511)*

1 teaspoon rosemary, finely chopped

Zest of 1 orange, removed with a Microplane

1 teaspoon honey

2 tablespoons aged balsamic vinegar

¼ teaspoon salt

5 turns of the pepper mill or scant ⅛ teaspoon black pepper

2 oranges

⅔ cup Salt-and-Butter-Roasted Pecans *(page 134)*

1 tablespoon olive oil for finishing

Buttermilk Blue Cheese Dressing
Makes 1½ cups

4 ounces high-quality blue cheese (I like Maytag)

½ cup buttermilk

¼ cup heavy cream

Make the dressing: Combine the blue cheese and buttermilk in the bowl of your food processor. Blend it till smooth. You'll need to stop and scrape down the sides with a spatula a couple of times. Meanwhile, beat the very cold heavy cream with a whisk until it reaches stiff peaks. I wouldn't normally recommend doing this by hand, but it takes less time to whip ¼ cup of cream with a whisk than to clean the mixer.

Turn the buttermilk blue cheese into the whipped cream and fold the two into each other gently. Whipping the cream and folding it into the blue cheese is best done just before serving. The dressing loses some of its fluff over time.

Assemble and serve: In a medium bowl, stir together the beets, rosemary, zest, honey, balsamic vinegar, salt, and black pepper. Supreme the oranges over the bowl with the marinating beets and let the orange juice drop into the party. Set the oranges aside and let the beets marinate for at least 30 minutes and up to 2 hours at room temperature.

Spoon a nice dollop of dressing on the bottom of your plate. Top with the marinated beets, oranges, and pecans, and drizzle with the finishing oil.

Grilled Lamb Kebabs with Beet Tzatziki

Serves 4

WE'VE MADE BEET TZATZIKI at Chef and the Farmer for close to eight years. I thought I was clever to switch out cucumber for beets but recently learned this is actually a traditional condiment in the Eastern Mediterranean. It's wonderful with flatbreads and grilled meats. But be ready for its wild, almost hot pink color.

Grilled Lamb Kebabs

- 1½ pounds lamb leg
- ¼ cup balsamic vinegar
- Zest and juice of 2 lemons
- 2 tablespoons chopped rosemary
- 3 tablespoons chopped oregano
- 1 tablespoon ground coriander
- ½ cup plus 1 tablespoon extra-virgin olive oil, divided
- 3 teaspoons salt, divided
- 10 turns of the pepper mill or ¼ teaspoon black pepper

Beet Tzatziki

Makes 3 cups

- ⅔ cup full-fat plain Greek yogurt
- Zest of 1 lemon
- ¼ cup lemon juice
- 1 garlic clove, grated on a Microplane
- 2 tablespoons extra-virgin olive oil
- 2 tablespoons chopped parsley
- 2 tablespoons chopped mint
- 1 tablespoon chopped dill
- 1 teaspoon honey
- ½ teaspoon salt
- 3 medium beets, roasted and cut into ½-inch wedges (about 2½ cups) *(page 511)*

Make the tzatziki: Whisk together everything but the beets. Stir the roasted beets into the yogurt mixture. This can be made up to 2 days in advance and stored in the refrigerator. Serve at room temperature.

Marinate and grill the lamb: Cut the lamb into 1½-inch cubes and transfer to a baking dish just large enough to hold them in a single layer. In a small bowl, whisk together the vinegar, lemon, herbs, coriander, ½ cup olive oil, and ½ teaspoon of the salt. Pour the marinade over the lamb and refrigerate for a minimum of 1 and up to 3 hours.

Preheat your grill to medium high. Thread the lamb onto 6-inch bamboo skewers, covering each skewer entirely with lamb. Season both sides of the lamb with the remaining salt and the pepper. Just before grilling, brush the grates with a paper towel soaked with the remaining 1 tablespoon olive oil. Drop the kebabs and cook 3 minutes each on all 4 sides. Remove the kebabs from the grill and serve with the tzatziki.

Chocolate Orange Beet Cake
with Cream Cheese Walnut Icing

Chocolate Orange Beet Cake with Cream Cheese Walnut Icing

Makes one 8-inch-round 3-layer cake

BEETS AND CAKE HAVE A HISTORY—not the one I'm about to lay out here, but a history nonetheless. About ten years ago, I was digging around in cookbooks when I learned that during World War II, cooks substituted beet juice for red food coloring in their red velvet cakes. This thrilled my vegetable-loving, connection-driven mind, and I set out to make a red velvet beet cake.

I failed. The cake we made never matched my red velvet memory stamp, a bloodred, subtle-flavored masterpiece. But what we came up with was actually really good, so we went with it. We decided to play off things that went well with both beets and chocolate. Creamy cheeses, orange, and walnuts became our muses, and this layer cake is the surprising result. If you make this cake once, you'll make it again.

Chocolate Beet Cake

- 3 medium beets
- 4 ounces semisweet chocolate
- 1 cup vegetable oil, divided
- 1 tablespoon orange zest
- 1 tablespoon vanilla
- 1 cup all-purpose flour
- 1 cup cake flour
- 2 teaspoons baking powder
- ¼ teaspoon salt
- 3 eggs
- 1½ cups sugar

Orange Syrup

- ⅓ cup orange juice
- ¼ cup water
- ¼ cup granulated sugar
- 2 teaspoons cocoa powder

Chocolate Walnut Icing

- 16 ounces cream cheese
- 12 tablespoons (1½ sticks) butter
- ⅓ cup sour cream
- ¼ cup cocoa
- 2 teaspoons vanilla extract
- 3 cups powdered sugar
- 2 cups walnuts, chopped roughly with a knife

Make the syrup: Whisk together the orange juice, water, sugar, and cocoa in a small saucepan. Bring it up to a boil and reduce by half. Set aside.

Make the icing: Combine the cream cheese, butter, sour cream, cocoa, and vanilla in the bowl of a mixer fitted with the paddle attachment. Paddle until things are velvety and soft. Add the sugar, a cup at a time, lowering the speed each time you make an addition to avoid a white mess. Scrape down the sides, and add the nuts. Paddle again for about 15 seconds.

Make the cake: Preheat your oven to 375°F, and spray three round 8-inch nonstick cake pans thoroughly with pan spray.

Cover the beets by 1 inch with water in a 4-quart saucepan. Cover and bring them up to a boil over high heat. Cook at a rolling boil for 30 minutes. Test the beets for doneness by sticking a knife in the center of the largest one. It should slide in with little resistance. Once the beets are completely cooked through and cooled, peel and cut them into rough cubes. You should have 2 cups of cubed beets. If you have more, use them for something else. If you have just a little less, roll with it.

In a small double boiler, melt the chocolate with ½ cup of the oil. Combine the beets with the remaining oil, orange zest, and vanilla in a high-powered blender. Process until the mixture is completely smooth and add the melted chocolate. Pulse to combine.

In a medium bowl, sift together the flours, baking powder, and salt. Set aside.

In a mixer fitted with the whisk attachment, beat the eggs and sugar until they are light and fluffy, about 1 minute. Slowly add the chocolate-beet mixture and continue whisking to fully incorporate.

Add the dry ingredients in 3 batches and just incorporate. You're going to end up with a batter that is slightly thicker than most you're used to seeing. Don't worry.

Turn ⅓ of the batter into each of the greased cake pans. Slide them onto the middle rack of the oven and bake for 15 minutes. Test the center of the layers with a toothpick. If it comes out clean, you're good. If not, bake a few additional minutes.

Turn the layers out onto a rack and cool about 30 minutes. Once they are cool, brush the syrup over the bottom of each layer. Try to use all the syrup.

Ice the cake: I'm not great at decorating cakes, so I love the naked-side look. To accomplish this, just divide your icing into 3 parts and spread it to the edges of each layer, stacking one on top of the next. Easy.

Cumin-Crusted Pork Belly with Sweet and Sour Beet Bottoms and Tops

Serves 4

I FORCED LOTS OF PEOPLE TO TRY beets during Chef and the Farmer's early days by giving them a buttery, sweet and sour treatment and spooning them over a pork chop. I can't tell you how many people tried to order that dish without the beets, and I just said no. This is an homage to the original treatment, where the sour notes from the beets cut through the fat of the pork belly.

Let it be known you could omit the pork altogether and have a satisfying supper, but pork belly done this way is unctuous, easy, and impressive.

1 heaping tablespoon cumin seeds

1 heaping teaspoon coriander seeds

2 teaspoons salt

1 teaspoon mustard powder

1 pound pork belly, portioned into 6 x 2-inch rectangle

Sweet and Sour Beets

2 medium beets roasted (page 511), cut into ½-inch wedges or ½-inch dice (about 1½ cups)

Zest of 1 orange, removed with a Microplane

Juice of 2 oranges

⅓ cup red wine vinegar

3 tablespoons honey

½ teaspoon chili flakes

¼ teaspoon salt

2 tablespoons cold butter

Water if needed

Beet Greens with Garlic

2 tablespoons vegetable oil

3 or 4 cloves of garlic, sliced thin

8 to 12 ounces beet greens or the greens from one bunch

1 teaspoon salt

¼ cup white wine

Roast the pork belly: Toast the cumin and coriander seeds in a medium sauté pan till fragrant. Transfer to a spice mill and grind to a medium-fine texture. In a small bowl, stir together the ground spices, the salt, and the mustard powder. Pour the spice mix onto a plate and roll all sides of the pork belly around in it, completely covering each side. You should use nearly all the mix.

Preheat your oven to 350°F and bring the pork belly up to room temperature. Lay the pork on a baking sheet and slide it onto the middle rack of the oven. Roast for 1 hour. Remove it from the oven and let the belly rest for 5 to 10 minutes.

Cook the greens: Cut the bottom 2 inches off the stem of the greens and discard. Then cut the remaining stem without greens into ¼-inch pieces. Set those aside. Then roughly chop the leaves.

In a 10- to 12-inch sauté pan, heat the oil, garlic, and chopped stems over medium heat. Once it starts to sizzle, add

the greens. Top the greens with the salt and turn them over with a pair of tongs a few times to get everything all mixed in. Add the wine and cook about 5 minutes. The greens will release some liquid and become limp. Continue to toss from time to time so that things cook evenly.

If I were eating these all on their own, I might add a knob of butter and a squirt of lemon juice just before serving, but because I'm pairing them with the awesome stuff above, I let them just be themselves here.

Glaze the beets: Just as you get ready to take the pork belly out of the oven, combine all of the ingredients for the beets except for the butter and water in an 8-inch sauté pan. Bring it up to a quick simmer and let it cook down to a glaze

consistency or until the liquid coats the back of a spoon. Give the beets a stir from time to time during this process to make sure there are no lonely glaze-less beets. This will take about 8 minutes.

If you let it go too far and the glaze becomes sticky, just whisk in a tablespoon of water to bring it back to where it needs to be. Just before serving, remove from the heat and swirl the butter into very hot beets. At this point you could also adjust the consistency with a little water and heat. It's surprisingly forgiving.

Serve: Slice the pork belly into ½-inch slices and serve with a bed of beet greens and a big spoonful of beets.

MUSCADINE GRAPES

MUSCADINE SEASON is the season of fresh starts. A new book bag, clean tennis shoes, a stack of fresh folders, and that first nip in the morning air—these, the sensations of a new school year, mean that muscadines are ripe. In early September, when backyard gardens turn tired and brown, we shift our focus to the twisted, mottled-green arbors nearby. Thick-skinned, seed-filled, foxy-sweet muscadines are just what we call grapes here. Wild and prolific, muscadines roamed Eastern Carolina before we did—before barbecue, cornbread, tobacco, and textiles. And they'll probably continue to wind in and out of overgrown woods when pig pickings and the golden leaf, our region's symbols, are things of the past.

Growing up, it seemed like everyone I knew, whether living in a trailer park or a sprawling farmhouse, had a grapevine...except for us. My great-uncle Bunk had several acres of scuppernong vines right down the road from our house. He and my Aunnie, as I called her (a cross between Auntie and Annie), never had children and were in their sixties when I came along. My mom says I was a good distraction for them. I spent many afternoons at their house, watching the stories (what we called soap operas), eating fried eggs, and playing in their sprawling manicured yard.

For kindergarten, my parents drove me to school, but at the dawn of first grade, I wanted to ride the bus, where I wouldn't be humiliated by my dad's pickup truck. It was littered with Pepsi bottles, honey-bun wrappers, and mail. But on the first day of school, despite my efforts, I missed the bus and had to ride to school in my dad's caked-with-mud truck. Determined to break the cycle, I rode the bus home. All went as planned. I grabbed a shiny brown seat with my best friend, Renee, and we bounced along as the bus drove through crossroads and over dirt paths on its way to Deep Run.

I sat in a window seat, head back, nose in the air, catching the breeze and thinking first grade was going to be great. Then we turned right onto my road and the stench of hog manure rushed in through the open windows. Bus number 24 erupted in nose-pinching disgust.

In addition to farming tobacco, my parents had a growing pig business. At that time, in the square mile surrounding my house, we probably had close to a thousand pigs—some of them on the ground, some of them in houses, and all of them smelly. As the bus slowed to a stop in front of my house, I saw the pointed fingers, and the accusations that my house smelled like a pigsty rang in my ears. I grabbed my book bag and rushed out. Down the stairs and across the road I ran, sure I'd never step foot on bus number 24 again. Halfway down our driveway, tears streaming down my face, I ran straight into the back of Uncle Bunk's denim-blue truck.

"Come on, girl. Get in. Let's go pick some grapes."

My great-uncle by marriage, Uncle Bunk was slimmer than my dad's people. He had an angular face, pointed features, and wavy silver hair. I'm not sure what he did for a living, but I know he had an "office" in a ramshackle shed in his backyard where there were lots of postcards, magazines, and pictures of girls in bikinis.

"How was your first day?"

"Awful…well, school was fine. Ms. Smith is nice, but the bus was awful. They said my house stunk. It does stink! I'm never riding the bus again!"

Uncle Bunk chuckled and pulled slowly down the driveway, his truck moving with the sound and speed of an old man getting out of bed. "You know, Vivian, next time you just need to tell 'em they're smelling money."

As Uncle Bunk drove toward the grapevines, my six-year-old subconscious floated from the bus disaster toward excitement for the sweet syrupy orbs in my future. Howard family legend has it that my first word was *pop*. The story goes that I said it the September after I was born, when Granddaddy Currin took me out to the grapevines and popped the muscadine pulp in my mouth over and over. I find the tale dubious because that would have put me talking at seven months old, and, as a parent myself, I would no more projectile-pop grapes into my babies' mouths than give them plastic bags to play with. But times were different then.

Uncle Bunk parked the truck under a massive oak and came around to the passenger side. I waited because we had done this before, last year at the start of kindergarten. He handed me a shoe box with no top, hoisted me up on his shoulders,

MUSCADINE WISDOM

What Is a Muscadine?

MUSCADINES ARE THICK-SKINNED, musky-fleshed grapes that grow all over the Southeast. They are indigenous to this region and are the state fruit of North Carolina. Muscadines are gold, bronze, black, and several shades of red. Their skin is incredibly tannic when eaten raw, so we don't generally do that. Their flesh is floral, syrupy, and reminiscent of honeysuckle. We like it a lot.

Concords Will Work

ALTHOUGH THEY DON'T have the aromatic traits of muscadines and their skin tends to be less tannic and thick, Concord grapes are a fine substitute for the recipes in this chapter.

Scuppernongs *Are* Muscadines

THERE ARE SOMETHING like three hundred varieties of muscadines out there, but confusion surrounds the scuppernong variety. Scuppernong muscadines were the bronze grapes French explorers wrote about when they came to the New World. They were the first muscadines cultivated, and their notoriety leads to the incorrect assumption that all bronze grapes in the Southeast are scuppernongs and all black or red grapes are muscadines. But scuppernongs are just one type of muscadine, like Sun Golds are one type of cherry tomato. In general, black muscadines with names like Nesbit, Noble, and Black Beauty are boozy, musky, and in-your-face. Bronze grapes, like the scuppernong varieties Carlos and Magnolia, are more elegant, fruity, and feminine.

Look for grapes that have tight, shiny skin; you can store them in the refrigerator for up to five days before they start to shrivel.

The Skin Is Good for You

MUSCADINE GRAPES have way more health benefits than common white and red seedless grapes. Problem is, most of their insoluble fiber, vitamin C, antioxidants, and manganese is in the tough, tannic skin or the seeds. And when we eat muscadines out of hand, we rarely eat either of those.

How to Eat a Muscadine

NO ONE EVER SAID that they love muscadines because they're easy to work with.

Point the stem end of the grape toward your mouth and pinch the opposite end with your thumb and index finger. The pulp and

and lumbered over to the middle of the arbor, where the vines were taller. Perched on his shoulders, I fit right under the vines with a view that revealed more bronze, plump scuppernongs than I could fathom. From there I picked and popped for as long as Uncle Bunk could hold me. My chin dripped with the wild sweet syrup of too many grapes, and my mouth itched, angry from their tannic skin. But I didn't care. The

juice will pop out. Slurp it up and suck the remaining nectar from the grape's cavity. Roll the pulp around in your mouth and fish out the seeds with your tongue. I spit the seeds out, but plenty of people eat them.

Straining the Pulp

NONE OF THE RECIPES in this chapter call for using only the flesh of the grape. But if you wanted to do that, the best way to separate the flesh from the skin and seeds is to heat the entire grape over medium heat until the skins burst and the pulp begins to break down, about ten minutes. Transfer the skins, seeds, and pulp to a medium-mesh strainer and press down on the pulp and skins using a ladle. Following a little elbow grease, the pulp and juice will have passed through the strainer, leaving the skin and seeds for you to discard. Use the strained pulp and juice in grape-flavored glazes, vinaigrettes, or jellies.

Sugar Makes the Skins Tough

ANY TIME YOU PLAN on using the skins for any reason (grape-hull pies, mulled muscadines, grape-hull preserves), it's important to cook the skins till they're tender before adding any sugar. Sugar added too early will make the skins tough.

RECIPES

Grape-Hull Preserves

Kid Juice and Adult Juice

*Horsey Arugula
with Muscadine Vinaigrette,
Parmesan, and Pecans*

*Mulled Muscadines and
Whipped Feta Toast*

*Grape-Roasted Brussels Sprouts
and Sausage*

*Muscadine-Braised
Chicken Thighs*

Triple-Decker Grape-Hull Pie

muscadine nectar was just too good to let a little rash slow me down. By the end of it all, I had a wet shirt, a sticky neck, a red face, a swollen belly, and a shoe box full of grapes.

Three decades later—this year— my four-and-a-half-year-olds, Theo and Flo, started school for the first time. I'm shocked at how much it's affected me. I'm not sad they aren't babies anymore. I'm excited for them to experience school—it's almost like I'm starting school again myself. Shopping for backpacks, meeting their teachers, signing up to be the event mom at school functions, early mornings, a nip in the air, ripe muscadines—the sum of it all reminds me of what it's like to be a kid. It offers me, the old person, the opening to do better this year—to be a better mom, a more thoughtful wife, a more patient daughter, an inspiring teacher. I fall for a fresh start every year. This year, I fell hard.

Grape-Hull Preserves

Makes 1 pint

YOU CAN, OF COURSE, USE ALL BRONZE GRAPES or all black grapes to get the job done, but I prefer a ratio of two-thirds bronze, which I think have a subtle flavor, to one-third black. The two balance each other and the combination results in a pleasing purple end product.

This is a traditional, no-frills recipe, but feel free to jazz it up with some lemon zest or warm spices. You already know these preserves are an obvious choice for biscuits and toast, but consider swirling some into the pan drippings left from roasting a chicken, or make the assertive muscadine vinaigrette on page 536.

8 cups whole muscadine grapes, washed (about 2 pounds)	2¼ cups granulated sugar	2 teaspoons lemon juice

Squeeze the pulp and seeds of the grapes into a 2- to 4-quart saucepan. Reserve the skins. Bring the grape guts up to a simmer and cook for 5 minutes. The flesh will lose its form, and some of the seeds will start to slip away willy-nilly. Transfer the contents of the pan to a medium-mesh strainer or a colander whose holes are not large enough for the seeds to pass through and push down on the pulp and juice till it passes and all you're left with up top are the seeds. Discard the seeds.

Transfer the strained pulp, the skins, and ½ cup water back to the original saucepan. Bring it up to a boil and cook for 5 minutes. Add the sugar and cook an additional 10 minutes. Check the consistency of your preserves by chilling a small plate or bowl in your freezer then bringing it out and spooning a little of the preserves on the cold surface. If it jells up and wrinkles, your preserves are ready. If not, cook another 3 to 5 minutes. Stir in the lemon juice.

If you make only this tiny amount, there is absolutely no reason to can it in a hot-water bath. Just store it in a sealed container in your refrigerator for up to 3 months and bring to room temperature before serving. However, if you choose to do more, follow the directions for canning (*page 16*) and process for 10 minutes.

Kid Juice & Adult Juice

THREE DAYS AFTER the *Chef's Life* muscadine episode aired, I got a care package and a note from Regina Stroud, a former teacher and wife of a muscadine grower in our community. She wanted to share some of her muscadine recipes and tips with me. I've received plenty of feedback and family recipes from viewers, but rarely have I learned so much about an ingredient I thought I already understood.

Ms. Stroud is how I learned that adding sugar too early in the cooking process makes the skins tough and that just a few dark grapes will color a whole batch of preserves. She also gave me a jar of what I've chosen to call Kid Juice. She labeled it grape juice because that's kind of what it is. I was so taken with the technique and taste result, I conducted my own twenty-jar experiment by adding honey to some, aromatics to some others, and vinegar to yet others. The star was what you'd call a drinking vinegar but I'm calling Adult Juice. It's bracing, refreshing, and addictive.

Kid Juice

Makes 4 quarts

THE FLAVOR of muscadines is elusive, like that of a peach or strawberry—it tastes one way raw, another way once you add heat. This juice reminds me more of the musky honey-like first slurp of eating a raw grape than any other muscadine recipe I've ever made. It's hard to understand how it happens, but it happens.

Because you can't just buy it at the store, this juice is a treat in our house for tea parties or celebratory snacks. We've also been known to swap it for the OJ in a mimosa.

8 cups whole muscadine grapes (2 pounds)

2 cups granulated sugar

4 1-quart mason jars and lids

Wash the grapes well and add 2 cups grapes and ½ cup sugar to each sterilized jar. Fill the jars with boiling water. Put the lids on and process in a hot-water bath for 10 minutes (*page 16*). The juice will be ready in 2 to 3 weeks and will keep for a year. Serve over ice.

My kids like it so much we add more water and sugar to the jar, let it sit overnight, and have a second-rate second batch.

Adult Juice

Makes 4 quarts

FROM THE NAME, you probably think this is about booze, but it's not. Instead, it plays on the popularity of the old-fashioned tradition of diluted sweetened fruit vinegars, called shrubs.

Why, you might ask, wouldn't I just make a muscadine shrub and dilute it? Well, I tried that, and the result tasted like something I mixed together instead of something that came together. It's kind of like seasoning a pot of soup in the end instead of seasoning it all through the cooking process.

Serve over ice.

- 8 cups whole muscadine grapes (2 pounds)
- 2 cups granulated sugar
- 2 cups white wine vinegar
- 4 1-quart mason jars with lids

Follow the instructions for Kid Juice, but add ½ cup vinegar to each jar before pouring in the water.

Same aging and shelf life apply.

Horsey Arugula with Muscadine Vinaigrette, Parmesan, and Pecans

Serves 4

"HORSEY" IS WHAT MY FRIEND WARREN calls any tender, sweet vegetable that stayed out in the field past its tender, sweet stage. Most of the time this is not a desirable situation, but when arugula is set against assertive components like the ones here, I prefer it horsey.

In most cases, muscadine hulls are hard to eat raw. But I've found if you use the largest, firmest ones you can find and slice them into thin rounds, the skins are actually a nice balance for the sweet flesh.

If all the stars align and give you horsey arugula and giant muscadines, then you're lucky. If not, take what you can get. Tender arugula from a bag and small grapes work too.

- ½   cup sliced large muscadine grapes, about 2 cups whole
- 5   cups mature arugula
- 2   tablespoons olive oil for finishing
- ¼   teaspoon salt

- ½   cup grated Parmigiano-Reggiano
- ½   cup Salt-and-Butter-Roasted Pecans *(page 134)* or Viv's Addiction *(page 133)*

Vinaigrette
- 2   tablespoons Grape-Hull Preserves *(page 533)*
- 1½ tablespoons lemon juice
- 1   teaspoon Dijon mustard

Make the vinaigrette: Put the Grape-Hull Preserves in a small food processor and blend till they're roughly chopped. Transfer the chopped preserves to a small bowl and whisk in the lemon juice and Dijon. Set aside. The dressing will keep sealed in the refrigerator for up to 1 week.

Assemble the salad: To slice the grapes, you're gonna need a small serrated knife

and large firm grapes. Slice the stem end off the grapes and discard. Then cut ⅛-inch-thick rounds till you hit seeds. Once you reach seeds, stick the tip of your knife in there and pry them out, then keep slicing till you get to the end. Discard the end slice.

Just before you're ready to eat, toss the arugula with the sliced grapes, olive oil, salt, dressing, and half the cheese. Sprinkle the top with the remaining cheese and pecans.

Mulled Muscadines and Whipped Feta Toast

Makes 12 toasts

THIS IS SOMEWHERE BETWEEN a chutney and a fruit preserve, and I called it a mull only because I included ingredients reminiscent of mulled cider. Despite its quirkiness, the recipe is versatile. Here, I serve it over whipped feta and olive oil–fried bread, but at the restaurant, we might swirl the mull with a little stock and butter, then spoon it over pork chops. Sometimes we throw a cup or so into the braising liquid for pork shoulder, and it pairs perfectly with fried chicken.

If I were making one and only one preparation with the beloved muscadine, it would be this one. With minor tweaks, it can go anywhere.

1 cup Mulled Muscadines	***Mulled Muscadines***	2 strips lemon zest, removed with a vegetable peeler
½ cup extra-virgin olive oil, divided	Makes 1 cup	½ cup orange juice
1 baguette sliced into ½-inch-thick slices	2 cups muscadines, split and seeded	3 tablespoons lemon juice
1 teaspoon salt	4 cloves	1 tablespoon apple cider vinegar
1 cup Whipped Feta (*page 458*)	1 2- to 3-inch cinnamon stick	⅛ teaspoon salt
	4 black peppercorns	1 teaspoon minced ginger
	¼ cup honey	1 sprig rosemary
	2 strips orange zest, removed with a vegetable peeler	

Make the muscadines: In a 2- to 3-quart saucepan add the grapes and 1 cup water. Bring it up to a boil over medium high heat and cook uncovered for 5 minutes. Tie the cloves, cinnamon stick, and peppercorns up in a sachet and add them and all the remaining ingredients to the pot. Lower the heat to medium low and simmer for close to 20 minutes. The mull will reduce and become syrupy. You're looking for slow, deliberate bubbles that rise to the surface of the entire mull, not just the perimeter.

Let the sachet cool in the cooked grapes and store sealed in the refrigerator for up to 2 weeks. Ideally, I let the mull rest for a day in an effort to allow all the flavors to mellow. Before serving, bring the mull to room temperature so that all the warmth and spices have a chance to open up.

Assemble the toasts: In a 10-inch sauté pan or skillet, heat ¼ cup olive oil over medium heat. Add half the baguette slices and brown on one side. Flip, season the top with salt, and brown on the other side. Drain on paper towels. Add the remaining oil and fry and season the rest of the toasts. This can be done up to an hour before serving.

Just before serving as an appetizer or snack, smear roughly 2 tablespoons feta on each toast and top with an equal amount of mull. Serve at room temperature.

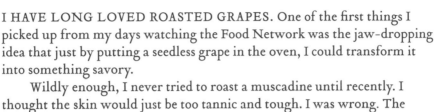

Grape-Roasted Brussels Sprouts and Sausage

Serves 4

I HAVE LONG LOVED ROASTED GRAPES. One of the first things I picked up from my days watching the Food Network was the jaw-dropping idea that just by putting a seedless grape in the oven, I could transform it into something savory.

Wildly enough, I never tried to roast a muscadine until recently. I thought the skin would just be too tannic and tough. I was wrong. The skin holds its shape but loses its chewy brawn, and the flesh becomes the jammy essence of muscadine. If the seeds weren't such a pain to extract, I'd probably put roasted muscadines on everything from ice cream to steak.

This mixed roast pairs caramelized muscadines with toasty Brussels sprouts, link sausage, and Dijon mustard. It hits every element of taste we humans have. Serve it in early fall with roast meats, all by itself, or next to a bowl of greens.

- 2 cups muscadines, halved and seeded
- 2 cups Brussels sprouts, trimmed and halved
- 8 ounces of your favorite link sausage, cut into ½-inch rounds (about 1 cup)
- 2 tablespoons extra-virgin olive oil
- 1¼ teaspoons salt, divided
- 15 turns of the pepper mill or scant ½ teaspoon black pepper
- 3 tablespoons smooth Dijon mustard
- 2 tablespoons lemon juice

Preheat your oven to 425°F. Toss together the muscadines, Brussels sprouts, sausage, olive oil, 1 teaspoon salt, and pepper. Spread the mixture out on a large baking sheet in a single layer. Do not crowd the pan. Slide the baking sheet onto the middle rack of your oven and roast for 25 minutes.

As it roasts, whisk together the remaining ¼ teaspoon salt, the Dijon, and the lemon juice. As soon as you take the grapes out of the oven, slide a metal spatula underneath it all, and scrape up any caramelization that's accumulated on the pan. You want that sugary stuff to be a part of the final dish, not a part of your roasting pan. Serve warm drizzled with the Dijon dressing.

Muscadine-Braised Chicken Thighs

Muscadine-Braised Chicken Thighs

Serves 4 to 6

I HAVE A FANTASY that looks like this: I pick my kids up from school. We go home. They play outside while I put together the beginnings of a sensible but creative supper, like chicken thighs braised in muscadine grapes. I slide the thighs in the oven along with whole sweet potatoes and call Theo and Flo inside. They come running and we do homework to the chorus of a crackling fire and the smell of a home-cooked meal…

I've always been a dreamer.

This dish fits the fantasy because it cooks in the oven for forty minutes, which is really as long as I like to help with homework. It's also aromatic with warm spice, and because it uses the grapes' nutrient-packed skin as well as the flesh, I feel like I've really done something when I feed it to my family.

Cooking the chicken along with the grapes softens the skin's texture and transfers its bitter tannins to the sauce, making this recipe a little like braising chicken in wine with fiber, vitamin C, and antioxidants.

2 teaspoons extra-virgin olive oil	2 to 3 leeks, sliced into ½-inch rounds, white and light green parts only (about 2 cups)	2 sprigs rosemary
4 to 6 chicken thighs		½ cinnamon stick
3 teaspoons salt, divided		3 star anise
2 teaspoons black pepper	5 cloves garlic, sliced thin	2 cups chicken stock, preferably homemade
⅓ cup all-purpose flour	2 cups muscadine grapes, halved and seeded	1 cup apple cider
	6 sprigs thyme	¼ cup cider vinegar
		1 tablespoon butter

Preheat your oven to 350°F. In a 12-inch cast-iron skillet or brazier, heat the olive oil over medium heat. Season the chicken with 2 teaspoons salt and the black pepper, then dredge in the flour. Beginning skin-side down, brown the chicken for 3 to 5 minutes, then flip it over and brown the other side an additional 3 minutes. Remove the chicken from the pan and set aside.

Pour off all but 1 tablespoon of fat. Add the leeks and the remaining 1 teaspoon salt. Cook the leeks for 3 minutes until they start to brown. Stir in the garlic and the grapes. Cook an additional minute. Add the thyme, rosemary, cinnamon stick, and star anise. Put the chicken back in the pan, skin-side up, and pour the stock, cider, and vinegar into the pan, making sure it does not submerge the chicken. You want the

skin exposed. Bring it up to a simmer on the stovetop, then slide it onto the middle rack of your oven and cook for 40 minutes uncovered.

    Take the braise out of the oven. Remove the thighs and set them aside. Pluck out the rosemary, thyme, cinnamon stick, and star anise. Over medium heat, reduce the sauce by about half, till it's

thickened and will coat the back of a spoon. Swirl in your butter and return the thighs to the pan to keep warm till you're ready to serve.

    Serve with Turnip Roots and Greens (*page 68*), Dirty Faro (*page 373*), or Stewed Rutabagas (*page 470*).

Triple-Decker Grape-Hull Pie

Makes three 8-inch pies

IF YOU'RE GONNA GO TO THE TROUBLE of making a grape-hull pie, you might as well make it in a major way. Based on Edna Lewis's apple pie of the same stature, this is basically three small pies stacked on top of each other to create something akin to the wedding cake of pies.

A joy to look at, this pie is for those who love crust as much as they do filling. I love a tall slice with vanilla ice cream because it marries the savory notes of lard with the tart foxy sweetness of grapes in a union that tastes like a happy memory.

Note: *Yes, you could just make one pie by dividing the recipe in three.*

Grape-Hull Filling
- 4½ quarts whole muscadine grapes
- 3 cups granulated sugar
- ½ cup cornstarch
- 1 teaspoon nutmeg
- ½ teaspoon salt
- 2 tablespoons lemon juice

Crust
- 5 cups unbleached all-purpose flour, plus more for dusting, sifted
- 1 teaspoon salt
- 1⅔ cups almost frozen lard, cut into small pieces
- ¾ cup ice water

Make the filling: Using your fingers, squeeze the pulp from the skins. Put the pulp, juice, and seeds in a 4-quart saucepan and the skins in a separate bowl. Bring the pulp up to a simmer and cook for about 10 minutes, or until the pulp breaks down and the seeds break free. Strain the cooked pulp through a colander into the bowl with the hulls and discard the seeds.

In a medium bowl, stir together the sugar, cornstarch, nutmeg, and salt. Transfer the pulp and hulls back to the saucepan and cook over medium heat for about 5 minutes or until the hulls are soft. Stir in the sugar mixture and the lemon juice and set aside. If you choose to make the filling a day or two before you make the pies, store it in a sealed container in

your fridge. Make sure the filling is room temperature before you assemble the pies, otherwise they will not warm all the way through.

Make the crust: Put the flour and salt in the bowl of your food processor and pulse to combine. Add the lard a few pieces at a time and pulse till the fat is just combined with the flour. Add the water and continue pulsing just till you have a sticky dough.

Flour your work surface. Turn the dough out onto the surface and dust the top with flour. Using your hands, work it up into a ball and let it rest for about 20 minutes in a cool spot in your kitchen.

Keep in mind while you're doing this that you're just making three pies and stacking them on top of one another. That

Cut the larger portion into 3 equal rounds. Roll them out and lay them in your pie pans. Because this pastry is more sticky than a lot of pie crusts, store the rolled-out dough in your freezer till you're ready to fill and bake. Roll out the tops and lay them in between waxed paper. Chill them down also.

Assemble and bake: Preheat your oven to 425°F. Divide the room-temperature filling among the three pie shells. Moisten the edge of the crust with a little water and lay the top crust over the filling. Seal the top and bottom by pressing the edges together with your fingers or a fork. Cut 5 half-inch vents on the top of the crust. Place the pie pans on a baking sheet and bake in the center of your oven for 40 minutes. Unless you have two ovens, you'll have to do this in two batches.

Let the pies cool completely in their pans. Then carefully turn them out and stack them on top of each other. Let them sit for an hour before slicing with a careful hand. Serve at room temperature, never cold.

should help me explain the next part. Divide the dough in 2 unequal portions. The first will be for the bottom crusts and should weigh about 30 ounces. The second will be for the top crusts and should be about 18 ounces. If you don't have a scale, eyeball it and split the dough unequally, ⅔ for one part and ⅓ for the other.

Ben Knight: If I don't thank anybody else for anything, I'm thanking you, my partner in parenting, business, and all the murky stuff in between. Your steadfast commitment to our families at work and at home have made this book and all the wild stuff that comes with it possible. I love you.

Theo and Flo: I wrote much of this book with an eye toward how I hope you will one day remember me, your grandparents, and the place you grew up. Thanks for giving me the perspective to connect our past to your future.

Mom, Dad, Leraine, Currie, and Johna: I grew up thinking I could be president, a professional dancer, even a beauty queen if I worked hard enough. I also grew up knowing that nobody would push me toward those triumphs and soothe me during the inevitable disappointments more than my family. Thank you for the steady belief through both.

Cynthia Hill: We all know that without *A Chef's Life,* nobody would be interested in a Vivian Howard book. Thank you for believing in the project and in me from the beginning. The show we've made is important, but the friendship we've forged while making it is invaluable and among the greatest gifts of my adult life. You're the best storyteller I know.

Rex Miller: The first day we started shooting *A Chef's Life,* you said to me: "Vivian, even if you don't think you can do it, act like you think you can." I used that advice not only in the show but the whole time I wrote this book. Thank you first for that. And thank you for taking more than just beautiful pictures of food as you chased "magic hour" around Eastern North Carolina for close to three years in pursuit of storytelling. Your dedication, keen eye, and the fact that you always want to eat make working with you an absolute pleasure.

Amelia Foran: The nights I work late, I never worry whether my children are read to, fed well, or adequately snuggled. I don't worry because I know you love Theo and Flo like they are your own. Thank you for being a constant in our lives and for being a darn fine disciplinarian.

Holley Pearce: Thank you for doing so much more than going to the grocery store. I know it's not typically a good idea to have your right hand also be your close friend, but with us, it works. Thank you for making me laugh, putting me in my place, connecting the wildly disparate dots, and answering my texts.

Justise Robbins and John May: When I told y'all I was going to write a cookbook and it would probably take me out of the restaurant some, I was wrong. It took me out of the restaurant almost totally for close to a year. Thanks to you, nobody knew I was gone.

Angie Mosier: Lordy, I love working with you. Thanks for contemplating how to capture the individual spirit of all two hundred dishes. I was fatigued by it long before you.

Kim Adams, Allen Tracy, Kristen Whitfield, Susan Fakowski, Beth (Bonnie) Thigpen, Angelina Mendoza, and Jason Kops: Some of you have been at Chef and the Farmer since the day we opened. The rest of you have also been there a long damn time. Thanks for sticking around and for giving a business that was destined to fail your full selves. Chef and the Farmer, Ben, and I needed every bit of it.

Lillie Hardy and Warren Brothers: I'm honored to call both of you teachers and friends. Thank you for your generosity, wit, knowledge, and patience. The two of you, plus your mothers, Mary Vaughn and Annette Brothers, allowed me my first glimpse into Eastern Carolina home kitchens beyond the one I grew up in.

Josh Woll, Tom Vickers, Selena Lauterer, Amy Shumaker, Margaret McNealy, Shirlette Ammons, Jenn Cromling, Blair Johnson, Jason Hill, Un Kyong Ho, and Christine Delp: You are the best people in television. Seriously. We make a show that changes people's lives for the better. Thank you for being creative, sensible, tenacious, and ambitious. I hope I get to make good stuff with you for a long time.

Anna Moriah Myers, Michelle Gans, Leslie Zapatero, Logan Wolfram, and Sheri Castle: Thanks to all of you for cooking through these recipes...some of them many times. It's important they work in home kitchens, and your tweaks and observations are why this book will work for real-live people at home with cups and teaspoons.

My publishing team: Thank you to everyone at Little, Brown and beyond who helped produce this book, especially **Don Morris,** for a design that made me jump for joy; **Tatsuro Kiuchi,** for paintings that reveal these ingredients as the heroes they are; **Sara Smith,** for drawing where I came from; **Stacey Van Berkel** and team, for the glamour shot; **Jayne Yaffe Kemp** and **Tracy Roe,** for helping me color within the lines of grammar; **Lisa Ferris,** for making sure it got printed; **Zea Moscone, Pamela Brown,** and **the Door** for getting the word out; and **Reagan Arthur, Judy Clain, Craig Young, Heather Fain, Michael Sand, Nicole Dewey, Melissa Nicholas, Mario Pulice,** and everyone else who stuck their necks out for me.

David Black: Agent, advocate, friend, straight shooter, and hotelier—you're a master of many trades. Thanks for believing that I could do this. That conviction made it possible.

Michael Szczerban: I better hurry up and start on my next book so we don't lose touch. My time with you has been a gift wrapped in new friendship and a mutual love for food, family stories, procrastination, and Instagram stalking. Don't you ever leave Little, Brown or I'll kill you.

Vivian Howard grew up in Deep Run, North Carolina, and is the chef and owner of the acclaimed Chef and the Farmer and Boiler Room restaurants in Kinston, fifteen miles away. She trained as a cook in some of New York's finest restaurants before returning home in 2006 to open Chef and the Farmer. Vivian is the cocreator and star of the James Beard and Emmy Award–winning PBS series *A Chef's Life,* which tells stories about the people, food, and culture of the Carolina coastal plain. She is the first woman since Julia Child to win a Peabody Award for a cooking program. This is her first book.

Rex Miller is the Emmy Award–nominated director of photography for *A Chef's Life* and the documentaries *Private Violence* and *The Loving Story,* and he is the director of *Althea, Behind These Walls* and *Somay Ku: A Uganda Tennis Story.* His photography has appeared in the *New York Times, Rolling Stone, Time, Spin, Forbes,* and other publications.